The Day The
Devils Dropped In

Fear knocked at the door
Faith opened it
And there was no one there

(Part of the 9th Parachute Battalion Padre's
pre D-Day sermon)

THE DAY THE
DEVILS
DROPPED IN

The 9th Parachute Battalion in Normandy
D-Day to D + 6

The Merville Battery to the Château St Côme

NEIL BARBER

Pen & Sword
AVIATION

First published in Great Britain in 2002
Reprinted in 2003 and 2004
Published in this format in 2007 by
PEN & SWORD AVIATION
an imprint of
Pen & Sword Books Ltd
47 Church Street
Barnsley
South Yorkshire
S70 2AS

ISBN 1 84415 045 3

A CIP catalogue record for this book is
available from the British Library.

Printed and bound in Great Britain
By CPI UK

Pen & Sword Books Ltd incorporates the Imprints of
Pen & Sword Aviation, Pen & Sword Maritime, Pen & Sword Military,
Wharncliffe Local History, Pen & Sword Select,
Pen & Sword Military Classics and Leo Cooper.

For a complete list of Pen & Sword titles please contact
PEN & SWORD BOOKS LIMITED
47 Church Street, Barnsley, South Yorkshire, S70 2AS, England
E-mail: enquiries@pen-and-sword.co.uk
Website: www.pen-and-sword.co.uk

For Caroline, James and Max

CONTENTS

Foreword 8

Preface 11

Acknowledgements 12

List of maps 13

List of abbreviations 14

Chapter 1. 'An Elite Club of Volunteers' 15

Chapter 2. Ready to 'Go To It!' 31

Chapter 3. 'Gentlemen, The Operation is On!' – Monday 5 June 41

Chapter 4. The Drop – Tuesday 6 June 46

Chapter 5. The Attack 69

Chapter 6. Onward 98

Chapter 7. Consolidation – Wednesday 7 June 125

Chapter 8. The Château St Côme; Opening Skirmishes – Thursday 8 June 136

Chapter 9. Pressure Mounts – Friday 9 June 150

Chapter 10. Onslaught – Saturday 10 June 163

Chapter 11. Tragedy – Sunday 11 June 177

Chapter 12. Day of Decision – Monday 12 June 182

Chapter 13. Relief – Tuesday 13 June 197

Aftermath 202

Today 202

The Fates of those mentioned in the text 204

Appendix 1 – The continuation of Private Fred Glover's
                      story after capture 206

            2 – The Commando liberation of
                      Amfreville/Le Plein 207

            3 – The continuation of Private Terry Jepp's experiences
                      after reaching the Vermughens 208

            4 – The continuation of Lieutenant Douglas Martin's story
                      following his serious wounding as recalled by his wife, Eileen 209

            5 – Controversial issues surrounding the Merville Battery 211

Sources 216

Notes 217

Index 223

FOREWORD
by
Brigadier S James L Hill DSO**, MC
Commander, 3rd Parachute Brigade 1943-45

It is a great pleasure for me as an ancient warrior to be given the opportunity of paying my tribute to a remarkable bunch of men who in the days now 'far away and long ago' gave their all and then more, in a just and noble cause.

The occasion was the protection of the left flank of the Allied Armies during the invasion of Normandy, the dates described were 6-13 June 1944.

The account is centred on the men of the 9th Parachute Battalion of the 3rd Parachute Brigade of the 6th Airborne Division.

The 9th Battalion task during those seven days was to 'take out the German coastal defence battery at Merville' before dawn on D-Day, then capture the Le Plein feature and having handed it over to Lord Lovat's Commando Brigade, to proceed south through the village of Breville to the Château St Côme which they were told to hold as a part of the vital ridge overlooking the 6th Airborne Division's objectives (including Pegasus Bridge) and hence the left flank of the Allied Armies!

I found it intriguing, that the author who was born sixteen years after the battle he describes took place, should devote all his spare time for the last six years to collecting the individual experiences of those still living who took part in the battle.

He then had to correlate stories in chronological order to match the war diaries and histories already written. No mean task there! Indeed a labour of love as he himself described it.

Previously he had become an addicted historian visiting and reading up on the battlefields of the First and Second World Wars and by somewhat remote family links, he had been led to study of the Battle of the Château St Côme.

The author must then have caught a glimpse of the unseen forces that moved these young men to perform deeds of courage and endurance far beyond normal expectation and this motivated him to produce this story in a rather unusual format.

As Commander of the 3rd Parachute Brigade, I do not recognize some of the 'slants' on the battle given here and I suspect it may be difficult for the average reader to follow the sequence and importance of each individual's actions to the battle as a whole, as one becomes glued to each gripping story be they great or small. However, they do paint a remarkable picture of what fighting is all about. Anyone who wishes to study the psychology or art of command in battle can do well to 'read-mark-learn and inwardly digest' the meaning behind the many pictures painted, as one turns the pages of this book!

I therefore ask the reader to relax and use the power of his imagination to the full and place himself in the position of the men of the 9th Parachute Battalion as around midnight preceding D-Day they found themselves flying across the Channel – penetrating the ack-ack coastal defences and parachuting into enemy infested territory by night. Remember: average age twenty-two, few had seen a shot fired in anger. Quite an ordeal!

Who were these soldiers? I found the parachute soldiers of the Second World War were of two dispositions. The soldiers of fortune who wanted to get dug into the battle and fight, I had many of these in the 1st Parachute Battalion which I commanded in the early days in North Africa, several of whom had received the Order of Lenin in the Spanish Civil War. My Canadian Battalion in the 3rd Parachute Brigade also has some of their soldiers from this category. They were splendid fighting material, always provided they were well disciplined.

The second disposition of parachute soldiers were usually drawn from County regiments and thought it their duty to volunteer for parachuting when their battalion were asked to do so – 9th Parachute Battalion were of this category and were borne from the 10th Battalion Essex Regiment.

It is interesting to note that the original three Battalions in the 3rd Parachute Brigade, which included the 7th Parachute Battalion (Light Infantry), 8th Parachute Battalion (Midland Counties), 9th Parachute Battalion (10th Battalion Essex) when asked, all volunteered to a man, some 550 men per battalion. After their initial physical and then parachuting training, an average of 156 men per Battalion survived to form the backbone of each parachute battalion. These men provided a magnificent rock on which to build the 3rd Parachute Brigade. In May 1943 the 7th Parachute Battalion was withdrawn to provide the nucleus of the 5th Parachute Brigade, newly forming and were replaced in the 3rd Parachute Brigade by the 1st Canadian Parachute Battalion – newly arrived from Canada, fully up to strength and itching to go!

Each battalion therefore had a year to train itself for the great day. That year was not wasted! Their targets for achievement were speed, control, simplicity and fire effect!

A premium was placed on physical and mental fitness, hence the capacity to endure. All men were volunteers and a great leadership potential amongst all ranks was there for development. Example – example – example, became the watchword and a great band of brothers was formed as each man became self-sufficient and trusted his leaders, be they section, company or battalion commanders. No man would ask another to do anything that he was not capable of doing himself.

Since the war I have often reflected on how it was that the 3rd Parachute Brigade, who bore the brunt of the battle for the ridge, were able to see off their opposition, a first class German Infantry Division, 346 Panzer Grenadier Division, complete with tanks and mobile 88mm guns etc. After the Battle of Breville on 12 June the German Division retired to lick its wounds, never to return! Now I think I know!

The men of the 9th Parachute Battalion, in spite of their heavy loss in numbers due to their scattered parachute drop and casualties at the Battery, were capable of 'breaking the sound barrier' of normal human endurance and lived to fight on when there should have been nothing left. I witnessed this same phenomenon in both the Canadian and 8th Parachute Battalions further along the ridge. Battle fatigue was not a word in the Divisional or Brigade dictionary!

I feel it would be helpful here to make three comments. The first on the scattered drop suffered by the 9th Parachute Battalion, the Canadian Battalion and the headquarters of the 3rd Parachute Brigade on D-Day. Originally there were only sufficient aircraft to fly in one brigade and the 3rd Brigade was given the task of seizing Pegasus Bridge. I then asked for a *Coup de Main* party of three gliders to help do the job. Approximately six weeks before D-Day the Divisional Commander was informed that Bomber Command would produce additional pilots to enable the whole of the 6th Airborne to be flown in, in two lifts. The 3rd Parachute Brigade tasks were then changed to ones further airfield.

There was little or no time to practice. This contingency proved an increasing worry to me as the days went by so on 5 June I addressed as many officers and sergeants as possible in their staging camps in the following lines:

> Gentlemen, in spite of your excellent orders and training, DO NOT BE DAUNTED IF CHAOS REIGNS. It undoubtedly will.

This warning proved to have been most helpful to many people.

The second comment is on the orders issued for the attack on the Merville Battery which have often been criticized for being far too complicated and far from simple. It must be remembered that the young men of the 9th Parachute Battalion taking part were intelligent and would willingly tackle any task provided there was an answer to the problems facing them (however formidable those problems might be), such as deep barbed wire walls, minefields and tank ditches sixteen feet deep and fourteen feet wide and steel doors to their gun casements, to say nothing of the weapons defences. The answers were provided and practiced. In Lieutenant Colonel Terence Otway they found a

Commanding Officer who was an outstanding trainer and resolute commander of men, hence morale remained at the highest level during the final days of waiting.

The final comment. If you are to fight a long war, it is essential that the noble integrity of your cause be built upon a rock. You cannot train and lead intelligent young men to surrender their lives in battle for less!

Those of us who had been fighting the German Army from the beginning knew and appreciated the qualities of their soldiers and sensed a change in the autumn of 1944. For the German Army, from their Generals down, began to realize that Dr Goebbels, their propaganda minister had been feeding them a pack of lies! The cracks in morale started to show!

The depleted numbers of the 9th Parachute Battalion depicted in this story returned with the 6th Airborne Division to their wartime home in Bulford in early September 1944. The half-empty barrack rooms resulting from the absence of so many smiling faces emphasized the price of war. Life was never quite the same again.

However, there were two more campaigns to be fought. The Ardennes (Battle of the Bulge) and the Rhine crossing followed by the drive through Germany to Wismar on the Baltic. Training recommenced in earnest, the new intake were happily absorbed and the monstrosity of Hitler's desires made all concerned more determined than ever to see the thing through to the end. Morale was high.

Today, fifty-eight years on, some forty-five men of the 9th Parachute Battalion who caused the story to be written, survive. We surely owe them our love and gratitude, together with their Normandy brothers in arms from all formations who fought in that battle in the 'far away and long ago'.

PREFACE

This narrative follows the paths of the men of the 9th Battalion, The Parachute Regiment, during the first week of the Normandy invasion. It attempts to address the Battalion's drop, its primary D-Day task of silencing the Merville Battery, the action at Amfreville/Le Plein later in the morning and the subsequent unpublicized but hugely important battle at the Château St Côme on the Breville ridge.

Six years ago, having become interested in the Merville Battery and St Côme actions, I went in search of information and subsequently read all of the various published books. However, impressive as they were, a feeling of dissatisfaction prevailed. Something was missing. I realized that what I actually wanted to read was a detailed account in the words of the men who were actually there and not a narration of their experiences by an author. This, along with the deliberate omission of hindsight, therefore dictated the goals of the research and the format of this book.

As with all such attempts to chronicle historical episodes, it is never possible to uncover the complete picture. One can only portray the events and try to get as close as possible. In my efforts to do this, I have interviewed as many 9th Battalion veterans as I could find (around fifty), plus many of those formations who fought alongside them in the area. A wealth of correspondence was also gathered from other survivors. In addition, the 9th's Reunion Club allowed me access to the accounts written for John Golley's 1982 book on the Battalion, *The Big Drop*. These were vital in seeing the actual words of many who are sadly no longer alive. (Unfortunately, this did not include a dozen accounts that were lent to Robert Maxwell in the 1980s and lost when the receivers moved into the *Daily Mirror*).

Another essential piece of information was a detailed account written by one of the officers, Major George Smith, in 1946. This formed the backbone of Lieutenant General Sir Napier Crookenden's book, *The 9th Parachute Battalion, The First Six Days*, and later, part of Dropzone Normandy.

Also vital in piecing together events was a report made in 1946 by the medics entitled, *The Red Devils – The Story of 224 Field (Parachute) Ambulance*. This was doubly useful as it helped to highlight the bravery of the medics, a matter that all of the fighting men were anxious to emphasize.

Using all of these resources, I have therefore been able to construct, correct and expand on much of the existing published information. Naturally, several very interesting incidents have proved impossible to confirm against a precise time or day and have consequently been added in calculated positions, but as general comments. Having said that, I believe I have tried to employ every available source to confirm the book's accuracy and any errors are therefore my sole responsibility.

I hope that people who visit the area and especially those who stand in front of the memorials at the Merville Battery and the Château St Côme, may now have the chance of a clearer idea of the terrible struggle which took place on this small piece of Normandy countryside.

Neil Barber
Belvedere
Kent

May 2002

ACKNOWLEDGEMENTS

There are five people without whose help this book could not have been produced. Therefore, firstly I would like to express my gratitude to Brigadier James Hill DSO** MC and Lieutenant Colonel Terence Otway DSO, for patiently vetting each draft, their encouragement and hospitality. I am also thrilled that James Hill has written the Foreword.

Similarly, to Lieutenant General Sir Napier Crookenden KCB DSO, for advice on many things, including the draft and also permission to quote Major Smith's correspondence and pieces from his book *The First Six Days*.

Finally to Sid Capon and Gordon Newton who contributed in so many ways that it would be impossible to list them all!

Amazingly, all of these men never once tired of my (almost) incessant questions. Again, I am extremely grateful.

I would like to say thank you to Bill Mills, Aubrey Lees, Tony Lea, Ken Walker, Len Daniels and Tom Hughes of the Battalion's Reunion Club Committee and particularly Mike Woodcock, who allowed me to see written accounts at no small inconvenience to himself.

Also, to Ron MaCaffrey, now of the Pegasus Memorial Museum whose assistance and patience knew no limit.

To the veterans themselves (listed at Sources), thank you all again for your time, hospitality and co-operation. It has been a privilege and of course an education.

The many other people to whom I owe a debt of gratitude are as follows:
Dr Toby Haggith, Matthew Lee and the staff at the IWM Film Archive; Mrs Beech at Keele University, and Diana Andrews, Alan Brown and Tina Pittock at the Airborne Forces Museum.

Colonel David Benest OBE, of the Airborne Assault Trust Normandy and Alex Taylor, who has always provided long and thought-provoking correspondence!

For various pieces of assistance over the years, Ian and Jan Bayley, Nigel Bewley, Ian Clark, Joan Delsignore, Colin and Ian Dewey, Mrs Garrett, Andy Goodwin, Johnnie Johnson, Chris Johns, Ron Kennedy, Neil Kerr, Michael Knight, John Magill, Max Orkamfat, Paul Parris, Ian and Tracy Pieri, Keith Ponsford, Carl Rymen, Fred Scott, Stan Scott, Pat and Denzil Slade, Mrs Stroud, Joan Tugwell, Richard and James Tudge and Mrs D Woodcraft.

Of the French people involved, my appreciation goes to Monsieur Andre Miguet, the owner of the Château St Côme, who has put up with my multitude of walks around his property over the years. To Louis Adelin, a great friend of the Battalion for many years, Monsieur Lechartier, the former Mayor of Breville, Madame Anne-Marie Trevel, the Mayor of Gonneville and Monsieur Olivier Paz, the Mayor of Merville, who has championed the cause of the Merville Battery for many years. Also, Monsieur Bernard Saulnier, Maurice and Rolande Dufour and Monsieur and Madame Jacques Courcy. Merci, Messieurs et Madames!

To those at Pen and Sword, Charles Hewitt, Brigadier Henry Wilson, Barbara Bramall, Jon Wilkinson and especially Tom Hartman and Sylvia Menzies.

I must mention my uncle, Jeff Haward MM, formerly of the 1/7th Middlesex Battalion, without whom my interest in the war and particularly Normandy, might not have been what it is! Also, to his former carrier driver, Dennis Daly and other Normandy comrades, Arthur Berry, Billy Noblett and dear, now departed, Alan Carter and Bill Jones. The trips to Normandy would not have been the same without you.

To Neil Leonard for producing the terrific maps, patiently and exactly to my requirements.

To my parents, Bob and Joan, and brother Colin for all the support and encouragement over the last forty-odd years!

Finally, and particularly, to my dear wife Caroline, who has had to endure my many absences from home.

List of Maps

The Invasion 23
The 6th Airborne Divisional Area – East of the River Orne 24
The Merville Battery Assault Plan 34
The Assault on the Merville Battery 83
The Le Mesnil Crossroads Area 130
The Château St Côme/Bois des Monts Area 140
The Black Watch Attack on Breville 178

Photographic Credits

9th Battalion Archive (59 Upper, 102 Lower, 116, 150 Upper), Mrs R. Abel (110), Louis Adelin (29, 113), Airborne Forces Museum (15, 161), Rob Baldwin (72), Neil Barber (145 Lower, 173 Lower, 202, 203), John Britton (18, 21, 124, 141, 153, 193 Lower, 215), Sid Capon (46 Lower, 85 (both), 101 Upper, 122, 124, 154, 159 right, 173 Upper, 193 Upper), Ian Clark (via Johnny Walker) (56), Msr Courcy (198, 200 Lower), Lt Gen Sir Napier Crookenden (182, 184 Lower, 197), IWM (117, 127, Lower, 133), Len Daniels (20, 21), Joan Delsignore (78), Harry and Sheila Eckert (93), Robert Ferguson (157), Mrs F. Garrett (52), Gonneville Mairie (96, 102 Upper), Derek Higgins (152), Terry Jefferson (formerly (Jepp) (120, 121, 189 Lower), Bob Jenkins (112 right), Neil Kerr (80), Tate Gallery (158), Michael Knight (48), Mme Lecomte (136), Msr A. Miguet (137 Upper), Fred Milward (84, 167 Lower), MoD (70, 82), Paul Parris (99), Geoff Pattinson (26/27), Ron Phelps (145 Upper), Public Records Office (22, 171), Robbie Robinson (17 Upper), Bernard Saulnier (111, 127 Upper), Fred Scott (199, 200 Upper), Mrs D. Slade/Denzil Slade (115), John Speechley (26 Upper, 77), Mrs T. Stroud (126), Richard and James Tudge (131), Mrs D. Woodcraft (19), John Woodgate (137 Lower).

List of Abbreviations

ADS	Advanced Dressing Station
BHQ	Battalion Headquarters
CO	Commanding Officer
CSM	Company Sergeant Major
DSO	Distinguished Service Order
DZ	Dropping Zone
FOB	Forward Observer Bombardment
FOO	Forward Observation Officer
GSO	General Staff Officer
KB	Kitbag
LMG	Light Machine Gun
LST	Landing Ship, Tank
LZ	Landing Zone
MC	Military Cross
MDS	Main Dressing Station
MG	Machine Gun
MM	Military Medal
NAAFI	Navy, Army and Air Force Institutes
NCO	Non Commissioned Officer
'O' Group	Orders Group
OC	Officer Commanding
PHE	Plastic High Explosive
PIAT	Projectile, Infantry, Anti-Tank
POW	Prisoner of War
DAA & QMG	Deputy Assistant Adjutant and Quartermaster General
RAP	Regimental Aid Post
RASC	Royal Army Service Corps
RE	Royal Engineer
RSM	Regimental Sergeant Major
SB	Stretcher Bearer
VC	Victoria Cross
III/857th	3rd Battalion of 857th Regiment (German formation)

CHAPTER ONE

'An Elite Club of Volunteers'

On 5 November 1942, the War Office authorized the formation of a brigade to strengthen the existing British Airborne Forces, namely the 1st Airborne Division. As part of this expansion, the 10th Holding Battalion, The Essex Regiment was chosen to be converted into a parachute

Major General Frederick Browning.
Taylor Library

unit. Major-General Frederick 'Boy' Browning, the 'father' of the Airborne Forces, subsequently visited the battalion and gave a talk about the objectives of a parachute force, and from a strength of 644 all ranks, 567 volunteered. However, before acceptance, the men were required to pass stringent mental and physical criteria. This began with a two-week selection course at Hardwick Hall near Chesterfield, which involved a strict medical, rigorous physical training and various tests. The survivors then went on a further two-week course for parachute training at Ringway in Manchester.[1] The first week was devoted to learning and practising the drill and culminated in two jumps from a balloon at 700 to 800 feet. During the second week the trainees had to make five jumps from aircraft. Around 150 successfully completed the course, and were duly presented with the coveted wings. One of them was Company Sergeant-Major Jack Harries:

Certainly the issue of Para wings, the Airborne shoulder flash and the red beret seemed to transform men almost overnight, and suddenly you were part of an elite club of volunteers.

Most of this successful group were experienced pre-war regulars, 1940 conscripts or members of the Territorial Army, and these formed the backbone of the 9th (Eastern and Home Counties) Battalion, the Parachute Regiment.[2]

The new brigade was designated as 3 Parachute Brigade and was completed by the 7th and 8th Battalions.

The structure of a Parachute Battalion basically consisted of a HQ Company, three Rifle Companies, 'A', 'B' and 'C', and the Reserve Company. HQ Company dealt with the administration of the Battalion and included the signals and intelligence sections plus an MG platoon of four Vickers heavy machine guns and a mortar platoon of six three-inch mortars. Each Rifle Company comprised of five officers and 120 men organised into Company HQ and three platoons of thirty-six men each.

'Home' for the 9th Battalion was Kiwi Barracks in Bulford Camp near Andover in Wiltshire, and Lieutenant-Colonel Tom Hearn, the greatly respected Commanding Officer of the 10th Essex, briefly continued in this role, but had to relinquish command as he was too old to jump. Colonel Stanley James Ledger Hill was appointed.

James Hill's path to the Battalion had been eventful to say the least. While commanding the 1st Parachute Battalion in North Africa, he had been shot three times when leading a raid behind

James Hill.

15

enemy lines. One bullet went straight through his chest, while the other two hit him in the neck and shoulder. He was placed in the sidecar of an Italian motorcycle with his badly wounded adjutant and rapidly driven back to Beja where he was operated upon by a forward parachute surgical team. Here, his life was saved and after three weeks in a casualty clearing station, was evacuated to a hospital in Algiers. To regain fitness, as soon as he was able, at night he started slipping out of the French windows of his room for illicit walks in the hospital gardens. Seven weeks later, considering himself fit enough, he just walked out of the hospital and set off to report to his superior, Brigadier Edward Flavell. The front had by then moved on into Tunisia, a journey of 400 miles. He hitchhiked the whole distance. Unfortunately, Flavell could not return command of the Battalion to him so he put Hill on a plane back to England, whereupon he was immediately sent to hospital in Tidworth.[3] Whilst here he received the offer of the 9th Battalion, but his first problem was getting passed fit to command again. He was friendly with the hospital's commanding officer, Major Salmon, and so one afternoon, while she was at dinner, he left a note saying that he apologised for missing her, but that General Browning required him back immediately. He also asked that a medical certificate be forwarded to him.[4, 5]

Hill duly assumed command of the Battalion and his impact was immediate. The officer commanding 'A' Company was Major Allen Parry:

> The Colonel invariably picked on a different officer each day and said 'Come along and walk to the office with me.' The walk was a breathtaking experience. James Hill invariably carried a thumb stick, which increased the length of his stride. His speed of movement often left the unfortunate officer trotting a couple of paces behind his master, trying to answer his questions but with insufficient breath to do so. The Colonel quickly earned the name 'Speedy' from the soldiers.

Sergeant Doug Woodcraft, 'A' Company:

> When Colonel Hill took over the Battalion, he took us all on a forced march. At the end he addressed us, saying 'Gentlemen, you are not fit, but don't let this worry you because from now on we are going to work a six and a half day week. You can have Saturday afternoons off!'

And he meant it! Even Sunday Services at the Garrison Church provided only a brief respite. Company Sergeant Major Harries:

> We were required to attend in full battle order with weapons and leave them outside on the lawns, and at the end of the Service Brigadier {sic} Hill would arrive and suggest we all went on 'a nice stroll' before lunch. No one could refuse of course but the stroll usually consisted of anything up to ten miles which usually developed into more of a run than a march, such was the pace of Brigadier Hill at the front.

Hill placed great emphasis on both physical and mental endurance. Everything was done 'at speed', and all movement during working hours was carried out at the double. This was necessary because when the men initially went into battle, they would be carrying all of the Battalion's equipment and ammunition with them, and would also be facing numerically superior and more heavily armed opponents.

*

On 23 April 1943, the War Office issued orders for the formation of the 6th Airborne Division, which was to comprise of 3 Parachute Brigade, transferred from the 1st Airborne Division, and two new brigades, 5 Parachute Brigade and 6 Airlanding glider-borne Brigade.[6]

The Divisional Commander was Major-General Richard 'Windy' Gale, a veteran of the First World War and a straight talking 'soldier's soldier' who set the tone for the character of

Major-General Richard Gale. *Taylor Library*

9th Battalion officers.

the Division when he introduced the motto, 'Go To It!':

> *This motto will be adopted by 6th Airborne Division and as such should be remembered by all ranks in action against the enemy, in training and during day to day routine duties.*[7]

James Hill was duly promoted to Brigadier and given command of 3 Parachute Brigade.[8] Colonel Martin Lindsay, another experienced parachutist, became the new CO of the 9th Battalion. Training continued with the same intensity, under the watchful eye of his second-in-command, Major Terence Otway.

*

To bring the Battalion up to its fighting complement of around 650 men, successful applicants from a general request for volunteers gradually began to arrive.[9] Private Bill Stack, HQ Company, Signal Platoon:

> *We were brought up to strength by a new intake of young chaps and they livened things up greatly. We had a few of them in the Signals. Us older chaps got the job of training them, and as 'Speedy' had named us 'The Nucleus', we had something to live up to.*

Private Frank Delsignore of 'C' Company, was one of the new arrivals:

Signal Section.

'R' Section – Signals (trainees).

    The Battalion set about training with great enthusiasm, each man pulling his weight, trying to become the most efficient and fittest fighting unit in existence. For we all knew that for us it was not a case of one day you may be going into action, we knew we were going. It was just a matter of time, and we intended to be ready when that time came.

The training was intense. Private Ernie Rooke-Matthews, 'B' Company, Signal Platoon:

    We would have early reveille, a mug of strong tea (sweetened to hide the regulation dose of salts) and then on parade whatever the weather, often in the dark, in vests and shorts for physical training under the watchful eyes of Company Sergeant-Major Instructors 'Dusty' Miller and Bill Harrold. Sometimes it would be straightforward PT on the square, sometimes it would be a road run or cross-country run.

    We marched and marched, uphill and downhill until we knew every bend, every gradient on the roads around Bulford.

    Gradually the distances were increased and the time allowances were reduced as the loads we had to carry increased. Five and ten mile marches were routine, to be accomplished before breakfast. We worked up to twenty-five miles and then to fifty miles {in twenty-four hours with full pack}.

Corporal Doug Tottle, 'A' Company, Medical Section:

    All we did from Kiwi Barracks was run, run, run, march, march, march, drop, drop, drop, all over the south of England. We often used to march from Southampton, do three days street fighting and then march back to Bulford.

To familiarise the men with the problems of night fighting, at one stage the Battalion trained throughout the night and slept by day, and this was not over-popular. The only ones excused were members of the Battalion boxing team who were training for the Brigade and Divisional Championships. CSM Harries:

    Sergeant 'Dizzy' Brewster was a regular member of the Battalion team and could usually be found reclining on his bunk laughing his head off whilst the remainder of his colleagues were departing for night training in full 'Battle Order'.

    Sergeant 'Dizzy' Brewster suggested to Sergeant 'Ginger' Woodcock that he should have a go if he wished to avoid night training. The idea was sold and 'Ginger' volunteered. On the night of a battalion competition we all paraded for a night route march leaving 'Ginger' Woodcock reclining on his bed with 'Dizzy' Brewster.

Sergeant 'Dizzy' Brewster in the reclining position!

Upon our return around reveille the next morning, the sergeants of 'A' Company not unnaturally were hot foot for 'A' Company's sergeants room to wake up and sort out the two 'skivers'. The next I heard was much commotion and laughing and upon looking into the room I found them all surrounding 'Ginger' Woodcock's bed, who was sitting up with a pillow and one eye closed. The other sported a huge bruise. His nose was swollen with puffed lips. To add to this, one arm was in a sling with the thumb separately heavily bandaged and sticking upright like a sentry.

Needless to say, from that time 'Ginger' withdrew from boxing training.

The application shown by the men in training was recognised and duly rewarded. Ernie Rooke-Matthews:

We would go out on an exercise, perhaps for three days (and nights) finishing on a Saturday. Then we would march back to barracks arriving on our knees around the NAAFI break time to be told, 'Thirty-six hour passes at the office'. It was amazing how quickly we recovered, shaved, showered etc., changed into best battle dress and made either for the railway station, if affluent, or up the hill to the main road if hitch-hiking.

We made frequent journeys to London by train from Bulford Sidings. Most of the lads bought tickets, some used them more than once, others, if hard up, took a chance. At Waterloo, as the train from Bulford pulled into the platform, the ticket collectors would open the gates and stand back. Valid ticket holders took the flanks, other ticket holders took the inside ranks and the free riders the centre as the mass stormed through the barriers. On Sunday evening, masses of troops in red berets would congregate on the concourse at Waterloo by platform 11, bidding farewell to wives or girlfriends.

Secrecy was the order of the day – somewhere in England was our location. Then the dulcet tones of the announcer. 'The train now standing at platform 11, calling at...', the gates would open

Sergeant Albert 'Ginger Woodcock sporting his boxing injuries. Sergeant Doug Woodcraft stands beside him.

'B' Company.

up, a mass of red berets would tear onto the platform leaving the concourse empty save a number of smiling, weeping ladies.

Returning late to the barracks carried the punishment of a week's 'fatigue duties', so the last train to Bulford was always packed solid. A 'B' Company NCO and Private Derek Vincent evolved their own solution to this problem:

> We used to come marching up to the barrier. 'Escort and prisoner.' They used to unlock a special carriage and lock the door [behind them]. We had these seats in this carriage all to ourselves! It worked every time. Nobody twigged it.

This shared hardship of training, plus camp life and the inevitable humour, gradually helped to knit the men together and imbue an immense pride in the Battalion. CSM Harries:

> The emphasis was certainly on work hard, play hard, and despite quite heavy drinking and social occasions, such was the fitness and power of recuperation that it seemed to have no effect on the performance of all concerned. In fact it seemed to pay dividends and the spirit of Esprit de Corps was quite fantastic.

Captain Havelock Hudson, better known as 'Hal', assumed the high-pressure role of Battalion Adjutant in August 1943:

> There are great advantages in serving in a unit the personnel of which are all volunteers. The senior officers of what was the Airborne Division went to some lengths to foster the idea of a Corps d'Elite, and a good deal of exhortation, admonition and advice was published in the form of pamphlets and brochures. For 3 Para Brigade the epitome of all this literature was embodied in what was known as 'The Blue Folder'.

A Signals Platoon training drop.

The Merville Battery detailed with photographic interpreter's marks. *(P.R.O. DEFE/2/375)*

The large scale model of the Merville Battery. *(P.R.O. AIR40/1959)*

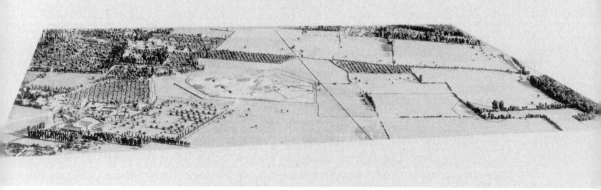

The contents of the folder consisted of contributions from Browning, Gale, Hill and Lindsay. Captain Hudson:

> *This was issued by the Brigade Commander, Brigadier James Hill who, as far as 3 Para Brigade in general and 9 Para Battalion in particular were concerned, was only very slightly less respected than God Almighty.*

*

Although no one in the Battalion, not even the CO, had been informed of their task in the forthcoming invasion, when the emphasis of the training changed, it was clearly apparent to the men. Frank Delsignore:

> *As 1943 came to a close and we moved into 1944 we became increasingly engaged in exercises with specific tasks and objectives. These included attacks on bridges, sometimes to capture and hold or destroy; attacks on set positions, eg gun batteries, and exercises where we were the defenders holding various positions, eg wooded areas, high ground, rivers etc.*

These exercises continued unabated well into 1944.

*

In April, Major Otway was summoned from leave for a meeting with Brigadier Hill, who informed him that he was promoted to Lieutenant-Colonel and was to take command of the Battalion forthwith.[10] He was also told that the 9th's main D-Day task was a 'Grade 'A' stinker of a job'; to neutralize the guns of a heavily defended coastal battery.[11]

Otway was driven to the Divisional Intelligence Headquarters in 'The Old Farm' at Brigmerston House, two miles north of Bulford. He was locked in an upstairs room, in which the walls were festooned with photographs, maps and diagrams. On a large table lay a model of the Battery and its surrounding area.[12, 13] He was left to study the information.

*

For Operation Overlord, the Allies had chosen to land on five stretches of beach along the Normandy coast. The Americans were to use the two most westerly beaches, code-named 'Utah' and 'Omaha', while to the east the Canadian beach, 'Juno', was sandwiched between two British areas, 'Gold' and 'Sword'.

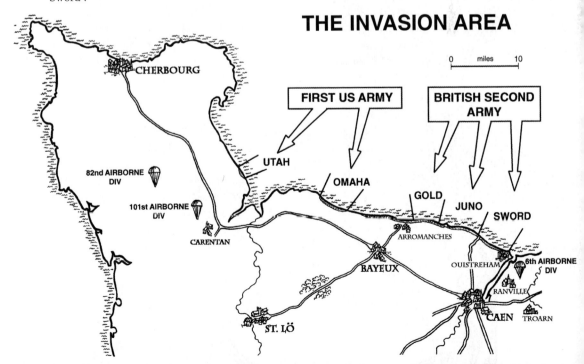

THE INVASION AREA

For the invasion to succeed, it was vital that the beachheads had enough unhindered time to establish and then build up men and materiel. As the two flanks would be the most vulnerable areas, hours before the landings, Airborne Forces were to be sent in to protect them. The American 82nd and 101st Airborne Divisions were detailed for this task in the west, and the 6th Airborne Division, the east. Major-General Gale:

> The left flank of the British seaborne assault was bounded by the double water obstacle consisting of the Canal de Caen and the River Orne. The ground to the east of the River Orne, though not high, was sufficiently dominating to overlook the left flank of the British assault. It was not desirable to extend the seaborne landings to the beaches east of the Orne in order to capture this ground, as the sea approaches to these would have come under the fire of the heavy defences of Le Havre. The river and the canal were obstacles of no mean order, and an attack over these would have been a costly and most undesirable operation. The quickest and surest way of seizing the dominating features east of the Orne was therefore, by means of an airborne assault.[7]

This area was one of open, rolling fields, punctuated by small villages and woods. Specific groups of these fields, known as 'Dropping Zones' (DZ's) to the Paras and Landing Zones (LZs) to the Glider Troops, were chosen for the Division's arrival. DZ/LZ 'K' was to the south of Escoville, DZ/LZ 'N' between Ranville and Breville, DZ/LZ 'V' at Varaville and LZ 'W' just to the west of the River Orne.

During the early hours of D-Day the Division had three primary tasks. The first was the capture, intact, of two bridges across the important waterways. These were three and a half miles inland, along

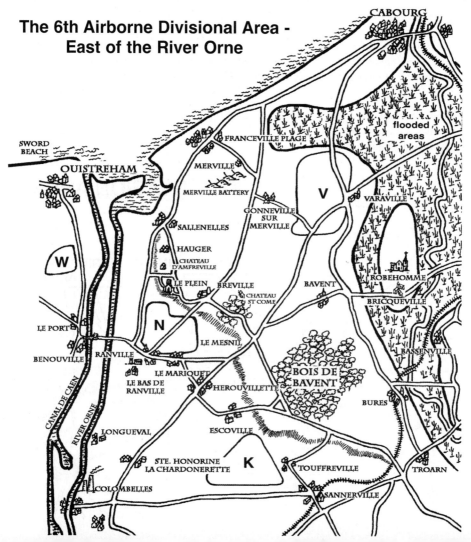

The 6th Airborne Divisional Area - East of the River Orne

an 800-yard section of road running east from the village of Benouville. Being the only crossing points before reaching the city of Caen, they were vital for the Division's reinforcement and supply. This task was the responsibility of 5 Parachute Brigade and was to be carried out by a *Coup-de-Main* glider party of Oxfordshire and Buckinghamshire Light Infantry, 'on loan' from 6 Airlanding Brigade.

A mile to the east the battalions of 5 Brigade were to land on DZ 'N' and take up an initial defensive position from the River Orne, through Le Bas de Ranville to Ranville, and reinforce the men holding the bridges. They also had to clear and protect LZs 'N' and 'W' because around seventy gliders were to land on LZ 'N' at around 3.20am. These carried 6 and 17 Pounder anti-tank guns and heavy machine guns to ensure that the Brigade was strong enough to resist the expected armoured attacks from the south. They were all to be in position by dawn.

A mile north of Ranville, the vital ridge began, running through the villages of Hauger, Le Plein, Breville, Le Mesnil, the Bois de Bavent to the outskirts of Troarn. The capture and domination of this ridge was imperative.

East of the ridge lay the River Dives valley, much of which had been flooded by the Germans to deter such airborne landings. However, this was to be put to good use by destroying various strategic river bridges to hinder the possible arrival of German armoured reinforcements from the east. This was one primary task for 3 Parachute Brigade, silencing the gun battery was the other.

*

This Battery was sited just east of the mouth of the River Orne, near the small village of Merville, and contained four casemates, each to protect a high calibre gun. The Battery's purpose was to cover the estuary, but its location had drawn it to the attention of the Allied planners. Major-General Gale:

> It was so situated that it could fire on the beaches, as well as on the sea approaches to them on which the I Corps assault divisions were to land. Our task was to seize and silence this battery before the assault craft came within its range. The sea assault was to be at dawn, and nothing could have been more awful to contemplate than the havoc this battery might wreak on the assault craft as they slowly forged their way in to the shore. It was, of course, hoped that bombing alone could achieve this. The actual guns were in enormous reinforced concrete casemates, and nothing but a direct hit from one of the heaviest bombs would knock them out. That meant that each gun in turn would have to be hit. One raid would never achieve this; and prolonged bombing of the battery would be the best way of indicating to the Germans the left flank of the Allied invasion. The whole of the northern coast of France was studded with such batteries. A similar treatment of the others as a bluff would use too much of our bomber effort which was required for a multitude of other tasks. For these reasons, a direct assault on the battery by airborne troops was necessary.[7]

James Hill now had the 1st Canadian Parachute Battalion and the 8th and 9th Battalions under his command, and he knew them well.[14] Each battalion possessed its own distinct 'character', and he had chosen the 9th for the task because he considered it to be:

> ...an extremely finickety battalion, masters of detail and management techniques. They had a Commanding Officer who was a remarkably good trainer.

*

After a week of analysing the mass of information, Colonel Otway and one of his officers, Captain Robert Gordon-Brown, had formulated an assault plan. Colonel Otway:

> The Battery contained four guns which were thought to be 150mm, and each gun was in an emplacement made of concrete six foot thick, on top of which was another six foot of earth. There were steel doors in front and rear. The garrison was believed to consist of 150-200 men, with two 20mm dual-purpose guns and up to a dozen machine guns. There was an underground control room and odd concrete pillboxes dotted about. The position was circular, about 400 yards in diameter and surrounded by barbed wire and mines. There

The Battery under construction.

was a village a few hundred yards away which might have held more German troops.

There were only two sides from which we could possibly attack. On the north there was a double-apron barbed wire fence, outside which was a minefield about thirty yards deep. Outside this again was an anti-tank ditch fourteen feet wide and sixteen feet deep, which we assumed would be full of horrors. On the south side there was the same double-apron fence and the same thirty-yard minefield, but instead of the ditch there was another barbed wire fence some twelve to fifteen feet thick and five to six feet high. The whole Battery was then surrounded by a minefield 100 yards deep which was protected by a barbed wire cattle fence, possibly electrified. Such was the nut to be cracked.

As we were to land to the south of the Battery I decided to attack from the south.

'A' Company.

Synchronised with the main assault, three Horsa gliders containing fifty-six men of the Battalion and eight sappers, were to land inside the perimeter:

> *The basis of my plan was surprise and the fact that I did not intend to allow the garrison to concentrate on any one point; they would have to look several ways at once.*

The men required for these assault gliders were duly chosen through a specific selection process. Private Fred Milward, 'A' Company:

> *The CO had us in the Mess Hall and said that we'd got a hush-hush operation to do. He said, "A' Company's the best Company I've got. I want them to do it, but they've got to volunteer, so all those who want to volunteer take a pace forward'. No-one stood still, everybody took a pace forward. Nobody was going to be a coward and stand there!*

No details were given about the mission and the feeling prevailed that it was 'a suicide job'. Major Parry whittled the volunteers down to the necessary number, selecting as many unmarried men as possible. To Fred Milward's relief, he was not chosen:

> *I didn't want to go in the gliders. I'd flown in one before. I had a trip in a Horsa and oh, the smell of vomit! It was the actual movement of the thing, because not only did you move up and down and side to side, you had the tugging. It wasn't a very nice feeling.*

This glider assault group was commanded by Captain Gordon-Brown and so became known as the G-B Force.[15] It comprised of two platoons, each organised as follows:

Captain Robert Gordon-Brown

RHQ	–	Platoon Commander
	–	Platoon Sergeant
	–	Batman
Three sections each	–	Section Commander
	–	Seven Other Ranks

The platoon commanders were Lieutenants Hugh Pond and Hugh Smythe. The engineers comprised of one officer and seven other ranks of No. 2 Troop, 591 (Antrim) Parachute Squadron RE.

*

Having outlined the method of assault, Colonel Otway decided that detailed training was required to familiarize the men with their specific tasks, deduce the necessary equipment, and add the fine detail to the plan. For this he required a full-scale mock-up of the Battery and the route from the DZ. Colonel Otway:

> The Brigade Major, Bill Collingwood, and I, flew over the area and we found this place near Newbury with a big hill. It's called Walbury Hill. It's a long ridge about 800 feet high, very narrow at the top, so it was absolutely ideal for live ammunition. Then I went to see the owner, who was a farmer. He was very good about it because we could have slapped a compulsory order on him. One landowner was a bit difficult. He happened to be a retired Lieutenant Colonel from the First World War, but I took him in and gave him a gin...!
>
> I had, in fact, to see seven people in departments about it, including the Civil Service who said 'You can't do this, you'll have to wait for permission...'. I said 'To hell with that, I'm doing it, and I'm doing it tomorrow!'

And so on the night of 8 May the Battalion marched to the area and set up camp in the hedgerows of a field at nearby West Woodhay, this being the same distance to the mock-up site as that of the DZ to the real Battery.[16] Private Ron Tucker, 'C' Company:

> At one corner of the field a large marquee had been erected, and when we had all settled in, it was here that the CO told us why we had come to this area.
>
> We learned all the details, except where in France, or on which day we would go to destroy the guns; but it was the middle of May, and we expected it would be only a matter of days.

Also taking part in the training were various units attached to the Battalion specifically for the attack. These were one section of the 4th Airlanding Anti-tank Battery RA to deal with the steel doors of the casemates, the sappers to destroy the guns, and medics of 224 Field (Parachute) Ambulance.

This unit contained a nucleus of fully trained personnel to carry out major operations if necessary, and at the same time treat and dress the more normal wounds suffered in battle. It had three sections, each comprising of twenty men including a Medical Officer and a driver. One section was attached to each of the battalions in the brigade. These were to form Advance Dressing Stations (ADSs) where necessary, each being responsible with its corresponding Regimental Aid Post (RAP) for the treatment of its battalion casualties until they could be evacuated to the Main Dressing Station (MDS). This was to be set up by the main body of the Field Ambulance. The battalions themselves each had a medical officer and medical personnel mostly divided amongst the companies. One MO was attached to Brigade HQ.

Captain Ian Johnston commanded No 3 Section, which was allocated to the 9th Battalion:

> Fifteen of my section, i.e. with the exception of the NCOs, were conscientious objectors and did not carry arms. The section carried medical and surgical equipment, our job being to set up a dressing station just outside the Battery, as we expected heavy casualties and did not expect to be able to evacuate them quickly.

A farm along the road running south from the Battery was earmarked for this dressing station.

*

The morning after arrival the Paras proceeded to help the Royal Engineers construct the position using tubular scaffolding covered with canvas to represent the constructions. All the features such as minefields, tank traps, trenches and wire, plus hedges, trees and tracks on the route to the Battery, were also accurately reproduced. Training then commenced. Ron Tucker:

> *At first we simply walked into the attack to make sure of our movements; then we made it as close to the real thing as we could without firing a shot.*

Nine rehearsals followed, five by day and four by night:

> *By this time everyone knew just where he was supposed to go, where the enemy troops would be and which ones each of us were detailed to kill. The only things we did not know were their names and the colour of their hair![16]*

Security during this period was stringent, however the Colonel decided that it was vital for the men to be given the chance to unwind before D-Day. Certain that they realized the importance of secrecy, he gave each Company in turn, twenty-four hours leave to spend in the local town. However, to double-check he went so far as to:

> *...employ some thirty attractive, well-dressed WAAFs in civilian clothes in order to test whether the troops could keep a secret. All concerned had an excellent time and the integrity of the troops was proved to be complete, at any rate as regards security![17]*

The Battalion returned to Bulford camp and on 19 May were given three days leave, again vouched for by the Colonel. They knew it would be their final leave before D-Day. Upon their return they went straight into a three-day exercise involving the whole of the 6th Airborne Division. The Battalion again ended up attacking the mock-up in darkness and with live ammunition. This was the final preparation for the invasion.

*

With such a short space of time to D-Day and particularly with the task in hand, the transition of commanding officer had needed to be smooth. Captain Hudson:

> *The relationship between CO and adjutant is very close; closer than that between CO and second-in-command very frequently. It says a great deal for Terence that, in those hectic days before 6 June 1944, he managed to overcome my feelings when he took over from Martin Lindsay. Those feelings are best expressed by the Master in the parable of the talents:*

> *'Thou knowest that I am an austere man, taking up that I laid not down, and reaping that I did not sow'.*

> *Thus he continued what had been begun, and we provided, I think, the central cohesion that was required from Battalion HQ.*

Otway, a professional soldier since 1933, had

Lieutenant Colonel Terence Otway

joined the Parachute Regiment from the Royal Ulster Rifles. He had spent the pre-war years with them in China, Hong Kong and India:

> We spent four months in Shanghai, and we were bombed, shelled and machine-gunned almost every day by the Japanese, whilst guarding the International Settlement. We then moved to India. We'd hardly arrived before we were involved in putting down riots in Rawalpindi. Then we moved up to the North-West frontier and we were there for a year on active service. Not a week passed without us having a scrap with the tribesmen, and some of the scraps were hand-to-hand fighting with knives and swords. So that was so-called peace!

The Colonel was a tough, forthright, determined man and his drive to get the Battalion to the state of preparedness he required did not endear him to some of the men. Sergeant Len Daniels, 'B' Company:

> Colonel Otway was a very hard man, very stand-offish, naturally as you'd expect your Commanding Officer to be. No tolerance for a fool whatsoever. You daren't make a mistake with the Colonel.

This did not bother him unduly. Colonel Otway:

> I wanted to be respected and I wanted to be considered to be a fair person, but I wouldn't go out of my way to get popularity. I wanted an efficient, well run, happy Battalion, and I reckon I had it.

'C' Company.

CHAPTER TWO

Ready to 'Go To It!'

In readiness for D-Day, on Thursday, 25 May the Battalion began moving to Broadwell Transit Camp near Cirencester. This was close to RAF Broadwell, the aerodrome of departure. Ironically for the Colonel, the bell-tented camp was shared with the 1st Battalion, Royal Ulster Rifles of the 6th Airlanding Brigade.

Since the turn of the year all of the officers had been extremely busy. Lieutenant Douglas Martin, the liaison officer with Brigade, had married Eileen Hart in February and following their forty-eight-hour honeymoon had only seen each other on two weekends since. Arrival at Broadwell did not signal a let up in the preparations, especially for Colonel Otway who was also appointed OC Transit Camp, ie. of all the troops. His adjutant was almost as busy. Captain Hudson:

When we moved to the Transit Camp I was approaching mental and physical exhaustion. The problems of Airfield Procedure, the absolute necessity of attending to what are now known as logistics – Bangalore torpedoes, containers, ammunition, scaling ladders and so on, allowed me no respite.

Briefing for the operation began, and the companies took turns to visit a heavily guarded room to study aerial photographs, models and maps of the area, the DZ and the objectives.

Accordingly, all contact with the 'outside world' was cut. Corporal Doug Tottle, 'A' Company, Medical Section:

There was not a lot to do. We played football most of the time. Local village girls used to come up to the camp and gaze through the barbed wire, only to be chased away by the scores of 'Red Caps'. We were not even allowed to talk to the NAAFI girls, only to order your beer or tea and wad. The 'Red Caps' were watching you.

Dougie and Eileen Martin on their wedding day.

This routine continued until 30 May when the CO, assisted by the Intelligence Officer, Lieutenant Worth, informed the whole Battalion of the plan for the main landings and again went through the detail of their own assault.[1]

The nearest suitable dropping zone for the Battalion was DZ 'V', 2,400 yards east of the Battery. This DZ was to be captured and the immediate area secured by 'C' Company of the Canadian Parachute Battalion which was jumping at twenty minutes after midnight, half an hour before the main drop. Also jumping at this time were Pathfinders of the 22nd Independent Parachute Company who were to set up various navigational aids to identify the DZs. This entailed placing battery-powered fluorescent tubes known as

Lieutenant Joe Worth.

holophane lights at twenty-five yard intervals in the form of a 'T'. The stem indicated the line of flight and each DZ/LZ had its own colour-coded light forming the tail of the stem. This 'T' was used by the Pathfinders to flash the DZ/LZ code letter. A small rectangular box with a collapsible aerial was placed around 100 yards forward of the 'T'. This was a homing beacon called 'Eureka'. Fifteen minutes before the main stream of aircraft was due, the Pathfinders would switch them on. As the transport planes approached the coastline a Rebecca transmitter/receiver set fitted in the aircraft was turned on. This emitted an impulse that caused the Eureka to respond automatically, allowing the aircraft navigator to check his bearing and distance from the DZ. To prevent confusion, each DZ was allocated a different frequency, and, to avoid saturating the Eureka, Rebeccas were only used by group and flight leaders and any pilot who lost his formation.[2]

Also jumping in advance were 9th Battalion Troubridge (Reconnaissance) and Rendezvous (RV) Parties.[3] On landing, the Troubridge Party was to head straight for the Battery to 'confirm the enemy's positions and defences and discover the best approach into the objective as made by OBOE [A bombing raid on the Battery at 0030 hours], ie. whether OBOE has cleared the mines and wire'.[4]

The RV Party prepared the DZ for the arrival of the Battalion. A red Aldis lamp indicated the initial Battalion RV point, while red, blue, green, yellow and maroon lights, as well as white cloth markers, would be set up to identify the individual Company RVs.

Transport gliders carrying the Battalion's heavy equipment were to land on part of the DZ. These contained three jeeps and trailers, a lightweight bridge for use, if required, on the anti-tank ditch, and two six-pounder anti-tank guns. Although eight sappers of 591 Parachute Squadron were in the G-B Force, the majority of the Troop would be jumping with the 9th Battalion. Some of their special 'General Wade' charges could be taken in the G-B Force gliders, but the explosive was too dangerous to jump with and so most of them also had to be carried by the transport gliders.

Thirty-two aircraft were to ferry the bulk of the Battalion, which was to begin jumping at 12.50am. The first out would be members of a Taping Party and those of a duplicate Troubridge Party to cover the possible non-arrival of the original. Upon landing, the Taping Party was to confirm with those at the RV point that the original Troubridge Party had landed successfully and then head straight for a rendezvous with them at a road junction just outside the Battery perimeter.[5] The party would then continue to the Battery and begin clearing and taping three lanes through the minefield up to the perimeter wire using approaches as advised by the Troubridge Party. The duplicate Troubridge Party would instead check the authenticity of a suspected dummy battery to the north-west of Gonneville.[6]

Once on the ground, to help rally the mass of men in the darkness, officers were supplied with a variety of instruments that simulated bird-noises. There was also a password, 'PUNCH', to which the response was 'JUDY'.

It was calculated that the Battalion would take about an hour and a half to assemble and organize on the DZ, and so the advance to the Battery was planned to begin at 2.35 am. Along the way the Battalion would meet the Troubridge Party at a crosstracks one thousand yards south-east of the Battery, where the results of the reconnaissance would be conveyed.[7]

'A' Company of the 1st Canadian Parachute Battalion was to assist in this approach march by protecting the Battalion's left flank. This entailed clearing Gonneville and establishing a security post at the crosstracks rendezvous until the 9th had passed through. The Canadians also had to neutralize an enemy position south of the Battery, and protect the flank during the assault by holding the area from a road junction 700 yards to the south, the site of a Calvary Cross, and the 9th's proposed 'Firm Base'.[8] This was an area along the road east of the Battery that was to be occupied by a Firm Base Party led by the 9th's second in command, Major Eddie Charlton.[9] The party consisted of HQ staff, 2 Platoon, 3 Platoon less one section, Battalion medical personnel and No 3 section of the Field Ambulance. Its task was to hold the area as a rallying point following neutralization of the Battery.

Merville Battery

N

DZ/LZ Area

DZ 'V' to the Merville Battery. This is the actual photograph used by Private Derek Higgins.

Colonel Otway planned to reach this 'Firm Base' at somewhere between 4.10 am and 4.20 am. An 'O' Group would immediately be called and orders issued to the various Company Officers and NCOs. These would return to their sub-units with orders to report by runner when ready to move.

A Diversion Party and two Sniping Groups would then be sent forward. The Diversion Party, led by Lieutenant Browne, consisted of 4 Platoon, less two anti-tank sections, plus two German-speakers. It was to create the diversion by neutralizing a

Lieutenant Brian Browne

33

THE MERVILLE BATTERY ASSAULT PLAN

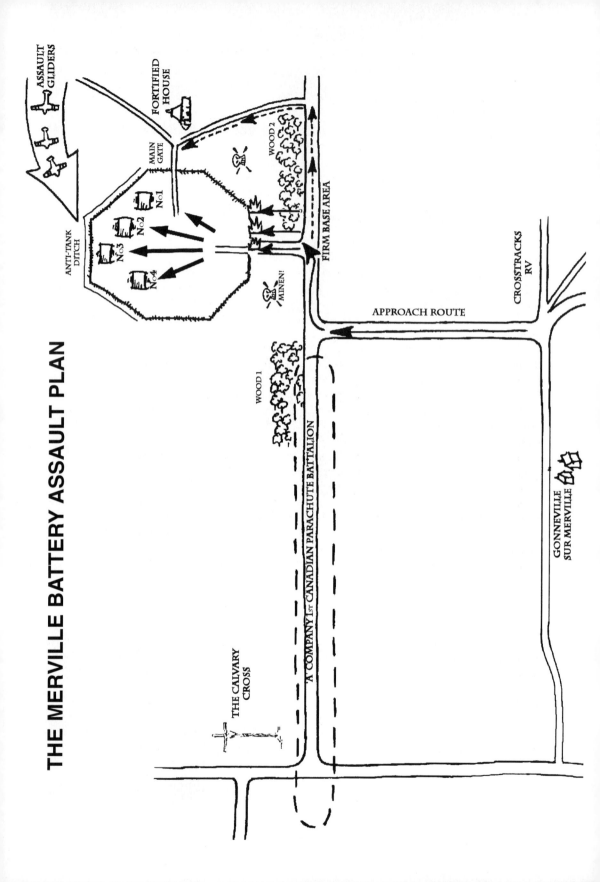

ASSAULT GLIDERS

FORTIFIED HOUSE

MAIN GATE

ANTI-TANK DITCH

No1

No2

No3

No4

WOOD 2

MINEN!

FIRM BASE AREA

WOOD 1

APPROACH ROUTE

CROSSTRACKS RV

'A' COMPANY 1st CANADIAN PARACHUTE BATTALION

THE CALVARY CROSS

GONNEVILLE SUR MERVILLE

fortified house on the northern edge of the perimeter and by forcing entry at the main gate. The German speakers would 'create their own havoc'.

The Sniping Groups comprised of:

1st Group: Commander: CSM Jack Harries
               Troops: Three 'A' Company Bren detachments
                               One Anti-tank section of 4 Platoon with anti-tank rifles
                               Three 'A' Company snipers
2nd Group: Commander: CSM Barney Ross
               Troops: Two 'A' Company Bren detachments
                               One 'C' Company Bren detachment
                               One Anti-tank section of 4 Platoon with anti-tank rifles
                               Three 'C' Company snipers

Snipers of the 1st Group would target the pillboxes and protected machine-gun emplacements, while those of the 2nd were to concentrate on the flak towers.

One section of 3 Platoon would neutralize anti-aircraft positions to the north-west of the Battery.

When all sub-units were ready for the assault, Colonel Otway would order the 'A' Company contingent to move forward onto a cross-tape on either side of the cleared lanes.

'B' Company would then move forward to the outer wire, where they would position Bangalore torpedoes and wait.[10]

If it was necessary to use explosive to clear the mines on the line of advance and surprise lost, or if time was short, the CO would order the bugle-call 'CHARGE', to indicate the 'NOISY' method. On this call the 6-Pounder anti-tank guns of 4th Airlanding Battery section, plus 2 Platoon, the Sniping Parties and 4 Platoon were to open fire. Simultaneously, if they were not already there, the 'B' Company Breaching Parties were to double forward to the wire and lay the Bangalores. They would then lie down, ready to light the fuses and await the arrival of the G-B Force, which was scheduled to land inside the perimeter at 4.30 am.

Having been guided to the site by a Eureka beacon set up close to the Battery, at 4.24 am these gliders were to be released at 5,000 feet, each flashing an 'M' on an Aldis lamp. One and a half minutes later, Otway would order the bugle-call 'REVEILLE'. On this call, Lieutenant Peters, the mortar platoon officer was to order his men to change over to one detachment firing 3-inch star shells to illuminate the whole area. At the same time a Regimental Police detachment was to stand by to supplement the star shells with 2-inch mortar flares should it be necessary. The signal for this would be a 2-inch mortar flare fired by the Colonel.

With two and a half minutes to go, the tug aircraft would signal the letter 'M' on their headlights. On receiving this signal, or at the appointed time, Otway would order the bugle-call 'FALL-IN'. All fire with the exception of the Diversionary Party and flares would cease.

The gliders would then land inside the perimeter. When the third glider was down, the Colonel was to order the bugle-call 'LIGHTS-OUT' and the star shell fire would cease.

Simultaneously, 'B' Company would light the Bangalore fuses and blow the gaps in the wire. Red, white or blue lights were then to be placed to identify the successful gaps. Should one gap be unsuccessful, the light from that gap was to be moved over to the next gap and placed beside it, indicating that troops must switch. As soon as the inner gaps were blown, Otway would order the bugle-call 'REVEILLE' on which the area would again be lit up by 3-inch star shells. On this call, 'C' Company was to assault. 'A' Company was to follow through and take up position inside the wire on either side of the centre gap, and while some 'B' Company men went forward to protect the gaps against any German infiltration around the flanks, the remainder of the Company was to withdraw. The Sniping Groups were to join 'A' Company inside the wire.

Following the successful capture of the casemates, the sappers would blow the barrels off the guns using the General Wades and destroy the recoil mechanisms with purpose-made

PHE charges. Colonel Otway, after inspecting the guns, would then send up a success signal of red-green-red 2-inch mortar flares, followed by the bugle call 'STANDFAST', on which all the troops were to immediately reorganize where they were.

Navy signallers jumping with the Battalion would send a success signal by radio to HMS *Arethusa*, lying off the coast. If by 5.30 am the cruiser had not received an acknowledgement signal, it was to open fire on the Battery.

Meanwhile, 'O' groups were to report to Colonel Otway who would either be inside the centre gap or on the road.

On ascertaining the strengths of the Companies and general position, the CO would order the bugle-call 'COOKHOUSE'.

On this call 'B' Company parties covering the gaps were to turn the lamps to face inwards and the troops would then withdraw to the Firm Base area in the following order:

Royal Engineers
'C' Company
'A' Company
Advanced Battalion HQ
'B' Company gap protection detachments

As Otway passed through the centre gap he was to inform the 'B' Company officer in command of the gap protection detachments to withdraw behind the Advanced Battalion HQ.

The Battalion was then to rendezvous to the south, in the area of the Calvary Cross.[11]

*

Almost immediately after silencing the Battery, the Battalion would have to begin its remaining D-Day tasks. These were to block roads leading from Franceville Plage to Le Plein, capture a German Naval HQ/radar station at Sallenelles, and seize and hold the village of Le Plein until relieved by the Commandos of the 1st Special Service Brigade.[12] These were to arrive at the Benouville bridges via Sword Beach at around noon. To aid in this link-up, Lieutenant Peter Winston and Marine Donald of 45 Royal Marine Commando would be jumping with the Battalion. Signallers Bill Stack and Reg Sherwood, whose 68 radio set had been netted to the Commando system, would accompany them to the bridges.

Bill Stack.   **Reg Sherwood.**

The other battalions of the 3rd Parachute Brigade also had plenty of tasks to achieve. The Canadians, besides supporting the 9th, were to protect the 3rd Parachute Squadron engineers while they blew two bridges, one over the River Dives at Robehomme and another over its tributary, the Divette, at Varaville. Finally, they were to hold the centre of the ridge at the Le Mesnil crossroads.

The 8th Parachute Battalion, landing on DZ 'K', was to provide protection for the engineers while they destroyed two bridges over the River Dives at Bures and another at St Samson (Troarn), and prevent the enemy from capturing the Bois de Bavent along the southern part of the ridge.

*

Six pilots of 'B' Squadron, the Glider Pilot Regiment, were handpicked for the G-B Force, and although they were taking off from RAF Brize Norton, Staff Sergeants Baldwin, Bone and Kerr and Sergeants Michie, Dean and Walker, stayed with the 9th Battalion in the Transit Camp. They had been informed that the three best Horsas in the Regiment would be supplied for the operation and in addition, be specially modified with the Rebecca equipment and an arrester parachute.

Unfortunately, training for the use of the Eureka-Rebecca equipment had somehow been overlooked, and so on 1 June the co-pilots were ordered to attend a course at Netheravon. Sergeant Joe Michie:

> We got to Netheravon and were shown into an ante-room and finally saw two grizzelled old pilots who must have been in the Royal Flying Corps in the First World War.

They were then informed that the course involved two weeks of instruction!

> We knew that D-Day was two or three days away, so we had to go out of Netheravon to a phone box just outside the camp, and in guarded tones tell 'B' Squadron that they didn't seem to know when D-Day was coming up. Anyway, the next day, they'd obviously been told and everybody ran around in small circles.

The course was hastily compressed.

*

During the afternoon of 2 June General Gale arrived at Broadwell and spoke to the assembled camp. He received a rapturous response when describing the airborne assault. In typical fashion he said, 'The Hun thinks only a bloody fool will go there. That's why I'm going!'

The station commander of RAF Broadwell also received a loud cheer when he came to wish the Battalion good luck and stated that his pilots had never missed a dropping zone yet, or even been late over one. However, this did not quite give the full picture. The newly-formed 46 Group RAF was dropping the Brigade and, due to a shortage of transport plane crews, had been forced to draft in a large mixture of hastily trained airmen and experienced bomber-crews and consequently many of them had little or no experience of dropping parachutists. Later in the evening, to try and help alleviate any fears about the drop itself, the aircrews of 512 Squadron, which was transporting the 9th, met the men and chatted for about an hour.

Another problem was that the Group had insufficient transport aircraft to ferry the whole of the Division in one operation. And so most of the 6th Airlanding Brigade was to arrive during the evening of D-Day, using LZs 'N' and 'W', while the remainder landed by sea on D+1.[13]

*

The following day, most of the men travelled to the airfield to load their kitbags and draw parachutes. The Paras marked the chutes with the last two digits of their serial number and placed them on the planes. Ditching drill and the use of 'Mae Wests' was practised in the event of a plane crash-landing in the sea.

Forty equipment containers were also attached to the aircraft.[14] These containers each had four built-in lamps that lit up on striking the ground, so that in whatever attitude they landed one would be visible. To readily identify the contents, various coloured discs were fitted to the lamps.

A special lightweight version of the Bangalore torpedo was being taken. These had been designed so that the scaffold-like lengths, when connected together, would not bend as much and so make them easier to pass through the wire. However, while attempting to load them, another problem came to light for Captain Hudson. The cradles designed to carry them beneath the Dakota wings were too long, and as the torpedoes were vital to the operation, immediate modification action had to be instigated.

Departing earlier, the RV and Troubridge Parties had to fly from RAF Harwell. Major Parry was given command of the RV Party:

Ten of us had visited the airfield to 'bomb up', collect and fit parachutes and meet our pilot. We were the only ten of the Battalion to depart from this airfield, from which also flew the Pathfinders of 22 Independent Parachute Company and Divisional Headquarters.

Major George Smith was assigned to command the Troubridge Party:

Together with two Company Sergeant Major Physical Training Instructors [‘Dusty’ Miller and Bill Harrold], I was to make a reconnaissance of the Battery, instruct a Taping Party, meet the Battalion, advise the Commanding Officer of the prospects of his plan, and lead the unit along to the assault by the best route. The other party consisted of an officer [Major Parry], his batman [Private Adsett], four sergeants [Easlea, Knight, Lukins and Pinkus] and a private from the Intelligence Section [Mason] who were to organize the Rendezvous for the Battalion by the time it landed on the Dropping Zone.

For the majority of men it would be their first time in action. This was certainly the case for Private Maurice Parris of ‘A’ Company. Twice he had joined up whilst under age and on both occasions his father had ‘dragged him back home’. When he made a third attempt and joined the Paras, his father had to resign himself to the fact that it was no use trying to stop him. Maurice was eighteen years old, yet his age was not unusual, in fact the majority of the others were not much older.

Sgt Lukins.

Sgt Pinkus.

A very special member of ‘A’ Company was Glenn, a German Shepherd Parachute dog. He had been trained to locate explosives, carry messages and detect the enemy in the dark, as each nationality of soldier had his own particular odour caused by such things as diet and clothing. His handler was Private Emile Corteil or ‘Jack’ as he was known (a bit of a ‘Jack the Lad’!). The dog, which actually enjoyed jumping, was well loved by many of the Paras.[15]

Although Private Stendall Brailsford of the Motor Transport Platoon had been at the dummy Battery for the rehearsals, he was possibly the only man who did not know his task in the assault:

Being MT, I didn't take much part in it at all. To be honest I knew nothing about how the operation was going to take place. At Broadwell, as far as I was concerned I was the QM's driver, who wasn't going.[16]

Lieutenant Christie, known as ‘Corpus’ Christie, ‘B’ Company, his batman went sick. I was so desperate to go that I immediately went and volunteered and I got taken on.

Brigade HQ was pitched among the tents of the Canadian Parachute Battalion at RAF Down Ampney. Brigadier Hill:

> *I put my headquarters there because perhaps they were the least experienced of the chaps. It was amusing, I remember I used to have strict rules that everybody would be in their tents, and lights out by 10 o'clock. And then of course, a football would hit my tent. They weren't fussy!*

The Brigade Administration Officer, Staff Captain John Woodgate, a former member of the 9th, shared a tent with his good friend Major Alec Pope, the Brigade Deputy Assistant Adjutant and Quartermaster General. Most of the Brigade Headquarters was taking off from RAF Down Ampney, but, due to logistical reasons, one stick had to go from Broadwell. John Woodgate:

> *That was going to be Major Pope's stick. We practised in that way, and the day before or so, the Brigadier decided he must have the DAA and QMG with him at the aerodrome he was going from. So we swapped over. It was rather nice in a way, going with my old Battalion.*

*

Broadwell Camp was now a hive of activity. Private Ron Gregory, 'B' Company, HQ Platoon:

> *Life in Transit was of unbelievable cramp, non-smokers smoking, non-drinkers drinking, non-believers believing. Everyone became so busy cleaning weapons, priming grenades, studying maps, photos and models, that time started to fly.*

Peter Neal.

With all this labour involving weaponry, accidents were inevitable. A grenade explosion killed several members of the Royal Ulster Rifles, and the 9th Battalion suffered its own tragedy. Lance Corporal Edward Hull was a member of the G-B Force. Private Gordon Newton, 'A' Company:

> *Hull and his friend Peter Neal were talking as they walked back from the Admin block to their tents. There was a football match going on to their left. Suddenly, Neal realized that he was talking to himself. He looked around and there was Hull lying on the ground. He said to Hull, 'What's up ?', to which he responded, 'I don't know'. Neal then saw that he had a wound in his neck. An officer on the far side had been cleaning his Sten when it had fired a single shot. The bullet went across the football pitch, missing everyone, and hit Hull. It was extremely bad luck. Even so, everyone thought he would be OK.[17]*

*

With D-Day only forty-eight hours away Colonel Otway imposed a drink ban in case anyone, under the strain of waiting, drank too much and went into battle with a hangover. Corporal Doug Tottle:

> *Then all we could do was lay on our sleeping bags wondering what was going to happen to us. I used to think of the girl I left behind at Crookham; the only pub at Bulford, the 'Rose and Crown', where there were fights every night (British v the Yanks).*

*

On Sunday, 4 June, the eve of D-Day, John Gwinnett, the Battalion Padre, held a final service. The Camp Commandant, Captain Peter Young, and his staff had presented the Battalion with a maroon flag that had a white silk 'Bellerophon' as in the Airborne emblem and a large '9' in the top left-hand corner. It had been made for the camp by the Women's Voluntary Service of Oxford, the men's wives having given up some of their clothing coupons for it. A deputation of camp administration staff asked Captain Young to present it to the Battalion to take into action and, although against regulations, this was duly done and Gwinnett carried out its dedication. It was given to Gordon Newton to take across with the G-B Force.

Later in the afternoon Brigadier Hill arrived and addressed his officers, proffering some final advice:

> *Gentlemen, in spite of your excellent orders and training, DO NOT BE DAUNTED IF CHAOS REIGNS. It undoubtedly will.*

*

The G-B Force co-pilots had completed the Eureka-Rebecca course and arrived at Brize Norton. Sergeant Michie:

> *The 2nd pilots were then sent off to collect the gliders for the actual landing..., to pick up four gliders, three plus a spare. These were to have radar installed with Eureka-Rebecca radar which meant they would have aerials on the leading edge of the wings, and arrester parachute under the tail.*
>
> *When we got there, the Flight Sergeant took us out to the gliders and said, 'Here they are, these are the ones with the parachutes.' I said, 'Well there don't seem to be any radar aerials on them'. Of course the security had been so good that radar had been fitted in four gliders and parachutes fitted in four others. Well, we happened to bump into, literally, Colonel Chatterton, told him about this and people tore around. Eventually flew back with the gliders correctly fitted.*[18, 19, 20]

However, Staff Sergeant Baldwin was very unhappy when he was confronted by the chosen three:

> *Two brand spanking new Horsas and one beat-up old one. The Major (Toler) did the only fair thing he could do; three sticks, the fellow drawing the short stick getting the old one. I need not tell you who that was. There was no time to take them up for a short flight. All the months of planning and now this.*[21]

To compound matters, some bad weather that had developed had now deteriorated into a storm.

*

Having completed their preparation, the Paras waited, listening to the wind and rain buffeting the bell-tents. Private Sid Capon, 'C' Company:

> *We were all set to go, ready to board the trucks. The rain was teeming down. Then word came that the operation had been postponed for twenty-four hours, so we went back to our tents.*

At 9.30 pm the members of SHAEF, the Supreme Headquarters Allied Expeditionary Force, met at Southwick House near Portsmouth, to discuss the situation. Group Captain John Stagg, the head of the Meteorological Committee, reported that when the present front had passed, an interval of fair conditions would prevail over the Channel until at least dawn on Tuesday. The commanders discussed the risks involved and General Eisenhower decided to issue provisional instructions for the assault to begin on Tuesday, 6 June.[22]

CHAPTER THREE

'Gentlemen, The Operation is On!'
Monday 5 June

At 4.15am the SHAEF committee again met with Group Captain Stagg who reported no change to his forecast of the previous night. The final and irrevocable decision was made to launch the assault on 6 June.[1] The order filtered down the chain of command and Brigadier Hill broke the news to his officers:

> *Gentlemen, the operation is on! We go tonight. The wind on the continent is from five to ten miles an hour.*[2]

The men were informed and began repeating their final preparations. Private Ron Gregory:

> *After spending some time on last-minute details and looking at aerial photos of the DZ etc., we had lunch and were ordered to bed for a few hours. I didn't need much waking! Another meal was ready for us, the cookhouse staff were marvellous... . Flasks of hot tea and jam sandwiches were collected for use on the flight, together with a lot of sweets, chocolate and gum. Early evening we spent on camouflaging faces and telling jokes, and at last the order 'Kit up' – a queue for the toilet!*

At 8.00 pm, after a last word of goodwill from the Colonel, the ten men of the RV and Troubridge Parties departed for Harwell. Major Smith:

> *We were boisterous. I do not think anyone felt unduly nervous, although none of us had previously done an operational jump. The meteorological forecast of the wind on the Continent caused considerable comment. It was quite strong here in England, and even the largest branches of the trees were dancing up and down. Surely the forecast was just a myth invented to spur us forward, and we should find a wind of at least twenty-five miles an hour gusting to thirty. Anyway, it was a relief to be out of the confinement of the Transit Camp.*

They arrived at Harwell at 9.20 pm. Major Parry:

> *Ever since returning from France in 1940 on the occasion of the Dunkirk evacuation, I had been apprehensive lest I should not one day be among the lucky ones to return. Thus, on the evening of 5 June I found myself at Harwell airfield waiting to emplane on what was to be the biggest operation ever undertaken by British arms. I was well aware of this fact, which added to my suppressed excitement.*

Meeting the aircrew, they chatted over a cup of tea. Major Smith:

> *The pilot told us we would be dropped about half a mile from the intended Dropping Zone as aerial reconnaissance showed enemy-dug positions in its vicinity. We were already aware of these positions but had had no confirmation that they were manned. It seemed to me that this was more of a military decision than one to be made by the Royal Air Force, but as we had studied the ground thoroughly and thought we knew it from all angles we did not argue.*

Major Parry:

> *Everybody was very calm, outwardly at any rate, and going about his business quietly. I stuffed my haversack into my leg kitbag in which I was also carrying an Aldis Lamp. Seeing me do so, my batman, Private Adsett did likewise; so did one of the sergeants. I told them I couldn't guarantee they would see them again but they appeared to be quite content to take the risk rather than strap them to their stomachs for the jump.*
>
> *A frightful job getting into one's harness. Although we had fitted chutes a couple of days before, mine didn't fit at all well now. After a few further adjustments, it fitted beautifully thanks to Adsett's*

Left to right: Lieutenants Bobby De La Tour, Don Wells, John Vischer and Bob Midwood, Pathfinders of the 22nd Independant Parachute Company, synchronize watches prior to emplaning at RAF Harwell. Taylor Library

beneficial advice. [The] Kitbag became a bit of a problem as the quick-release mechanism had come adrift and reposed in the bottom of the bag. As there was not sufficient time to look for it, I had to be content with tying the rope onto my harness.

Major Smith:

I placed my haversack and respirator under my jumping jacket, and this over my equipment, containing pistol, entrenching tool, grenades, rubber gloves, torch, binoculars, compass, overloaded map case, and numerous other contrivances I considered necessary, must have made me appear grotesquely comic, for everyone burst out laughing. Soon, some of the others looked very much the same as myself, but several of the RV Party had special kitbags containing necessary stores, and included in them their personal kit. These kitbags were strapped to their legs when they jumped. On the parachutes opening, they pulled quick releases and let the kitbags down on ropes called static lines, to dangle twenty feet below them, thus hitting the ground first and relieving the parachutes of the extra weight before the men landed.[3]

The pilot told us that, as there was a following wind, he would not take off until nine minutes after eleven, nine minutes later than the time scheduled. We were not to worry as he guaranteed he would drop us accurately at twenty minutes past midnight.

Back at Broadwell, as the main body of the Battalion had boarded the trucks taking them to the airfield, they had been 'serenaded' by the G-B force with a chorus of, 'Oh What A Lovely Hole in the Elephants Bottom!' And when the time came to depart they received a rousing send-off as the trucks passed through an avenue of administration staff, NAAFI girls and Royal Ulster Rifles.

After a short journey the convoy arrived at the approach road to RAF Broadwell. WAAFs and aircraftsmen were walking in the opposite direction, heading for billets, the local dance hall or the nearby pub. The trucks entered the airfield and the men dismounted beside the planes.[4] The atmosphere was subdued. Sipping tea, they waited. Like many others, CSM Harries went through yet another mental check of his equipment:

A Sten gun, which would eventually be stuffed inside the parachute harness, against my chest. Webbing equipment and small pack which contained so much that I intended to jump with this in my arms with it attached by a length of strong string to the 'D' on my parachute harness so that I could let it down after I was free of the aircraft, so that it would hang below me and I would hopefully find it on landing at the end of the string. Four Sten magazines filled with 9mm ammunition, a spare small box of 9mm, two '36' Mills grenades, one phosphorous grenade, two sticks of plastic explosive for the anti-tank grenade, mess tin, knife, fork, spoon, 24-hour ration pack, map, message pad, entrenching tool, parachute helmet, maroon beret, mirror, bootlaces, spare socks, singlet and briefs, small towel and washing and shaving kit, pay book, handkerchiefs, writing paper, envelopes, pen, pencil, binoculars, torch, French money, field dressing, one packet (three) contraceptives, toilet paper, boiled sweets, camouflage smock, boot polish/dubbin, blanco and brush, comb, plus of course any personal items.

In addition to this there were the escape gadgets hidden around the clothing – two brass buttons sewn into the flies of my trousers which, one balanced on the other, formed a compass, a small metal saw about four inches long bedded in rubber and sewn into my trousers, a small compass sewn into the lining of my jumping smock together with two silk maps of the area. A bonus tucked into my smock was half a bottle of brandy which had been issued to officers and senior NCOs for 'medicinal purposes'.

At around 10.30 pm the RV and Troubridge Parties began boarding their Albermarle. Major Parry:

This was most difficult as we were all very heavily laden. The only entrance was the aperture in the floor of the aircraft. One had first to crawl under the fuselage, grab a doubtful ladder and then, by using every ounce of strength, lever oneself into the interior. When all ten of us were in, we were sweating like pigs and cussing each other because of our extreme discomfort. I found it quite impossible to strap my kitbag to my leg so had to be content to secure it with but one strap round my right ankle, and praying to God it would not slip off before I wanted it to. Sergeant Easlea spent several minutes swearing at the crush.

At the same time, the men of the main body were ready to board their Dakotas. Captain Albert Richards was a war artist attached to the Battalion:

There was no joking. We all had too much on our minds. Our Captain Quartermaster, who had told us a thousand times that none of us would ever make real soldiers, broke down and wept.
The CO wished us, 'Happy landings.' His optimism was infectious.[5]

CSM Harries:

A glance at my watch showed that it was 10.30 pm and from the movement of the chap in front I could see that he was trying to climb the short ladder to the aircraft door. He needed a shoulder beneath him as the weight he was carrying prevented him climbing in unaided. In fact, all required assistance.

Now to look for our seats and 'chutes with the chalked number. Despite numerous rehearsals all seemed chaos for a while with people standing up and trying to fit 'chutes before they could sit down and hook up. It seemed pretty dark in the aircraft but soon one became accustomed to it and was able to recognize others. Most were having difficulty as some harnesses required adjustment due to the large loads and extra equipment each was required to carry.

A thought came to me that our earlier commanding officer, who objected to the use of Anglo-Saxon swear words, would need to cover his ears if he was in this aircraft!

Things now seemed to be settling down and a sure sign was the red glows of cigarettes here and there. Some rations were put aboard together with sick bags and a tin for urine. It was always a standing joke that having fitted a 'chute to do a drop, one always wanted a 'panic piddle' which is no doubt due to nervous tension. I guess if anyone wanted one right now it would be extremely difficult and no doubt most would need to control it or have damp trousers.

Shortly after 11.00 pm six Albermarles, each carrying ten Pathfinders of the 22nd Independent Parachute Company, began taking off from Harwell. The 9th Battalion plane was among fourteen Albermarles of 295 and 570 Squadrons carrying the advance parties of 3rd Parachute Brigade HQ, and the Canadian's 'C' Company. Major Smith:

Once inside we closed the doors and crowded forward as far as were able in the approved take-off positions. It was half-light when the aircraft taxied clumsily to take up its position at the beginning of the runway. Suddenly the engine revolutions increased and the plane rapidly gathered speed and took to the air. We did not as usual circle the airfield, but went straight off as though determined to finish this thing as soon as we could.

At Broadwell the 9th was similarly ready. CSM Harries:

The aircraft started to whine to life and move off to the take-off position. A glance at my watch confirmed it was just after 23.00 hours, so we were right on time.

After a few minutes we taxied again and then it seemed we were on the take-off runway as the engines were now straining and I wondered if we'd get off with the weight.

Fifteen minutes later the Battalion's Dakotas were airborne. They formed up in 'vics' of three, flying at thirty second intervals. Visibility was quite good, although 10/10ths cloud obscured the moon. With forming up they faced a flight of just over an hour and a half. Colonel Otway fell asleep.[6] With all the planning and training he had been close to exhaustion, and the day's delay in going had been a very welcome relief:

I woke up shortly afterwards because I saw us crossing the British Coast. I had a bottle of whisky with me. Passed it around.

The bottle went through twenty pairs of hands. When it returned he found there had been few 'takers'. He went back to sleep.

Ahead of the main body, the planes of the advance parties had taken up position in a bomber stream to disguise their approach. The RV and Troubridge Parties had settled down. Major Smith:

> *I had brought with me some jam sandwiches without butter. They were supposed to be a safeguard against air sickness. This I did not fear, but considered it was better to fight with a full stomach than otherwise. They were offered around, but nobody fancied any. I managed to eat one, but it was most distasteful, and I had to eat slowly and force down each mouthful.*

Back at the Transit Camp the G-B Force had been left feeling rather alone. Sapper Alex Taylor, 591 Parachute Squadron RE:

> *The stillness of the area had become depressing, almost as if we had been left out of things and left behind.*

Eventually they departed for Brize Norton:

> *Our spirits rose, we were on our way at last after the delays. None of us expected to survive the night.*

The journey gave the Paras plenty of time for such thoughts and they prepared themselves in their own different ways for what was to come. Private Jack Humfrey, 'C' Company:

> *It's only if you're scared about getting killed that you get unhappy. If you can tell yourself, you aren't going to come back, do the best you can ever do with it, suddenly you get a little bit of peace, and it wasn't so bad. But I was psyched-up for the fact that I wasn't going to return.*

Sapper Alex Taylor.

Private Ron Phelps, 'A' Company HQ:

> *I didn't feel scared at all, which is a bit strange. I think the main thing is you're in with your mates and you can't sort of show them you're a coward or something like that. So that's what really keeps you going in those situations.*

Ron Gregory:

> *A letter from Mum saying that my brother serving in the RAF had been posted missing over Germany was enough to gear me up.*

CSM Harries:

> *I wondered about my wife and little five-year-old daughter, who had no idea where I was at this moment. I wondered if they were having an air raid, which was usual being only some twenty-five miles from central London. If that was the case then they would no doubt be in the Morrison shelter in the living room, which doubled for a table. I knew it was no picnic having to spend so much time in an air raid shelter, particularly as our second baby was expected in about six or seven weeks. When would I see the new baby? I told my wife I was volunteering for parachuting and asked her if she minded. The reply must have been typical of many wives – 'If that's what you really want to do and it helps to finish the war any quicker, then I don't mind'.*

The airborne armada swept on.

CSM Jack Harries

CHAPTER FOUR

The Drop
Tuesday 6 June

Just after midnight the advance parties began to ready themselves for their exit. Major Smith:

Soon the navigator informed us that we were approaching the French coast and advised us to open the trap doors. This was more easily said than done, encumbered as we were with parachutes, equipment and the kitbags. There was little enough room, and it was only with facetious and rude remarks that I eventually persuaded the others to move up sufficiently to allow me to get off the doors and open them, pinning the flaps against the inside of the fuselage. I sat on the forward end of the hole and swung my legs through it. The slipstream blew them back, so I rested them on the narrow ledge each side.

Suddenly the coast came into view, and away to the right I could see sudden bursts of flame which arose and died away almost immediately. The bombers were softening up the beach defences.

Major George Smith.

Five minutes to go. We began to prepare our positions for the jump. CSM Miller took up position to the rear of the hole. I stood over the centre of it with my legs astride, each foot balanced precariously on the narrow ledge at the base of each door, whilst CSM Harrold stood similarly over the rear of the hole. This was not the orthodox manner of jumping, but one we had worked out as the best method for a quick jump, most likely to land us on the ground close together. The usual method in this type of aircraft is to bunny-hop down the fuselage from the forward end and through the hole in turn. We had not been able to practise our new method, but the theory seemed good.

We passed over the coast at about 700 feet. One minute to go. There was no flak to mention, but streams of tracer began to pass us. Most of it was below or in the rear. My job was to watch the lights near the roof of the fuselage, so I was unable to watch the tracer for long. The red light would come on for four seconds

CSM Bill Harrold.

as a warning and then change to green; the order to jump. It was a very long minute and I remember my hands were sticky with sweat. The red light shone.

With a sudden flick the red light disappeared and the green took its place. I closed my legs, clutched the harness about my chest, and felt myself sliding down the slipstream. I clearly remember saying to myself, 'Well, you can't climb back now!'

Directly Miller had seen me close my legs he had jumped at me, and Harrold had thrown himself at Miller's disappearing head. There was a gentle tug at my shoulders, the clack of the silk canopy opening, and I was floating majestically to earth.

The RV party followed. Major Parry:

Major Allen Parry.

We couldn't get out fast enough. I eased my way towards the aperture and just fell out. Catching my KB [Kitbag] on the port side of the aperture caused numerous twists in my rigging lines, a sight that perplexed me slightly. Worse still, I couldn't reach sufficiently far down to release my KB.

Sergeant Sid Knight:

Unfortunately for me I was number ten in the stick and when I went to jump out, I couldn't move; somehow my harness had hooked onto a handle on the door leading to the pilot's cabin. Anyway, I hammered on the door and I just saw a chink of light when the door opened and I was loose, so I slid out.

Major Smith:

It was a perfect descent. We were not being fired on, although tracer could still be seen firing in an arc further and further away, apparently still at the aircraft.

There was no moon, but we had been sitting in the dark for an hour and our eyes were adjusted for night vision. I could see a large building about half a mile away half-left and another about three-quarters of a mile half-right. I decided the former was a place known as the Varaville Headquarters, a German Military Headquarters. Next, I found it swept from sight by the tops of trees, and I hit the ground with a thud, rolling over onto my back in a manner which would have made the instructors of the Parachute Training School weep with shame.

I sat up, twisted and punched my harness quick release until it dropped free, pulled out my leg straps, and ripped open the zip-fastener of my jumping jacket. I was ready for action. I could not understand why somebody was not shooting at me, or some burly figure had not hurled himself upon me.

I looked around. Four yards away a figure was struggling with his harness. 'Who is that ?' I whispered. 'Dusty Miller,' came the answer. Another figure emerged from the shadow of some trees fifteen yards away. It was Harrold. Our method of jumping had proved better than we expected. I had not seen them in the air as I had been too busy trying to locate my position to look up. If we had jumped in the usual way we should have been from twenty to forty yards apart, and possibly more. There would also have been thick hedges between us. As it was, we were all in the corner of a field surrounded by a thick hedge, closely treed. There was no sign or sound of any members of the other party.

CSM 'Dusty' Miller.

We went close to the hedge to get our bearings and discuss our plans. It was twenty minutes past midnight by my watch, so the pilot had kept his promise. Further, there was little wind and our doubts of the meteorological department had proved misplaced.

As Major Parry came down, he continued the struggle to free his kitbag:

I was beginning to think I had 'had it', when with a final effort, I succeeded in releasing it. All this took time and I didn't once look down to see how I was doing. It was, therefore, with a considerable shock, both mentally and physically, that I touched down. My legs must have been miles apart.

Before landing, however, I was conscious of hearing bullets and made up my mind then and there that they were all destined for me. I felt a devil of a target sitting on the ground, ridding myself of my harness and emptying my KB.

No more than two or three aircraft had dropped before us so we could claim to be among the first forty or so to land in France.

He had no idea of his whereabouts and so studied a map and two aerial photographs with a torch. Still none the wiser, he began 'quacking' with his Bakelite 'duck' whistle, but after a few minutes of this, no 'lost ducks' had responded and so he set off on a compass bearing to the west and hopefully the RV.

For Sergeant Knight those few seconds delay in getting out of the plane had resulted in landing quite a distance off target, in a field full of cows.

All of the 3rd Brigade's advance parties had made their jumps, but, owing to their pilots having taken evasive action to avoid some flak, the Canadians were dropped over a wide area. Only about thirty of them actually landed on DZ 'V', but fortunately very little resistance was met.

The Pathfinders, led by Lieutenant Don Wells, managed to set out two green holophane 'T's and erect one Eureka beacon on the DZ.[1]

The bombing raid to 'soften up' the Merville Battery was due to begin at 12.30 am. Major Smith:

We had intended to lie up in a ditch and wait for it, stuffing our ears with cotton wool and lying in an anti-blast position. The Battery was 2,400 yards away and we should have been fairly safe. The temptation to get going was too great, so we decided to get going and take cover when we heard the Lancasters approaching. We kept in the shadows of the hedges and went at a good pace until we heard them. A shallow ditch was handy and we took up our positions in it. Suddenly there was a harsh tearing sound as the bombs began to fall, and then terrific explosions. I could not resist putting my head up to have a look. The bombs were falling halfway between it [the Battery] and us. There was a large field in front of us, which we had either to cross or make a detour around. I shouted to the sergeant majors, 'Let's run across the field whilst the Huns are taking cover from the bombs,' and we darted out of the ditch in a bunch and began to run.

We were not halfway across the field when there was a terrible screaming sound, like twenty expresses tearing past one another on adjacent tracks. We threw ourselves to the ground, clasped our hands round the backs of our necks, with the forearms pressed over our ears, and our elbows lifting our bodies slightly from the ground. Bombs crashed before us, to the right, left and behind. The earth shook as though in the hands of an angry giant. Great trees fell and huge clods of earth showered about us as craters opened up, each large enough to bury a suburban villa. Even above the din and chaos I imagined I could hear my heart pounding against my chest.

Major Parry:

Many of the bombs dropped in the field in which I found myself. I took cover in a ditch and, whilst hoping for the best, feared the worst. I was scared out of my wits. I bit the dust and there prepared to meet my end.

Sergeant Sid Knight.

Sergeant Knight:

I had a terrific sense of loneliness. It's funny how things come into your mind, but as these bombs were coming down and the cows were being blown to bits and bellowing like mad, I suddenly thought of this old Cadbury's advert which said 'Where is your chocolate? It's with the soldier, alone in an empty country.' That was me ![2]

The bombing continued for ten minutes. Major Smith:

Suddenly this man-made eruption ceased. Aeroplanes could be heard going into the distance, and a haze of smoke and dust obliterated everything. We sat up. A feeling of stupidity overcame me and then cleared as I realized how lucky we were to be alive. The others were getting to their feet as though surprised to find their limbs still worked. Miller uttered a single word of blasphemy.

Again we started for the opposite hedge at a steady double. On the other side of it was a rough track. I had expected to find a good road. We stopped to check our position. Both of the other fellows were convinced this was not the road. The types and thicknesses of the hedges about agreed with the picture in my mind, and I decided that the maps and aerial photographs we had studied over-emphasized this track and made it appear like a road. We set off on the field side of the hedge and fortunately my surmise proved correct.

We had not gone far when a voice from a ditch ahead halted us. I recognized it as the voice of the batman of the officer commanding the RV Party. [Nineteen year-old George Adsett]. He seemed a little bewildered and very excited. He had met none of the other six in his party and was lost. I pointed out to him some trees which bordered the RV, instructed him to make his way there and get a message to the Battalion when it arrived that the Recce Party had landed safely and started off on its job.

Major Parry had also survived the bombing:

When they ceased to fall I breathed a sigh of relief. In contrast to this noise, the next I heard was a rustling in the hedge. I lay very still for a few moments and breathed yet another sigh of relief when I heard whispered 'Punch', to which I replied enthusiastically 'Judy'. At long last I was no longer alone and joined up with two Canadians who were as lost as I was.

As they had lost their weapons and Parry could use his pistol, he passed them his Sten gun. The three of them carried on through the darkness.[3]

The Troubridge Party also struggled on. Major Smith:

The next hedge junction we met was too thick to get through. This meant going away from the road, and we walked a good hundred and fifty yards before I decided to break through it and chance the noise alarming the enemy. To do so we had to cross a deep ditch and break through a hedge comparable with those in Kent, when we found ourselves in a three-yard wide belt of shrub, with yet another hedge to cross. I threw myself at it only to find nothing beneath my feet, and I was falling and falling. I landed in an incongruous heap at the bottom of another ditch. It was of exceptional depth and only by stretching my arms at full length above my head could my colleagues grasp my hands and pull me out through a tearing mass of brambles and rose thorn.

Another similar double-ditched, double hedge a little later made us decide to try the track at any future hedge junction. We could not afford the delay caused by breaking through the hedges and in any case the noise breaking through them was, if anything, more dangerous than moving on the verge at the side of the track occasionally.

Soon we did come to another hedge junction and we found a gap onto the track. I decided it would be better going on the other side of the track, ran across it and threw myself into a ditch about five feet deep. There, not five yards from me were two German soldiers. They were not in a prepared defensive position and I grasped that they were still frightened and sheltering from the holocaust of bombs which had been let loose. I had been using both hands to gap the hedges and wire fences, and my pistol was still in its holster. Anyway, my immediate job was reconnaissance and to avoid conflict with the enemy. I leaped back out of the ditch, a large stone came against my hand as I did so, and I threw it at the Germans. They must have thought it was a grenade for they threw themselves flat. All this took about half a second. I joined the other two across the track and we made a small detour.

Next we had to cross about six hundred yards of open country. We found our starting point and set off on a compass bearing which, if correct, would bring us out at a hedge gap. Thirty yards into the field we found two posts about fifteen yards apart. They were solid affairs, whole trees with the bases sunk well into the ground, and the other ends about fifteen feet high. Between them a piece of wire was stretched, starting at a height of six feet on one and ending three feet up the other. The wire was of exceptional thickness and it would have been impossible to cut it with ordinary issue wire cutters. We ducked under it and continued on our course, only to find the field full of these posts, and all were joined by the thick wire at varying heights, from the ground level to ten feet up. They were German defences against glider landings.

We were nearly across the open space when flak guns along the coast began to open up. Almost immediately the dark silhouettes of Dakota aircraft appeared and continued to appear for the next fifteen minutes. They were at heights from five hundred to fifteen hundred feet, rather more hidden than we expected. I could have jumped for joy. This was the Battalion.

It was 12.45am.

The drop that had dominated the Paras thoughts for months had finally arrived. On a five-minute warning they stood up and those that had not already done so began hooking up their parachutes to the static line. The red warning light was to come on at four minutes but many of the stick commanders had made private arrangements with the pilots to reduce this to a single minute. The Number One stood in the doorway with the stick packed tightly behind him. They awaited the green light. Conditions for the pilots were difficult as a twenty-five knot cross-wind had developed, and confronting them was a huge dust cloud stirred up by the wayward bombing raid. Flak began to rise and for many the sheer quantity of it was a big shock. Private Derek Vincent, 'B' Company:

All of a sudden there was a sort of a lurch. It wasn't taking evasive action... . It must have been ack-ack stuff, must have blown the aircraft about a bit. I went over and got picked up quickly, before the jump started, but that started a bit of chaos.

Some pilots did instinctively begin to 'zig-zag' the aircraft in violent evasive action, with the result that many of the Paras ended up on the floor. Private Tom Stroud, 'C' Company:

We were, with some difficulty, able to get to our feet to hook up our static lines and take up positions ready to jump with our kitbags strapped to our legs.

With DZ 'V' arriving literally sixty seconds after crossing the coastline, it gave little time for directional correction or for the men to recover. Tom Stroud:

Red light on, green light on, and out of the plane, shortly to feel that reassuring snatch of the shoulder harness as the 'chute developed fully, quickly controlling the 'chute while what appeared to be golden chains drifted slowly up towards me, before rapidly and thankfully passing; my first experience of ack-ack whilst hanging from a parachute.

Company Sergeant Major Harries, 'A' Company:

I could see men falling through the door and being whipped away in the slipstream. Suddenly, I seemed to be doing a balancing act, as gone was the support of the person in front and then had a yard or so to go to the door... . The RAF dispatcher hooked up in the tail by the door grabbed me by the shoulder and guided or pushed me towards the door, and he was so close that I was able to hear his shouted message to me which was 'Hurry up, we want to get back.' Needless to say he had a reply which was 'Bollocks! You'll be back for supper.' I doubt whether he heard me as the next moment I was feeling for the edge of the door to get a good push off; the other arm was occupied holding my pack to my chest. I must have gone out like a sack of rubbish but at that stage the slipstream took over and I was plucked from the aircraft and seemed to be falling headfirst. Within a few moments I felt my chute crack open and develop and my speedy descent was suddenly slowed down. There seemed too much flak from anti-aircraft shells and some were much too close for comfort and made a hell of a noise accompanied by a whine as they whistled past.

Behind his friend Les Cartwright, Private John Speechley of 'C' Company could see the flak as he neared the doorway:

All you see is a little orange spark getting bigger and bigger, and VROOMF, it's bloody there ! The pilot heeled over away from where all the crumping was going on. Of course we keeled over. I fell backwards, he fell out.

The plane righted itself and Speechley got out:

It was bright, the wind was high, plenty of cloud but it was really moving, and I saw this pom-pom gun and it was really having a go down on my half-right. It was firing... one, two, three, four and every fifth or sixth was a tracer, so you got some idea where he was panning, and he was going from left to right. I'm drifting towards him. I thought 'This is handy!' He must have seen me but he saw so many in the sky he didn't make a beeline for me. They were crumping all over the place.

Fred Milward, 'A' Company:

Standing in the doorway ready to go, and all I could see below was water! The red light was on; I waited, head up, for the green. Suddenly there was a loud bang and the aircraft dropped, flinging me out.

I felt a blow on my helmet which was ripped off, probably by the tailplane; lost my kitbag on my leg, went down and that was it, I was on the ground.

Corporal Jim 'Marra' McGuinness, HQ Company:

Flak, ack-ack, it was awful. I closed my eyes, but as we got lower, we came out of their fire, they were in the next field, you could see them. I lost my pack and rifle coming down. The cord I had, snapped. I must have released it too quick.

Ernie Rooke-Matthews struggled to the doorway with a giant-sized kitbag attached to his leg. It contained a wireless set, headphones and other equipment:

Hands firmly on the rope at the top of the kitbag, I swung my right foot with the bag forward and stepped out assisted by the weight of the kitbag. For once I made a perfect exit, keeping my arms in and legs together. My body went horizontal and then that reassuring tug, and the chute opened up fully and I floated down. Then I opened my eyes again. The air was full of activity, planes and parachutes everywhere.

The two signallers, Reg Sherwood and Bill Stack, who were accompanying the Marine Commandos, readied themselves. Bill Stack:

Those with the heaviest loads always jumped first. I went at number three. I had the set in a kitbag. 'Sherry' was behind. He had the spare batteries in a satchel. There were two chaps in front of me with 3-inch mortars. Lieutenant Winston and his batman were somewhere behind us.

It was a Canadian crew manning the plane. One of them stood by the door and when the green light came on and we started to go, he slapped us on the back and shouted 'Good luck' in our ear. It was lovely and quiet after the noise of the plane.

Sergeant Bob 'Paddy' Jenkins of 'B' Company, was the stick commander of his aircraft. Privates Harry Harper and Reg Osborne, a Canadian signaller, were in front of him. Harper jumped and then came Osborne's turn, but the plane tilted and he was thrown backwards onto the sergeant. 'Paddy' Jenkins:

One of the Canadian crew shouted, 'Come on, come on, get out.' The next thing, the plane tilted and he went out and I was thrown back. The plane did another tilt and I was thrown out. We were behind the rest of the stick because of this delay; just a few seconds and you're well away from the stick.

He began to let his rifle down on its line:

Like so many others, mine went 'whoosh' and it was gone. The force and weight of it and it's just gone. I looked down and thought 'Oh no, (I was coming towards a road) I can see it now, I'm going to be lying there with a broken flipping leg or something.' I managed to heave and pull [on the lift webs], and there were these high hedges, it was more or less all orchards where we dropped, and the next thing is my knees came up and into my chest. It winded me for a while. If anybody had been there, I couldn't have done a thing. As I lay on the ground there were planes criss-crossing everywhere.

The noise of the flak caused Glenn the parachute dog to cower beneath one of the wooden benches. 'Jack' Corteil and Private Jim Baty dragged him out and literally threw the dog out of the plane. Corteil followed and just as Baty went to jump the aircraft banked, throwing him to the floor. By the time he got back into the door the DZ had passed, but he jumped anyway and landed in deep water. Corteil and Glenn were safely reunited on the ground.

Sergeant Fred Garrett of 'B' Company was the stick commander of a Dakota nicknamed 'The Molly-Oh'.[4] The men on board all belonged to his platoon apart from Privates Hart and Dugan who were signallers, and Terry Jepp, a medic whose younger brother Ron served in the MG platoon. Garrett had been briefed to dispatch ten men, release some bundles of Bangalore torpedoes held in the containers and then resume the jumping. Theoretically, with the bundles in the middle of the cycle, each half of the stick would then go towards the centre of the DZ, pick up the Bangalores and head for the RV. Private Terry Jepp:

There was a slight delay in ditching the Bangalores. Jumping recommenced, but a further and more serious delay occurred when number thirteen, Page, became stuck in the doorway. It appeared that his rifle,

51

Private Hart.   **Private Page.**

presumably attached to his leg, had become loose and was jammed across the door. By the time he had freed himself with the help of number fourteen, the red light had come on, but he jumped anyway.

They had passed the DZ so Garrett stopped the remainder from jumping:

Sergeant Fred Garrett.

I unhooked myself and I went forward to the cockpit to the pilot, explained what had happened and asked him to go round again. He flatly refused and explained that we were on our way home. I explained that it was very important that I should jump as I was carrying detonators for the various types of grenade carried by the platoon. I had detonators for the Hawkins grenades, the bundles of Bangalore torpedoes, also the '77' phosphorous grenades. Why I had to carry those I don't know – but that was an order.

After some time he said, 'I'll drop you here.' He gave me my position but I declined it as I wouldn't have known where it was. The offer would have been absolutely, completely, mysterious to me as we worked on a grid reference. He then agreed to go round again. I explained the drill; give us a two-minute run up, a five-second red light and then the green, and the rest would be up to me. I returned to the fuselage and found the green light was on and the chaps were making every effort to get to the door to jump. I got into the door and I stopped them jumping; it was totally wrong.

Terry Jepp:

> There was an immediate and very angry reaction from the rest of the stick, the general opinion being expressed in very unmistakable language that we hadn't undergone months of uncomfortable and arduous training just to land tamely back in England and miss 'the Big Show'. Every man missing from the assault (each one trained not only in a specific task but in at least one stand-by job) would make the capture of the Merville Battery less likely to succeed, and how would we face our mates when it was all over ?

Sergeant Garrett:

> I went back to the pilot, explained, and he flatly refused to jump us. I then sat down and I was really at a loss to know what to do.

The problem of items jamming across doorways was also occurring in other planes. Private Cyril Thwaites, 'C' Company:

> There was about eight or nine dropped immediately before me. As I went to jump, the Para in front of me went to jump and he momentarily stopped. As he jumped, his rifle had come off his leg... . As he went down, the rifle caught across the bottom of the door.

The Para was hanging outside the plane, caught in the slipstream, with his own weight holding the rifle in place.

> No way was I going to jump over him, so he had to be freed. It was just deathly silent, nobody had said a word, they were just watching me trying to pull the rifle up to free him.

It seemed like an eternity before the rifle and the Para were freed. Thwaites jumped straight after him.

Sergeant Doug Woodcraft of 'A' Company suffered from air sickness and so had not been included in the G-B Force. He was the stick commander of his plane and so the last to exit:

> I had an entrenching tool secured to my right leg, which somehow got caught up in the strops at the same time as the pilot started to take evasive action. Arse over tip I went, with my head and shoulders out in the slipstream, wondering just what the hell had happened to me. It took the combined efforts of the dispatcher and navigator who came back to help to get me on my feet, by which time the pilot was heading off back to England like a bloody homing pigeon. My request sent by the navigator that he should turn and take me in again was met by what I still consider an impolite reply of just two words!

Company Sergeant Major Frank Stoddart was number thirteen in the CO's plane:

> The plane did a lot of rocking and rolling, flak coming up. Number one to go was the CO's batman, Lieutenant Colonel Otway was number two. The batman got wedged in the door, having his kitbag strapped to his leg. He had to be helped out.

Just as the Colonel passed the whisky bottle to the RAF dispatcher, a shell exploded behind the aeroplane, throwing Otway out. A Stirling immediately passed beneath him and then he became aware of the flak rising:

> There were incendiary bullets coming up at me and actually going through my chute, which was disturbing, in fact I was bloody angry about it!

The moonlight and the reflected glow of the searchlights on the clouds lit up the ground. Familiar field configurations became apparent and in particular a farmhouse that he knew was a German battalion HQ. To compound matters, the wind was forcing him towards the building.

Captain Hudson was in one of the last of the Battalion's Dakotas:

> The soldiers were singing 'There'll always be an England, and England shall be free.' I recall being surprised by the emotion that these soldiers put into the banal verse, being of course, an upper class twit. But I rather liked it. Through the windows one could see jetties on the coast burning, and soon the flak started. Almost at once the red light came on and we staggered to our feet, only slightly put out by the bumping from the anti-aircraft fire.

The slipsteam hit me in rather an exhilarating way. I was isolated in the sky, dropping to battle.

Before those of Brigade HQ began jumping, Brigadier Hill prepared to carry out some 'allotted tasks' for the Canadians:

Before we set sail on D-Day, in order to amuse them I produced a football and had it painted phosphorous with a picture of Hitler on the outside. I told everybody, as we went over the defences that I was going to drop this football on the beach defences. The Canadians produced bricks for me to throw!

Then we came to the beaches, so I threw out my football (I like to imagine it bouncing up and down and when they went to retrieve it, the face of Hitler!), kicked the bricks out to drop, also on the beaches.

He then made his jump.

All of this had happened in a matter of minutes. On the ground Major Smith had watched the drop:

From near and far German machine gunners came into action spitting streams of tracer at the dark shapes above. We saw very few parachutists descend. Just two sticks to our left. They were difficult to see in the darkness and were bad targets, descending quickly, and being visible for only a few seconds. The firing was heaven-sent to my party for we were able to pick out all the machine-gun nests in the vicinity and particularly ahead. Some were surprisingly near and we were able to adjust our route to avoid them.

As the Paras started to arrive on the ground, for most, their troubles were only just beginning.

Colonel Otway had tried to manipulate his parachute away from the German HQ, but, with the strength of the wind, little could be done. He rammed straight into the wall of the house at first floor level, dropped to the ground and got out of his harness. He seemed to be in a garden, a corporal and a private were already there. An upstairs window was thrown open and a German leaned out to see what the noise was. Not having time to get a grenade out, the corporal picked up a brick and threw it. There was a crash of glass and they sped to the front of the house, got out of the garden and followed a track, at the end of which was a road. The field opposite was flooded, but the Colonel knew that he was only about 400 yards from the south-eastern edge of the DZ, so he turned left, taking an indirect route in case any Germans decided to follow.

The HQ building had an attached greenhouse and his batman, Corporal Wilson, had crashed through the roof. Suffering only a slight cut, he also headed towards the track. During all of this, German soldiers had poured out of the front door and as Wilson turned a corner he saw them doubling down the track. Accordingly, he fell in behind and followed them until the road, where he broke away and set off for the RV.[5]

Sergeant Daniels of 'B' Company had had a good jump and landing:

The first chap I met when I hit the ground was a signaller. His '18' set, a big important set, was hung up on some high tension cables. He had it in a kitbag and he had come down one side of the cable and the kitbag swung over the other side. He was damned lucky to be alive. No way could he get his radio down. He said, 'Well I can't go without it,' and I said, 'There's no way you're going to get it down.' So I stuck half a dozen rounds through the radio set. If we weren't having it, Jerry was certainly not having it. We scarpered from there on.

I didn't know where I was. The instructions were if you were off the DZ, look up and see which way the aircraft were flying and you'll know where to make for. Well the aircraft were flying all bloody ways!

They continued walking, meeting various people until they had built up a group of around twenty men.

Private Jimmy French was a signaller attached to 'B' Company:

It was a very quick drop. I hit the deck with my bag still on my leg; as quick as that. I was rather shaken. I wandered around a field until I found a road. I was wondering which way to go. I heard a noise coming along the road and a German soldier appeared on a pushbike, no lights, just on his own, his rifle slung across his shoulders, quite nonchalantly riding along. I thought 'He's a German and I'm here to shoot Germans', so I was just about to when about twenty yards behind him came another three!

He let them pass and waited to make sure they did not return before moving on.

The Battalion had actually been dispersed over a wide area and, to compound this, the men encountered various other unforeseen problems. Major Harold Bestley, Officer Commanding 'B' Company:

I was not expecting Salisbury Plain but fields divided by hedges, clearly visible on the air photos. What I did not realize was the height and density of each hedge, making each appear by night like the edge of a wood.

Another shock was water-filled ditches that bordered the fields, which had either not been noticed by aerial reconnaissance or deemed unimportant. They were extremely difficult to traverse and became major obstacles in reaching the DZ. Perhaps the biggest problem faced those dropped east of the DZ, over the area flooded by the Germans. Five-feet four-inch John Speechley was one of them:

John Speechley.

As I was going down I could definitely hear voices of alarm and trouble. I heard a mass of glass go, that was to my left.[6] I was looking at the ground, and I said to myself 'Bloody hell, I'm looking at the reflection of the moon on the water. Bugger this!' So I turned my cords 180 degrees to have a look around the other way, and it's still all reflection. 'Shit! I'm in trouble.' I thought I was on the edge of the sea.

He prepared for a water drop. This meant inflating his life jacket, then hitting the quick release button on the harness and gripping the cords, while gradually sliding out of the harness and eventually holding on with one hand. At about fifteen feet from the water it was imperative to let go, otherwise the canopy could smother him:

My heart's beating, I can't swim, not with this bloody lot [pack, etc]. I let go. I went in and I sat on my arse, looked up. I could see this green flickering, it was the moon shining up top. So I felt down; this was grass not mud, and I realized it was a flooded area. I stood up and I'd got the water just by my Adam's apple. Bloody hell! I heard people in trouble. You could hear 'Help, bubble, bubble', y'know, one here, one there.[7] It's just a case of survival now. I walked this way, I walked the other way. I walked another way and made a bit more headway, and I got it down to my ammunition pouches. I'm looking around and I went right round 360 degrees. I can't see a bloody thing; a top of a tree, a row of trees... I looked in one particular direction and it looked too straight. That's a railway line, got to be. So I made my way there, slightly to the right, bit to the left, bit too deep. I was following the contours of the meadow. In the end I got almost to it and it turned out to be a road.

He had ten yards to go:

A bloke said, 'Halt, who goes there?' Well, now I've got to think. There's that much been going on, what with the aeroplane noise and firing. I heard the click of a rifle bolt. Got it. 'PUNCH'! 'JUDY'! Well it was Corporal Dowling. He said, 'Don't bugger around in there, get out!' 'That's all right for you. I can hardly bloody walk.'

Robert Ferguson.

Peter Dowling.

> *So he said, 'Get hold of this,' and he gave me the butt of his rifle. I took one stride to get hold of it and went straight under. I didn't realize there's a drainage ditch been built in it, all of eight feet deep plus the flooding. I'm crawling among the reeds and I came up. He hit my helmet, I felt where his butt was and he got me out. My head was really pounding. I was loaded, had to let the water out of my trousers. This mud, oh it stunk!*

When Corporal Robert Ferguson of the Medical Section came down he saw that he was fast approaching a five-bar gate and so raised his legs to avoid it:

> *I was thinking great, I've got over it. The next thing, I couldn't breathe, and I didn't believe it. I was under water. I was struggling like hell, I'd got my pack on my back and where I put my feet out there was nowhere to crawl upwards anywhere. I noticed that the chute wasn't coming down any farther so I struggled like hell, climbing up it and each foot I went up I dropped three or four inches. It was a case of what was going to hang out, the strength [of the chute] or my muscles. I got my head out of the water and I just hung on for five minutes to get my breath back. I thought 'It's alright this bloody war!'[8]*

Bill Stack had also landed in the water:

> *By the time I sorted myself out and stood up, I was in water up to my waist, and alone, not a soul in sight. There was a few flashes in the distance and one or two bursts of fire, but nothing close at hand. And then 'Sherry' found me. There was no sign of Lieutenant Winston or his batman.*

A large proportion of the Battalion had landed in this flooded area.

Signals Sergeant Johnny Britton was luckier and landed in about four inches of water:

> *I stood for a short time trying to decide which way to go, then a bird noise came from the far corner of the field. With some relief I started to slosh in that direction. When I got there the noise had stopped and there was no one there, but it started up again at the other end of the field I had just left, so off I plod back again. On reaching there it stopped again, and still there was no one to be seen, and believe it or not, started up again at the other end. What the hell was happening? Anyhow I decided to go back for the last*

time, then I waited for a few minutes and heard a slight rustle behind some bushes. I could just distinguish two black faces and the whites of four eyes. Hesitating a moment or two, I decided to give the password 'PUNCH' and back came the reply 'JUDY'. Was I relieved. I had bumped into two Canadian medics. I found out later that my bird noises turned out to be bull-frogs having me on!

Brigadier Hill was another dropped over the flooded land:

Sergeant John Britton.

I saw exactly where I was coming down, about a quarter of a mile from Cabourg, and I suppose about three miles from where I should have been. Anyhow I splashed down in the water, and there one was in four and a half feet of water. I had tea bags sown, being a very professional soldier all round, in the tops of my trousers!

The land had deep irrigation ditches and of course, if you're walking in water you can't see. We gradually gathered the chaps together. We realized we couldn't get on by ourselves, so we all carried toggle ropes. If one chap went down in one of these ditches, which were ten feet deep, of course with all your kit on you couldn't hope to get out. You could tackle it together, or if you went into the wire, because the wire was mostly under water.

With a mixture of men from various battalions and Brigade HQ 'toggled together', they headed north-west in search of Varaville. The Brigadier's prophecy of chaos had already become unerringly accurate.

In the approach to the French coast, various planes had become disorientated, perhaps mistaking the River Dives for the River Orne, causing their occupants to be dropped vast distances from where they should have been. Some landed in the Trouville area, fifteen miles east of the DZ. Somehow, this was where the two Marine Commandos, Winston and Donald landed.[9] Corporal Mick Corboy of 'C' Company was another:

I swung down into a small orchard with a building, completely surrounded by my first sight of the bocage hedgerow. No pretty lights, no flares or beacons. Well that's a good start, lost already! I clambered out and headed up a hill to where I could see two figures silhouetted against the night sky. When I pointed this out to them in a critical fashion, one said, 'Well we're in no danger from you Corp, you've still got your rifle in your leg bag!'

They set off southwards, not having a clue where they were.

The 3-inch mortar platoon had been scattered. One of them, Sergeant Doug Smith, had no idea why he had landed in complete silence. No aeroplanes, no firing, nothing. He found three others from his plane, but that was all. Another mortar man, Private Don McArthur, had landed in a hole that appeared to be ready for an anti-glider pole:

Releasing my catch, and a quick glance showed that the mortar company container, which had followed me out, was approximately 100 yards away. As I approached this I heard someone approaching and so I dived into the nearby ditch. It was the stick number eleven, and on the password he joined me. A short while later two others arrived, and together we opened the container and took out two pieces of the 3-inch mortar each and started to head away. Instead of being in an area where there should have been more landing activity, we were in a field with hedges etc. Thinking we were on the edge of the DZ we did as suggested

Don McArthur.

Doug Smith.

in England, ie, go in the direction of flight in.

After a while, with the ground showing no familiar landmarks, they also began to realize that they had absolutely no idea where they were.[10]

Some of the Battalion *had* fared better. Captain Hudson had landed on the DZ, though in a tree:

Convinced that some fat German was sitting at the bottom of the tree with his rifle aimed at my backside, I disentangled myself from the harness in double quick time and dropped safely to the ground. As I was in the last aircraft bar two, I knew that by the time I arrived at the RV the Battalion would be deployed and Battalion HQ set up. I set off across the field, following the ditch I knew so well from the aerial photographs and the model, and arrived at the Battalion HQ RV. Nobody was there.

A feeling of horror washed over him, combined with a rapid draining of self-confidence.

Could I have completely misread the topography? There seemed to be no other explanation. After a minute or two I retraced my steps along the ditch when suddenly a figure appeared out of the shadows. I threw myself to the ground and said in the best barrack-room style, 'Halt, who goes there?' The figure replied, 'It's me, Sir.' The tension of the last few minutes caused me to lose my cool. 'Don't be so bloody silly', I said. 'You're supposed to say 'Friend' and then I ask you to give the password.' 'Sorry Sir,' he said, 'V'. 'For Victory,' I said and felt better.[11]

Company Sergeant Major Barney Ross, 'C' Company:

I dropped within fifty yards of the little hut that was on the Dropping Zone, which was the kind of marker. I must admit, when I hit the ground and looked around, I thought I was the only bugger there! It was so quiet. There I was with grenades strapped all around me, Sten at the ready... . Not a soul!

We had these clickers, and then I heard one of these clickers going and it was the Doctor... [Captain Harold Watts] *'You're bloody handy to have!' He came with me and we got to the Rendezvous and looked around for the rest of 'C' Company... I think there was two blokes.*

Private Frank Delsignore, 'C' Company:

As I floated down I could see a wooden hut and the surroundings, just as I was told there should be. I had a good landing and quickly released myself from my parachute, removed the protective cover from my rifle, put one up the spout and slipped the safety catch on, all while still lying on the ground. I knew I was in the right area and which direction to go to the Rendezvous.

I then dared to get up on one knee and instantly saw someone coming towards me. I slipped the safety catch off on my rifle, but even as I did so I recognized 'Johnnie' [Harold] Walker, one of my section, another good friend, who had jumped just behind me from the aircraft.

Sid Harmon.

The actual RV point was identified by a solitary tree in a hedgerow on the western edge of the DZ.[12] Fred Milward had landed nearby:

I could see somebody down in this bomb crater, with his 'chute all wrapped round him. I said, 'Is that you Sid?', no password or anything! He said, 'Yes.' I'd found Sid Harmon, he jumped number two. The earth was warm and smelly and all loose. He couldn't climb up so I pulled him up on the 'chute. We were right on the edge of the DZ. It was more or less as if I'd been there before. It was only moonlight. We'd seen so many models and so many maps that it was second nature. There was the tree and we knew where we'd got to go.

Although Sergeant Knight of the RV Party had been dropped wide, the briefing had been so good that he knew exactly where he was:

The first bloke I saw was Sergeant Hugh Salter, so we ran together to the Rendezvous. When I arrived, there was hardly anyone there at all. Then one of my mates turned up plus a few more.

Sergeant Hugh Salter.

Lieutenant Dennis Slade, HQ Company:

I landed on the DZ, but, when my chute developed, the rigging lines were screwed down on my head and I slowly revolved before hitting the ground. This was not helpful in establishing where I was. Again, how or why I know not, but my battledress trousers split from the crutch to gaiter.

Colour Sergeant Harold Long of 'C' Company had landed close by in a ditch full of nettles:

> *The first person I saw was Mr Slade. He had dropped over the opposite side of the road. We could spot the lights flashing at times, but were very disappointed at the amount who had turned up.*

Major Parry and his two Canadian companions were still trying to reach the DZ:

> *By this time, 01.00, I was getting a little agitated at the passing of time and still I hadn't made the RV. I collected about a dozen other chaps and eventually saw a red light. For the third time, I breathed a sigh of relief and approached the red light which was held by the inevitable Joe [Lieutenant Worth, the Battalion IO]. Sergeant Easlea was there, waving his torch, also Charlton and Hudson, but precious few others.[3]*

He began looking for the RV point:

> *I eventually found the tree I was looking for and was amazed to see my batman was already there. His direction finding at night was evidently better than mine. I congratulated him and he said, 'Good evening Sir. What kept you then?' I replied, 'I had one or two little jobs to do on the DZ and here I am.' That didn't impress him either!*

Adsett kept conspicuously silent about his own ordeal! Major Parry:

> *All this time I had been lugging the heavy kitbag with which I had jumped. It contained an Aldis lamp which I was to flash to mark the RV for the Battalion... I knelt to unpack the bag, pulled out the lamp and my haversack. To my surprise there was another haversack. Adsett, who was leaning over me, said, 'Thank you very much Sir, I believe that one is mine!'*
>
> *I said to Private Adsett 'Now you go up that tree and I will hand you the lamp, and when I give you the word you can start flashing.' He said, 'Oh no, you're OC Party, you go up the tree and I will hand YOU the lamp.' So up the tree I shinned and he handed me the lamp.[3, 13]*

He then began signalling.

Learning that the Troubridge Party had set off successfully, Lieutenant Slade, CSM Stoddart and the Regimental Sergeant Major, Bill Cunningham, left to check the authenticity of the suspected dummy battery.

Elsewhere, Ernie Rooke-Matthews had landed safely with his cumbersome kitbag, but hadn't a clue where he was:

> *I had just started to move off when a voice, which I instantly recognized, boomed at me 'Where the f...... hell do you think you're going?' 'To the RV, Corp,' I replied. It was Corporal McGuinness, our provost NCO. 'If you keep going that way you'll end up in the sea,' he said. Mac was a little annoyed. Apparently as I came crashing to earth (as he put it) my kitbag was swinging violently (as I knew) and he was unable to avoid it and he got a direct hit. Being hit with a swinging kitbag fully loaded, weighing perhaps eighty to one hundred pounds, would at least give you a headache (even when wearing a steel helmet). Then to my astonishment he helped me carry my load of equipment from the DZ to the RV.*

Corporal McGuinness:

> *I then made for the RV and I asked Captain Hudson if it was Battalion HQ. When he said it was the Battalion I could have dropped with shock. I said to him, 'What's*

Ernie Rooke-Matthews.

happened to the rest of the Battalion, Sir?', he just said, 'God knows, McGuinness.'

Many planes had had to turn around and make further runs to drop their Paras. The Dakota carrying Major Dyer, the Officer Commanding 'C' Company, and the members of 14 platoon, was among them:

> *The aircraft went over the coastal batteries and they fired up at us {The pilot took evasive action, but couldn't find the DZ} and went back out to sea again, turned round and came in, again trying to find the run-up. In the end he simply put the green light on and we tumbled out.*

Private Walter Johnson jumped from around the middle of the stick. He lost his rifle and landed in the top of an elm tree:

> *After a few vigorous swings back and forth I managed to grab the tree trunk. I undid my harness and slid, with my hands tightly around it, down, and it seemed twenty-five feet, maybe thirty feet. Anyway I found myself in a wooded area. My hands were skimmed from sliding down the trunk but it didn't worry me too much as at least I had landed with no other injury. Drawing my fighting knife from its sheath, I started to advance towards the direction of the rendezvous.*
>
> *Everything was so quiet until I heard cows mooing nearby... . Which way to go was a problem, so I just followed a track. Next thing, I fell in a ditch full of water. I could have done without a bath really. I kept going and eventually met up with more Paras. Who they were I didn't ask. You just kept very quiet and followed in their wake.*

Ron Tucker jumped number thirteen from the same aircraft. During the descent he could see that he was over the flooded area:

> *I could see a small track below and luckily for me I landed on it. As soon as I got out of my parachute I heard the sound of boots running towards me. There was a small hedge about four feet high and I jumped over that and got as near underneath it as I could. I held my breath and listened to the soldiers talking and examining the 'chute. There were three of them. I pulled out the pin of a '36' grenade. If they wanted me I was at least going to take a few of them with me. Another soldier arrived on a bike, obviously an officer because he gave an order and they began to search for me, peering over the hedge. One of them stood so close to my face that I could smell the dubbin on his boots. It couldn't have been long but it seemed like ages, when suddenly the officer gave another order and they ran off down the road. I put the pin back in the grenade, removed my rifle from its protective sleeve and went off down the road in the opposite direction. Shortly after, I met 'Jock'*

'Nobby' Kightley

Lepper my Platoon Commander and my friend Gus Gower with three other lads.

They soon located Major Dyer who had found two others using his 'peewit' whistle. However, they could not determine their whereabouts and so this group, which included Privates Berry, Arthur 'Nobby' Kightley, Derek Higgins and Peter Bowden, set off to the north-west in an attempt to get clear of the water.

Captain Robinson, second in command of 'C' Company, had also endured a hazardous drop:

> *The Dakota was hit and seemed to be out of control, but eventually we received the green light and made our way with great difficulty to the door. I was in the middle of the stick and landed in several feet of water, about*

Peter Bowden

500 yards from the coast between Franceville Plage and Cabourg. Since the general direction of flight was north to south, I fear that most of the earlier stick numbers (One to seven) must have landed in the sea.

'Robbie', as he was affectionately known, found a few others and moved on:

Saturated to the skin was most uncomfortable but there were several injured in the vicinity who required attention and they were moved to a farm nearby. They were given First Aid and left in the care of the farmer and his wife. By this time about a dozen paratroops had converged on the farm, since it formed a small island in the flooded countryside. Obviously we were out of the Merville Battery battle and so made our way, wallowing in the water, in the direction of Varaville. We soon had the good fortune to bump into James Hill with a similar party.

They joined the group, which now totalled around twenty men.

Sergeant Garrett and Terry Jepp had been stuck on their plane with the pilot refusing to round again. Fred Garrett:

Warrant Officer Mercer, part of the aircrew (he was the only Englishman in the aircrew) came back and said that the pilot would go around again, and this time he gave us the correct drill, and on the green light we jumped.

The number fourteen, Corporal Penstone went first, followed by Lance Corporal Green, Privates Duce, Atkinson, Jepp, and Backhurst, and finally Sergeant Garrett:

I got into the air and was absolutely flabbergasted as I couldn't see another parachute in the sky, and on looking down all I could see was water. I thought 'Bloody hell he's dropped us in the Channel.' I landed and promptly submerged. On standing I found that the water was about three to four feet deep. I looked around. There was not a sound or a sign of anyone, I was completely alone.

Terry Jepp:

Crouching low, I pulled out my Colt.45 automatic pistol and looked around me. I couldn't see a living soul, no sign of the other six men at all! I stood up and took a few tentative steps forward and found that I was in a slight hollow and by moving carefully I was able to reach slightly higher ground and the water was only waist deep. After a few moments of silence I heard quiet splashing sounds nearby. Crouching low again, and very quietly, I gave the unit's password, 'Punch'. There was no reply and no further movement, so once again, and in a slightly louder voice, I called again, 'Punch'. By now I could see more clearly and located a solid shape about twenty yards away. I said again, 'Punch, give the countersign or I shoot.' A very tremulous voice answered 'Judy', and I was confronted by a very scared young Company signaller, Private David Duce. Just a few moments later we were joined by Doug Penstone and 'Mitzi' Green, but

David Duce. **'Mitzi' Green.**

of Backhurst, Atkinson and Sergeant Garrett there was no sign at all.

Fred Garrett:

I walked about, but each time I tried to leave the field that I was in I floundered about in very deep and very muddy ditches, and these were quite dangerous. I thought I was going to drown. I nearly wept with helplessness and exhaustion. I wasn't a kid, I was twenty-six years old. I hunted about and eventually found a tree lying across a ditch. I crawled across the tree, and found myself on a hard track. I went moving along the track and all of a sudden somebody said, 'Is that you Sergeant?' No countersign, no password, no nothing. Just 'Is that you Sergeant?' It turned out to be one of my platoon, David Backhurst, who jumped number nineteen just in front of me. Together we walked along the track, and eventually we came to some large iron gates. We went through the iron gates and up a drive, there was a big house there; crawled up to the house and we could hear the Germans talking inside. I thought 'This is no place for us', so we withdrew and we came back down the track, didn't know where we were, didn't know quite what to do. We came to a cow byre, so I said, 'Let's get in here, at least we will be out of the water', so we got in the cow byre and we laid down in all the muck and mess. Eventually we drifted off to sleep.

David Backhurst.

At the RV a trickle of men continued to arrive. One of them was Sergeant Jenkins who, after his bad landing, had recovered his breath and quickly moved towards the DZ:

I wondered what was wrong because as we went along I was picking up stuff. I remember picking up a 2-inch mortar, I thought that's better than nothing. When we got there [the RV] I was hearing exactly the same story. They were picking up different weapons as they went along, from where somebody else had dropped them. So we landed with so many bits and bobs. I thought 'Whatever has happened here?' What a shambles.

Reg Osborne had jumped just in front of the sergeant:

I made sure I did everything right so as not to get hurt on landing, ie, feet and knees together, but where I got down, I landed in long grass, and the ground was uneven, so I broke my ankle. I laid there for a while to get my bearings and see what was going on when Harry turned up.

Harry Harper helped him limp to the RV.

Sid Capon of 'C' Company had fallen out of his plane 'like a bloody sack of coal', but had a beautiful landing in a field near a hedgerow and road. He didn't know where he was, but then saw a parachutist come down nearby and went over to him. They subsequently met another 'stray' and then a group of six men led by Lieutenant Mike Dowling of 'B' Company, who were lying in some stinging nettles. Sid Capon:

We found our bearings and we were on the DZ. Then down this

Reg Osborne

63

narrow road came a lorry load of Germans, but we let them off the hook because we mustn't engage in private battles. So we laid in the hedgerow and they never saw us. We got across the road and there were these Pathfinders and we got to the RV.

The Colonel had hammered a rule into their heads. 'Get to that RV. You are not to have any private fights. You get to the RV and THAT'S IT!'

Elsewhere, CSM Harries had crashed through a tree, and as he lay on the ground, a welter of apples fell around him. Luckily he only suffered scratches to his hands and face:

I was now in a small garden close to a house... . I certainly didn't recognize the surroundings as there was never a house and garden on the DZ, to say nothing of the manor road which ran past the house.

Around the garden was a thick blackthorn hedge, but luckily was a bit thin at the bottom, so I scrambled under into a deep ditch and was immediately up to my ankles in mud and water with very high growing stinging nettles which gave me a sting or two on the hands. I was now on the edge of the narrow road and was about to cross through a gateway into a field on the other side. I quickly stopped as the sound of a vehicle was getting louder and I had to nip back into the ditch as a flat-topped vehicle with no roof came down the road. I was up to my ears in stinging nettles as it went by and in the back were German troops, most of which were standing up and holding onto each other and surveying the countryside.

The lorry passed, but he realized that his 'medicinal' brandy bottle had fallen out of his pocket on landing, and so set off back to the apple tree.

Corporal Tottle, the medic, had landed in a field of tall grass:

By now all the planes had gone and the ack-ack had stopped. There was a deadly silence, all I could hear was the wind blowing through the grass. This was the moment I was really scared. I expected to find the field full of my own mates.

We were told that on landing, to look for a church steeple. I couldn't see a steeple anywhere, but I did hear about five minutes later 'duck quacks'. Well, being a bit more brave now, I pushed my head up through the grass and started to crawl towards the so-called 'ducks'. A second later something got hold of my foot. I think I nearly died of fright, but it turned out to be one of my own lads... . So both of us, not speaking but very glad to be together, crawled our way towards the 'quacks'. We then heard a few whispering voices in a copse, so we laid still, trying to find out what language they were talking when all of a sudden a bloody great corporal with a Sten gun nearly on my temple whispered, 'Halt'. God what a fright, I thought it was Hitler himself. I managed to get the password out then everything was OK. I could then see, more or less, that there was a single line of men in the copse, how far the line stretched I don't know. I was sent one way and my friend the other. On getting to where I was sent I found my medical officer, Captain Watts and only about four other medics instead of thirty.

Nearby, Captain Hudson had been busy:

After making a few casts in the Battalion HQ area we found elements of several platoons. I then went back to the area where I had landed and was relieved to see one or two containers with their lights showing and troops taking them up. At this point seven civilians, two women and five men, suddenly appeared, apparently returning from the village. By this time several 9 Para soldiers were with me on their way to their respective RVs. I therefore accosted the civilians and, in my usual execrable French, demanded to see their papers. These they produced and I examined them in the light of my pencil torch. They meant nothing to me, but I think I impressed the wretched civilians.

Colonel Otway's small group had slowly made its way towards the DZ, wading through chest-high water. After escaping it they had had to endure another harrowing experience:

We saw two men come down by parachute and land in the marshes. We tried to pull them out by their parachute harness but it was useless. With their sixty-pound kitbags they sank out of sight at once and were drowned in the mud and slush.

Further on, two rather stout Germans appeared on bicycles:

> *Home Guard types, old enough to be my father. They said they were 'Sick of the SS dressing up as Paras and please let them get back to barracks.'*

Otway managed to convince them of his nationality, threw their rifles into the water and let them ride off. The group then arrived at the DZ. Staff Captain Woodgate, Brigade HQ:

> *I met Colonel Otway on the Dropping Zone and we helped one another over ditches. Went up to the 9th Battalion RV where Allen Parry was flashing a lamp, and I thought I'd better go off to where Brigade Headquarters was supposed to be meeting. When I turned up at the rendezvous outside Varaville, there weren't any Brigade Headquarters chaps at all. So I set off through the woods towards Le Mesnil crossroads.*

Colonel Otway:

> *We arrived at the Rendezvous at 1.30am... . There was desultory firing going on but otherwise everything was quiet except for the moans of a sapper with a broken leg.*[14]

The first man the Colonel recognized was his second in command, Major Eddie Charlton, who greeted him with 'Thank God you've come, Sir.' 'Why?' 'The drop's been a bloody chaos. There's hardly anyone here.' It was shattering news. Suddenly Otway noticed Joe Wilson standing next to him, proffering a small flask 'as if it were a decanter on a silver salver.' Colonel Otway:

> *He said 'Shall we take our whisky now Sir?'*[15] *He was a professional boxer, and then he turned valet. Flat nose, big cauliflower ears, the sort of man you'd think hadn't got a brain in his head. In fact, he was extremely intelligent and he knew me backwards.*

Captain Hudson returned to the RV:

> *When I got back to Battalion HQ several people had arrived, including the CO, who said, 'Where the hell have you been?' After a bit of explanation, I told him about the civilians and asked him what to do about them. 'Shoot them,' he said.*
>
> *I do not normally dispute orders from my superiors, nevertheless I demurred. 'If they were not people the Germans trusted,' said the CO, 'they would not be allowed in this area. Shoot them,' he said. He was under some tension at the time.*
>
> *Back I went to the civilians. It was a worrying moment. By chance there was a sort of a barn nearby. I herded the civilians into this barn, told them that a sentry was posted outside and that if they showed themselves in the next four hours they would be shot at once.*

*

During all of this chaos the three-man Troubridge Party had continued its trek to the Battery. Major Smith:

> *We reached a crosstracks, one of which led straight to the outer perimeter of the Battery about six hundred yards away. The country was very open except for the small hedge and ditch alongside the track. We slipped quietly along the hedge.*
>
> *It had been our intention to cross the open country on a compass bearing to bring us out at a certain wood, known to us as Wood Two, but there was a wire fence with a wooden board hanging on it. This board merely had the sign of a skull and crossbones roughly painted on it, a sign we knew denoted a minefield. We were already aware of the existence of mines, for aerial photographs had shown some small craters equal distances apart and in rows. They had been set off by a stick of bombs which had fallen near. We did not know, however, that the minefield was so extensive. Across the track was another wire fence with a notice saying 'MINEN', another minefield. We decided prudence was better than valour and crept along the ditch.*
>
> *The six hundred yards seemed very long, and we certainly did not cover it quickly. At last we came to a track running across the top of the one we had crawled along. On the other side was the cattle fence*

marking the outer perimeter of the Battery. Wood One, inside the perimeter, started in front of us and went away to our left. Wood Two could be seen about a hundred and fifty yards to our right. We knew we should now have to cross a minefield, and, to confirm this, more of the skull and crossbone notices hung upon the fence. Running by Wood Two we expected to find a track leading into the heart of the Battery. There would most certainly be a heavy guard on this, and no guard at the moment would be anything but very alert. I decided to leave Harrold in the corner of Wood One to watch and report if we got into trouble. He had a lonely job. We dumped our haversacks with him to lighten our load and keep him company.

The pair headed for Wood Two.

*

Back at RAF Brize Norton, at around 1.30 am the crews of the three G-B Force assault gliders had completed their final briefing. As they would be landing among the Germans inside the Battery perimeter, the occupants required some form of identification that would be recognizable to the rest of the Battalion in the darkness. Captain Gordon-Brown had been the one to come up with an idea. Private Gordon Newton, 'A' Company:

We were ordered to put a skull and crossbones on the left breast, which was done in luminous paint. They gave us the paint but they didn't give us any brushes. We had to use a shaving brush or a toothbrush. There were no stencils, you just did it yourself. Some were bigger than others. Then we got onto the airfield and they said, 'They're all luminous!' Of course, they had to be I suppose! So we all started to rub dirt on to get the luminosity out of it!

The glider pilots arrived at the runway. Staff Sergeant Baldwin:

The Parachute Regiment men were waiting to board the gliders. While I was counting them on, I noticed that each man, in addition to his normal kit, was also carrying a spare small haversack. I asked one what they contained and he replied, 'Grenades'. As I counted thirty men aboard I was convinced then that we were grossly overloaded. With just minutes to take-off there was absolutely nothing I could do. No one in his right mind would dare tell the officer in command that some of these men must remain behind, or alternatively, they must leave the extra small kits behind.

The gliders were veritable arsenals. Gordon Newton, who was carrying a flamethrower, was on board Gordon-Brown's glider:

The gliders each had two men with flamethrowers. The flamethrower guy had a 17lb flamethrower and his personal weapon was a pistol. If you carried a specialized weapon you carried a pistol. They gave us two sets of equipment. We had our own equipment, which was two pouches of Bren gun magazines, and I had a rifle and two bandoliers of ammunition, and a small pack. So when the assault was finished we changed our equipment into a rifleman's, mortar man's or Bren gunner's. All those who didn't carry flamethrowers or have a Sten gun had extra bandoliers and a bag full of grenades, and various other bombs and things. Being a big boy I always got to carry the heaviest things. What I had to do was get all these together and put them under the seats of the glider.

In addition were the Royal Engineer's plastic high explosive (PHE) charges and General Wades. These comprised of a curved segment to wrap around the gun barrel and a cylindrical piece placed in the bore.

At 2.15 am they were ready to take off. Glider No 28, piloted by Staff Sergeant Bone and Sergeant Dean, in which Captain Gordon-Brown was travelling, took off just after 2.24 am, followed seven minutes later by No 27 of Staff Sergeant Kerr and Sergeant Walker with Lieutenant Pond's men. At 2.37 am came No 28a of Staff Sergeant Baldwin and Sergeant Michie, containing Lieutenant Smythe's platoon. Their tug pilot was Flight Sergeant Dennis Richards. Arnold Baldwin:

We began to trundle forward. After using the usual amount of runway I pulled back on the stick but there was no response. A little further on I tried again - still no response. Then Dennis asked me rather sharply over the intercom, when I was going to lift off. I told him I couldn't get off. A few more yards and then Dennis said with great urgency that if I didn't lift off we would be going through the hedge at the end of the runway. At that moment she lifted very slowly and we both cleared the hedge. Almost immediately the port wing began to slowly drop. I tried to correct it with aileron but it still continued dropping so I applied opposite rudder. At first there was no effect, and I feared that, being so near to the ground, the wing-tip might strike, so I steadily increased right rudder till it was fully extended and slowly the wing came up again. Then I realized that we would have to make the whole flight with full right rudder. I tried to speak to Dennis on the intercom cable running through the tow-rope, but there was so much noise on the line, possibly caused by the strain on the tow-rope, that we could not hear each other. Before long my right leg became so painful that I asked Joe to put his foot down. Fortunately, he was a hefty lad with stout legs and he was able to take most of the strain off my leg. We flew like this for some time in fairly clear conditions, but the effort to keep such an unstable aircraft going was a great strain on both of us and the inability to tell Dennis of our problems made matters worse.

The G-B Force was on its way.

*

At the 9th Battalion RV, stragglers were still arriving. Ernie Rooke-Matthews:

From time to time men would come into the Rendezvous, some alone, others in groups. As each man came in he was greeted like a long lost brother such was our mutual feeling of relief at arriving safely.

After successfully finding his brandy bottle, CSM Harries had returned to the road, passed through the gate and began moving alongside a hedge. He then saw that he was not alone:

Two figures were moving some yards in front and did not seem to notice I was around. They certainly weren't wearing parachute helmets or our red berets, but, having moved closer to the hedge and moving forwards just quickly enough to keep them in sight, I found they were Germans wearing field caps. At the junction of the hedge was a type of pillbox, which provided a field of fire on both sides of the hedge. I was then surprised to see them disappear into the pillbox but could not figure out the reason. They certainly couldn't fire at anyone, as it was quite dark. After a few moments I decided to by-pass them but felt the opportunity too good to miss, so I quickly assembled a '36' grenade and having got close enough I lobbed it through a slit on the way past. My progress from then on increased, but having gone some twenty yards I heard the grenade explode and could only hope it served some useful purpose.

Moving on I met Sergeant Dorkins and we were quickly joined by some three or four others... . The general opinion seemed to be that we were heading in the right direction and after about another half-mile we were greeted by someone performing with the 'Bakelite duck'.

By the appointed time of 2.35 am only 110 men had reached the Battalion RV. No transport gliders had arrived. They had also encountered the huge smoke and dust clouds caused by the bombing raid, and with the strong wind, the pilots struggled to control their gliders. One carrying a party led by Colour Sergeant Davies had come down in the sea. All were lost. The others had landed to the south-east of the DZ among the anti-glider landing poles, causing seven deaths and many casualties. Consequently, the Battalion had no anti-tank guns or any of its heavy equipment and no charges to silence the guns. There was no signalling equipment, no engineers or Field Ambulance surgeons, although the doctor and six medical orderlies appeared with their First-Aid kit, no

Colour Sergeant Davies

Navy signallers and no Commando Liaison people. The Bangalore torpedoes had been dropped, one bundle of ten lengths to a chute, but only one bundle out of six had been retrieved. The 3-inch mortars and Vickers heavy machine guns had also been dropped by parachute, in metal containers, but no mortars had been recovered and only one machine gun.[16] Finally, no contact had been made with the Canadian covering party.

Colonel Otway faced a decision that had immense repercussions, not only for his few men on the DZ and in the gliders, but perhaps more importantly for the seaborne forces. He had to wait for as long as possible to allow other stragglers to arrive, while taking into account the mile and a half to reach the Battery and the arrival time of the assault gliders. On top of all this, the Germans must now surely be alert. He had not told a soul but in his plan he had allowed a 'window' of fifteen minutes for problems and so waited a little longer. The only man to whom the Colonel showed his concern was his batman, when at 2.45 am, the time for the final decision had arrived. Colonel Otway:

> I said, 'What the hell am I going to do, Wilson?' 'Only one thing you can do, Sir, no need to ask me.' And he was right. What else could I do? If I gave up I wouldn't be able to face my colleagues again.

He ordered Wilson to get the officers and NCOs together for a move in five minutes.

In these final few minutes, vitally, about forty men arrived to raise the strength to around 150. Among the late arrivals was a group to which Sergeant Daniels belonged. En route they had also experienced a close encounter:

> We bumped into one patrol going to the RV. We heard voices and one or two guttural words and down we'd gone, into the grass verges. Jerry got level with us, fifteen or twenty of them, on bikes. They laid the bikes down and had a slash, and one of the blokes was pissed on! The Jerries got on their bikes and away they went. Our objective was the Merville Battery and nothing could deter us from getting to the RV. We could have cleared that little lot off but what good would we have done? We'd have lost a few men who we couldn't spare at the time.
>
> We got down to the RV. What they'd got of the Battalion there was just beginning to move off.

Another late arrival was Stendall Brailsford who, having found no trace of his officer, Lieutenant Christie, had made his own way to the DZ.

They formed up in single file, as in the planned sequence for the assault. Major Parry, Lieutenant Worth and thirty men of 'A' Company were in front, followed by the Colonel, the weaponless anti-tank platoon, and half of one of the diversionary groups under Company Sergeant Major Harries. Then came thirty men of 'B' Company carrying the few Bangalore torpedoes. Two Company officers, Major Bestley and Lieutenant Dowling, were among them. Twenty men of 'C' Company followed, again with only two officers, Lieutenants Parfitt and Jefferson. Bringing up the rear were Battalion HQ personnel, including Major Charlton, Captain Hudson, Lieutenant Halliburton the Pioneer Platoon commander, Lieutenant Loring the Signals Officer, Captain Richards, the war artist, the MO Captain Watts, and six orderlies.[17]

At 2.50 am they began to leave the RV.

CHAPTER FIVE

The Attack

At the Battery Dusty Miller and Major Smith had started their reconnaissance:

The area was strewn with bomb craters. We had expected to find them but were amazed at their size. We reached the track through the Battery; it was wired up and another mine sign hung upon the wire. The main and inner perimeter defence was two hundred yards away. Wood Two stretched for half this distance. We decided to cut the wire just inside the corner of Wood Two and keep near its edge. We had been warned that this was a likely place for anti-personnel mines. It is, however, more comfortable with trees around one. If seen, one is more likely to get quick cover from view, and even at night it is darker beneath trees than elsewhere, and observation more difficult. We cut the wire and crept into the wood.

We were not frightened of anti-tank mines as it is unlikely that the weight of the body will set them off, although there was some danger that the bombs dropped near may have made them super-sensitive. This was a chance that had to be taken. Our main fear was of the anti-personnel mine, of which the Germans had numerous types, some difficult to detect without an electrical mine-detector, a piece of equipment we had considered bringing but decided was too burdensome.

Our present plan was to keep as far apart as possible and work forward level with each other so that we would not both be injured should a mine go up. The moon was beginning to rise and we found we could just see each other at thirty yards. If anything was to happen to either of us, the other was to go on and complete the job, heedless of the other's need for assistance. We went forward on hands and knees, feeling with our hands and making paths for our knees. We reckoned that if a mine went up or one of us was seen it would attract considerable fire, but the enemy would not venture onto their own minefield and come to close quarters.

We soon discovered why the track leading into the Battery had been wired off. Three heavy bombs had fallen on it, making it quite impassable and beyond repair without a considerable amount of labour. A bulldozer might have done the job but then the mines on either side of the track would soon have settled the account of the bulldozer.

Before we had gone far there was a noise of people on the track we had left, but there was no undue disturbance and we pressed on.

We met a number of wires of the loose variety. They were probably attached to anti-personnel mines worked on the pull principle, and we either cut them or passed over the top. They were close to the ground so this was not difficult.

At length we reached the inner edge of Wood Two. Here was another cattle fence in which we cut our separate gaps and went into the open on the last hundred yards of our journey. It was not long before we passed into long coarse grass about a foot high. Going through this even stealthily seemed to make a great deal of noise, but we were probably more than sensitive to noise at this moment. I could see the black dome of Miller's back moving slowly above the top of the grass.

Eventually we reached the wire and, as arranged, kept flat and still for five minutes, listening. Nothing could be heard, but the dim outline of the huge encasements could be distinguished.

We crept towards each other and listened for another five minutes. A wide anti-tank ditch ten feet deep had been started with the intention of encircling the Battery, but it had got only halfway round before the excavating machine had been taken away. We had watched its progress on aerial photographs. It had not reached where we are now. Most of the Battery also had two thick belts of wire entanglement about thirty yards apart forming the inner perimeter. This was the only place where there was one. Bombs had broken it and made large craters where it had been, but the Germans had joined the wire together around the inner sides of these craters, leaving peculiar indentations.

The Merville Battery area.

To discover whether or not there was anything strange or helpful we each went one hundred and fifty yards along the wire in opposite directions. The type of ground was the same everywhere. I passed what had been the entrance of the track, but the gap there had now been firmly wired. Soon after it the second fence started, running out at a gradual angle from the first fence, until it was thirty yards away when it ran parallel. I returned and found Miller already waiting for me. He had also found the second fence soon started. Why this gap had been left was beyond my comprehension. The defences here were stiff, but nothing in comparison with those on the side facing the sea.

The Battalion was to make three gaps through the wire and I decided the best locations would be on the track, about seventy yards to the right by a telegraph pole, and about seventy yards to the right again. This was more or less as we had rehearsed the operation.

There was still not the slightest sound and I began to wonder whether the place was deserted. I decided to make sure by going inside through the wire. It would have been unwise to have thrown away the knowledge of the layout we already had, so I decided to send Miller back to join Harrold and meet the Battalion should anything happen to me.

I waited until Miller had disappeared before I began my journey. The wire was about five feet high and fifteen wide. It seemed to be made to no particular pattern, but was thick with many supporting stakes. Cautiously I began to push various strands of wire aside and hook them back. Crawling half on my side and half on my back, I crept carefully into the hole I was making. My body was not more than half under the wire when I thought I heard a click, a familiar noise often made by a fidgety sentry knocking his rifle. I listened and heard it again probably within thirty yards. At crawling level there was a small rise hiding the ground in the direction of the noise from my view. I could not be certain of its origin and decided to carry on. I felt it imperative for me to be certain whether or not the Battery was held, and if so more about its ground defences. I continued my crawl.

It was slow and tedious work. Even on a dark night, if the head is held low, the wire can be seen against the sky. Twisting loops back and fastening them down was a simple but slow job. The main trouble was the numerous pieces which seemed to pop up from nowhere and catch on the rest of the body after the head and shoulders had passed.

I was a good halfway through the wire when I suddenly heard excited voices half-right about two hundred yards away, inside and towards the main entrance of the Battery. A tug aircraft and glider came into view from the right, flying at about eight hundred feet. This started a frightful hullabaloo in the Battery, which wakened to life as a sleeper with a bucket of cold water thrown over him. There were shouts and cries from everywhere, deep guttural voices booming out orders, these being relayed and acknowledged. I imagined all the available firepower being organized to meet this solitary invader, who was already being chased by a stream of tracer from more distant weapons.

Almost simultaneously, four machine guns inside the Battery opened fire with tracer. Neither the glider nor the aircraft faltered, but flew straight on, right over the centre of the Battery. Not more than thirty yards from me a 20mm flak gun opened up. The bang, bang, echoed in my ears and I saw the tracer-lit shells following each other upwards. This, with the machine guns, lit the place until to me it seemed like daylight. It seemed as though someone must see me in my insecure position. I suppose they were all too busy with their target, for I was not bothered, and keeping perfectly still I noted the positions of the ack-ack weapons which were bound to have a ground role as well.

The aircraft passed and the firing stopped. It must have been hit, but not sufficiently to bring it down, and I saw it disappear, still on the same course, at the same height, and on an even keel. A good pilot.[1]

I now decided I had sufficient knowledge. The Battery was most certainly occupied and I knew the state of its defences. Directly the firing stopped I began to get from under the wire, whilst the Germans were still excited, and their attention more in the air than on the ground. To get clear of the wire took a good five minutes, after which I dropped into a crater, and then began my journey to rejoin my two partners on this mission.

*

71

On the advance to the Battery the Battalion remnants had also encountered the mass of bomb craters. In the darkness people just suddenly disappeared into them.

CSM Barney Ross:

> *They made gaping great holes in the ground, and half the time we were going down one side trying to get up the other. You couldn't really walk around them because you'd be far too exposed if anything was to happen.*

The group had reached about the halfway stage when the aircraft towing the Divisional gliders began passing overhead. A hundred yards away an anti-aircraft battery opened up and every time a gun fired its crew was caught in mid-movement by the flashes. The Paras skirted around them. CSM Harries:

> *Some intermittent rifle and automatic fire was coming in our direction and quite suddenly a few heavy shells were also added which made it necessary to quit the track, and my party, together with others, hastily moved through the hedge and wire fence on our right. We soon wondered whether we had done the right thing as the field contained a herd of cows, some of which had obviously been killed, perhaps by the aerial bombardment. The remainder decided at that moment to stampede, and all one could see and hear was a herd of cows tearing round the field like mad things.*

At the noise, some of the Paras tensed, ready to open up, but the Colonel ordered them to hold their fire. A Pathfinder Officer, Lieutenant De La Tour, who was due to set up the navigational aids at the Battery, had been sitting down before the rumpus began, and had just disappeared. Colonel Otway:

> *He had fallen into what was a dry well in which the farmer dumped everything from their outdoor toilet. He was covered in it, and consequently smelt decidedly unpleasant! You can imagine his reaction as an ex-Guardsman!*[2]

They resumed the march along the bomb-cratered lane. Shortly after, they heard the sound of approaching troops and guessed that it was an enemy patrol. The Paras got down into some of the craters and around twenty Germans walked around them, suspecting nothing.

*

While things were going badly on the ground, the ageing, overloaded assault glider flown by Staff Sergeant Baldwin and Sergeant Michie, which had been airborne for about thirty minutes, had run into further trouble. Joe Michie:

> *We headed for a very heavy thick black cloud which Dennis Richards, our tug pilot, managed to avoid, great lumps of cumulus which looked pretty threatening at night. Then eventually he said over the intercom through the rope, 'I'm sorry we can't go round the next lot, we'll have to go through it', so we went straight into this large black cloud.*

Arnold Baldwin:

> *How long we were in that cloud I cannot tell, but it was quite the most frightening experience I have ever had. We bounced and bumped around with no idea of our relationship to the tug and a terrible fear that we could go completely out of control at any second. After what seemed like ages we emerged from the cumulus and there, right ahead of us and in the right position, I could see the tug.*

Staff Sergeant Arnold Baldwin.

Joe Michie:

> *We came out under this black cloud which was like a ceiling and just as we came out, the rope parted with a sigh more than anything.*

Arnold Baldwin:

Sergeant Joe Michie.

> *I felt physically sick. Although we had only been training for this job for about three weeks, all the previous months of training that led me to feel that the end of this flight would mean France, and at first I couldn't accept the fact that we were off tow and still over England. I slumped in my seat feeling utterly dejected and said to Joe, 'I don't give a f... what happens now.' When he responded, with a great deal of feeling 'Well I do and I expect those fellows in the back do as well', I came out of my trance and began to think about what to do. The ASI read 140 so I eased back on the stick very gently and had a look around. There, to my amazement and great relief, I saw a runway's lights just off our starboard wing-tip. Fortunately, I had a good deal of night-flying experience and it looked like a normal circuit and landing to me. We were flying cross-wind to the runway and I thought 'Just continue a bit further on this leg, then a down-wind leg, another cross-wind and a nice turn in to the runway.' However, I had barely commenced the down-wind leg when the runway lights went out. I thought they must be flying Ops to France and wanted no strangers coming in. It was now very dark, the moon being obscured, but I felt pretty optimistic now about a safe landing. Another look at the ASI still showed 140. I knew that couldn't be right, but I also knew with our overload that we would have a much higher stalling speed than normal so I did nothing to change the glider's altitude. Turning across wind when I judged the aerodrome to be a little way behind us, I made my turn and then again, as I believed, into the wind. We now had very little height and I was pretty shaken when I dimly saw the outline of a building on either side of us. By a very lucky fluke, we passed between two hangars. Then we were bumping along on the grass and I had a similar loss of concentration to that when the tow-rope had broken. Fortunately Joe had his wits about him and quickly applied the brake. Even so, we made a long run down the field before stopping.*

They had landed at RAF Odiham in Hampshire. It was 3.20am.[3]

The two remaining G-B Force gliders survived the cloud and rain, but, as they continued, ran into 'severe bumpiness'. No 28 developed a problem. Gordon Newton:

> *We knew that something was not right. The glider was 'crabbing' from side to side. We didn't realize what the problem was but the light went on and the co-pilot came through, very very calm and collected, and said, 'A knife please, any sort of knife, as long as it cuts.' I was sitting in the back seat. He said, 'Just a minute mate,' and pulled the back door open and cut the arrester gear off. We were about ten feet off the Channel.*

The rough ride had caused the arrester parachute cable to stream prematurely. This led to severe jerking and practically stalled the combination. The tail plane was damaged, the flying controls became sloppy and the starboard undercarriage was lost, but, in spite of the glider continuing to 'crab', the tug managed to pick up flying speed, regain height and continue towards the Normandy coast.[4]

*

Outside the Battery, Major Smith rejoined Dusty Miller and Bill Harrold:

> *The Taping Party, whose job was to clear a lane through the mines and mark it with white tape, should have now arrived.*

I decided to return to the point where I was to meet the Commanding Officer. This time I took Harrold with me, leaving Miller to meet the Taping Party and give it the layout. I had barely started, however, when I saw shadowy figures sliding down the lane towards me. I waited for them and challenged the leading figure softly. 'Paul, is that you?' 'Yes, old boy.'

It was Captain Paul Greenway, the officer leading the Taping Party.

'Is everything OK?' 'Yes, but there are very few of our lads at the RV.' 'Is your party complete?' 'No, we're about half strength and we haven't got any tape or mine detectors. Hell of a drop, all over the place.' 'Well, you'll have to devise something. It's pretty easy here.'

With that I told him the layout, left Miller to give him any further advice and set off. I was supposed to meet the Battalion at the first crosstracks where I had encountered the first minefield.[5] As I approached it there was a sho-o-oing noise like an amplified lavatory cistern and a shattering bang. A cloud of smoke and dust arose in front of us. This was followed by more. The Huns were shelling the crosstracks. If this place was being shelled by the enemy, it was most likely he had none of his own men there. We got to our feet and moved at a good pace past the crosstracks. The Battalion was not there.

Time was getting short and I was more than worried. I had not long to wait, however, for soon the head of the column approached. We remained still, in cover, until they were nearly on us, then I whispered the password and showed ourselves.

He met Major Parry, the leading figure. Major Smith:

The Commanding Officer was not far behind, and I met him and told him that things were going well and it should be easy.

He reported his findings at the Battery and also that only Captain Greenway and two men of the Taping Party had arrived, without any mine detectors or tape. The Colonel then confirmed the bad news of the drop, but it didn't really worry the Major:

Perhaps I was elated by having completed my task, but I was cheerful and certain we could manage the job as we stood.

I was sent forward to lead the Battalion. The crosstracks was still being shelled spasmodically, but now most of the shells were falling a little plus, and we got by safely.

It was now 4.00 am. They advanced in single file up the lane towards Wood One:

The Taping Party were awaiting us where Harrold had laid up, and this place was immediately made into a strongpoint.

The Colonel called the 'O'Group while the men stayed in the lane. Captain Greenway, CSM Miller and the two Taping Party men had managed to crawl through the outer minefield and clear four paths of around four feet width by searching for the mines with their fingers and defusing them one by one. These routes had been marked by producing furrows in the earth with spades or by simply dragging their heels. The two men had been left in position to pinpoint the lane entrances.[6] Otway issued orders for the assault. Major Smith:

The Commanding Officer was calm and unperturbed. He gave his orders concisely and clearly, as though he were standing giving orders on a training demonstration. Looking back, it seems incredible that everything was arranged and organized on the spot, amidst what seemed the most awful chaos. It took only a few minutes. The CO's calm set a fine example which was followed by all ranks. His thoroughness in training paid a fine dividend, the troops were on their toes and ready for the job.

The Diversionary Party was to carry on as planned and kick up as much noise as possible over to the right at the main gate. However, Lieutenant Browne was missing, in fact the only member of the party to reach the Battery was Sergeant Knight, so he would first have to round up a few men. The detail of the assault itself also had to be changed. Major Smith:

The Breaching Company, now thirty strong, should blow two gaps in the wire instead of three, and for this purpose it was split into two groups of fifteen.

Major Parry:

The CO decided that I must lead the assault in the absence of Ian Dyer, OC, 'C' Company, and that 'A' and 'C' Companies would constitute the Assault Party. The signal for the assault to begin would be the blowing of the torpedoes.

This Assault Party was to comprise of about fifty men and be split into four groups, one for each gun, two groups passing through each gap. With no engineers or special charges to destroy the guns, they would have to rely on those carried in the assault gliders, or just the men's initiative.

The remainder of the force was under Colonel Otway for mopping-up purposes.

The officers returned to their depleted companies and relayed the orders, which were passed backwards by word of mouth.

Private Ken Walker was supposed to be part of the Firm Base Party, but again, due to the lack of men, he did not know what his role was to be:

It was then that Captain Hudson, the Adjutant, said we, Battalion HQ, are going in after the original assault. Well to my memory, he said Battalion Headquarters, I think there were only three of us. Him and three soldiers!

Instead of going around to the right as planned, the role of CSM Harries' 1st Sniping Group was altered:

I found that my small party was to move up to the Battery perimeter wire with the Main Base party and as the assault groups moved forward, to move and support them by fire as the actual guns were dealt with.

Major Parry began organizing the Assault Party. He formed two groups under Lieutenants Jefferson and Dowling to attack No. 1 and No. 2 casemates respectively. CSM Ross was supposed to be leading the 2nd Sniping Group around to the left, but hardly any of his men had turned up, so he had no idea what he was going to do until, approaching Major Parry, he heard him say, 'Any other NCOs? Oh you'll do, Barney'. He was assigned command of the No 3 casemate group.

Colour Sergeant Harold Long was given responsibility of the group attacking No. 4 casemate, while the Major himself would lead another in behind the initial parties. Fred Milward:

My original job had been to be in a Firm Point as reserve, but as there were only 150 of us this was all changed. Major Parry tapped me on the shoulder. 'You're with me,'he said. 'No 1 gun'.[7]

Major Parry:

There was no time for anything more than cursory orders. I explained that there would be no communications, as we had no wireless and that each party would have to go independently. I arranged a signal for the assault to begin [a blow on his whistle to detonate the Bangalores] *and we deployed along the line of the cattle fence which marked the perimeter of the minefield.*

Another major problem remained the lack of a 3-inch mortar to illuminate the Battery for the gliders, but there was no option, the pilots would

CSM Barney Ross.

just have to rely on the other aids and make their best attempt.

Meanwhile, Sergeant Knight had assembled a few men including Sergeant 'John' Walker, but was still looking for more. Tom Stroud:

> *I should have attacked No. 1 casemate but at this stage Sergeant Knight told me to go with his small party to attack the main gate.*

Ernie Rooke-Matthews:

> *As the groups were moving off to their positions ready for the assault, Sergeant Sid Knight, whom I knew as our musketry-training instructor, came over to me. 'What are you doing laddie?' 'I'm a signaller. I was with 'B' Company but I was told to come up here with BHQ.' 'But you have no contact?' 'Right Sergeant.' 'Then come with me,' he said. With my wireless set still on my back and armed with a .45 revolver, a couple of grenades and magazines, I followed the Sergeant.*

Sergeant Knight:

> *There was hardly any noise whatsoever, and the Battery loomed out of the darkness. You could see the*

Sergeant 'John' Walker.

outlines of the four big guns facing the sea. We'd come over the barbed wire and there was an old perimeter track leading up to the Battery, so I started to make a movement around this road when machine guns opened up from both sides.

Colonel Otway shouted, 'Get those bloody machine guns!' Major Smith:

> *Ten enemy machine guns opened fire, four from inside the Battery position and three from each flank outside. Colonel Otway ordered the Vickers crew to knock out those on the left and told Sid Knight to take some men and silence those on the right.*

Ernie Rooke-Matthews:

> *As we dashed across the perimeter the sergeant told me to stay by the main gate [track entrance to the east of the Battery] and to give warning if any reinforcements were to come in my direction. The sergeant, with his section, went in to put the enemy machine guns out of action. I stayed at the gate surveying the road for any movement.*

Tom Stroud:

> *The Battery was on our left and as I had the only Bren gun, Sergeant Knight told me to knock them out. He was next to me when I opened fire from the hip at the first gun. It was very easy to locate as it was firing a heavy concentration of tracer bullets, apparently on a fixed line of fire. After two short bursts of fire from the Bren, the gun did not fire again.*

Sid Knight:

> *We found there were three guns, one outside and two inside the perimeter, in front of No 1 Battery [casemate]. I got the bloke on the outside corner by the forming-up point, then went into the Battery.*

They began moving along a lane that led to the main gate in order to attack the remaining machine guns and create the diversion.

Those on the receiving end of the machine-gun fire from the left had been fortunate. Sergeant McGeever, Corporal McGuinness and Private Fenson were carrying the solitary Vickers gun. Jim McGuinness:

Main gate area of the Battery. Sgt Knight's party followed the curved path along the line of trees, top right.

> *We were at the rear of the Battalion. As we came into the open field, Jerry opened up with his machine gun. A good job he used tracers, he missed us by about three feet, everyone including myself jumped into a bomb crater. But when McGeever called to get the bloody gun in action, Fenson ran out, mounted the tripod, I put the gun on, he loaded and McGeever gave the range, then the order to fire. We heard no more from the machine gun.*

The Vickers crew remained where they were.

In the meantime, the move through Wood Two had begun. Major Smith:

> *The Breaching Parties followed in single file after the guides from the Taping Party. They disappeared into the darkness carrying their few Bangalore torpedoes, and were closely followed by the Assault Parties. The second in command [Major Charlton] stayed at the strongpoint with a mere handful of men and the medical officer [Captain Watts] who was in a large crater rendering first aid to a few wounded.*

Private Bob Abel was in Captain Greenway's group to blow the left-hand gap, on the track itself:

> *We just ran through the perimeter wire, which was already down and just followed the path through the minefield.*

All the parties took up position among the bomb craters at the 'start line', about fifty yards from the

Frank Delsignore.

barbed wire. Frank Delsignore looked about him:

I thought it looked a very thin line compared to the one I was used to when practicing at Newbury. I wondered how I would react when the signal did come. I knew I was afraid that I may be killed within the next few minutes, and I suspected there were others like me. As I lay there thinking about it, I knew I would have the courage to overcome the fear when the time came. I consoled myself with the thought that if a man can overcome his fears, then he is as good as the naturally courageous man.

Over to the right, Sergeant Knight's small group began the diversion. Colonel Otway:

They loosed off everything they could, not towards the casemates, but in a north/north-westerly direction to stop hitting us in the side. They threw grenades, made a hell of a row. It made the Germans go and find out what was happening.

They didn't seem to know where we were, didn't concentrate their fire. They didn't send anyone out to the wire to find out [if anyone was there].

Pushing the Bangalores in front of them the Breaching Parties crawled forward to the Battery wire. The party to blow the right-hand gap comprised four men led by Sergeant Len Daniels:

We connected up the Bangalores and slipped them under the wire; put in a GC primer in the end, detonator into GC primer, and a little igniter.

Leaving a man at each gap to detonate the torpedoes, the parties withdrew. As all of the blast was going upwards, Sergeant Daniels was lying only three feet away from the end of the Bangalore.

Readying themselves for the left-hand gap, Derek Vincent and Ron Gregory of the Breaching Party were ordered by someone to go up to the gap and hold back the edges of the wire so that it did not curl in again and impede the Assault Parties. Derek Vincent:

He said, 'As soon as everybody has gone in, just get inside and any Germans you see, pop 'em off, any machine guns..., but by Christ sake don't shoot your own blokes! Keep there so that you can help them out again.'

Behind, the Assault Troops waited. Sid Capon was a member of the party heading for No 1 casemate:

To my right was Alan Jefferson, to his right was Eric Bedford, Frank Delsignore, 'Johnnie' [Harold] Walker and Les Cartwright. There was one other bloke... . [Private Morgan]. To my immediate left was Lieutenant Mike Dowling who was going into No. 2 gun with a similar group.

Frank Delsignore:

Alan Jefferson was quietly giving us a pep talk, telling those of us around him why, in the next few minutes, we should become ruthless, killing bastards and strike a blow for the bombings and killings that our parents, wives and girlfriends had endured for so long.

Jefferson also had a strictly 'unofficial' toy horn with which he was going to spur the men on. They waited for the gliders.

At this point Private Cyril Thwaites of 'C' Company, who had landed alone and headed directly for the Battery, arrived at the position and came across a Lieutenant:

Cyril Thwaites.

There was this old tree trunk. It was just as though someone had hollowed a bit out. He was crouching there with papers in his hand. I'd got to the Battery. I was pleased 'cos I thought I'd be the only bloody one missing! He said, 'Thank goodness, another one.' I thought, 'Another one? Who am I? A private out of nearly 700 blokes.' The next words he said to me were, 'Come on, let's get going 'cos the attack's going in now.' I said, 'What!' He said, 'Well, within a short period.' As we were walking he said, 'Do you know what, there's only about a hundred-odd of us.' What! No wonder he said another one!

He then tagged onto the back of a group waiting to go through the left-hand gap.

Suddenly the glider carrying Captain Gordon-Brown's party arrived overhead. Due to the low cloud base, it had to come down to 1,000 feet. The navigational aids were supposed to have been set up 600 yards south-east of the Battery, but none were apparent to the pilots.[4] Gordon Newton:

Then suddenly flak started coming up. It was coming through the floor and out the roof. Under the seats, which are along the full length of the glider, you had all the other equipment, and there were mortar bombs, high explosive, there were replacements for the flamethrowers... . The whole thing was not just a tinderbox, it was very high explosives, and if it had got a tracer in the right place it would have just disintegrated. Had we been sitting crossways, people might have got hurt. I was sitting in the back seat, the pilot put me there and I wasn't very happy with that. So I went and sat next to Foster, the other flamethrower, whereupon they opened the door. In order that I didn't get thrown out the door, I went and sat the other side. As soon as I did this, where my head had been, something came through the floor and out the roof.

With both glider and Albermarle under such fire, Pilot Officer Garnett continued to fly the tug around the area while trying to locate the objective. After four circuits, Staff Sergeant Bone spotted what he thought was the Battery and released the towrope.[4] Descending to 500 feet he realized that it was actually the bombed village of Gonneville and so banked the Horsa away. The men at the perimeter saw the glider for a few brief seconds. A 'posh' voice was heard to say 'It will be alright chaps, it will come back. The world is round!'[8]

Gordon Newton:

Through a window I could see a tree and I thought, 'Hello!' As it happened it went skidding across the water and the tail came off, and left it about seventy-five yards behind.

Gordon Newton.

79

They had landed some distance to the east of the Battery. Luckily no one was injured, but, Captain Gordon-Brown's party was not going to make it to the Battery in time.

Gordon Newton:

> *We got out into this water which was nearly waist deep. As we came out the glider I could see the other glider just casting off, the telltale lift of the nose, and then I saw it coming down. All the tracer shells of the machine-gun fire were going up, and there was a lot of shooting.*

The glider containing Lieutenant Pond's group had not been able to locate the target either. Staff Sergeant Dickie Kerr:

> *When we were in the approximate Battery area we cruised round looking for lights on the ground, but there were none. There were no parachute flares either and we were dead on time. Jerry meanwhile had been rather interested in us and was peppering the tug and glider with light flak.*

Sapper Alex Taylor, 591 Parachute Squadron RE:

> *Lieutenant Pond shouted that we had flown over the Battery and were turning to make another run. We were in trouble! The flak was catching us again. Holes appeared in the thin plywood fuselage of the glider. Our tug was taking evasive action, causing terrific stresses in the fabric of the glider.*

Dickie Kerr:

> *We continued to circle the target, however, for a quarter of an hour and at the end of which time a triangle of lights appeared on the ground pointing to the Battery and also a flashing recognition light {red 'A', the pre-arranged signal}. I pulled off as I saw these lights and proceeded to do a pretty snappy circuit*

> *of the Battery in order to lose height. Three light flak batteries were now engaging us and the glider was hit frequently. We were hit about eight times in the fuselage with bursts of tracer and twice by cannon shells. The wings got a lot of tracer too. I could feel them quivering as the bullets hit them. The glider remained fully manoeuvrable though.*

Inevitably, some of the Paras were wounded. Sergeant 'Dizzy' Brewster:

> *These bullets came through the floor. One went up through my leg, my knee and another through my hand.*

Private Fred Glover:

> *Suddenly, for some reason both of my legs momentarily lifted off the floor. I didn't realize at first that I'd been hit, there was no pain or anything.*

Dickie Kerr:

> *Visibility was bad and I could not make out the Battery at all. I only knew I was flying in the right direction because of the ground lights. At this point I could make out the ground and what I saw wasn't healthy. It was a field that was poled and from the information that I had been given was mined too. I decided it wasn't really an ideal landing spot and kept the glider flying as long as possible in the direction of the Battery.*

The glider passed over the casemates, the waiting assault troops and just above the head of Ernie Rooke-Matthews at the junction of the track and the road. Dickie Kerr:

> *We were now over an orchard and I could see we would not make the far side of it. I therefore told my second pilot to let go*

Staff Sergeant Dickie Kerr.

the parachute and I put full flap on. This brought the speed down nicely and as we sank onto the trees the parachute caught in the branches, acting as an anchor. This slowed us up still further and we landed not too badly in the trees.

Kerr was thrown through the front of the cockpit where the Perspex had been and landed in a bomb crater twenty feet away. Sergeant Walker was hanging in the co-pilot's seat. The Horsa had come to rest in an orchard 500 yards east of the Battery perimeter, facing south-west and lying around twenty yards from the lane up which the Battalion had arrived.[9] Alex Taylor:

The tail section of the glider was off, the wings were destroyed, the right side was open. Those who weren't wounded struggled to get out and feel solid ground. No hail of bullets met us as expected and there was no fire.

Fred Glover:

The tail section came adrift with Ron Sharp, a flamethrower under his seat, still strapped in and struggling to get free which thankfully he did. I dragged myself from the wreckage and was surprised to find that I could walk, albeit with some difficulty.[10]

Ron Sharp.

Dickie Kerr:

The flak had hit a box of smoke grenades in the glider and it was smouldering vigorously as we landed but as we moved away it burst into flames so we were unable to retrieve certain equipment and spare ammunition which had been left in it.[11]

Above the Battery there was no sign of the third glider and the assault could wait no longer. Major Parry blew his whistle. Everyone hugged the ground. Sergeant Daniels:

I just pulled a little piece of cord attached to the igniter, there's a second and away it went.

Major Smith:

There were two shattering simultaneous explosions, two gaps about twenty feet across appeared in the wire.

Sid Capon:

Otway was sitting just behind me and he said, 'Get in, get in!'

It was 4.30 am.[12] Without hesitation they began running towards the clouds of smoke. Frank Delsignore:

Alan [Jefferson] was the first one up on his feet and led us into the assault. Any fear I had was gone. We were up and running with Alan, firing from the hip as we went in. We knew there were land mines in the ground we had to cover.

With support fire blazing away, they headed into the minefield, yelling as they ran. Enemy flares went up and fire rapidly increased from various positions around the site. Lieutenant Jefferson was blowing his horn. Suddenly

Lieutenant Alan Jefferson.

81

he felt something strike his left thigh and he fell to the ground.[6] Frank Delsignore:

He was unable to lead us any further but he was not finished yet, for as we carried on I could hear him swearing and cursing about the Germans and encouraging us on.

Sid Capon:

I remember shouts from the left saying 'Mines!, mines!', and explosions. We carried on zig-zagging, running the gauntlet of the crossfire.

Private Walter Johnson:

I seemed to be deafened by the noise of the battle and confusion, which was now going on as I found myself running and looking for cover, seeing Germans running here and there in all this. All this in a matter of seconds, and as I made my way I was caught by a sniper. My hand was pinned to the butt of my rifle and down I went, and probably caught by an explosion, as my smock smelt as though it was on fire.

The groups led by Lieutenant Dowling and Major Parry followed through the right-hand gap. Fred Milward:

With shouts and cries and a few curses as well, we charged after Major Parry over the minefield, through the gap blown in the wire and straight for the guns just as fast as we could. I found myself spending half the time running up and down bomb craters. There were so many bomb craters overlapping one another and it was all loose earth.... If you ran down in one, you had a hell of a job getting up the other side. It was like trying to climb up a sand dune, everything was moving. I saw Major Parry go down and several of my pals hit as they charged forward.

The terrain faced in the attack.

THE MERVILLE BATTERY ASSAULT

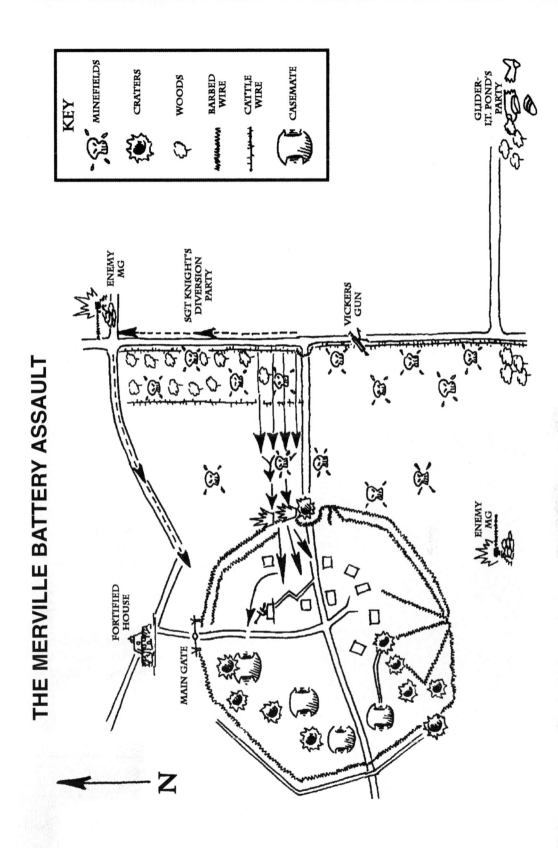

KEY

MINEFIELDS

CRATERS

WOODS

BARBED WIRE

CATTLE WIRE

CASEMATE

ENEMY MG

SGT KNIGHT'S DIVERSION PARTY

VICKERS GUN

GLIDER- LT. POND'S PARTY

FORTIFIED HOUSE

MAIN GATE

ENEMY MG

N

Major Parry:

> *I was conscious of something striking my left thigh, my leg collapsed under me and I fell into a huge bomb crater. I saw my batman, who was just alongside me, looking at me as if to say, 'Bad luck mate', and off he went.* [13, 14]

Seventy yards to the left the Assault Parties of firstly CSM Ross, then Colour Sergeant Long, went for the centre of the Battery, heading for Nos. 3 and 4 casemates. CSM Harries' fire support party followed them, taking up position just beyond the gap.

Over to the left an enemy machine gun opened up. Sergeant Daniels was at the edge of the wire:

> *There was a hell of a commotion. Grenades exploding, '77'phosphorous grenades going off, Stens were blazing away.*

Fred Milward negotiated another crater and came to a trench:

> *I could see it in the moonlight. There was some Germans up the other end and we started firing at them. I dived in one end and they came out the other and they were shouting something like 'Paratruppen, paratruppen'. I honestly thought 'The rest of the boys are coming in on the Battery,' so I looked up to see where they were! Of course, they'd recognized us! They disappeared into the darkness.*

To the rear of the Battery the G-B Force men had scrambled from the wreckage of the glider, dragging the wounded with them. Fred Glover:

> *There were quite big craters. The first thing I did was to tumble into one. One of the Pathfinders said, 'Up there, I'll help you', and we went towards the direction of the Battery. He was obviously aware of the situation... . I was a bit shocked of course, I knew I'd been hit but not the extent.*

Sergeant Harry Dixon was heading towards the lane when his attention was drawn to the field opposite:

Sergeant Harry Dixon.

> *This field was mined and it had a gate, and it had the skull and crossbones hanging on the gate, 'MINEN'. Three German soldiers came out of the gate and I gave them a burst and I must have hit two of them and they dropped down, but the third one, he skedaddled back in the gate.*

Hugh Pond's party then heard the sound of troops approaching up the lane from Gonneville and, realizing that it must be the enemy, got down into the ditches and hedges on either side of the lane and opened fire. About thirty yards away the Germans did likewise and a private battle developed. Having missed the Battery, it had turned out to be a very fortuitous position to land.

Behind them the battle was in full swing. Colonel Otway:

> *The garrison concentrated everything waist-high on the gaps in the wire, booby traps and mines were going off all over the place, the battle in our rear was going full tilt and fierce hand-to-hand fighting was taking place inside the Battery.*

Frank Delsignore reached No. 1 casemate to find the rear doors open:

> *'Johnnie' [Harold] Walker and I were the first to get to the gun emplacement. We got to the entrance and shouted for anyone still inside to come out. We got no answer, so we threw a couple of hand grenades inside.*

Then Sid Capon arrived:

> There were four of us, Eric Bedford was now the senior
> NCO, and there was Frank Delsignore, 'Johnnie'Walker and
> myself.... It suddenly seemed all quiet. We lobbed two grenades
> in there and all of a sudden heard movement inside. In the left-
> hand compartment, the Germans started pushing each other out
> and lined up opposite. I wasn't worried about the gun, I wasn't
> worried about anything, only the Germans. The last one wore
> glasses and I think he thought he was going to be shot.

Suddenly, two more jumped out of a trap-door with their
hands held high, their belts still full with stick grenades.
These joined the others outside. Fred Milward:

> I reached the massive casemate of No. 1 gun. There were
> loads of wounded lying around. You could hear the moaning,
> groaning, not only ours but Germans as well. I dived in
> through the open rear doors and, much to my relief I can tell
> you, found some of our lads already there. Perhaps they could
> run up and down bomb craters quicker than me! Went into the
> room on the left-hand side as you go in the casemate and had a
> go with the old Sten, no time for niceties, and came to the front
> of the casement to find the gun.

The group to which Cyril Thwaites had attached himself
arrived in the centre of the Battery just as a large number of
Germans came around the side of one of the casemates. The
Paras engaged them in hand-to-hand fighting.

Colonel Otway had moved forward and was standing at
the right-hand gap in the wire, a position that enabled him
to observe both left and right:

> As it got lighter I could see. I had to be able for example,
> looking to my right to see Sergeant Knight and whether they'd
> managed to get in through the gate. Equally, I had to be in the
> best position from the machine gun on the left of the position. In
> addition, I had to keep on dodging this sod, a machine gun up on
> the tower, who was shooting at me. So I was moving in and out.

Sid Capon.

Sergeant Knight's diversion party had gradually worked its
way forward to deal with the machine guns near the main
gate. Tom Stroud:

> I moved forward and to the left, got down in a prone position
> and opened fire at the second gun. As before only two bursts were
> necessary to knock it out.

Sergeant Knight:

> It was very dark, but I could see that one of the gunners was
> by a whacking great lump of concrete that had been blown up.
> His tracer gave him away, so I got right round behind him and
> put my gun on him, which soon quietened him down. I had a
> go at the third one, whether I got him or not I don't know but
> it all went quiet.[15]

Sergeant Eric Bedford

Tom Stroud:

> *I again moved my position and opened up on the third and last gun. This too, quickly ceased fire. I looked round for Sergeant Knight and the section, only to find I was completely alone. I had no idea which direction they had taken so I reverted to my training at the dummy battery and ran towards No. 1 casemate.*

With more distance, and therefore wire, craters, trenches and enemy positions to negotiate, it was a very tough proposition for those men heading for Nos 3 and 4 casemates. CSM Ross:

> *The longer you was out there, the longer the bloody bullets and shit were flying about!*

With the firing and explosions continuing unabated, Otway decided to send in the remainder of his force:

> *Like many men, I suppose, I had no great fear of being killed but the horror of being mutilated swept over me when the moment came to go through the wire into the enemy fire. Quite irrelevantly, I wondered what Wilson would think of me. I shouted, 'Come on!' and ran for it. In the circumstances it was the only thing to do.*

They headed through the gap. In various places some of the men had to fall on what was left of the wire while the others ran across their backs. Major Bestley:

> *Terence Otway ordered me to sort out a machine gun half-left of the axis of assault. The rest of my company being committed to the gap they had blown, I set off with my batman in the direction indicated. I had not gone more than fifty to a hundred yards when a bullet clipped a nerve behind my left knee, incapacitating me.*

Beside the Colonel was Captain Hudson:

Major Harold Bestley.

> *I was just short of the gap in the wire when something hit my right buttock. I assumed it was a piece of earth, or a stone thrown up by mortar or shell fire. I was extremely surprised to find myself thrown on my back and assumed that some sort of blast must be responsible. However, on attempting to get to my feet, I found that I was unable to do so. I put my hand on my right buttock and was very surprised indeed to find it smothered in blood. I felt no pain, but a curious weakness. Lying on my back, looking towards the Battery through the gap in the wire made by the Bangalore torpedoes, I saw a stream of machine-gun tracer which appeared to be uninterrupted. Through this gap were pouring the assault troops.*
>
> *I could see German troops outside the gun emplacements, presumably others were in the casements. With infinite pains I took up my revolver, aimed carefully at the nearest German, and pulled the trigger. Unfortunately, the bullet went straight through my left foot. This self-inflicted wound caused me the most exquisite pain.*

Hudson did not realize how badly he had been wounded and was more concerned about his foot. Otway was very fortunate as one bullet hit his water bottle and another went through the back of his smock.

Having been wounded, Walter Johnson was making his way out:

> *Colonel Otway saw me and said, 'Get that wounded man out of it'. Tom Stroud said, 'What are you bloody doing, you're not wounded'. I said, 'I must be 'cos I'm covered in blood!'*

Indeed, apart from his hand injury, he was covered in shrapnel wounds, and the front of his smock was soaked in blood. Tom Stroud carried on towards No 1 casemate:

> *I was within a few yards of the door when I was knocked flat on my back by a bullet in my left upper*

arm. I lay there trying to locate the source of the fire before moving forward into the comparative safety of the door opening. Shortly afterwards one of our lads nicknamed 'Darky', I think his name was Colville, ran in, but as he appeared to have no weapon I gave him the Bren which I couldn't control as my left arm was now paralysed. Fortunately, I could still use my revolver in my right hand. Stupidly, I wondered if I could get a receipt for the Bren gun from 'Darky', but as things were still pretty hectic within the Battery I decided against it.

Ken Walker:

We were told that our job was to wipe out the German machine-gun posts which were inside the Battery, between No. 2 and No. 3 casemates – most of them were Schmeissers in pits. And then I suppose, in the vernacular, my bottle must have gone because things to me are virtually blank. There were two Germans with a machine gun, and myself and another soldier ran towards it, and as we ran towards it they upped and ran away. I fired my rifle and missed, did it again and I'd had all my ten shots, and I wasn't aware of firing them.

Walter Johnson.

Even those with the most severe physical difficulties tried to 'do their bit'. Reg Osborne limped in with his broken ankle and Private Tony Mead, who on landing had suffered the agony of a branch penetrating his abdomen, reached a pillbox, crouched beside the aperture and while holding his insides with one hand, fired the Sten with the other.[16]

Only about four of CSM Ross' party survived to reach a casemate. In the darkness and confusion, possibly No. 4:

The door was shut. It was a long way round to the front of the bloody things..., turning round the corner and shooting bullets into the eyelets. We were milling around the top. We were poking some grenades down the air vents. By the time we'd done this on the top, the door was then coming open and they were coming out.

CSM Harries had also made it to No. 4 casemate:

I moved to the entrance of the gun emplacement but there was plenty of activity inside with bodies milling around like a crowded railway carriage. Germans were running out of the exit and being picked off as they went.

Barney Ross:

I think there were a lot of Polish guys amongst them, all shouting 'Comrade, comrade', with all their bloody hands up. [17]

Tony Mead.

The enemy evacuated the casemate and the Paras went in to inspect the huge gun, only to be confronted by a wheeled 100mm Field piece on a platform. Following up, Sergeant Fred Dorkins of 'A' Company also reached No. 4 and entered the casemate:

There was CSM Jack Harries, another man and myself. We decided to elevate the gun. Damaged the elevating gear and placed a Gammon bomb on the breech block with a short fuse. It seemed to work, causing considerable damage.

In an attempt to get some PHE charges to the casemates, Sapper Alex Taylor had left the glider group and tried to approach the Battery:

Corporal Sanderson and myself decided to go for No. 1 casemate. We immediately came under fire, returned some fire with our Sten guns, but had no real target. We made slow progress towards the casemate from crater to crater, a distance of some 200 metres. From a bomb crater we realized we would stand little chance of reaching No. 1 casemate and we came under fire from the rear.

Sergeants Daniels and Novis, and Privates Mower and Hawkins of 'B' Company, were among those who had charged in with the Colonel, reaching a spot not far from No. 2 casemate. Mortar fire was now coming in thick and fast. Colonel Otway:

Mike Dowling came up to me by himself, with his right hand and arm over his chest.

Alan Mower was a few feet away:

He saluted and said, 'Battery taken as ordered, Sir.' Otway said 'Have you destroyed the guns?' 'I think so.' 'Bloody well get back up there and make sure those guns are out of action.'[18]

Mower, Hawkins, another Para and a Bren gunner continued towards No 2 casemate. George Hawkins:

We were going down towards it, and Lieutenant Dowling, Mike, he was twenty yards in front of us and a mortar just killed him outright.

It also killed his batman. The three men passed the prone bodies and veered left, towards Nos. 3 and 4 casemates:

The first casement we went into, this officer, he had the blinking thing undone..., the breech block. He seemed to know what he was doing.

This could possibly have been the party of Colour Sergeant Long:

We had no explosives with which to blow the guns. We removed the breech blocks, took them away and threw different parts in various directions.

Fleeting bodies, both Paras and Germans, were running about the place. Hawkins group headed over

Sergeant Fred Dorkins.

Lieutenant Mike Dowling.

to No. 4 casemate. Sergeant Johnny Novis:

After manoeuvring around the craters, four of us are in an area midway between two emplacements, and looking to my right I see Jock Hannen disappearing into an emplacement, totally oblivious to our shouts for him to wait for us. Making my way over to him, he suddenly reappears behind two prisoners, both as young as ourselves.

On reaching No. 4 casemate Mower left the Bren gunner and Hawkins outside, and went in to investigate. He also found the field gun:

The gun was fixed, you couldn't move it. You couldn't move it up or down or sideways. You couldn't turn any handles, it was just sighted on the beach. I saw this ammunition in this little recess... . There was all these boxes with the shells in.

As all he possessed were two '36' grenades, he had two ideas; put them in the wheels and try and bring the gun down, or throw them in with the ammunition. He went back outside and began to inform the others of his intentions:

Colour Sergeant Harold Long.

There was this explosion and we sort of fell in a heap together. I fell on the Bren gunner and it was obvious he was dead. Hawkins and me were just riddled with shrapnel. It caught me in the back, legs, arms and went through into the wall of my chest.

George Hawkins:

The boy on my left got it all in the face... . And I suppose the other boy behind, shrapnel came up and went right through his head, killed him outright. I just laid there. It just knocks you silly.

Sergeant Daniels arrived and leapt onto a concrete position. He saw Hawkins and so jumped down and knelt beside him:

His eyes were upside down so to speak, he couldn't move, he couldn't speak. Got a lot of dirt and what have you on him. I couldn't find a pulse and he was dead. I heard something and looked, and Sergeant Jenkins was standing up on this concrete position that I stood on previously. He'd got his rifle pointing up the hill. I looked to see what was happening and he shot, and a Jerry came rolling down off the casemate. He [Paddy] jumped over the top of us and rammed his bayonet into him.[19]

Amazingly, Hawkins was not dead.

Over at the main gate the machine guns had been silenced and the diversionary action completed. Sergeant Knight:

I went back to report to the Colonel and was just going towards the actual objective when I saw Major Parry on the right-hand side of the track wounded in the leg; on the left side was Captain Hudson and he had a terrible wound in his stomach. I carried on with my diversionary party inside the perimeter and as we reached the main gate we saw some Germans walking in, waving white flags. A

George Hawkins.

couple of our blokes were shouting out, 'Shoot them.' Of course, I shouted, 'You can't shoot them; they've got the white flag up', and so we rounded them up.

Suddenly another machine gun opened fire from a building on the right flank, outside the perimeter. Sergeant Knight immediately marched the prisoners straight towards the machine gun. Sid Capon:

At that he stopped firing and surrendered himself. He was a little blonde fella.

This signalled the last of the action within the Battery. Cyril Thwaites:

All of a sudden it came to a halt. It evaporated. It was fierce and then all of a sudden it was over.

Ken Walker:

When the adrenalin, I suppose, had returned to normal I found myself alone and although still inside the perimeter of the Battery, strangely lost. The ground and vicinity was virtually indescribable; large deep bomb craters, shell holes, freshly churned up earth, the smell of cordite and most horrifying of all, the dead bodies of the soldiers, both ours and German.

Sergeant Daniels:

The whole area was pervaded by this peculiar smell of freshly turned earth, torn flesh, that sort of thing. And it's a smell, you never forget it, almost like if you go into hospital for an operation, you smell the ether for the first time. You never forget it.

Colonel Otway:

I saw what I thought was a dog tied up outside a pillbox and went to investigate, but an officer who was lying nearby with a shattered leg shouted, 'Don't touch that you bloody fool, it's a booby trap.' It was Lieutenant Jefferson.

Jefferson, who was still lying wounded, had not realized that it was his CO.

Sergeant Knight went and had a look in some of the casemates, one being No. 2:

Some chaps put two shells in the gun; one at the breech and one in the barrel! When the gun fired, the shells blew the gun to pieces. I did not see the actual firing but heard the explosions.

Major Parry:

In the bottom of my rather personal bomb crater, I assessed my position. My left leg was numb and my trouser leg was soaked in blood. Having a minuscule knowledge of first aid I removed my whistle lanyard and tied it to my leg as a tourniquet. My knowledge was evidently too limited, as I applied it in the wrong place. Realizing, after a brief interval, my error, I removed it, thus restoring some form of life to my leg; sufficient at any rate, to enable me to clamber out of my hole and continue with my appointed mission.

He managed to get to the entrance of No. 1 casemate, where he saw a few Paras attending to the wounded, but there was no sign of his batman, George Adsett. The group of German prisoners was still stood there with their hands in the air:

Most of them were wearing greatcoats and soft hats and didn't appear to be expecting us.

As I entered the enormous casemate it was possible to discern only two or three of my party. I was somewhat weakened by the loss of blood and passed through the casemate to the firing aperture at the far end, where, to my intense dismay, I saw not a 150mm gun, as was expected, but a tiny, old-fashioned piece mounted on a carriage with wooden wheels. I estimated it to be a 75mm {sic} and it was clearly a temporary expedient pending the arrival of the permanent armament. This was an awful anti-climax, and made me wonder if our journey had really been necessary.

He sat for a moment on the sill at the bottom of the firing aperture and as he did so, there was an explosion immediately outside and he felt something strike his wrist. Fearing that he had lost his hand, he was relieved to see that it was only a small gash from a shell splinter. He proceeded to deal with the gun:

We all carried sticks of plastic explosive, detonators and fuse wire and I instructed a sergeant to make up a suitable charge which was placed in the breech of the gun.

Private Bill Picton:

> *I went in with 'A' Company under Major Parry, and a chap named Vic Simpson and myself were given the job of spiking the German gun which we did with Gammon bombs.*

Fred Milward:

> *We set up the explosive and then we were ordered outside and I curled up beside a wall. There was an enormous bang and smoke came curling out of the doorways.*

Major Parry:

> *We re-entered the casemate, now full of acrid smoke, and upon inspecting the gun I was reasonably satisfied that sufficient damage had been inflicted upon it to prevent it playing a part in the seaborne assault, which was due in two and a half hours.*

Having found that the suspected dummy battery's guns were indeed made of rubber, Lieutenant Slade's duplicate Troubridge Party arrived at the main gate. The scene in and around the entrance to the Battery was pretty shocking, with dead and wounded appearing to cover the ground. CSM Stoddart:

> *The lads had gone in and taken the Battery and the first thing I saw near the entrance was a number of wounded lying around the top of a bomb crater. I gave them a drink of whisky... . Seeing a few German prisoners and the wounded made me realize I was in the war.*

There were only a few medics on either side to help the wounded. Corporal Tottle was one of them:

> *My God, what a terrible sight. I thought I could stand anything like dead men, arms and legs blown off, men crying for their mums. I couldn't. It made me feel sick and I am sure I was. I then helped and did what I could with the aid of the other medics.*

Sid Capon:

> *We took the wounded out on sledges. I didn't know what these sledges were but was later told that they were ammunition sledges. I teamed up with Paddy Jenkins, 'Johnnie'Walker teamed up with Frank Delsignore, and we carried the wounded out.*

Major Bestley, known because of his youth as 'the Boy Major', was lying in one of the bomb craters. Sergeant Daniels:

> *Major Bestley was badly wounded in the legs. We put him in a builder's barrow. Major Bestley said, 'Leave me, I'm no good to the Battalion,'and threatened to court-martial us because we were disobeying orders by taking him out instead of leaving him.*

They picked him up and left him just outside the perimeter wire. Harold Watts, the Doctor, was treating the wounded in a bomb crater between Nos. 1 and 2 casemates.

Amongst all of this, the war artist, Albert Richards was running around, making sketches.

Major Parry decided to check the action carried out on the other guns:

> *I visited No. 3 gun after the party responsible for its destruction had withdrawn. Lieutenant Halliburton went to inspect No. 4 gun and reported to me that he considered it had been successfully neutralized. Whilst marshalling the prisoners prior to withdrawing, Lieutenant Slade came along and informed me that the position was due to be shelled in a very few minutes by* Arethusa. *I ordered Lieutenant Halliburton to lead numbers one and two parties back to the Battalion. At this stage I was feeling weak from a considerable loss of blood.* [20, 21]

In an attempt to give a success signal, Major Parry gave orders to begin lighting yellow smoke candles. These were to be let off at intervals of not more than five minutes, from thirty minutes after dawn, and would hopefully be seen by spotter aircraft that were due to arrive around that time. Although it would not stop the *Arethusa's* guns in time, there was also a more basic method of sending a success signal. Ernie Rooke-Matthews:

Lieutenant Jimmy Loring.

My Platoon Commander Signals Officer, Lieutenant Jimmy Loring, had carried a pigeon inside his battledress blouse. This bird had survived the flight, the drop and the mayhem and was still able to do its job. Jimmy withdrew the bird and despatched it on its way. Some 'wag' suggested that the bird was heading in the wrong direction![22]

Corporal Tottle continued moving around, busily attending to the wounded:

I glanced at the huge guns in the Battery itself and saw the lads marching out the German prisoners who had, after some hand-to-hand fighting, surrendered. At that moment I heard cries from within the minefield. It was Captain Hudson, the adjutant. Scared stiff, I ran through the minefield and did what I could for him.

Captain Hudson:

A soldier, I don't know who, stopped beside me and said, 'Are you all right, Sir?' I said I thought I was, but something had hit me on my right side. He bent down and looked. I can still hear his involuntary intake of breath.

At this point Terence Otway came running down the pathway through the mines. He stopped beside me and said, 'Are you all right?' 'I think so,' I said. 'He's been hit in the stomach,' said the soldier. 'Oh bad luck,' said the CO. 'We've got the Battery, Hal.' I take it as eternal credit that I did not say what he could do with the Battery.[23] From that time on, a dream quality invaded what remained of my life behind the German lines.

Because of the disastrous drop there was only one stretcher in the Battalion. They provided it for me, but I felt that it was wrong that this should be done, because by now I realized that I was very badly wounded indeed.

Whereas I did not mind dying from my wounds, I really disliked the idea of being blasted to pieces by British warships. So I asked them if they would move me to the orchard and leave me there.

A few wounded had been dragged or taken refuge in No. 4 casemate. Alan Mower:

I managed to crawl back inside and laid on a board, and Paddy Jenkins came in and I felt that bad that I actually asked him to finish me off. Then Sid Capon came in... . I got up and found I could walk a few steps and he sort of carried me out. They sat Hawkins up in there and he kept shouting, 'Don't leave us, don't leave us.'

Hawkins was too badly wounded to be moved.

Sid Capon helped Alan Mower across the Battery:

Then a couple of chaps came up with this bit of a door... . They carried me a little way on that and then once we got outside the wire some boys came along with this handcart. There was already another boy on there and they laid me on there and got me outside the Battery as far as we could go, and they left me then with Major Bestley.

Alan Mower

CSM Harries:

> *Glancing back, the Battery area was strangely silent, with men moving slowly out, some wounded and others quite still on the ground where they had fallen. The remaining German prisoners were being herded together and taken out of the Battery.*

Colonel Otway:

> *There were twenty-three German prisoners. I ordered them to show us the paths through the minefields. They refused so we fired into the ground behind them. Then they moved.*

Close by, Corporal Tottle was unable to move Hal Hudson on his own:

> *I looked up and the prisoners were being marched along the mine-free lane. I called out for some help and the Corporal in charge ordered the Germans over to help me. They refused to walk through the minefield. This was very soon sorted out by a few bursts of fire at their heels. With their help I managed to get Captain Hudson and a lot more of the lads out of the Battery area. There was a large shell hole on the edge of the Battery grounds and I managed to get all the wounded into this hole, at least I hope I found everyone.*

Unfortunately his task was impossible.

Colonel Otway went around checking the state of the guns himself:

> *It was a shambles, it was a mess. Then Dante's Inferno was let loose. The Germans began to shell and mortar us from neighbouring positions with complete disregard of their own troops. I personally took shelter in the first casement I could, and one had to move very carefully from casement to casement.*

The shelling, from another battery further along the coast, made it impossible to evacuate all of the more seriously wounded. Lance Corporal Stan Eckert of 'B' Company and Les Cartwright were among those who had to be left to be cared for by the Germans.[24] As tough a decision as it was, there was no choice.

Sapper Alex Taylor had got as far as the perimeter:

> *Shelling commenced, heavy and accurate. Our time had run out, our only chance of survival was to leave the Battery and get to the rendezvous area to the south. The time was 0500 hours. Troopers were leaving*

Stan Eckert (right) and George White. Both killed on D-Day.

the Battery so we joined up with a small party who were escorting about fourteen prisoners.

They started to make for the Calvary Cross, the planned rendezvous on the road to Breville. Sergeant Daniels:

> It was just a shambles virtually, coming out of the Battery and making your way back. Like people coming out of a football match. We didn't march out, we came out in a bedraggled line. Didn't exactly form up as such, the thing was we were so close to the knuckle that we'd got to get out as quickly as possible. There was one or two people going 'Come on, get on, get out quick'. We got out, and all followed along.... You met one, 'Is that you Joe?', 'Is that you Fred?' That sort of thing as you went along.

Fred Glover did his best to keep up as the remnants passed by but could not maintain the pace and had to sit down again:

> I set about examining and dressing my wounds. There were no bones broken and some of the splinters had passed right through, but the piece in my thigh was another matter.

Major Smith:

> I was sent to contact the Brigadier and a company of Canadian Parachutists who should have been guarding our left flank, about 500 yards away. With my batman I made my way to the position and was eventually challenged by a Canadian voice. I gave the password and introduced myself. There were five in all.... These Canadians had had several scraps and not seen the rest of their Company.

Stragglers continued to slowly leave the Battery. Major Parry:

> There were quite a few soldiers still in there and, as best I could, I shouted to them to make their way out. I felt weary and was not as mobile as I would have wished. Slowly, and with some difficulty, I made my way to the point of exit [a cottage to the north-east which was believed to be used as a guardhouse], where I saw what can only be described as an urchin's soap box on wheels. This seemed to me a godsend and I decided to mount it and begin my withdrawal. By lying on my back on the trolley, and propelling myself with the heel of my right foot, I was able to make very slow progress. It was, however, exhausting, and I considered my chances of reaching the rallying point remote. As I was reflecting upon my chances a sergeant of my Company came into view [Taylor], took off his toggle rope, attached it to my chariot and proceeded to drag me along the dusty track to the rallying point. During this journey, while shells were still landing nearby, I drank several mouthfuls of whisky from the flask which, attached to my belt, I regarded as an important part of my battle accoutrements.[14]

Private George Bosher saw Alan Jefferson struggling along:

> I tried to give a piggy-back ride to Lieutenant Jefferson, but he proved to be quite a burden and I had to leave him alongside a hedge.

In fact, Jefferson ordered him to put him down.

Corporal Tottle was still with the wounded on the edge of the Battery:

> What was left of the 9th, including my other medical friends were now marching off to their next objective. I had no hope of shifting the wounded. I had no transport whatsoever, but looking towards a farmhouse about 300 yards away I saw a large horse's cart (no horse though). So with the help of the prisoners we got the cart and loaded the lads who could not possibly walk on the cart. I keep saying German prisoners, but they could have walked away whenever they wanted to. I think what made them stay was that there were about five wounded German soldiers also in my cart.... Whilst loading the cart, four more Germans came to help us, where they came from I do not know.
>
> The lads in the hospital cart were very brave. I think that them knowing me, they had great faith in me and I kept them all well supplied with fags.
>
> We managed to pull the cart about three quarters of a mile, not meeting a soul, but there was lots of gunfire very close to us.

Men began to arrive at the Calvary. Ken Walker:

Here for the first time, I realized some of the horrors of war, never having been in battle before. I was absolutely exhausted and feeling depressed as if suffering from the after effects of an attack of influenza. Most of the soldiers appeared to be in the same state, which could also be described as total bewilderment.

Ernie Rooke-Matthews:

We were still standing around, some dazed by the events of the recent hours; little snatches of information passing around, 'The Major got hit in the legs...', 'Fred hit a mine...', 'I saw Joe go in...'

We were not at this stage very well organized; it was still dark although there were first signs of dawn appearing.

Sapper Alex Taylor:

Lieutenant Colonel Otway was already there with a small party just sitting around. I thought this strange at the time, they should have been in a defensive position. The prisoners were put in a bomb crater. I think they expected to be shot. I felt depressed about the guns.

I spoke briefly to Lieutenant Colonel Otway about the glider crash but he didn't respond. The time was about 0530 hours.

Ken Walker.

During the battle Lieutenant Pond's glider party had continued the action against the Germans in the lane. When the firing died down, a stand-off ensued during which each side had hurled insults at the other, but after a period of quiet, he realized that the Germans had actually gone. Shortly after, CSM Miller appeared in the minefield behind them yelling and waving to gain their attention. They began shouting at him to go back but Miller knew that it was a dummy minefield as he had seen two Germans walking through it earlier. Otway had sent him with the message for them to move to the Calvary.

Major Smith arrived at the Cross with the five Canadians and witnessed Major Parry's arrival:

We were no sooner settled than a figure appeared coming down the road from the Battery pushing a wheelbarrow containing one of the Company Commanders who had been shot through the leg. He took a brandy flask from his pocket, gulped a mouthful and beamed, 'A jolly good battle, what?' The grim faces of the men burst into smiles, and the sullen group of prisoners looked on in bewildered amazement. He

Lieutenant Hugh Pond.

'I saw the Colonel sitting on the Calvary
with his head in his hands.'

insisted on being allowed to stay with the Battalion, but the Commanding Officer ordered him to go to the Regimental Aid Post and he did so reluctantly.

All the wounded continued for 200 yards down the road to the farm that had been earmarked for the RAP. This was a stud farm called the Haras de Retz. Among twenty-two that had to be left were Majors Parry and Bestley, Captain Hudson, Lieutenant Jefferson, CSM Harrold, who had been wounded in both arms, Tom Stroud, Alan Mower, Walter Johnson and Tony Mead, who had actually carried a drum of cable to the RV! Three prisoners, a doctor and two big medical orderlies, 'whose uniforms hung on them like sacks', stayed behind to help Tom Stroud:

> *There we all helped each other as best we could. I was surprised when a German medical orderly took off my boots and produced a dry pair of socks which he put on for me. All my clothing was still wet from my ducking in the floods. All morphia had been used up on the more badly wounded. I shall never forget the agony of the Battalion Adjutant* [Captain Hudson], *but all were extremely brave. No one complained.*

Major Parry:

> *I lay on the floor next to Hal Hudson who had serious intestinal wounds. He was barely conscious and deadly white. Watts came in and dressed my leg, assisted I believe, by Private Comley. The MO had to leave hurriedly to rejoin the Battalion, but left us in the charge of two German medical orderlies who were awfully good, and couldn't do too much for us.*[25]

At the Calvary, Sergeant Daniels was taking stock:

> *Wandered up and down finding out what's what and who's there, and trying to organize bits and pieces, and that's when I saw the Colonel sitting on the Calvary, with his head in his hands. He had been through a tremendous amount. To take what few men he had in to attack that Battery, was beyond human expectancy. What he'd put up with. Organizing the job and then to do it with so few tools, and knowing full well we had a full day in front of us.*

CHAPTER SIX

Onward

All through the early hours the men of the 6th Airborne Division had been carrying out their tasks, attempting to reach their RVs, or purely trying to survive.

The 9th Battalion group led by 'C' Company's Major Dyer had waded around the flooded fields for several hours before finally coming to a road. As they began to cross it, about thirty Germans on bicycles came scooting out of the darkness, their rifles slung across their backs. One of them shouted at Lieutenant Lepper who responded with something unrecognizable in his Scottish brogue, but the cyclists just carried on into the night. After another encounter, this time with an anti-aircraft gun site, the Major decided to change tack and head south in an attempt to find the planned location for the Brigade Headquarters, just south of the Le Mesnil crossroads. To avoid detection they took to the ditches along the sides of the roads, but these were full of water, sometimes up to three feet deep, and progress was slow. This movement was incident free until two soldiers were spotted darting into

Major Ian Dyer.

a hedge about 200 yards away. Dyer sent Jock Lepper and Corporal Gus Gower to investigate but this resulted in the figures running off. Half a minute later they were seen again. Gower gave the password but there was no response and just as they began to run away again, Lepper shouted, 'Don't you know the password, you bloody fools?' The two men immediately stopped and came back. They turned out to be Paras of senior rank, one being the Division's GSO 1 (Operations), Lieutenant-Colonel Bobby Bray, General Gale's principal staff officer. Bray's glider had landed on DZ 'V' instead of DZ 'N' and was therefore on his way to Divisional Headquarters at Ranville. He had his leg pulled for not knowing the password, but in turn, he knew their location, which was close to the Varaville-Le Mesnil road. They headed directly for Brigade HQ.

On finally approaching the Le Mesnil crossroads the chimney of a brickworks could be seen. This was directly opposite the site for Brigade HQ, but, before proceeding, they had to pass a house on the right-hand side of the road. Privates Tucker and Berry were detailed to go forward and investigate. Backed by 'The highest ranked covering party ever', they climbed over a high wall that surrounded it and entered the building. Ron Tucker:

> *The house was in perfect order. The table was set for a meal, cutlery on the table and there was a vase with some flowers in it on the table, but there was nobody in the house at all. Went upstairs to a bedroom and saw some perfume. We had come out of the ditches covered in foul-smelling mud, so I gave myself a few squirts!*

The rest of the party then joined them in the house.

*

Brigadier Hill's group had taken nearly five hours to wade its way out of the flooded area and reach Varaville. The village had only been 2000 yards away. Brigadier Hill:

> *I suppose about a quarter past six or something like that, we struck dry land, and it was the edge of our Dropping Zone, where we should have been. I was able to contact the Company of the Canadian*

Battalion whose task it was to ensure the safety of the DZ, and who stated that they had captured the local German HQ there, but had not yet been able to winkle the enemy out of certain pillboxes on the perimeter.

The Canadians were positioned in and around a large gatehouse that acted as the entrance to the Varaville Château. The Château itself was quite a distance from the entrance, and so a few 224 Field Ambulance personnel had set up an Advanced Dressing Station in a small cottage near the building.

Brigadier Hill:

Then I thought what should I do now? I should be with my Brigade Headquarters on the ridge at four o'clock, and here it was at half past six and I was miles away, so I thought I'd go and see what had happened to the 9th Battalion. So I got hold of a party of very wet stragglers and we went on up towards where the 9th Battalion was, to find out if they'd been successful. My group was led by myself, my Defence Platoon Commander [Johnnie Jones] and one or two others, and we proceeded down a narrow path with water each side.

Forty-two men were strung out in a single file that covered a considerable distance of the track.

Among the Canadians had been a contingent of 9th Battalion men; Lieutenant George Peters and a few of the mortar platoon, Lieutenant Douglas Catlin and several of 'A' Company including Jack Corteil with Glenn, and they had joined the Brigadier's party. The column also included two naval ratings who were the Forward Observers Bombardment (FOsB) to direct the fire of HMS *Arethusa*, plus Staff-Sergeant Crisp, Lance Corporal Howard and Privates Ginn, Wright, Hutton, Sargent, Cracknell (who was acting interpreter for Brigadier Hill) and Driver Park, all of 3 Section of the Field Ambulance.[1]

Shortly after leaving, they witnessed the opening of the barrage on the landing beaches. Brigadier Hill:

It was about twenty to seven when it started and I'd never seen such a barrage, which was coming from the sea to the land. It did look like the most glorious and superb firework display, which is once seen never forgotten.

*

At the Calvary Cross the survivors had slowly begun to recover from the shock of the Battery assault, and the few remaining officers and NCOs went around, gradually restoring some semblance of organization. A defensive position based on a group of craters was established.

A heavy price had been paid to reach the casemates. Sergeant Knight had carried out a head count and found only seventy-five men still on their feet. Therefore, accounting for the wounded, around fifty Paras had lost their lives. Eighteen-year-old Maurice Parris, who had so much wanted to see action, was among them.

Colonel Otway pondered on what to do next. The lack of men made it impossible to carry out all of the Battalion's allotted tasks, even though the arrival of Hugh Pond's party had raised the overall strength to around a hundred men. Otway decided to concentrate on the next objective, the capture of Le Plein at the northern end of the Breville ridge, two miles to the south-west. Major Smith:

I was supposed to take a strong fighting patrol to this place, but owing to the reduced numbers the patrol was cancelled and a surprise assault planned. Instead I was sent with Miller and Sergeant Knight to see what was happening in the direction of the coast.

The remainder of the men moved off in sections along each side of a track leading west from the Calvary. The prisoners, in the

Maurice Parris.

charge of Dusty Miller, were escorted in the middle of the column.[2]

Major Smith set off on his patrol with instructions to meet the Battalion at Le Plein:

> *We had not gone half a mile when shots began to whistle by us. They were being fired from some distance and were not accurate but uncomfortable, and we went forward in short sharp bounds from cover to cover. At the end of one of these bounds we tumbled into a bomb crater on top of seven men. Fortunately they were ours, but from different units. They had been dropped astray and were lost. They had made their way in what they thought was the probable direction when the snipers had taken pot shots at them. When we arrived they had taken shelter in the crater and were working out a plan of action. I put them in the picture and directed them to join our unit. We put down a small smoke screen for them with phosphorus grenades and they darted away like a herd of young deer. We had seen a covered line of advance nearby and went in the opposite direction. We covered another 500 yards and being now on high ground we started to observe through binoculars. We took a short move to improve our position when again bullets came whistling between us. This time the fire was uncomfortably close and we dived into a ditch. At the slightest movement a bullet came 'zissing' over. There was only one thing to do, snipe the snipers. The first thing was to locate them, and this we could not do without them firing. Accordingly we took it in turns to expose ourselves for a fraction of a second, whilst the others peered through tangled weeds as the resulting bullets came over.*
>
> *The snipers were in an orchard, and try as we could we were unable to spot them. We were endeavouring to work out a flanking move when we heard the sound of masses of bombers flying at great height. I looked up and could see hundreds of American Flying Fortresses flying in massed formation. The unhappy thought occurred to me that we were the wrong side of the Bomb Line.*

This was supposed to be the limit of aircraft bombing and therefore a demarcation line for troops to avoid crossing.

> *It was too late to do anything about it, the bombs began to fall. All the bombs seemed to come down within a few seconds. The solid earth became like a jelly, violently shaking. There seemed no interval between the crashes of the bombs they fell so fast, and the earth was not given a chance to settle down for a fraction of a second. This was the famous American Pattern Bombing.*

It was around 6.45 am and all kinds of Allied aerial activity was in progress. Brigadier Hill's group had reached a point about halfway between Varaville and Gonneville: [3]

> *We heard this horrid noise, and I was experienced enough and had heard that sort of thing before. It was low-flying aircraft carrying out anti-personnel pattern bombing. So I shouted to everybody to get down. We all threw ourselves down and I threw myself down on Lieutenant Peters who was the Mortar Officer of the 9th Battalion.*

Unfortunately, the track had high hedges but none of the usual deep ditches. Captain Robinson, near

the rear of the column, fell flat on his face, protecting his eyes. The bombs fell right across the column in rapid succession. When the shattering noise finally subsided, Robinson got to his feet to find that he was concussed, could hardly hear and had lost the heel of his right boot, but was otherwise unhurt. The air was full of dust and the foul stench of high explosive. The lane was strewn with dead and wounded, others were buried or had vanished completely. Captain Robinson:

> *I went the whole length of the column. I found only six men and myself alive.*

Lieutenant Catlin, 'Jack' Corteil and Glenn were among the dead. Corteil was still holding the dog by its lead.[4] Of the

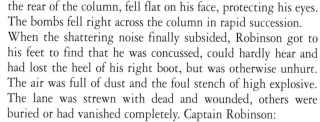

Lieutenant Douglas Catlin.

medics, Hutton was mortally wounded, and both Cracknell and Sargent had disappeared.

Finding no trace and therefore believing that the Brigadier was dead, they set off back to the dressing station at the Varaville Château. Brigadier Hill:

> *While the fumes were dying away the first thought that crossed my mind was that this is the smell of death. I looked round and saw a leg beside me. I thought 'My God, that's my leg.' I knew I'd been hit. Then I had another look at it and it had a brown boot on it, and the only chap in the Brigade who was wearing a brown boot, strictly against my orders, was Lieutenant Peters. He'd got his boots I think in North Africa from the Americans. I had been saved because I had a towel and a spare pair of pants in the bottom of my jumping smock, but my water bottle had shattered and I had lost most of my left backside.*

> *After stumbling to my feet, I found one other man who was able to stand, namely my Defence Platoon Commander, and the lane was littered for many yards with the bodies of groaning and badly injured men. We looked around, saw nothing of Captain Robinson or anyone at the end, and presumed they may have been bombed as well.*

> *What did you do next? As a commander you either had two choices. You could sit and patch up your chaps, or you can go on and do your job. So I had to go on and do my job. We took the morphia off the dead and gave it to those still living and injected them with their own morphia, and I*

Emile 'Jack' Corteil and Glenn.

> *suppose there was about a dozen people we did that to. That took us about half an hour. The thing I shall remember all my life is the cheer they gave us as we set off.*

Hill and Johnnie Jones continued west to find the 9th Battalion.

Major Smith, CSM Miller and Sergeant Knight had also survived their bombing. Major Smith:

> *As suddenly as it started, it ceased. We clung to the bottom of our ditch in case a few late bombs should arrive, but they did not. All was quiet except for the noise of the engines high above. Cautiously we poked our heads over the top of the ditch. It was impossible to see for more than a few yards because of the dust and smoke. The snipers were no longer active.*

> *I decided to rejoin the Battalion and we made a quick journey to our starting point. All the earth seemed dead. There was not a sign of friend or enemy, even the bird and animal worlds had taken to their hiding places.*

Lieutenant George Peters.

The temporary graves of those killed in the bombing of Brigadier Hill's group.

As the bombers had approached, those en route to Le Plein had set up yellow smoke recognition candles in the fields and fluorescent celanese triangles of material which they wore around their necks, but the planes had been too high to see them. The men jumped into the roadside ditches. Private Percy Hull, 'C' Company:

I had experienced the London Blitz. I had never been so frightened in all my life, and two or three of us virtually fought to get under a little wooden bridge for safety!

When they staggered to their feet they saw just how lucky they had been. Two sticks of bombs had landed closer than fifty yards on either side of them.

Continuing down the track they turned south-west into a field. Frank Delsignore:

As we moved forward we saw a field where many of the bombs had fallen. I do not know who it was, but a Cockney voice was heard to say, 'Blimey, we're not just liberating France, we're ploughing the f...... fields for them as well!'

*

Percy Hull.

102

Those members of the Battalion scattered far and wide had been having their own struggles in attempting to reach the Divisional area.

Having slept in the cow byre, Sergeant Garrett and David Backhurst had been wakened by the bombing. Fred Garrett:

> I went outside and the first thing that shot across the sky was a Spitfire, and I thought 'Bloody hell, I'm in France', and it really came over to me what had happened. Looking at my maps I found that they were totally useless as they had been folded to encompass the area of the RV and everything, and in the water they looked just like a bit of chewed string. But my compass was OK. We could practically see the Fortresses in the sky bombing, so I knew that was the direction I had got to head. So off we went, in and out of the water 'til we got to a hard road. We moved along the hard road and I was eventually heading north. We came to a farm and a young girl came out dressed in the first pair of hot pants I ever saw in my life. She went into the cow barn there, and was cleaning out the cows. So I went across the yard and I asked her, 'Were there any Germans about?' She said, 'No, the nearest village was Varaville.' I knew from the briefing where that was, so I thanked her and off down the road we went towards Varaville.

Corporal Corboy and his two companions who had been dropped very wide, had met a few more of their stick during the night. By the time it was light they were approaching Dozule, six miles east of the DZ. Mick Corboy:

> We couldn't chance taking the road through the village, so we followed the river to by-pass it. At this point our seven-strong team met up with Sergeant Bullock with about the same amount of men who had obviously spent the night as we had. Emboldened by the reinforcement, Sergeant Bullock took over my team and decided we would go through Dozule.
>
> We aroused quite a bit of interest. People were coming out and giving us milk and apples and the odd drop of cider. Sadly this idyllic phase was shattered by an unwary German car coming through the town. Suddenly the air was full of lead and to my surprise the car pulled up and two German soldiers got out and gave themselves up. Due to our incredibly high standard of discipline we stopped firing and as a tribute to our marksmanship neither had a scratch on him, in spite of all the flying glass. Both these soldiers were immaculate, fully armed with stick grenades stuck in their belts. I stuck one of the grenades in my belt.
>
> During the firing an elderly French civilian came out of the house, dashed to a car that was parked, picked up a bundle from the car and dashed back inside. What a lunatic! I investigated and found that the 'bundle' was a child of about four years of age. I tried to apologize but what can you do when you've only rehearsed the one essential French phrase, and it wasn't appropriate! Anyway, to show my admiration for the most heroic man I had met that day, I shook hands and saluted him.
>
> We gave the Germans' weapons to the villagers and carried on up the road with our two 'guests'.[5]
>
> About a quarter of a mile along the road, two cars came along. The first one, full of blue uniformed men, got away. I was glad because I thought they might have been French Police, but the other one 'copped it'. There were three high-ranking officers, and we shot them to ribbons. We collected their identity [papers] and I took a small Walther Automatic .75 from one and a Leica camera.

Mick Corboy.

103

Sergeant Bullock.

I messed about with this car that we'd stopped.... I drove it a few yards and noticed the other seat was full of blood. Well I thought 'Hell, if we can shoot this up they can shoot me up', so I got out and I followed on.

Sergeant Bullock at this point decided that the road had got 'too hot' and started moving off to the left. I didn't agree with this decision because I had seen a road sign saying Troarn. Anyway, I was the last one up the bank when I got my gear hooked on some barbed wire. Just then I heard a car approaching from Troarn. Panic stations! I decided to do a quick study on the stick grenade, which I had only seen pictures of. I unscrewed the base, revealing a double cord with a toggle. Not knowing if it was timed or impact, I pulled the cord and slung it. It vanished over the bank and made a lovely bang. Everyone came running back to see what the fuss was. The car, driven by a French civilian (it could have been a taxi) contained two German soldiers, done up to the nines, with two ladies, maybe their wives! We took the Germans prisoner and let the others go.

Corboy then managed to convince Sergeant Bullock that this was indeed the road to Troarn and so they began moving to the south-west.

*

Shortly after the bombing, Major Dyer's group arrived at the Le Mesnil crossroads. They joined some Canadians in a ditch alongside the road and also began digging in behind a hedge on the north-east side of the junction, about seventy-five yards from the crossroads. Two hundred yards in front was a farm.

It wasn't long before a truck could be heard approaching from Varaville. A bend in the road prevented anyone seeing it, but when it eventually emerged, six German soldiers were sitting in the back. Ron Tucker:

We opened fire when it was fifty yards away. It ran off the road into a ditch, and we crawled along the ditch to make sure they were all dead, and just as we reached them, one pulled a pistol from under his coat. It was an Italian 'Beretta' – he must have served in Italy. I shot him at close range, and when we turned him over he had a hole in his back as big as a fist. The truck, which was one that had been captured at Dunkirk, was recovered, and we sent it down to the brickworks.

*

Corporal Dowling and John Speechley had spent the night in a deserted farm and left in the early hours in case they had been spotted entering it during the night. They walked into Varaville and came across a few Canadians who were engaging a German positioned in the church tower. The two of them joined in the mêlée. John Speechley:

When we fired we were damaging the louvres round the bell-tower, and the pigeons were flying out left, right and centre. In the end he realized we were getting in down below and he was taken prisoner by the Canadians.[6]

Dowling and Speechley themselves took up post in the church tower:

Looking north I saw a German equivalent to a 15cwt truck with its arse facing us, and it was on a sort of a crossroads between the hedgerows and it was setting up a 3-inch mortar, either a 3 or a 6. It was a pretty large arrangement 'cos I saw the baseplate get positioned, then they put the tripod up and out comes the barrel.

He took aim at the truck:

The canvasses were drawn across, folded back either side, and I could see all the ammunition, three in a rack, in, like, fibreboard racks with a handle... . There was a mile of them in that truck. I was firing and I thought I've got to get one of the heads of those, 'cos they've got the charges in... . Do you know, I never got one! I could see the blanco on the canvas clouding off as you got the near misses. Anyway, unknown to us, in the town to our left the Canadians were forming up to move on... and they were saying, 'Who the bloody hell's making that row up there?' Every time we fired, course the soddin' bell was ringing. It was a giveaway. And of course we got a pile of shit coming back at us. Anyway they stopped us firing and we had to go down and form up with the Canadians.

They all then headed for the Le Mesnil crossroads.

Another party heading for the crossroads contained signaller Jimmy French, who had found his friend Bill Hurst and a group from various units including Major Alastair Young of the Field Ambulance. Jimmy French:

Our forward point had just gone round a bend when a car came towards us. You could hear it coming. We all took to the ditches at the side of the road. The Bren gunner in the point opened fire and he fired where the driver sat in an English car. He shattered the windscreen. The car stopped and a woman got out and she was on the other side luckily. She wasn't disturbed considering she'd narrowly missed being shot [The lady was slightly wounded in the wrist]. *She got out and talked to whoever was in charge of us and pointed the way we wanted to go. She was a member of the underground movement.*

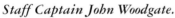

The two Divisional officers en route to Ranville had left Major Dyer's group at the crossroads and moved a hundred yards down the road. Opposite the brickworks they walked through a small wood, along a bumpy, winding drive which opened out into a farm. This was the Fromagèrie du Mesnil, the proposed spot for Brigade HQ. No staff had yet arrived. The Brigade Administration Officer, Staff Captain John Woodgate, was still making his way there from the DZ:

After a time I came to the Château Beneauville – Bavent and found some other chaps and civilians gathered in the grounds.[7] A field security chap was questioning the civilians. One was the Baronne

Staff Captain John Woodgate.

Chadenet. It was becoming light and I met some personnel from 224 Field Ambulance (one being its second in command, Major Alistair Young) as we set off along the road towards Le Mesnil crossroads.

This party also included some Canadian Battalion HQ personnel. Crucially, during the journey they met Captain Tom Gray, one of the two Field Ambulance surgeons.

They arrived at the crossroads at about 8.30 am. A sniper had just killed a Canadian officer and orders were given to disperse in the orchard on the north-east corner and lie down. After a while a Canadian Company Commander came over and Major Young explained their destination. The Canadian replied, 'Okay Doc, but step lively over those goddam crossroads'.[1]

John Woodgate moved down to the fromagèrie to find that he was the first of the Brigade Staff to arrive. The Barberot family, who owned the farm, were still in residence in the main building, the Château du Mesnil, so he decided to set up HQ in a small two-storey outbuilding just beside it.

About an hour later, Captain Tony Wilkinson, formerly the 9th Battalion's Signals Officer and now the Brigade Intelligence officer, arrived and assumed the duties of the Brigade Major.

*

Like most, the Paras of 224 Field Ambulance had suffered in the Brigade's scattered drop. Captain Johnston, who was supposed to have set up the ADS near the Merville Battery, had landed in the flooded area. He had been heading towards Varaville with a group of men when the bombing began, and this persuaded them to head for Le Mesnil instead. On the way he decided to commandeer a horse and cart, so he called at a farm where members of the party had obtained information earlier in the morning, and after a little negotiation they acquired 'Udine', a chestnut mare and a farmcart. The only problem was getting the farmer's wife, a Madame Eve, to name a price, but when reassured that the cost didn't matter as the government would be paying, she produced a chit: 'Pris: une jument, 65,000 frs; une vachere, 25,000 frs; un equipage, 5,000 frs'. M et Mme Arthur Eve, Robehomme, Calvados'. This was around £300. Several people with sore feet and minor sprains leapt into the cart. Everyone cast in their bundles, and the party headed for some high ground, eventually entering the village of Robehomme. They found a force of around a hundred men of the 1st Canadian Parachute Battalion under the command of Captain Peter Griffin occupying a strong position near the village church. Captain Johnston proceeded to set up a dressing station in a school just beside it.[1]

*

Following the crash landing of Captain Gordon-Brown's assault glider, his party had attempted to get to the Merville Battery but ran into opposition. Eventually, they did get close enough to find Fred Glover, who was still nursing his leg wounds. A few men spoke to him but they had to keep on the move. He forced himself to get up:

I followed them as best I could, but by this time my legs were becoming painful to the point where I could walk no further and so myself, together with another Para and two wounded Germans, were left as comfortable as possible while the group moved off. Rather stupidly, somebody got out a pack of playing cards, 'See if you can follow the trail. We've got to get on.' He was dropping bloody playing cards down!

A little later Glover spotted a British medic, who came over and did what he could for all four men:

Then we heard this shouting, and in the field in extended order there was a patrol coming across with an officer in front. He had a pistol in his hand and they were making their way towards these farm buildings. When this chap stood up and waved his yellow triangle, they swung round and came over to us. They wore the insignia of the SS.

There seemed to be a rather hostile atmosphere and I realized that it was the fighting knife fitted at my side which was the cause of the excitement. As one of them reached down to remove it, he noticed the Gammon bomb in my smock pocket and this created further angry remarks. I'd pushed some 9mm ammo into the plastic to aid its fragmentation. The tension eased when the least injured of the two Germans who had been with us apparently pointed out how they had been treated, wounds dressed, food etc., shared and I think most important, that morphine had been provided for his comrade. At this, the whole situation changed and with smiles and handshakes I was placed on a stretcher and transported to what I concluded was a field dressing station. On arrival, my legs were examined and dressed; the stay was very short because shells began to fall in the area and I was again in transit and wondering what the future held in store for me.[8]

Fred Glover.

*

With the early morning mist still rising, the 'main body' of the 9th Battalion had continued to move across country. About a mile from Le Plein they encountered a large field of shoulder-high corn and although a pre-determined route had been planned, time was getting on. So the column was divided into four sections and they headed off through the corn on a direct line for the village. This was going well when a Frenchman approached from a farm on their right. He gave them an enthusiastic welcome and supplied an invaluable warning that the village of Hauger, just north of Le Plein, was occupied by about 200 'Hiwis', Russian prisoners forced into the German Army. Otway therefore decided to give Hauger a wide berth and approach Le Plein from the east. Shortly after, a German machine gun began firing from a Château to the south-east, near the village of Longuemare, and the small Canadian group was ordered to clear it. This they did and rejoined at the rear of the column. Just before 9am they left to try and reach their own battalion at Le Mesnil.

At 9.00 am the 'B' Company point came out onto a road that led west into Le Plein. They advanced down both sides of the road with the prisoners on the left, still being led by CSM Miller. Fred Milward was behind them:

> *Two ladies of ill-repute came down the road. I should imagine they'd been up to the German barracks and were on their way home. They'd got painted legs, short skirts; I'd never seen anything like it in my life. Frightened me more than the Germans! There was a corporal in front with Dusty, a big tall bloke, but he told them to 'Arse off, get out of the way.' The women were laughing!*

The Paras continued warily. George Bosher:

> *We entered the village street and some Germans came round the corner on pushbikes. One was on the crossbar. Everyone just looked, until I remember CSM Dusty Miller's voice, 'Well shoot the bastards then', so someone did!*

Fred Milward:

> *When we got up to them, one had got a bullet through the shoulder and was bleeding like mad. The other one was dead. The one that was wounded was shouting, 'Hier Doktor, hier Doktor.' We thought he was trying to say that they were an orderly and doctor on their rounds but whether*

George Bosher.

107

they were or not I don't know. They hadn't got any crosses on their arms.

The move along the road continued. Just ahead of him, Fred Milward was keeping watch on the prisoners and CSM Miller:

> *There was a gate into one of the fields, and he walked them over towards the gate, and as they got to the gate they started jabbering. They saw a German coming down the other side of the hedge and ran over to the right, leaving me and Dusty standing there alone.*

Without knowing it, Miller and the German were approaching each other. Sergeant Daniels saw:

> *Dusty coming along with his Colt 45 and a Jerry coming the opposite way. A German officer with good fitting riding boots and quite a nice pair of riding breeches on. They stopped, looked at one another. Both fired a shot, turned and run. There were five or six blokes around me and they all had a bit of a giggle about it. Not a very good shot, Dusty!*

Slowly, they advanced again. As they approached a road junction, enemy fire erupted from directly in front. Colonel Otway:

> *I had half-a-dozen men up front leading the way. I was about fifty yards behind them, and when they went in where the houses came, some Jerries opened up with a light machine gun. Regimental Sergeant Major Bill Cunningham came up to me and I said, 'Go up and take charge of that lot and find out what is happening'.*

RSM Cunningham crawled forward towards a thick hedge that hid the German machine-gun position. Otway glanced to his right and saw a man in a blue suit, who greeted him with, 'A very good morning.' Colonel Otway:

> *This Frenchman asked if I'd like a coffee when it was all over! Standing up on the ground and I was in the ditch; bullets flying all around us, smoking his pipe. Not a care in the world.*

As Cunningham got close to the MG position he began shouting at a German there. Colonel Otway:

> *I actually could hear it, with his broad Belfast accent. 'You great big fat so-and-so, stick your f...... hands up or I'll shoot your guts out,' something like that, and the chap bolted. He couldn't understand English, but it was his tone!*

> *Then he found some more Germans. So we closed up and took up positions, the eight of us, on either side of the road, a ditch on the left, houses on the right.*

Johnny Novis, 'B' Company:

> *We came under enemy fire from a hedge which ran parallel to our position, and at a distance of approximately 150 to 200 yards. Their firepower kept us pinned down in a ditch by the roadside, bordered by a hedge. The situation was relieved by the use of a farmhouse approximately fifty yards inland from the road and overlooking the enemy position. The building was two-storied with an attic roof housing a glass window. Three of us made our way to the attic and managed to jemmy open the window through which one of us engaged the enemy with random fire along the hedge. This allowed our force to engage the enemy and resolve the situation.*

Johnny Novis.

Major Smith:

> *The enemy immediately in front then withdrew to other positions near a crossroads, and the leading Company attacked, dislodging them, capturing two machine guns and killing fifteen of the enemy. The buildings on the crossroads were seized.*

Sergeant McGeever, Corporal McGuinness and Private Fenson occupied a house on the left flank and set up the Vickers machine gun. About thirty to forty of the retreating Germans took up position at a road junction on the northern edge of Le Plein. As the Paras moved up they saw a large building surrounded by a high wall and it appeared to be unoccupied. Firing as they ran, Otway and the leading elements crossed a field and manned the wall. Major Smith:

> *I went forward to see what was happening. The CO called to me to cross the road. I did so as a hail of bullets chased me. The position was a strong one, being a large building with strong high stone walls. The enemy held a similar building opposite and a sniping battle commenced. A counter-attack suddenly developed on our left flank, but we saw it coming, held our fire until the enemy were twenty yards away, and then opened up with the Vickers. The attack was broken up and twelve bodies littered the ground.*
>
> *Twice more I had to cross the road to issue instructions for the Commanding Officer. It was rather like being a moving Aunt Sally. One side of the road was a deep ditch which gave cover, and the other side a high stone wall. One had to dash across the road, then along about nine feet of wall with bullets splashing against it, and finally crab-wise through an open door. Miller tried the dash and was unlucky to receive a bullet.*

However, the wound was not bad, the bullet having hit him in the fleshy part of the shoulder.

The village, which was 400 yards away, was actually called Amfreville. Le Plein was a large green in its midst with a church situated at its centre. The enemy could quite clearly be seen near this church, in a small farm on the left and in the area of a large building to the right. Movements in and out of this building confirmed that it was a key point in the enemy's defence.

A 'B' Company patrol of around ten men led by Lieutenant Tom Halliburton was assembled to reconnoitre this building. Colonel Otway:

> *I said to Halliburton, 'Take some chaps and go there and find out* [the enemy's strength]. *Do not get involved in any fighting. Come back here and tell me what the situation is.'*

Privates Joe Millward, Reg Osborne, Bob Abel and Roy Wright were at the front of the patrol. Nearing the building they came under sniper fire. Most of the patrol took to the right, but Wright and Abel went to the left. Bob Abel:

> *We got around the back of the Château {sic} into some sort of outhouse. The Lieutenant decided to make for a six-foot wall which was running round the outside of the Château.*

Reg Osborne:

> *The Germans were in an orchard surrounded by a high wall with two wooden gates, one of which was open and one shut, with a wooden bar across to support it. Our officer decided the only way was to charge them through the open gate.*

Roy Wright:

> *Me and Bob Abel, we went into one of these outhouses, looked through the boarded-up window and we see the machine-gun post and the mortar section. The machine-gun post was on the right and the mortars on the left. Before we could warn Halliburton, he'd gone round, straight in. He charged through there with his pistol, straight into a machine gun.*

Reg Osborne:

> *He went through and they dropped him a few yards inside. I was the next man behind him. I ducked under the bar and got caught on a nail. They opened up on me and I was saved by two Bren gun magazines*

Joe Millward.

Bob Abel.

in my pouches. By this time they were spraying the whole gateway with fire, so I ducked back behind the closed gate. I got splinters in my face as they fired through it. We were unable to reach the officer.

They made several attempts but it was impossible. The enemy's sandbagged position was backed up by men firing from the upstairs windows of the building on the opposite side of the farmyard. Others came into the courtyard itself. Roy Wright:

Me and Bob Abel were firing through the wooden slats and I was up in the aim [position]. The Jerry I was aiming at shot first. Just like in the films, I shot across this outhouse into the hay and I just passed out.

A bullet had gone through his collar, hit him on the left side of the neck and passed out just below his Adam's apple. Believing that his friend was dead, Bob Abel got out of the building:

Private Millward, who was giving us covering fire with the Bren, was hit in the face. With that we quickly doubled back behind the wall. Having considered the situation, the NCO realized that we could never get into the Château grounds without more fire support. We then made our way back to join the Battalion.[9]

The village was obviously heavily defended and so being outnumbered and outgunned, the Colonel had little choice but to try and consolidate in the position. Major Smith:

After a while the Commanding Officer instructed me to make a reconnaissance of the rear of our position, find a safe route and tell the second in command to bring the remainder of the Battalion into the position by it. I went alone and had to detour rather further than I expected. Nearing the end, I jumped through a hole in a wall onto a road. A burst of Bren fire passed me. I walked down the road to the main crossroads, where a sentry apologized for shooting at me, met the second in command and led the remaining companies into their new positions.

110

Château d'Amfreville.

It was about 9.30 am when the Battalion took up position behind the formidable walls of what was the Château d'Amfreville. Sentries were immediately posted to dig in and cover the flanks, and three or four men allocated to watch the road junction on the edge of the village that linked Le Plein with Hauger. Those supporting the Vickers remained in the houses at the north-east end of the village.

The Château buildings were searched and a couple of horses found in the stables, while Private Brailsford found an old Renault car and a motorcycle and sidecar in a garage. Major Smith:

> *The main building in our position was a German Army billet. All the personal belongings of the men were strewn about, even arms and ammunition. The larder was stocked with a magnificent supply of food, sides of beef, a barrel of butter, sacks of sugar, large stone jars of jam, a huge tub of pure cream.*

A large cider press and big vats of cider and Calvados were also discovered in the garden.

The prisoners were held in a tennis court at the rear, which had a strong, high fence surrounding it.

The Paras had no option but to sit tight and await the arrival of the Commandos on the ridge, hopefully later in the day.

The Colonel realized that, logically, the Germans should attack from the rear, but, although the enemy began to retaliate with mortar, sniper and automatic fire, nothing more developed. Due to the standard of some of the sniping it gradually became apparent that only a few were properly trained snipers, but casualties still slowly began to mount. Otway ordered that all spare ammunition was to be collected and given to the marksmen to root out the Germans one by one. Major Smith:

> *A number of shots came into our enclosure over a high wall, and it was obvious that they must come from a church overlooking us. One of the men spotted a loose slat in it which looked rather like a sniper's slit. Every time a shot came from it we sent back one in return and after nine shots from us it became quiet.*

In the outhouse of the enemy's fortified position, Roy Wright regained consciousness:

> *When I came to, I was covered in blood. I couldn't raise my head. I got to a farmhouse building a bit further away and went in there.*

He found a mirror to examine his wound:

> *I lifted my head up and just saw the hole (I didn't see the one in the side). I was breathing through it. It was funny 'cos all the blood was bubbling out. I tried to get a bandage around it, then I passed out. When I came to, there was this dirty great big Russian. He was Red Cross, a medic. Apparently one*

of the villagers had told him there was 'a wounded' laying down in the house. He looked huge, bombs all over him! He had Lieutenant Halliburton's pistol in his belt. He took me round to the enclosure where the machine-gun posts were.

At the entrance he saw Tom Halliburton, still lying where he had fallen:

Halliburton got a burst of machine-gun fire in the stomach. He'd had morphine and that, but they hadn't moved him. I could see he was going to die. He looked at me and smiled, but you could see that he'd had it 'cos he'd gone grey.

The Russian took Wright further into the enclosure:

He put me against a tree. He put a paper bandage, because they had no proper bandages, around my neck... and then I passed out again.

The stand-off at the position went on but the Paras continued to be bothered by snipers and automatic fire, and especially from a machine gun to their left. Lieutenant Slade, who, with Captain Hudson becoming a casualty, had taken over as adjutant, was in the area:

The barn from which we were endeavouring to silence a machine gun was set on fire over our heads by tracer, and efforts had to be turned to getting calves out of the bottom half.

In the end Colonel Otway had to physically haul him out.

With all the bullets flying about, trouble erupted among the prisoners, and when the Colonel went to deal with the situation he was confronted by a German officer who began calling Otway's attention to the Geneva Convention. Colonel Otway:

They were complaining about being left in the open and not protected. I said, 'You'll be killed by your own fire, not ours. If you're talking about the Geneva Convention, how do you explain this note which has Hitler's signature on saying that all members of the British Parachute Regiment were to be shot out of hand?'

There was no reply.

So I said OK, you can stay there or you can be locked up in a room in the Château. When the artillery opens up it is bound to be used as a point of reference. 'Which do you want to do?' They stayed there.

Roy Wright.   **Lieutenant Tom Halliburton.**

In the meantime Dennis Slade had gone out with a couple of men to destroy the troublesome machine gun. They had crawled along a ditch and, using grenades, silenced the enemy post. When he reported back, he handed over a piece of the machine gun as proof, but Otway was far from happy about him risking his neck and his men, and he let him know it![10] Colonel Otway:

> *Dennis was very inclined to go like a bat out of hell at everything. The sort of chap that get's the Victoria Cross. They always say that Victoria Cross people never knew why they got it!*

At around 10 o'clock Brigadier Hill arrived at the 9th Battalion First Aid Post:

> *I happened to bump into the Medical Officer who was a chap called Doc Watts, a splendid chap, older than most of the others. I think he was older than I was and I had a rule in the Brigade that nobody would parachute if they were thirty-two and over. He must have been among the ones who broke the rule. He was the only chap really of any consequence there, but I got the information I needed. The Doctor knew pretty well what was happening.*
>
> *Anyhow, he took a look at me and was unwise enough to say that I looked bad for morale. So I quickly cut him down to size and I told him what a bloody fellow he was, and if he'd had his left backside removed and spent four and a half hours in the cold water, he wouldn't look very good either! So that kept him quiet. He thought he'd better do something about this, so unbeknown to me he gave me an injection which put me out for two hours.*

*

Some three miles to the east the other survivors of the bombing had reached the Canadian First Aid Post at the Varaville Château. Captain Robinson, whose hearing had still not recovered, sat down by a hedge to study an aerial photograph:

> *I was about to return to the bombed area en route to Le Plein where I hoped to rejoin the Battalion, when the muzzle of an MG34 appeared at the point of my nose. The RAP and myself were prisoners.*

About forty Germans surrounded the whole party. These had entered the area while a battle was in progress at the gatehouse:[11]

> *Having disarmed us and having confiscated my Zeiss binoculars, the German patrol escorted us by way of Petiville, Bavant and Bures to Troarn. I became very concerned that this patrol, commanded by an NCO with one blue stripe and a Russian campaign medal, might typify the opposition.*

> *On the way we endeavoured to lengthen the column by those in front putting their best foot forward and those in the rear lagging behind, hoping thereby to give those in the middle an opportunity to bolt for it at a bend in the road. The Bosch were no fools. In fact their discipline, fieldcraft, battle drills and general demeanour were exemplary.*

*

After his escapade with the bullfrogs, Sergeant Britton and the two Canadian medics had been joined by two Commandos, Captain Haig-Thomas and his batman Sam Ryder, plus a Brigade signals officer, Lieutenant Douglas Smith.[12] Haig-Thomas was the liaison officer between the Commandos and the 3rd Parachute Brigade. Totally lost, they met a twenty-three year old Frenchman, Robert Godey. Haig-Thomas spoke French and they learned that they were in Petiville, a thousand yards south of the DZ. Very bravely, Monsieur Godey offered to guide them to the 'rue de l'Arbre

Robert Godey.

113

Martin' at Le Mesnil, from where they could find their way to Ranville. They gratefully accepted and set off in twos, one each side of the road, with the Frenchman and Haig-Thomas leading.

After a while, as they were walking along a sunken lane near Bavent, Godey noticed dark silhouettes a few yards in front of them. They were walking in the same direction and so the figures had not seen them. The Frenchman tapped Haig-Thomas on the shoulder and pointed. Lieutenant Smith:

Haig-Thomas shouted, 'Down!' and there was an enormous explosion followed by bursts of machine-gun fire.

Haig-Thomas was killed instantly and Godey threw himself flat on the ground, feigning death.[13] While the heavy firing continued one of the medics crawled towards them in the pitch darkness. Believing that both men were dead he returned and informed the others. John Britton:

We had to leave our two comrades and push on. Having lost our guide we really had no idea if we were going in the right direction, but at least we were still on the cart track.

They then found two engineers who were anxious to find their objective, 'to blow up a bridge.' After visiting a farm, they spotted a village and headed across a field towards it:

We were just about to get through the hedge onto the road when two German half-tracks entered the village, manned by about twenty men in each. They stopped about six feet from us. By this time we were flat down in the ditch, then the shouting of commands and they started to search all the houses. This went on for about half an hour. We still had not been seen and eventually, satisfied, they moved out of sight. We decided to follow the hedge down as far as possible.

Sergeant Garrett and David Backhurst were in the same area. Fred Garrett:

I bumped into a Sergeant and six men from the 2nd Ox and Bucks. He was their anti-tank platoon Sergeant and he had six men from his platoon with him, their glider had landed wide.[14] He happily joined us and I happily joined him. What was more, he had a Bren Gun, an automatic weapon which made us feel a little more comfortable. Anyway we had a discussion and we didn't quite know which way to go, so I said we would head south. Moving along the road we saw a church on some high ground and we thought 'Right we had better head for there.' Moving along the road to the church, who should be in the hedge but Sergeant Johnny Britton, who was the signal Sergeant of the 9th Battalion, so he joined us and we got into the village I later found out to be Robehomme. I found Captain Griffin of the 1st Canadian Parachute Battalion and some members of 'B' Company of that Battalion, and we joined them. He asked did I have any knowledge of a Vickers Medium Machine Gun and I said, 'Yes I have been trained on the medium machine gun.' They had nobody to work it. He put me in a position out on a piece of high ground that overlooked the Varaville road and, together with Johnny Britton, went there, covered ourselves up with a parachute and made ourselves comfortable.

*

Upon regaining consciousness Brigadier Hill found that he was unable to walk. It was imperative that he reached Divisional HQ and so Captain Greenway improvised a means of transport. Brigadier Hill:

Fortunately they found me a ladies' bicycle and I got a parachute pusher who pushed me down into Ranville, a distance of about two and a half miles, where I met General Gale and exchanged details. He told me the good news that my Brigade had taken all their objectives, so I thought that was heartening and I felt much younger![15]

The Brigadier then became the focus of attention of another medical officer, Colonel MacEwan:

I was seized by the ADMS who was the Head Doctor, and he was an old boy of the Division, who'd been in the First World War and was covered in decorations. He said to me, 'I'm going to take you off to the Main Dressing Station.' I said, 'You certainly aren't,' and he said, 'Well, you've got to have an op.' So I said, 'I'll have an op on one condition. As soon as its over, you'll promise to take me back yourself to my Brigade Headquarters.' So we struck a deal... . It was about one o'clock and I was being anaesthetized, chloroform, or whatever it was... and I heard a tremendous concentration come down on Ranville, and that was in fact the counter-attack by 21st Panzer Division. So I rather wondered if, when I came to after my operation, who would be in charge of the hospital!

After an hour or so I came to, and I looked round. They were still all our own medics.

An hour or so later Colonel MacEwan kept his promise and started off on a jeep for the 3rd Brigade HQ. Brigadier Hill, standing up, had a large bottle of penicillin strapped to his leg.

At Brigade HQ itself, personnel had slowly begun to arrive. Staff Captain John Woodgate:

Once we'd established ourselves in the early afternoon, people kept turning up. It must have been early afternoon when the Defence Platoon Commander Johnnie Jones turned up, and I told him to organize some all-round defences. Some of his platoon had also turned up.

In the Brigadier's absence Colonel Alastair Pearson, the CO of the 8th Parachute Battalion, was making the decisions. His battalion held the eastern end of the ridge, in the Bavent Wood.

The intended site for the Brigade's Main Dressing Station (MDS) had been a priory, a mile southeast of Bavent, but the enemy's continued presence in that area made it unfeasible. Consequently, in the absence of Colonel Thompson, the CO of the Field Ambulance, Major Young, had asked Colonel Pearson for permission to set up the MDS at the fromagèrie. He agreed, and an old house and a large barn opposite the Brigade buildings were immediately put into use. Unfortunately Captain Gray was only able to perform minor surgery due to the lack of an anaesthetist. It was the first instance of an MDS being set up so close to the front line.[16]

*

By late morning the Château d'Amfreville position had still not been attacked, although there had been heavy exchanges of fire. However, the overall situation had deteriorated because of the growing lack of ammunition. Patrols scoured the fields in search of stray containers but only two were found and these contained mostly mortar bombs. In a short space of time the situation would become critical. Colonel Otway:

At that time I was very, very down. I was almost on the point of deciding 'Do I go on or do I surrender and pack up?' That's when Paul Greenway who, although he was only a Captain, was a great friend of mine, said, 'Don't be so bloody silly. We've just got to go on.' So I came to my senses, took a brace of myself.

They conserved what ammunition they had and held on. Things quietened down.

Still sporting his 'ventilated trousers', Lieutenant Slade took time to explore the Château:

Château D'Amfreville produced a sewing machine to repair the trousers. Thank God for mother's training, although I almost convinced myself that there would be a counter-attack and that I should be captured with the indignity of my trousers down!

*

Shortly after 2.00 pm gunfire suddenly erupted from Le Plein. It was not being directed towards the Paras, but to the west. It could only be the Commandos. Colonel Otway made his way down the hill to find them. Reaching the Ecarde crossroads at the bottom of the slope, he met Lord Lovat. Then the leading party of No. 3 Commando, the bicycle-mounted 3 Troop under the command of Captain Roy Westley

Lieutenant Dennis Slade.

The scene on the road outside the entrance (centre-right) to the Château d'Amfreville.
(IWM-FLM/3457)

arrived. Lovat stopped him and the second in command, Lieutenant Keith Ponsford:

> *Otway explained his position. He was trying to do the impossible task of capturing the village with a handful of men. Lovat told us to attack Amfreville and asked Otway to conduct Roy and me on a recce of the area that he and his men were now holding close to the Château d'Amfreville. This we did and Otway agreed to give us covering fire from this position when we attacked.*

The two Commandos returned to the bottom of the hill.

At around 3.30 pm, the Paras saw the Commando Troop come up the road to attack the village. Firing broke out for a short time behind the houses at the top of the road and then stopped. After a while the firing restarted and the sound of it gradually began to move east. It appeared that the Commandos had pushed the enemy out of the village.[17] Colonel Otway decided to find out what had happened for himself:

> *I said to Wilson, 'We're going down there.' Everybody said, 'You're mad, you'll get killed, but I said, 'It's a risk I've got to take', I hadn't got any alternative. Wilson had got hold of a motorbike, so Wilson drove the motorbike, I sat in the sidecar, and we went down there.*

They crossed the green in front of the Château and passed a number of dead Commandos, including a Troop Sergeant Major in the area of the entrance. They then drove down the hill and on reaching the crossroads, heavy mortar fire began to fall so they took cover in a ditch. This barrage began just as Lord Lovat had brought up elements of No. 6 Commando. Colonel Otway yelled out:

The Amfreville/Le Plein area. The Château lies in the centre (circled) with the village to the right. Le Plein can be seen in the centre of the village. Bottom left is the Ecarde crossroads.

One of your Commando units has just had a sticky time. If you wish to talk to me, come down here because I'm not bloody well coming up there!

Lovat joined them in the ditch and was informed of the situation. Although its defence was still precarious, Le Plein had been taken. With No. 6 Commando taking up position at the southern end of the village, Lovat stated that to support the 9th Battalion, No. 4 Commando would occupy Hauger during the night.

The Commando attack had meant liberation for Roy Wright, who had awoken during the noise of the attack:

I came round and I see a '36 come over the wall, land, roll towards me and just for a split second I thought 'I've had it.' I just got around this side of the tree and I got the blast and out I went again. I was deafened. The Commandos came in and mopped them up. Got me out, took me to the medical section, pulled the bandage down. 'Oh, there's nothing I can do for you.' Cheered me up no end!

He was then transported back to the beach.[18]

*

During the late afternoon CSM Harries was given a special task:

I was ordered to take a small patrol back to the Battery to see if it was still out of action or had been reoccupied, although I couldn't imagine of what use it would be to the Germans. I collected four men, plus Sergeant 'Busty' Taylor, and we headed back across country to the Battery, and en route came across small units of Germans moving in other directions, usually at high speed. These we avoided as our task was to obtain information and not engage in a small skirmish. In any case our number was too small. We eventually moved through a wood approaching some rising ground towards the Battery, but upon reaching the edge of the wood, we were fired upon. Luckily, we were able to locate the fire and it transpired that we were being fired upon by Commando troops... . By waving our red berets we were able to convince them we were on the same side and after a shouting match, followed by closer contact, we were able to learn that at that stage the Battery was still out of action. In fact it could be seen quite well from the slightly higher ground occupied by the Commandos.[19]

Sergeant 'Busty' Taylor.

Mission accomplished, they returned to the Château d'Amfreville.

*

Brigadier Hill had continued his journey to Brigade HQ with the ADMS and his batman. They were heading along the road leading east from Ranville. Brigadier Hill:

Just ahead of us, a number of Germans ran across the road and to my annoyance and consternation the ADMS and his batman left me in his jeep and pursued the Germans into the wood in an endeavour to make a capture. This effort was unsuccessful and at four o'clock that afternoon I reached my destination, some eight hours behind schedule.

He was taken to the HQ building and led up an outside staircase to a small room where the medics took another look at him. John Woodgate thought that he would surely have to be evacuated. James Hill was adamant that he was going nowhere!

Another vital arrival at the fromagèrie was Captain Chaundy and his party of the Field Ambulance. He was one of the anaesthetists and so from this point on the MDS could truly start to function.[1]

Further along the road, at the crossroads Jimmy French had joined Major Dyer's group:

Each man carried a Hawkins grenade which was like a talcum powder container with a metal bracket, beneath which was placed a detonator, or two to be certain. These grenades could be linked together to form what was known as a 'necklace'. To cover the road on our left, a 'necklace' was placed across it.

There had been no major enemy attack, but a series of 'minor' incidents, and this 'necklace' proved vital in one of them. Jimmy French:

A German 3-ton truck, open-backed, came roaring down the road. The German driver must have been an experienced soldier because he realized what they were and slammed the brakes on. All the men jumped out and into the roadside ditches on either side, except one. He ran directly across the field about forty yards in front of our hedge. We all began to take pot-shots at him, like at a fairground. About halfway across he went down, and we thought we had him. He was rolling around on the ground, but as it turned out he was just getting rid of his equipment! And then he got up and carried on running in the same direction. Again we started firing at him, but as he approached the wood on our right we ended up cheering him! He made it to the wood. He had a charmed life.

*

It took the Germans most of the day to lead Captain Robinson and his fellow prisoners to Troarn. Each time Allied aircraft had appeared overhead, the whole party had taken cover in woods and ditches, but by 4.00 pm they had passed through the village itself. 'Robbie' Robinson:

Captain 'Robbin' Robinson.

About a mile south of Troarn, on the Janville road, they took up a defensive position on some high ground, this being the point where transport was due to meet them. The Germans, even more whacked than we, relaxed for the first time. I took a running jump at a hedge. Fortunately, having burst through the hedge, there was a recessed lane which I followed, going 'like a lamp-lighter' (one of James Hill's expressions), until I found a temporary hiding place in a pond. I was saturated to the skin anyway, so I took this opportunity, hoping that if the Bosch followed they couldn't find me. Well they didn't. I had however, been spotted by a Frenchman pottering about in his orchard. He came over to see me, and went forward to find a covered route back to Troarn.

Half an hour later he returned and signalled him to follow. Keeping well behind, Robinson finally reached a farm on the south-east edge of the village, where he was given bread and milk. A large number of civilians began to gather round him and he was led in triumph through the town.

The reception they gave me was both overwhelming and embarrassing. All the girls persisted in kissing me on both cheeks and the male population wrung me by the hand. I kissed innumerable young children and babies. I was handed a bouquet of roses, and bottles of wine, and cognac appeared. They even gave me some half-ripe strawberries and coarse granulated sugar. We were all having a grand celebration when a very agitated civilian rushed up with the news that the Germans had re-entered the town. The crowd simply dissolved, and I was told to hide in the church. I streaked over the church wall and made towards the porch. The latch clicked, the door opened and I was pulled inside and guided down into the crypt. Since no further move during daylight was feasible, I investigated my 24-hour ration pack. It was soggy and muddy, but, in the circumstances, edible. I then slept for an hour or so.

*

Terry Jepp, Doug Penstone, David Duce and 'Mitzi' Green had spent most of the day in the flooded region, and having been briefed that the Commandos were to advance along the coastal road and capture Cabourg during the evening, they had decided to head north. On the way they found a deserted cottage in which a few hours' sleep were gained. Terry Jepp:

Doug Penstone.   **Terry Jepp.**

Feeling a lot more refreshed, we decided to make a further attempt to reach the coast. From our vantage point we could see, almost due north, the tower and spire of a church which I recognized from one of the picture postcards on display in our briefing tent. It was the church at Cabourg, about two miles away at my guess, and that gave us a fair idea of our position. To have reached the area where the 6th Airborne Division was expected to be, we would have to traverse almost the full width of the flooded area, and it seemed more logical to head for the coast, where we would at least find a dry road running west, hopefully under the control of the Commandos. The only snag was a large ominous looking building, apparently a farmhouse, on our line of march. It could well be a German strongpoint, but after a short discussion we decided to take a chance. With only two rifles and one pistol between us we were hardly a force to be reckoned with, especially as none of the others had any previous experience of active service. And so with hearts full of hope, but in some trepidation, we sallied forth.

Fortunately the water was not particularly cold, but after another hour we were once more very wet and miserable. Then we saw a remarkable and almost unbelievable sight. Coming towards us across the water from the direction of the farm was what appeared to be an Indian canoe, propelled by a single person sitting in the stern, wielding a paddle. It headed straight for us, and when it stopped alongside, the occupant, a Frenchman of about fifty to fifty-five years of age rattled away in his native tongue (which none of us understood) and indicated that one of us should get into the canoe 'Vitement, vitement', and with gestures which suggested that we shouldn't waste any time in so doing! As usual, I was the one to stick my neck out, so leaving the others ready for trouble I clambered into the boat and was paddled, feeling more than nervous, towards the farm.

I was told the reason for the boat, 'Petite rivière, petite rivière', with gestures indicating that the little river between our group and the farm was too deep to cross. Shortly afterwards the boat grounded on the edge of what appeared to be an apple orchard, and a few moments later I met the two bravest people I have ever known.

Adrien Vermughen, the owner of the farm, was a tall and heavily built man with a neat hairstyle and the healthy look of a man whose life was spent out of doors. He didn't look anything like the

120

stereotypical French farmer, flat cap and cardigan, wrinkled trousers, big boots and scarf round the neck! Instead he was more like the so-called 'Gentleman farmer' of the English shires, neatly dressed and cleanly shaven, but with the unmistakable handshake of a man who was not only used to working with his hands but had the confidence of someone sure of his own ability. He greeted me warmly, and, with words and gestures, asked where we had come from and how many of us were there. A dozen questions in thirty seconds!! He then introduced himself, his twelve year-old daughter Monique, and his wife Yvonne, who was anxiously standing by, tut-tutting about my soaked clothing and somewhat dishevelled appearance. Georges Duval, who turned out to be the farm foreman, had meanwhile made three more trips into the marshes to pick up the other three Paras, whilst 'Mustique' the dog charged around sniffing and wagging as though we were his best friends. Madame Vemughen made signs that we should take off our wet clothes, and gratefully we all removed our boots and socks and placed them on a nearby window sill to dry out.

And then consternation! 'Mustique' began barking and ran out into the lane alongside the farm which at that point and for about 100 yards back into the marsh was above water. From the farm gate and heading towards the coast and the nearby village of Bas Cabourg, the lane was more or less dry, but when Madame V went to see what had upset the dog she ran back, white and agitated, saying, 'Allemands, Allemands'. We didn't need any translation, and shepherded by Adrien we quickly ascended a ladder into a loft over the dairy attached to the main farmhouse. Fortunately, I was last to ascend and just as I reached the top I thought 'My God, the boots'. With Adrien still holding the ladder, I shot down, scooped up four pairs of boots and seven socks into my arms and looking into the room behind the window I saw an old fashioned cider press. I hastily chucked my burden behind it, and because there was no room for me to hide, and Mustique was still 'going mad', I shot out of the room, round the corner and up the ladder, which Adrien promptly chucked across the passageway to lean against the loft over the cider press. I just had time to flatten myself along the floor of the loft when there were German voices in the yard. By then I was lying along the lip of the loft floor, about three feet back, with a Mills grenade in one hand and a basket of strawberries in the other. My gallant companions were lying behind me with their rifles and pistol at the ready, using me as a parapet. There was no thought of surrendering; after all, the Vermughens were already compromised by hiding us. However, the panic was all for nothing. The Germans were not a fighting patrol at all, just a couple of fellows from the nearby unit on the outskirts of Cabourg, looking to buy fresh milk and eggs. PHEW![20]

*

Yvonne Vermughen.

Adrien Vermughen.

East of the flooded area, Sergeant Bullock's men had continued their long march towards the Divisional area. They decided to take a rest. Corporal Corboy:

We all sat in an open field bordered by a road. We had been trained in fieldcraft and I pointed out that we should have a lookout. The answer was 'Fine, if you want to be it, OK.' So Mick went and sat by the roadside. Sure enough, around the corner came this Jerry 'blood wagon'. It must have seen everyone sitting there. Well I thought 'If they get away we'll be cooked.' I fired the gun across his front and suddenly it swerved over and into the hedge. I couldn't understand first of all why it had done that 'cos I thought I'd hit the passenger. It wasn't till later that I realized it was a left-hand drive car! Hit him in the left arm, it looked just like a little hole in his arm. Out jumps one, but gives up when he sees everyone running up.

Just after that a French farmer came along with a horse and cart and we didn't want to be lumbered with too many prisoners, so as they were Red Cross men we let them go.

*

Captain Gordon-Brown's assault glider party had also been walking all morning and into the afternoon. Gordon Newton:

Fortunately we came into contact with some Canadians who were just walking up the road between Le Mesnil and Cabourg. We walked back with them and got to Brigade Headquarters, where there was a wide variation of people, glider pilots, medics from all different units, military police, parachutists. They all knew it was a safe haven to get to.

It had been an eventful day for the 9th Battalion Padre, John Gwinnett. He had landed in the flooded area and gradually collected a few men of the Battalion before leading them westwards. After a fifteen-hour journey across country, during the course of which they were fired on by several groups of Germans, he found Brigade HQ. Here he learned of the men who had had to be left at the Haras de Retz. He immediately borrowed a Wehrmacht Morris 4-cwt truck and Private Allt to drive it. Along the road to Breville they met Tom Stroud and some walking wounded who had left the Haras de Retz in order to try and reach Brigade HQ:

We were near the Château St Côme when we met the Padre in a captured German vehicle with hundreds of bullet holes in it. The Padre asked about the more seriously wounded we had left earlier, before directing us to the shortest route to Brigade HQ and the field hospital, before he set off to collect the wounded.

They arrived at the Haras de Retz at about 6.00 pm. Reverend John Gwinnett:

Shall I ever forget linking up with CSMI Bill Harrold... . His parting crack to me when he left Broadwell was, 'See you on the other side Padre, I'll have a cup of tea waiting for you!' It was some eighteen hours later that I found him near the Battery with a couple of dozen wounded; they were being looked after by one of our medical orderlies and a German. Bill Harrold had been shot through both arms and hands. We were loading some of the wounded in a captured vehicle when he came towards me muttering, 'Your tea Padre.' He was holding a mess tin in his teeth. Unashamedly the tears came into my eyes.[21]

The vehicle only had room for four men, and so they took Major Bestley and three others, stating that they would return for the rest.[22]

*

Reverend John Gwinnett.

At the Merville Battery George Hawkins and his two companions had laid in No 4 casemate, sleeping fitfully through the day:

> *The Battery had been silent and there was no sight or sound of anyone until around 8.00 pm, when there was a lot of shouting. I thought it might be troops from the beach. All these bleedin' Germans came, about twenty of them. This sergeant, Feldwebel, he had a Spandau and I think he wanted to shoot us. They had a big conflab and waving arms. Anyway, they got us some bedding, well, mattresses and blankets, gave us a bit of food and drink. They did what they could. They had no medics there or anything. This German put a bit of wood on my arm.*

They were left in the casemate.

*

At around 9.00 pm, the troops in the bridgehead were confronted by an awesome spectacle. Ernie Rooke-Matthews:

> *We witnessed a sight which filled us with elation – the arrival of the 6th Airlanding Brigade... . Planes towing gliders filled the sky. We stood and watched and cheered as the aircraft veered away having released their gliders and the gliders swooped in to land.*

Over 250 gliders ferried the Glider troops, better known to the Paras as the 'Chairborne Airborne'.[23] Among them were the 9th Battalion men of the 'A' Company assault glider whose tow-rope had broken.[24]

Ironically, Sergeant Doug Woodcraft was also on the glider. Having been forced to return to England, he saw the occupants of the glider when they had arrived back at the camp, and so hitched a lift with them:

> *I remember thinking what a bloody fine time I had chosen to make my first flight in one of these things. To say I was unhappy is putting it mildly. The unaccustomed motion of the glider soon had me more airsick than ever and without a parachute on my back I felt naked and vulnerable.*
>
> *And then out of the haze the coastline of Normandy appeared. Looking down I could see the huge collection of shipping offshore. Suddenly, the whistling noise ceased as the tug cast us off. There was a heart-stopping dive to earth, then we levelled out and made a safe, lumpy landing in a cornfield.*
>
> *We tumbled out, took up a position of all-round defence and then a section at a time went back into the glider for other equipment and then we were off, running through the corn, making for the chimney on the skyline which belonged to the brickworks at Le Mesnil.*

They took up position in the ditch beside the road to the west of the Le Mesnil crossroads. Facing them was a lightly treed orchard where several horses were grazing peacefully.

*

At the Haras de Retz, the wounded continued to await the return of Gwinnett and Allt. They were not disappointed. The small bullet-ridden, open-backed truck arrived again. Major Parry, Lieutenant Jefferson and Walter Johnson were helped on board and, by necessity, Hal Hudson. It was his only chance of survival.

They set off. Hudson knew that he was dying:

> *It is something which is impossible to describe to people who have never experienced the near certainty of death, or whose imagination cannot bridge the gulf between acceptance of the reality of the human situation and the immortality of the human soul. When one is in a situation in which one knows that one is dying or likely to die, one fights against death in two ways. First, by physical endurance, and second by the power of the human spirit. I myself, because of the Blue Folder, and the certainty that Brigadier Hill would not approve of any succumbing to physical difficulties, was not prepared to give up the physical struggle. But there is something else. I knew that I was going to die. But there was time for communication. For communication, I suppose, with the living. For some reason I put out my hand, quite indiscriminately.*

Alan Jefferson took it, and Hudson held on grimly.

The journey was not straightforward. Major Parry:

123

We nearly ran into an ambush en route and sheltered for half an hour at a Château in which refugees had collected. Hal was taken out of the car but nothing could be done for him. A French doctor there had lost all his belongings, including his instruments, as a result of the Allied bombing. A woman in the Château hastily made us a Red Cross flag which we gave to a German orderly to hold. We placed him on the nose of the vehicle as a precaution. We hoped, by this, to avoid getting shot at should we encounter an ambush. As luck would have it, we had no trouble and arrived at the MDS at 2130.

Hal Hudson was still holding Jefferson's hand:

I had decided that I was going to live, come what may. But the reason was something to do with this contact with the living.[25]

*

Captain 'Hal' Hudson.

In the crypt of the Troarn church a Frenchman arrived to help Captain Robinson continue his escape. He was guided around the eastern edge of the village and as far as the open country to the north:

At dusk I set course through the Bois de Bavent for Le Mesnil and Le Plein, still hoping to rejoin the Battalion. Before leaving our transit quarters in England I had been given a collar stud with a compass concealed in the base, and this proved invaluable.

He headed off, taking a north-westerly bearing.

*

It *had* been a long day. Brigadier Hill:

I took stock that evening. Alastair's 8th Battalion was about 280 strong; the Canadian Battalion was in very good order and had captured their two bridges, and were now digging in at the Le Mesnil crossroads, about 300 men in all.

The 9th Battalion, consisting of ninety good chaps, was still on the Le Plein feature. The only snag from my point of view was that they were supposed, that evening, to come into the Château {St Côme} which was part of our Brigade Defensive Plan. Of course, they didn't turn up, and the reason they didn't was that the Commandos, who were supposed to come and take over from them were held back at the bridge by General Richard Gale because the situation there was extremely uncertain and unstable. So he held them back there as a reserve.[26]

My Brigade Headquarters was depleted. I had no DAA and QMG, no Brigade Major and no Padre, no Commando Liaison Officer and no sailors. The two sailors who were to direct the guns of the Arethusa *had been killed in the early bombing raid.*

In spite of the chaos, the 6th Airborne Division had achieved all of its primary D-Day objectives. The Merville Battery had made little or no contribution to the defence of Sword beach, the bridges over the Orne and Caen Canal had been captured intact and all five bridges had been destroyed. The defensive perimeter had also been formed, based on a series of pockets. The southern part was held by the 2nd Ox and Bucks in Herouvillette, and the 7th and 13th Parachute Battalions in the Ranville area, the 12th at Le Bas de Ranville, and the Royal Ulster Rifles and a single company of the 12th Devons in the Longueval sector. To the north No. 4 Commando was in Hauger and elements of the 9th Parachute Battalion and Nos. 3 and 6 Commando were in Amfreville/Le Plein. To the north-east, at the Le Mesnil crossroads, was the 1st Canadian Parachute Battalion, and in the Bavent Wood, the 8th Parachute Battalion.

CHAPTER SEVEN

Consolidation
Wednesday 7 June

A s dawn broke on D+1, few of the men holding the Airborne bridgehead knew how the invasion had fared, but they did know that whatever had happened they would now have to face the inevitable German onslaught. Consequently the area was a hive of preparation.

At Le Mesnil the 3rd Parachute Brigade HQ had become more established in the outbuilding of the fromagère. Staff Captain John Woodgate:

> *There was a staircase leading up to it and the signals were underneath. We had our sort of office on the first floor. I suppose being the first person to arrive there, I took what was available and didn't think of moving into the main house.*
>
> *It wasn't a very convenient place. Of course we all had slit trenches outside in the wooded part.*
>
> *Our first wireless set was opened up by a chap from Divisional HQ called Hampton... but to start off with our signalling was a bit haywire, having lost our two signals officers.*

Some of the senior Brigade staff had now arrived. The Brigade Major, Bill Collingwood, had attempted to jump on D-Day, but whilst in the doorway, the plane was hit by flak and he was thrown out. However, he did not get very far as somehow he became entangled and was subsequently dragged along in the slipstream, his legbag having dislocated his right leg. He hung outside the plane for more than twenty minutes before being recovered and by then it was returning home. After landing at RAF Odiham and commandeering a jeep to Brize Norton he met Major Crookenden of the 6th Airlanding Brigade, who took him on board his glider. Brigadier Hill:

> *Collingwood arrived at Brigade HQ with his dislocated leg. I had him evacuated thirty-six hours later because I couldn't have a Brigade Major with his leg sticking out!*

Staff Captain Woodgate's friend, the DAA and QMG, Major Alec Pope had still not arrived.[1] John Woodgate:

> *The administrative matters therefore fell on me, but I was ably assisted by the Brigade Royal Army Service Corps Officer, Captain Donald Cooper.*
>
> *We set off from England with two 24-hour ration packs each. We had, therefore, to seek and deliver rations very soon after the landing.*

A few yards from Brigade HQ the Field Ambulance personnel worked busily in the MDS building. Tom Stroud:

> *They were very well organized in the circumstances.... . I was taken to the dairy and placed on the dairy table. This made an excellent operating table as it was tiled all over and could be easily washed down. The doctors and medics had also been dropped all over the place and had lost much of their equipment. They had no instruments, but used razor blades most effectively, no sutures for stitching up the wounds, so in my case they used plaster of Paris to hold my upper arm together. It must have been much more difficult for stomach or body wounds.*

Captain Hudson's turn 'under the razor' came at around 5.00 am, twenty-five hours after being wounded. Lieutenant Jefferson:

> *The A/ADMS, Major Alastair Young, at first felt that Captain Hudson stood no chance but then decided that the operation must go ahead. After the operation Major Young gave me a tiny shake of the head as if to say that Hudson would not live.[2]*

The main MDS building, Le Mesnil.

Hal Hudson:

> *Naturally, they did not expect me to live and I was put with the others in similar case. John [Gwinnett], what a marvellous man he was, came up to do what was necessary for a person who was a member of his church. Fortunately, he was accustomed to miracles. He never turned a hair when, clad only in a string vest and swathed in bandages, I said, 'Where is the loo?' And John said, 'Just spend a penny where you will, nobody will mind.' I did.[3]*

Tom Stroud was woken by an enemy mortar bombardment to find himself, Tony Mead and other wounded laid on the grass outside the 'operating theatre':

> *I well recall trying to stand as the bombs began to fall, but the effect of the Pentethol anaesthetic was similar to unwise use of alcohol. I staggered all over the place and eventually slept where I fell.*

In the early part of the morning John Gwinnett returned to the Haras de Retz, picked up the remainder of the wounded and brought them back to the MDS.

At 10.30 am No. 8 Field Ambulance formed the first ambulance convoy to leave the MDS, taking sixty-four

Tom Stroud.

126

casualties to the beachhead where a Field Hospital had been established.[4]

*

Having left the Church crypt at Troarn the previous evening, Captain Robinson had, using his small compass, finally reached the Airborne perimeter:

> *It was the early hours of the morning when I bumped into the 8th Parachute Battalion a few hundred yards south of Le Mesnil crossroads, and then moved on to HQ, 3 Para Brigade, opposite the brickworks. Here I was delighted to hear of the success of the Merville Battery battle and to find James Hill firmly established, having survived the Gonneville bombing.*

'Robbie' then walked up to the crossroads to join Major Dyer's men, and his arrival was a very welcome surprise. Ian Dyer was in a shell scrape at the junction of the road and the hedge:

> *He just appeared and said to me, 'For Christ's sake give me something to shoot with!'*

*

In the Amfreville area the Commandos were gradually establishing, and things were relatively quiet. Major Charlton, Reg Vallance and Ken Walker were ordered to take the 'liberated' Renault and scout the area while Colonel Otway led some men into the village. Passing dead Germans, horses and shattered carts at the entrance to the Château he headed for the church. Believing that the priest had co-operated with the Germans, Otway forced him up the stairway to the tower and shoved the man in through the doorway just in case any snipers had survived, but, the Battalion's counter-fire had certainly been effective. Six bodies lay there in pools of blood.

The church at Le Plein.

9th Battalion men mingling with Commandos in Amfreville. (IWM-FLM3449)

Along with the Commandos, a house-to-house search of the village ensued. Arms, ammunition and military papers were found, as well as further prisoners. Colonel Otway:

These were mainly Russians being forced at gunpoint to fight. This is what most prisoners stated, that they were either Austrian or Russian, but on examining their pay books some of them had difficulty in explaining their place of birth!

Private Durston of 'A' Company with a prisoner at the Ecarde crossroads. Note the skull and crossbones, denoting that he was a member of the G-B Force, in this case Lieutenant Pond's glider party. (IWM-FLM3021)

East of the flooded area, Sergeant Bullock's group had spent the night in a disused farmhouse. They recommenced their trek towards the Airborne positions during the morning. Corporal Mick Corboy:

> *We followed a railway line, with all the rails removed, which we later found were used for sea defences. We then came to the blown-up bridges over the River Dives. There was a crashed glider by the bridge where they'd blown it up.*

Clambering over the remains of the bridge, they continued west.

> *It was around this point I noticed a building along the line that looked like a halt, with 'Robehomme' painted on the wall.*

Now knowing their exact location, they made their way directly to Le Mesnil.

The Canadian group in Robehomme itself had risen in number due to the arrival of various stragglers, including some medical personnel led by Captain Bobby Marquis, the officer commanding 2 Section of 224 Field Ambulance, and they joined Captain Johnston's dressing station.

*

At around 2.00 pm the three wounded Paras remaining in No. 4 casemate of the Merville Battery began to hear the sounds of fighting. Commandos were attacking and George Hawkins could not understand why. Men of 4 and 5 Troops of No. 3 Commando were carrying out the attack because of a report from Sword beach complaining about the shelling it was suffering, supposedly from the Battery.

Shortly after, several Commandos came into the casemate. George Hawkins:

> *This Colonel said, 'I've got a jeep out here and we'll have you back in Blighty before long.' Then he came back again about a quarter of an hour later and said, 'I'm sorry, the opposition's too strong, we can't hold the position, we must withdraw.'*

The German response had gradually increased. Two self-propelled guns had been brought up and a heavy bombardment was now landing on the position. The Commandos were forced back, suffering heavy losses and several were taken prisoner. The wounded Paras remained in the casemate.[5]

*

The position at the Le Mesnil crossroads had been strengthened in the early hours by the arrival of engineers of 6 Section, 2 Troop, 3rd Parachute Squadron, who had dug in close to Major Dyer's men, and came under his overall command. The crossroads was of great importance. Sitting as it did on the ridge, it was formed by the lane from Breville to Troarn cutting the main Cabourg to Benouville road. Being the most direct route to the bridges across the River Orne and Caen Canal, heavy attacks were expected, and although it had been a quiet morning, enemy activity began to increase during the afternoon. Lieutenant John Shave, Officer Commanding 2 Troop, 3rd Parachute Squadron:

> *The first sight I had of the enemy in broad daylight was at about 1500 hours... . A movement some 300 yards away in the direction of Breville disclosed a small German recce patrol. Since they were obviously on the lookout for us, we lay still and watched their progress without disclosing our position. The patrol was then chased away by the troops on our left and we saw them no more. We knew that we should not have to wait long after this recce and we were right.[6]*

Jack Humfrey of 'C' Company had arrived at the position and been pushed forward into the house on the road that Ron Tucker had investigated early on D-Day morning. At 5.00 pm the enemy returned:

> *I was put into this house as a post, and looking through the window I could see Germans jumping across this gap [in the hedge across the road]. There was no chance of hitting them, I tried obviously, but you*

THE LE MESNIL CROSSROADS AREA

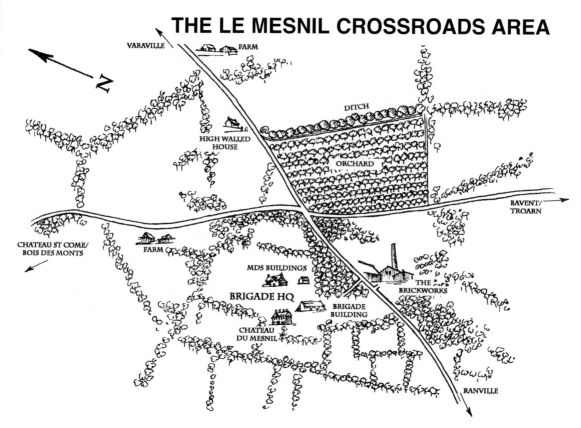

VARAVILLE • FARM
N
DITCH
HIGH WALLED HOUSE
ORCHARD
BAVENT/ TROARN
CHATEAU ST COME/ BOIS DES MONTS
FARM
MDS BUILDINGS
BRIGADE HQ
THE BRICKWORKS
BRIGADE BUILDING
CHATEAU DU MESNIL
RANVILLE

knew you weren't catching any of them. There must have been twenty got across that road and I knew that once across they were going to come behind this house, and there was me trapped upstairs in the bedroom. Two of us were up there. Well I thought we must get out. Came down, and there they were, all coming round the back of this house. I threw a smoke thing [grenade] in the road and ran across to where Corporal Dowling was with his machine gun. I came across thanking my lucky stars I'd got away with it and I got into this ditch.

There was a wall alongside the house, and this German tried to walk up the road with a grenade. He wasn't trying to hide up anywhere, in plain view of everybody. Couldn't believe it! He should have been knocked out first time, but he kept coming. He kept coming and coming, and old Corporal Dowling knocked him out.

Lieutenant Shave:

At 1700 hours we were brought to our toes by the homely chatter of a 'C' Company Bren in the position we were supporting. We were behind and to the left of 'C' Company, and it was a few minutes before the battle worked its way around to us. A few yards down the road towards Bavent was a small hamlet whose houses extended right up to the 'C' Company position. The Germans occupied a commanding house and from it proceeded to give the 9th Para Battalion a very hot time.

Jack Humfrey:

We were in this orchard and lined up. I remember these

Jack Humfrey (centre).

130

concrete posts being part of the fence. We all got behind these. I met my friends Len Tudge and Harry Dunk. We heard these Germans across the road, they were fifteen yards across and they were shouting fire orders as clear as anything. The mortars were the dangerous thing, but they weren't using the mortars then, probably they were too near to us and they could have got injured themselves, but they used machine guns, and all the apples were falling off the trees.

All of a sudden Tudge shouts, 'I've been hit, I've been hit.' I said, 'You'll have to wait a minute 'cos I can't do anything at the moment. I'm not very happy myself!' In the end he was totally in pain, I could see he was. It crossed my mind, 'What'll I do? I'll take him to the First Aid post.' But to do this I had to go out of this field in the corner, through the gate, up to the First Aid post. I had to carry him while it was all going on... . I got him on my shoulder and took him down. When I got to the gate I saw this old bicycle there with a carrier on the front of it. I put him in this carrier. Oh, he screamed blue murder. So that was that. Put the bike back and said, **Len Tudge.**

'Come on' [back on the shoulder]. So we got up there, up the road, there was no point in hiding, try being furtive. The Germans were there, just across the road, but never picked me off or anything like that, right to the top of the hill.

They reached the MDS and Tudge was sat down amongst the wounded. Humfrey obtained some cigarettes to replace his 'soggy stock' and set off back to the position.

Lieutenant Shave:

The battle went on for most of the evening but the only real excitement we got out of it was when a zealous sniper worked his way up a ditch some eighty yards to our left front and proceeded to use our slits for target practice. Such behaviour was all very well, but we were not being paid for that sort of work and so Lance Corporal Hurst, my LMG group commander, picked him off with one rifle shot. As soon as the attack had been driven off, we occupied that ditch and took him as our first prisoner – he was only

wounded in the leg. To my surprise we found the man was terrified, and when his pals were retreating he yelled as loud as he could for them not to leave him. This thug was a corporal and sported a Russian campaign ribbon; however, I suppose we did look a bit rough in our grime and sweat and two-day old camouflage. Little did he know that we were a bit shaky ourselves until he had been relieved of his Schmeisser machine carbine.

The battle died down at around 8.30 pm.[6] Jack Humfrey:

When I got back it was all quiet, tranquil. But unfortunately, of all the chaps lying there one was Harry Dunk, but lying there dead. I remember I put something over his face, and there were two or three more there with him from other companies, because you were all a mixture of everybody.

Harry Dunk.

131

Private Alex Durham, 'C' Company:

Harry Dunk was being employed as Company runner and had been killed during a mortar attack.

During the lull a section under Sergeant Harper was sent forward to re-occupy the house up the road. Around 9.00 pm a German motorcyclist scout came straight down the main road. He would have been allowed to pass unharmed so as to lure on the main body, but unfortunately he spotted Corporal Dowling, who shot him. The main body then came into view about 250 yards up the road and were engaged by the Brens of Major Dyer's force. The enemy's leading machine-gunner boldly got his weapon into action on the edge of the road and the Germans attacked immediately, straight at Sergeant Harper's section in the house. They withdrew to the main platoon position and the enemy's attack was halted. The Germans drew off and moved to the left flank, where they were met by heavy fire from the glider parties of Captain Gordon-Brown and Lieutenant Smythe.[7]

Hugh Smythe's men, being further down the road, had had a relatively quiet day. Private Reg 'Knocker' Knights:

Alex Durham.

We were mortared several times and received machine-gun fire on our right flank. Some mortar bombs fell short and amongst the horses across the road who scattered briefly and then surprisingly, resumed grazing even though they had some nasty shrapnel wounds on their flanks. Our main problem was attempting to stop small groups of enemy, ones, twos and threes, from infiltrating across our front from right to left.... A very difficult task with our weapons. We were not very successful.

After being forced to land back in England, Lieutenant Smythe had ordered them to leave their Battery assault weapons behind and just take their normal kit. 'Knocker' Knights:

I had left my Bren gun behind. We were now equipped entirely with ultra-short-range weapons – Stens. Excellent for close combat in dense woods or in confined spaces, but useless against an enemy engaging us with rifles and machine guns from eighty yards and beyond. This was the very uncomfortable position we were in. Luckily there was no concerted attack on our position.

*

During the early evening the Canadians at Robehomme received orders to move to Le Mesnil.[8]

It was dark by the time they set off. The medical party brought up the rear of the column, with the casualties travelling in the farm cart pulled by Udine and a car supplied by the local parson. Despite continuous flak and distant shellfire, it seemed that the noise of the column and the clatter of Udine's hooves must surely attract the enemy's attention. However, they entered a silent Bricqueville and halted.

The next part of the journey, between Bricqueville and Bavent, was the most dangerous because it was known that the Germans occupied this area in some strength and that a pillbox was sited at the crossroads south of Bavent. Patrols went on ahead and the column continued. The medical party heard the sound of firing and explosions up ahead, and as they reached the bridge on this critical stretch of road they saw a German vehicle which the Canadian point had just dealt with. There were several corpses in it, and in the dyke running parallel with the road another corpse was sitting up in the water, his white face staring at them. The group began to run, taking turns to push the cart. Up ahead at the crossroads the lead platoon was challenged by enemy sentries and a firefight erupted. Again, by the time the medics had got there the fighting was over and the shattered pillbox was the only evidence of the action. They turned left on the road to the Bois de Bavent, eventually entering the outskirts of the wood. They then had to run to force the cart up a steep track. The next two hours seemed interminable, as there was the constant feeling that they would be fired at from the trees on either side of the track. Deep ruts made life very uncomfortable for those in the cart. A family that Captain Johnston had treated in Robehomme had given him a bottle of Calvados as a thank you and to his amazement it was found to possess unexpected recuperating powers. Ian Johnston:

> Later in our journey when the horse Udine, pulling a cart full of casualties, became tired, we gave it a shot of Calvados and Udine took on a new lease of life!

At last they reached the spot where patrols from Brigade HQ were scheduled to meet them, but there was an hour to wait until the arranged time and Captain Johnston decided to push on to Le Mesnil. Unescorted, the cortège stumbled on with Johnston and two others walking in front brandishing Red Cross flags.[4]

*

On the western part of the ridge the Commandos had been shelled and mortared several times and continuously pestered by snipers, but on the whole the day had remained comparatively quiet. The post-office in Amfreville had been turned into a First Aid post and the French flag once again flew outside the Town Hall.[9]

The French flag flies again outside Amfreville Town Hall. (IWM-FLM3252)

It was not until 9.30 pm that the remainder of Lieutenant Colonel Young's No. 3 Commando arrived to relieve the 9th Battalion. Colonel Otway:

> They had hardly arrived when my orders came through on their radio to go to the Château St Côme. I was actually talking to Peter Young. A radio chap came up and said, 'A message for Colonel Otway,' and I was given my orders. They said, 'Go to the Château St Côme. Just take up position and hold at all costs.'

Those final four words needed no elaboration.

A gap of over a mile existed between the battalions of the 3rd Parachute Brigade at the Le Mesnil crossroads and No. 6 Commando in Amfreville. In between, Breville was held by the Germans, but from there to Le Mesnil was 'No Man's Land'. Here stood the Château St Côme.

Although this move was in the Brigade's pre-D-Day plan, Colonel Otway had no idea what the position was like, so he ordered Major Charlton and his batman to reconnoitre the area for the Battalion's arrival, and they duly set off in the Renault.

The Colonel decided on a route for the march, traced it on his map and issued the details to his officers. He did not know whether the Château was occupied and so rather than march to it directly, along the road from Breville, he decided to approach from the south-west by ascending the ridge, out of the possible sight of any Germans.

They left the Château d'Amfreville at 11.30 pm, with Lieutenant Pond and members of 'A' Company leading. Colonel Otway:

> My instructions to Hugh Pond were to carry on, and every time we come to a junction or crossroads, you stop. You do not cross. Don't go past any junction or crossroads without first reconnoitring that we can do so safely. So when I was satisfied that it was all right, I sent Hugh on. There was a runner who went backwards and forwards.

Major Smith:

> The column snaked silently through the night, men walking silently on the verges at the sides of the road. But in the centre of the column came the ludicrous sight of a lumbering farm cart, drawn by two white horses, with the Machine-Gun Sergeant driving and a man with the gun balanced on a pile of ammunition boxes. After this came a well-laden hand cart drawn by ten men.

The farm cart was actually an old wooden brewer's dray that had been appropriated by the 'B' Company Sergeant Major, Wally Beckwith, and Sergeant McGeever. Corporal McGuinness was put in charge of this transport. Blankets were wrapped around the horse's hooves to keep them quiet. Ernie Rooke-Matthews:

> The move to this position around midnight was quite eerie, progress was very slow – stop, start, stop, start – and we were somewhat tired. Some men had great difficulty in staying awake as we halted while the way ahead was reconnoitred. There was the inevitable howling dog adding to our concerns, breaking the otherwise silence of the night.

Corporal McGuinness:

> On our way the column kept stopping, sometimes five minutes, sometimes half an hour, so we all sat down. Fenson, Davies and myself fell asleep. When we woke up, the others had gone. When they moved off, someone in front of us should have told us. We were into our third day without any sleep. We had the gun, the others the ammunition.

Major Smith had known that the cart had been getting stuck, and so sent some men back with orders to find them and unhitch the horses for use as pack mules. Ken Walker:

> With Lieutenant Slade and Reg Vallance we made our way to locate them, and find them we did or more correctly they found us as the noise we made caused them to open fire. Fortunately it was with small arms and they missed. Eventually, peace was discussed.

Along the outskirts of Breville a British lightweight motorcycle was found in its parachute-dropping frame, and this was added to the growing Battalion transport section!

At the Breville crossroads they turned right, went down the hill leading to Ranville until reaching a track that ran east.[10]

As they moved along it, a German column suddenly appeared out of the darkness, forcing the two leading men to freeze. About two companies of enemy soldiers, marching in threes, tramped straight past. Somehow, McGuinness managed to keep the horses quiet by stroking their noses.

The Paras continued along the track which became steeper as it veered north. Trees appeared on either side until after a short distance it developed into a sunken lane, at points about fifteen feet deep by twenty feet across. A canopy of branches grew overhead. At the top of the slope the lane met the road connecting Breville and the Le Mesnil crossroads, and as they approached it Otway saw Major Charlton waiting, totally unconcerned and plainly visible in the moonlight:

> *He was walking up and down that road smoking a cigarette. I thought he must be mad. I said, 'Are you crackers?' He said, 'Why?' 'I could see the butt up the lane, what about the Germans in the Château?' He said, 'There aren't any Germans in there.' He was right, they'd got out.*

In fact, he and his batman had driven directly up the road from Breville without incident. Charlton reported that all was quiet. It was around 1.30 am.

The Château St Côme was 250 yards in front but too far away to be seen in the darkness. The Colonel took no chances and did not venture towards it. Instead, twenty yards to their right, along the road, they opened a gate and spread out into a wood that bordered the sunken lane. Inside, they came across a small bungalow. Brandishing his pistol, the Colonel knocked on the front door. A woman put her head out of a window and asked in French what he wanted. He replied that they were British parachute troops and that the invasion had started, but obviously being wary she responded:

> *Please go away! I'm fed up with you German troops and your exercises pretending to be British soldiers. We want to get some sleep!*

He replied:

> *Madame, we are British soldiers. Unless you come down and let us in, I'm afraid we are going to force an entry and I wouldn't want to wreck your house. If you will kindly come down, you will see for yourself.*

She replied, 'Oh all right!' The lady, accompanied by her husband, opened the door and Otway entered with a few men to search the building. He and Wilson went into the drawing room and, using their torches, looked around. Flashing his light at a photograph on a piano the Colonel recognized a chap that he knew from his time at Sandhurst. He asked the lady, 'What are you doing with a picture of Edward d'Abo?' Amazingly, it was her nephew, and she was finally convinced of their authenticity. The couple turned out to be the Mayor of Breville, Monsieur Magninat, and his half English-Danish wife, and this was their summer residence called the Bois des Monts. The Frenchman then stated that he worked for the resistance and he led the Colonel to the bathroom whereupon he produced a radio secreted beneath the floorboards.[11]

Outside in the grounds the men were very busy digging slit trenches. Sergeant Daniels, 'B' Company:

> *Several officers who were really on the ball were dashing round, saying, 'You chaps here, you there...' The RSM, Cunningham, was another very busy man. When you got settled it was 'You two chaps come with me', and you were moved around until I suppose we were all-round defence.*
>
> *'B' Company had men eight to ten feet apart. Just about close enough to speak to one another.*

Ron Gregory:

> *Digging with an entrenching tool was at most a very hard task, but in a wood with dry ground and roots, dog-tired and hungry, it proved most difficult. However, I was able to get down about twelve inches by daylight and all this being done as quietly as possible.*

The men at the Bois des Monts were left in no doubt as to their task. Sergeant Daniels:

> *Our instructions were quite simple. It will be held regardless, and to the last man and last round we'd hold that ground.*

CHAPTER EIGHT

The Château St Côme: Opening Skirmishes
Thursday 8 June

At daybreak the importance of the new position became immediately apparent to Colonel Otway. The view to the south and west was panoramic. If the Germans could capture the Bois des Monts they would be able to shell the River Orne and Caen Canal bridges accurately and eventually attack down the slope, and break across them. This would be catastrophic, as they would then be in a position to 'roll up' the beachhead by attacking the flank.

The presence of the 9th Battalion protected the Le Mesnil flank, reduced the length of the Breville gap and hampered German aspirations as to the capture of the bridges from the north.

*

With digging in and sentry duty there had been little opportunity for the men to get any sleep. Ron Gregory did manage some, but was woken by CSM Beckwith. He was wanted for an 'ad hoc' patrol:

> *CSM Beckwith said to me, 'Come on 'Greg', we're off,' and we walked straight up the driveway and into the Château, and through the rooms. We weren't looking for anything in particular, just to make sure it was unoccupied. We were amazed at what we saw. It seemed that the Château was in fact a German HQ and that they had just taken off. Food and drink were on tables ready to take, everything in a shambles. Outside we found a motorcycle and sidecar which the CSM quickly drove to the front entrance.*

The driveway.

This we loaded with tins of food, German sausages, mostly with black bread. The Germans had old 'cooler' jars, they used to tie them down with rope, looked rather like a large jam jar tightened down with a rubber band on top. They were sealed and then whatever was in them like fruit or vegetables was boiled. That was dessert. They were very keen on this bottled fruit.

I picked up an MG34 with boxes full of ammo, and we quickly headed back down the driveway.[1]

Shortly after, Lieutenant Slade led seven men across the road to carry out a more thorough investigation of the building. Stendall Brailsford:

As we got up to the Château a Frenchman approached us, spoke a little English, and started to tell Lieutenant Slade that in the fields to the rear... there were two gliders landed, and landed safely. So I said to Slade, 'I'll take two or three men and go and see what's in the gliders,' while he went in the Château.

Slade's men surveyed exactly the same scene as witnessed by Beckwith and Gregory, and then moved upstairs. Ken Walker:

On the first floor with Slade we entered an office, which I should have thought had been occupied by the German officer in charge. There was a large desk near the large window that overlooked open fields to Breville. On this desk was a cash box with the lid partially open. To me this seemed to be a classical booby trap. Slade decided to look and I left the room in a hurry. It was found to contain a German payroll... . Another room which was full of a big suitcase and ladies' clothes, reeked with scent, the bedclothes were thrown back on the bed. In that room was a massive great case filled with Marks. We searched throughout the premises which contained many other items that would have been useful. In actual fact Slade took for his own use an excellent officer's sword.

On our return to the Battalion and our report that there was no trace of the enemy in the Château, Colonel Otway ordered patrolling of the area around, and the [placement of the] Vicker's machine gun at the entry to the driveway, on the main road.[2]

This solitary heavy machine gun was located in what was an old dry pond on the left-hand corner, to cover the north-east.

Stendall Brailsford's small group had continued beyond the stables, crossed a couple of fields and found the abandoned gliders:

We found them intact with the tails 'blown off'. One had got the ramp already down and one hadn't. We got the jeep and trailer out of the first one, with ammunition and all supplies. One of the lads took over that jeep. I went into the other jeep and said, 'Come on, get the ramps down.' As we were doing that, we were fired on by a group of Germans coming across the field, so I said, 'Bugger the ramps, out of the way, I'm coming straight out!' And I drove straight out. It was about four feet off the ground and we bounced out. I said to the other driver, 'You follow me, we'll head back,' so we shot across the fields and we found an open gate. I went through the gate, turned left. I didn't know where I was.

Found myself on the outskirts of Breville. As we drove through Breville there was a group of Germans smoking and talking against somebody's window sill. They were just as surprised as we were! Got to the crossroads, turned left and straight into our area at the 'cottage'. That re-supplied us with a bit of ammunition. There was also a news cameraman's camera on it as well.

From the information brought back by the patrols, plus his own inspection of the immediate area, Otway gained a good idea of the position. The Château St Côme was a three-storey, rectangular building approximately thirty yards long by ten yards wide, giving an excellent view of the Breville area and the surrounding countryside. Like many of the residences in the area it was a stud farm, and the horses were still in stables to the north and west of the main building.[3] Paddocks surrounded the site.

Ideally the Colonel would have liked to occupy both the Château area and the Bois des Monts, but the lack of men prevented it. After liaison with Brigadier Hill, he therefore chose the wood because it was a naturally strong defensive position. This meant that the Château and stables would act as

The St Côme area.

The Bois des Monts bungalow. Monsieur Magninat stands outside.

cover for the forming up of any German attack, but he planned to try and deny the buildings to the enemy by patrolling, and whenever possible send two-man teams forward to act as an 'early warning system'. In any case, the Château was an obvious target for German artillery and aircraft. Otway redeployed his force around the Bois des Monts perimeter.

The stone bungalow was in a clearing in the midst of the wood, giving it a view south to Herouvillette and beyond. One room was turned into the Battalion HQ and Captain Watts' First Aid team was installed in the kitchen. A tool shed thirty yards away was converted into a Dressing Station. The solitary 3-inch mortar was dug in on the slope just below and a few yards east of the bungalow. This was well sited because the ground fell away at that point, ensuring that they were completely hidden from the enemy.

Fifty yards west of the bungalow, among the trees, was the sunken lane. Beyond it on the edge of the wood, was a large overgrown hedge followed by around thirty feet of grass, then a ditch. Sergeant Daniels, 11 Platoon, 'B' Company:

Our little platoon were dug in, in that ditch. The trees were sort of small stuff, more bush type stuff than trees. I had a pair of MG42s at the time, they were just in the hedge. Just in front of the hedge was a bit of blackberry scrub or something similar. To see over that, I had to expose rather a lot of myself. So we had quite a few sandbags, filled them with earth and built up a little bit of a sandbag parapet in front of this pair of MG42s.

This flank was designated as the 'B' Company area, but there were only enough men to occupy a length of about a hundred yards. The field of fire was around 250 yards across a gently sloping field down to the next hedge. Beyond that, another smaller field could be seen rising to the Breville crossroads. To the south-west was the glider-strewn LZ 'N' and Divisional HQ at Ranville. Their view to the right was of hedges bordering the Breville road.

At the top of the sunken lane the remnants of the anti-tank platoon led by Sergeant Knight were positioned to cover the road and Château driveway with their PIATs. The driveway was lined on either side by a wide grass verge, a row of trees, a ditch and a low fence. These ran parallel for its whole length until reaching the start of a road loop, behind which stood the Château.

As the Breville road ran east it became a winding lane through a no-man's-land of thick woods until reaching the Le Mesnil crossroads, three-quarters of a mile away. This road was bordered along its whole length by ditches and hedges.

The remainder of HQ Company was dug in among the trees behind the Bois des Monts hedge which followed the curve of the road. Directly opposite they were faced by a high bank with a double hedge, and beyond it an orchard.

East of this orchard a dense wood stretched up to the Château itself and for 400 yards along the road to Le Mesnil. Much of the undergrowth was so thick that it was almost impossible to move through it except on hands and knees, and then not in a straight line. Although there was virtually no field of fire, it was quite an obstacle for an attacker to penetrate, and as Major Charlton had found a ditch that bordered its western edge, Otway used a few 'A' Company men to occupy it. There was also another reason. He had concentrated his meagre amount of weaponry along a length of fifty yards stretching east from the driveway. Colonel Otway:

I made that little area the firepower base and I put every Bren gun and all the machine guns I got eventually, facing across that open ground... . I positioned my troops like this so that the Germans were 'funnelled' into the position; a killing zone. I wanted to lure the Germans into that. The one thing I didn't want them to do was to come creeping down through the wood on the right.

If the Germans attacked from the Château area they would be forced to cross the open ground and run straight into the combined firepower of the road position plus that of the 'A' Company ditch.

The eastern flank within the Bois des Monts was taken up in another wooded area. Some of the 'A' Company contingent of around twenty men was dug in among the trees. Ron Phelps, the

THE CHATEAU ST CÔME/BOIS DES MONTS AREA

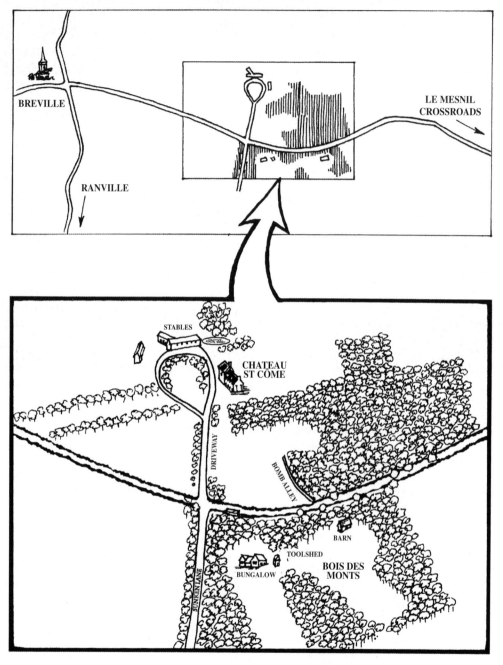

Company clerk, took up residence in his 'own little 'Company Headquarters":

> *I found what was probably a shooting hide, a wooden structure on legs about four feet off the ground, which I used as a store later for rations and spare ammo, a very meagre amount of which came.*

Several yards behind them, a barn was turned into the Company HQ. The remaining few of the Company were behind the roadside hedge.

'A' Company's Headquarters. The barn at the Bois des Monts.

The southern part of the position was 'C' Company's particular area of responsibility and this was to be covered by small 'standing patrols'. They were also dug in below and east of the bungalow and were to act as a mobile reserve to reinforce a flank as required and fill any gaps that appeared in the defences of the other Companies as the battle progressed.

The Colonel gave strict orders that the men were not to show themselves under any circumstances and not to fire without his permission unless the enemy approached to within twenty to thirty yards. If the order to fire was given before this, to disguise the lack of men, Bren gunners were only to fire single shots until necessary.

*

Later in the morning, a small patrol led by Lieutenant Gordon 'Ginger' Parfitt was organized. Sid Capon:

> *Parfitt was always one that said he would get the VC, but I hoped not at my expense! Otway said, 'Go and find out where the Germans are,' and Ginger took me and about three others.*
>
> *Our patrol crossed the road and stealthily advanced to the left position of the Château and we passed a British Major who was dead. Rigor mortis had set in. We had probed to the left and beyond the Château and came to a white double gate to a field, and there were the Germans on the left-hand side having a wash and brush up alongside the hedgerows. I'd say there was a couple of dozen or so, about platoon strength. We got spotted and split our formation up. Parfitt said, 'Quickly, back to our position'.*

They ran back across the fields and jumped into one of the driveway ditches:

> *We came under heavy gunfire and fortunately for me I never had the chinstrap to my helmet fastened. I felt a sudden crack from the gunfire on my helmet which fell off, and I didn't stop to pick the bloody*

thing up! The idea was to get the information back about where the Germans were. Mind you, they knew where they were then!

We finally dashed across the narrow road and through the opening [Bois des Monts gate], and I was bloody glad to get back there.

The Germans now had a rough idea that there was opposition in the St Côme area, although not the strength. The Paras waited.

*

At the Le Mesnil crossroads during the early hours the engineers of 6 Section, 2 Troop, 3rd Parachute Squadron, were moved into a line of trees across the road from Major Dyer's group. During darkness they had sown a minefield in the road, behind and to the left of the 9th Battalion men. The job was completed just before dawn, but before a marking fence could be erected, enemy mortaring began and they were forced to take cover. Lieutenant Shave, 3rd Parachute Squadron RE:

The time was 0530 hours and just as we were feeling relieved that a minebelt now lay between the enemy and the important crossroads, we heard a noise that almost froze us to the earth on which we lay. It began as six awful long-drawn-out shuddering groans, followed by a ghastly warbling which came hurtling through the air towards us with the speed of an express train. As this noise, like the knell of doom, reached its horrid climax, the six heavy rockets burst all around us.

This was the infamous German Nebelwerfer, a six-barrelled rocket launcher, to be christened the 'Moaning Minnie' or the 'Sobbing Sisters' by the troops.

Along the road on the western side of the crossroads, some Canadians had occupied a farm. Reg 'Knocker' Knights had just walked there to obtain some water when the Nebelwerfers opened up:

I thought 'What the hell was that!' Then one crashed in the farm courtyard with such a noise and smoke and fire, I thought 'Those poor Canadians, the whole farm must be wiped out.' But when the smoke cleared, there, nonchalantly walking up the steps of a building was a Canadian carrying a bucket of water!

The blast from these rockets was tremendous. However, they did not fragment into small shards of shrapnel but 'bloody great pieces, lumps as big as a bucket'. Their bark was literally worse than their bite and if the men remained underground only a direct hit would cause injury.

As the barrage receded, about 200 Germans appeared from a wood north-east of the crossroads. These were men of the III/857th Regiment who had only just begun to arrive in the area, having cycled from Le Havre. They began walking towards Major Dyer's thirty men hidden behind the hedge. Ron Tucker:

Major Dyer said, 'Do not open fire until we can see the whites of their eyes'. I remember thinking I had heard a similar order given in a movie picture. I must have had the first pressure on the trigger for two minutes or more, with the selected German in my sights getting larger and larger until at last came the order to fire.

Letting loose with everything they had, the Paras halted the advance, forcing the survivors to crawl back into the woods. The Germans then switched their point of attack and gradually began to reappear, attempting to make for the house on the road. Major Dyer ordered Lieutenant Lepper to occupy it, so he took Tucker, Gower, Fenton and Undrill, a Bren gunner, and dashed for the position. They came under fire and felt the bullets whistle past their ears, but all made it safely inside, shutting a pair of large doors behind them. The enemy closed up and a fire-fight ensued. Ron Tucker:

The Germans were firing through the windows from the ditch opposite. They were belting away and the ceiling was coming down on top of us. And then they came over and threw stick grenades. We only had the furniture to hide behind, pretty solid pieces of wood, sideboards and things.

The Germans gathered around the back of the house and began to approach the crossroads. John Speechley was in a ditch on the left-hand side of the road:

The Krauts put in a full company attack coming from half-left.... We heard the Sergeant or whoever was in charge say 'Schnell' or whatever, you could hear his voice. We saw smoke zapping down all over the place. We knew it was to cover us up. That moment you get the wind up then. There was Captain

142

Robinson; he said, 'Now come on lads, fix bayonets and wait for it.' I thought no way am I going to have a go at that, I only had a bloody 6-inch 'stick' [bayonet], bugger that! So as soon as anybody appeared in the smoke... as soon as I saw a shadow, I just let him have it with automatic. [Capt. Robinson said] 'Having a war on your own there Speechley?' I said, 'Yeah!'

Lieutenant Shave:

The method the enemy used in these attacks was simply designed to swamp us with lead. The attack was preceded by groups of men all squirting out bullets from Schmeissers; they were given very good covering fire and had the support of mortars in addition to the 'Sobbing Sisters'.

Our view to the front was limited to 100 yards of open field with a tall hedge and trees the other side of it and the house.

Our Troop LMGs were sited down the road some fifty yards to our right... Manned by Sappers Green, Tillbrook, Hurst, Reynolds, Smith (G), and others, they chattered steadily throughout the action. The fire which came back at them was the most intense we ever experienced, and could not be compared with the proverbial swarm of bees, being much louder and more consistent.

For hours that morning Sergeant Docherty maintained a constant supply of Bren gun magazines to our guns. In one very exposed position we had to lob them over a hedge from a prone position into the slit trench the other side. The 9th Battalion went into action all around us with such good effect that we saw very little of the enemy until the attack was nearly over. At one critical phase it appeared as if 'C' Company was being overrun.

However, they held on and the Germans were eventually forced to fall back. The situation at the crossroads quietened and just as the Paras began to attend to the wounded, a jeep came roaring down the road from the north. John Speechley:

I heard the engine and thought 'One of ours, that's alright', and WALLOP! I've never been so near to an explosion. I was in that natural ditch, and the pressure on my head was terrible. I jumped, and couldn't hear. I saw the jeep just rolling over in mid-air. There was a big tree and the tyre was alight in the tree, dripping molten rubber.... Bits and pieces were coming down towards me.

I ran across the road, dived in the ditch. The engine block stabbed in the ditch [a couple of feet away]. One fellow, I think he was a goner without question, but one of them in the front, driver or otherwise, he was running around screaming, 'Help me, help me'. Every time he run around he was roaring like an oil rag. I thought to myself 'Once he stops, grab him', but the shit was flying 'cos the bang excites them all. Everyone starts firing and there's no way you are going to stand up on the crossroads to get him. Too much shit flying about. Then he collapsed. He was smoking, he moved a bit but that was it.

Jack Humfrey was also in a roadside ditch. Initially, he could not understand what had caused the explosion:

I thought it was coming from the Germans, a big shell from a tank or something. It was such an explosion. I was right beside it. A sheet of flame shot by me. It was land mines put in the road by British soldiers, and a medical jeep had gone along and that went up in the air and came down. All its tyres were burnt off completely, there were three or four men running around alight. I've never seen anything like it. It was terrible. 'Help me, help me,' and we tried to. Skin was hanging.... We were all equipped with a couple of tubes of morphine and we did, in our way, I mean we weren't expert medical people...

Captain Robinson:

I was able to pull one lad out, I don't know what his name was, carry him down into the ditch and put out the flames. He was saying, 'Captain 'Robbie', Captain 'Robbie', for God's sake shoot me.' I pushed my ampoule of morphia into his arm, and that put him to sleep a few minutes later. As he fell asleep he said, 'Thank you Captain 'Robbie'.' I said, 'See you back in Bulford old chum, good as new', and I had him carried back to the RAP.[4]

This jeep party, which had made a couple of trips to a house along the Varaville road, contained twenty-year-old Raymond Garrett of 224 Field (Para) Ambulance, six wounded and the 9th Battalion's Corporal Tottle:

> *We were doing about seventy miles an hour when we hit the mines. The jeep with all eight of us on board must have been blown about ten yards into the air and was one mass of flames including us eight. On landing, although I was a ball of fire I managed to get into a ditch beside the road and after quite a long time I got my clothes off and put myself free of the flames. I remember I was in agony and enemy bullets were spraying the hedgerow. I could not see a thing now as the burnt skin had sealed my eyes.* [5]

During the furore that followed, Doug Tottle lay undiscovered in the ditch.

While the German attack had been going on, they had also tried a wider 'right hook' and infiltrated the area between the Bois des Monts and the Le Mesnil crossroads, thereby threatening the road link and Brigade Headquarters itself. During the morning a radio connection had been established between the 9th Battalion and Brigade HQ, and Brigadier Hill made a personal radio call to Colonel Otway requesting help. The Colonel immediately rounded up a force from 'C' and HQ Companies, led by Lieutenant Christie who had found his way to the Battalion earlier in the morning, after his wayward drop. There was also a fire group of two MG42s under Major Smith:

> *The Commanding Officer decided to attack the rear of the attacking enemy. He sent a party of twenty-two men round to the left flank to make the assault. I took two Sergeants, each with a German machine gun, and three private soldiers to form a covering party. I went down the strip of wood bordering the road on our right flank, but was unable to obtain a field of fire. I climbed a small tree to get a better view, but could see nothing but trees. Suddenly we were fired on. The enemy must have heard us and fired in our direction. We returned fire and bounded forward twenty yards. This we repeated on two or three occasions making headway safely, for the enemy seemed to duck for cover and stop firing whilst we were doing so. To my distress both the German machine guns jammed, and I left the sergeants tugging at their guts whilst I went forward with the three privates. We fired our Sten guns instead of the Spandaus and dashed forward in the same manner, occasionally throwing a grenade forward as far as we could. We no doubt sounded quite a strong force. Anyway, eighteen Germans fled from us, darted down a hedge, away from the wood right towards our flanking party who had no difficulty in shooting the lot. I did not know this at the time, and thought the firing on the left was nothing to do with me.*

Major Smith's small group continued to advance:

> *We came to a tough fence. Across the road was a small cottage. The enemy might be in it, so I threw an anti-tank bomb at the wall and charged to the gap it made. There was a howl from inside, and I was just about to throw in another hand grenade when I saw it was a goat.*
>
> *An officer from Brigade joined me and I agreed to let him join the party. I gave the direction of our next bound, up a ditch on the side of the road opposite the strip of wood. Moving off, the officer from Brigade darted in front of me. I was a little annoyed for it rather hindered my seeing ahead, but I admired his keenness.*

This was Captain Tony Wilkinson, the Brigade Intelligence Officer, who had been at the Bois des Monts when the Brigadier's call had come in. He wanted to obtain a prisoner and so joined the patrol. Colonel Otway had taken a few men along the roadside ditch:

> *He was on the other side of the road and he came over to me, and it was right on a corner. I came up, put my head around the corner to have a look and see what the Germans were at. They immediately opened fire. I went back and told Wilkinson to come back, and I suppose it was instinct, he then looked and got shot in the head. It wasn't a question of disobeying orders or anything, it was purely instinct.... . The sniper was very quick. He nearly got me.*

Major Smith came up the ditch:

> *I told him to keep still and I would send the SBs directly we had finished. He spoke perfectly calmly saying I need not do that for he was going to die, which he did almost immediately. His body blocked the ditch, so we went back about ten yards and dashed across the road into the same wood again as the enemy.*

Here we found two Canadians sheltering in a ditch, wondering what it was all about. They had been adrift since the drop and were just finding their way back. I told them to join forces with me and the chase continued in the same manner. Suddenly one of them said the Huns were behind a high bank which they had slipped behind hoping we would pass. I threw over a couple of grenades and told them to surrender. The grenades did the job for there was only one of seven men left standing. He was a Sergeant Major from Dresden. One badly wounded fellow begged to be shot, but someone jabbed him with morphine and told him to wait for the stretcher-bearers. We collected two more Spandaus, for this was a fire group, and then our assault group turned rather red in the face after having lost direction in the woods, but bringing news of the Germans we had driven out onto them.

The enemy had been cleared from the area, if only temporarily, but it eased the pressure on Brigade Headquarters and Otway's force returned to the Bois des Monts.

A party of stretcher-bearers from the MDS was sent out on a jeep to attend to the German wounded. On board were Captain Johnston and Private Bramwell, one of the Field Ambulance pacifists. To try and give themselves some sort of protection, Padre Gwinnett sat on the bonnet waving a Red Cross flag. Along the route a Para in a trench saw this and shouted, 'Don't matter. Jerry don't recognize no f...... Red Cross. Look after yourself mate.' The jeep continued to the scene of the action. James Bramwell:

Captain Tony Wilkinson.

The entire field was surrounded by a German patrol that had been wiped out by our people. What struck me as so horrific was that it was like a tableau, this kind of death dealt by machine guns, very rapid firing. One was gazing down his machine gun, the other was about to throw a grenade, his arm arrested in the air by rigor mortis. One was leaning back trying to get a grenade from his belt. All in these grotesque attitudes.[6]

Not a single man had escaped, and only about twelve were left alive to be taken to the MDS.

Captain Wilkinson's body was taken into the Bois des Monts. One of his intelligence section, Corporal Tilley, a stonemason by trade, sculpted a stone cross for his grave.[7]

*

Captain Wilkinson's stone cross in the Bois des Monts.

At noon a strong German force went into action further along the ridge, attacking the Commandos at Amfreville and Hauger. Simultaneously, at the Bois des Monts a patrol of around platoon strength appeared in the field to the north-west. Fred Milward:

> During the attack on the Battery at Merville, if you shot anyone it was a shadow, but now we could see field grey uniforms coming towards you and you knew you would be killing them. At that moment I had no thoughts of dying myself. That was to change very quickly as the battle for St Côme went on.

As the enemy approached, the Paras remained silent, awaiting the order to fire. It came with the enemy at less than fifty yards. Sergeant Daniels:

> The Germans were so close that when I fired my machine gun, I could see the dust bouncing off their tunics as the bullets hit their chests.

Ron Gregory:

> I went into action for the first time with my MG34. The small MG Platoon led by Sergeant McGeever had chosen to set up position directly in front of 'B' Company and the driveway. He was pleased to let me join them. The MG34 could only be used properly with a No 2, and Jock Skene came forward to help.

Ron Gregory.   *Jock Skene.*

The patrol was seen off. Subsequently McGeever and Gregory discussed the defence of the driveway and decided that, if an attack came from that direction, the Germans would surely approach using the ditch on the right hand side, especially if they were supported by a bombardment. Ron Gregory:

> Between us we suggested that the MG34 I had, be put on fixed lines to shoot all the way up it. There was a definite bank there, [on the Château side of the road] and you could lay on the bank and fire over the top of it. All you had to do was pull the trigger and all the ammunition ran up the ditch. This MG position was only about ten yards or so from my trench position so that I could snatch a few minutes' sleep when the attacks stopped, and also dig deeper!

The piecemeal German reinforcements were arriving in the area and immediately being fed into attacks without artillery or mortar support. The first came in through the Château wood, but the 'A' Company men held this attack, firing by sound into the heavy undergrowth in front of them. This was followed shortly after by two more attempts from the north-east. Sergeant Daniels:

> These were '1914-18 style'. They came straight at us up this field of hay, open order.

146

This continued until 1.25pm when the Germans suddenly withdrew. Things became quieter, but the enemy remained far from idle. Sergeant Jenkins, 'B' Company:

> I was actually in the trench with the rest of the platoon when I happened to look down to my left. We had quite an isolated place to our left, right down the road. I thought 'I don't believe this.' There were these Germans next to me, about six feet away! You could just see them through the bushes. I thought I was seeing things. There were about six to eight of them; they had crept through and were observing [the area of the bungalow]. They didn't realize we were actually there. Somebody shoved a grenade in there and captured a few of them, although I think a couple of them got away. They didn't get time to see what the situation was like.

*

During the afternoon there was a timely arrival at Brigade HQ when vehicles of the Field Ambulance seaborne party drew up in the yard. They had brought stores of all kinds and, vitally, a great stock of plasma. The MDS had only one bottle left. Also on board were the big packs containing personal kit. These were unloaded and a crowd immediately gathered around the pile, each man searching for his own pack. It was strange for them to see the names on the packs of those who were still missing. Perhaps, until that moment, many had been too preoccupied with their own jobs to notice just how many had failed to arrive. However, for those who had lost all their kit, the extra supply was very welcome as it enabled them to change out of their D-Day clothes, which still stank of the swamps.[8]

*

In the late afternoon, having returned from Robehomme with the Canadians, Sergeants Garrett and Britton headed for the 9th's position. Sergeant Garrett:

> Got back to the Battalion, had a look around and thought 'Crumbs, talk about out of the frying pan, into the fire!' We were absolutely horrified, there was hardly anybody there. I got some tea, met Sammy McGeever and he says, 'Ere you are, get down 'ere mate', and there was a shell trench there. I got down in that and stayed there, had some biscuits.

Sergeant McGeever had established the Vickers position and kept his team busy, preparing for the next assault. Corporal McGuinness:

> McGeever had us loading Jerry ammo, we'd found a few Jerry MGs in the Château. We were at it all afternoon. Then he told us to go and wash and shave, and would inspect us at 5pm. I had just finished washing when we heard small arms fire. Jerry was putting a counter-attack in, so I ran out with McGeever to the crossroads [driveway], he had the two front legs of the tripod on the edge and I was holding the rear leg and watching the belt. McGeever was firing, it seems there was a field full of Jerries. Mac and me couldn't see them but Russell was up a tree in a field opposite, giving us directions. Later on he slipped and fell to the ground, so it was home for him.

The Germans retired again.

*

Fred Garrett and John Britton had been among a slow trickle of stragglers that had begun to arrive in the Bois des Monts and these were not purely of the 9th Battalion. One of them was an experimental parachute tester whose unit had been drafted in to back up the Pathfinders of the 22nd Independent Parachute Company on D-Day. Harry Gray:

> We were extra ones under Captain Graham and there were only eight of us. 3X we were called.
> We were dropped near Colombelles. I never saw any of the other lads again. It was very, very tall grass. I knew we had to get up to the high ground afterwards. By hook or by crook I got up there. I got the shock of my life when I came across the 9th Battalion. They put me in a trench with 'A' Company![9]

147

Harry Gray.

Sid Capon had several stray Canadians dug in near him:

Harvey tied up two cows to a tree and relieved their laden udders. We filled our mess tins and opened tins of sardines. We had no hot food and drank the milk straight from the cows. What a mixture, sardines and biscuits and warm milk!

Fred Milward:

We had a peaceful evening and brewed up our tea. I had a piece of German cheese dished out when we were at Le Plein, so had an evening meal of biscuits, cheese and chocolate, washed down with tea made from cubes the size of an Oxo, containing sugar, milk and tea - but it was a drink! Washed and shaved, we settled down for the night, taking turns at sentry go.[10]

*

Although supplies were short, earlier, Staff Captain Woodgate, had managed to make a delivery to the Bois des Monts:

These had to be collected from our Divisional Maintenance area, which was located in a quarry a mile or two the other side of Ranville, and then delivered to units. The journey to the Divisional Maintenance area was hazardous, as Germans were all over the place and the road was under continuous bombardment. A lot of weapons were lost on the drop, and the Division was re-supplied by air each night, the drops being made on the Main Dropping Zone just outside Ranville. The supplies were gathered in by Divisional RASC. The Brigade and Commando Administrative Officers used to meet at Divisional HQ each day and the A/Q Divisional Staff used to allot the supplies to the Brigade representatives, and we used to return to our HQs with those and distribute them to our units. The 3rd Parachute Brigade had lost more than the other Parachute Brigade. So many people were dropped astray and in the flooded marshes.

Critically, the supplies included two 3-inch mortars and three Vickers machine guns. These arrivals allowed the Colonel to organize a platoon of four machine guns under Sergeant McGeever and a mortar section under Sergeant Hennessey. Nearly all of the trained machine-gunners and mortar men were still missing. Hennessey was actually a Rifle Company sergeant, but the Battalion policy was to train reserves for the specialist platoons and carry them in the Rifle Companies, from which they were taken in such emergencies as this. They set to work training the novice crews.

Of the Vickers machine guns, the original gun remained on the left-hand corner of the driveway covering the road from Breville. Another, in the charge of Corporal McGuinness was positioned at the junction of the road and the 'A' Company ditch along the edge of the wood, to cover the road from Le Mesnil. Sergeant McGeever mounted

Sergeant Hennessey.

another weapon on one of the jeeps, using sandbags to make a solid firing platform. This was to provide a mobile support and also give the impression of a larger force. The final gun was kept in reserve.

These reinforcements greatly increased the Battalion's capability to defend the position.

*

During the day, the Le Mesnil crossroads had again borne the brunt of the enemy effort, and probing continued in the evening. Gordon Newton was still dug in behind the road, just to the west of the crossroads. He was ordered to relieve two men who were in a ditch across the road, one of them being a sniper, Private Geoff 'Jock' Pattinson. Gordon Newton, 'A' Company:

> *Pattinson was lying on top of the bank smoking. I said, 'All right?' He said, 'Yeah, nothing going on,' and he flicked his cigarette up into the trees and promptly went back, whereupon a machine gun started firing across the field. In front of us was very, very, high corn. Standing out in the open was a German officer, and he was shouting at us. So I said to Dan Slater, 'Look, you'd better go back and tell somebody,' so he went back and told Gordon-Brown, whereupon Sergeant Woodcock came over and said, 'What's up mate?' At that point I could see soldiers jumping up in the corn, running, criss-crossing and getting down again. I said, 'Look, there are Germans out there.' He looked around. Nobody there. Every time he looked away they jumped up. Three times this happened and he never saw them. And with that, one jumped across the bloody hedge and I let him have it. Fortunately, the corn stopped quite a few yards in front, so in front was pretty clear.*

The Germans came on, and Newton and Woodcock began trying to pick them off:

> *When you're aiming, if a man's walking across, you slowly keep pace with his movement and aim one body width off, fire and follow through. If a man's running, aim two widths, pull the trigger with the rifle moving.*
>
> *We sat there for the best part of an hour firing at these Germans and they must have thought it was getting a bit dicey, so they withdrew.*

*

As darkness descended, the enemy remained a nuisance at the Bois des Monts. They were firing indiscriminately and throwing grenades. Major Smith:

> *The Germans came near to our position and called out in English. The objectives, I believe, were twofold; to keep us awake and to make us fire and disclose our automatic weapon positions. Our fire control was excellent and nothing was given away.*

The Germans had, on hearing the shouts of 'Stand To', responded by shouting 'Stand Down!' Gradually they retired. Ernie Rooke-Matthews:

> *The order came for us to 'Stand Down'. We had had no sleep on the night of 5th/6th June, and only a few hours on 7th/8th. The Sergeant [Paddy Jenkins] came along the bank giving his men their orders, organizing rest breaks etc... . We signallers were operating as a two-man team and I was on the bank in the forward position just across the sunken road; my mate was inside the garden of the bungalow. 'Get some sleep in,' said the Sergeant, 'I'll wake you if I need you.' I unrolled my gas cape, laid it on the ground and curled up, wrapping it around me for warmth and to keep out any rain or dew. Given the chance I could sleep on the proverbial clothes line - I was soon out to the world.[11]*

CHAPTER NINE

Pressure Mounts
Friday 9 June

The enemy activity during the night was partly successful in that it again prevented the Paras getting much sleep and just before dawn they were back again. Ernie Rooke-Matthews:

> *Someone was tapping me on the shoulder – it was the sergeant with a finger on his lips, 'Shush', warning me not to make a sound. 'It's 'Stand To.' I think we've got company,' or words to that effect – straight out of the films. I rolled my gas cape, checked my bits and pieces, nipped quickly across the road to check with my mate and straight back to the bank. It would soon be first light.*

Paddy Roche.

In the distance they heard the distinctive sound of mortars being fired. The men edged lower in their trenches and waited. As the bombs arrived overhead many began to detonate high among the thick foliage, showering the ground with broken branches and so reducing their effectiveness. However, some did get through and cause casualties. One of them, Private Tom 'Paddy' Roche, was hit in the back by a piece of shrapnel.[1] The Germans also used Nebelwerfers. Ernie Rooke-Matthews:

> *I needed no telling to keep my head down but watched in amazement and admiration as Sergeant Jenkins and another senior NCO moved calmly among us encouraging us, talking all the time, 'Keep your heads down lads', 'Keep your eyes open', 'Hold your fire, this will lift shortly.' He obviously had decided that this was one of those bombardments laid down to keep our head down while the enemy advanced to attack our positions.*

Sure enough, German infantry appeared in strength from behind the thick hedges to the north-west, again approaching 'HQ' and 'B' Company areas from each side of the Breville road:

> *We could now see the German troops advancing to our positions. As the sergeant had predicted, the bombardment had stopped. Still the sergeant moved among us, and I assumed our officers and other NCOs were performing a similar role. It just happened that this time the sergeant was right by my position.*
>
> *On they came – 'Hold it....' Then FIRE !' All along that bank and hedgerow our lads were firing rapid volleys. At the same time defensive fire was being put down in front of our position on the attackers.*

This supporting fire from the 3-inch mortars was welcome help and a distinct boost to morale. The Germans were within fifty yards of the wood. CSM Stoddart and his signal sergeant were firing at them when an enemy mortar bomb exploded nearby:

> *When I looked at Charlie, Sergeant Best that was, blood was*

Sergeant Charlie Best.

150

gushing from his ear. I was in such a panic that when I tried to get a field dressing out very quickly, it took even longer. Eventually I covered up his ear and he went back wounded.

Sergeant McGeever was firing the Vickers on the left-hand corner of the driveway when it just suddenly stopped. To the consternation of his No 2, Sergeant Garrett, instead of short-cutting to what might be the cause, McGeever began to calmly perform the Tests of Elementary Training; 'open the cover..., check for an empty cartridge case..., straighten the belt...', as if he was on a barrack square. There was no panic, even with the Germans so close. He did it the correct way, the way he had been taught. A soldier of the old school.

Sergeant McGeever.

Once more the Germans were forced to retire. Uniformed bodies littered the fields. A search began for any wounded among them and to gather information. On one corpse, a *Hauptmann* who had been hit by eight bullets, they found a copy of the instructions from Hitler stating that all captured parachutists were to be shot and a letter to his wife which forecast how he would drive the 'English' parachute troops back over the Orne.

On the Château side of the road, an untended double hedge had overgrown, creating a kind of tunnel. Stendall Brailsford found a wounded Polish soldier sheltering inside:

> *I took him back to the 'cottage'. It was drizzling. I stood him under the eaves of the 'cottage' and one of the lads came in with a Sten gun, and I'd got a .45 automatic, and he started to cry. He took out a photo of his wife and children. 'Mein Kinder, mein Kinder,' he was going. So we told him he was all right, we weren't going to shoot him as he'd been told.*

He waited to be interrogated. Private Max Hutton, a German Jew who had escaped from Germany just before the war, was the Battalion interpreter. Private Derek Higgins shared a trench with him:

> *When he was old enough he joined the Army and volunteered for the Para. He changed his name from Horwitz to Hutton after his favourite film star Betty Hutton! He interrogated all German prisoners before they were sent to Brigade HQ.*

When the order came to 'Stand Down', a 'skeleton force' was left to guard the perimeter while the remainder took the chance for a quick

Derek Higgins.

151

A photograph taken from a prisoner by Max Hutton.

wash, shave, a clean of the weapon and boots, and a bite to eat. Tea laced with Calvados was passed around. Ernie Rooke-Matthews:

> *Whilst the mortars were bursting around us I had felt a whack in my left leg, near my knee. I assumed it was obviously only blast because there was no indication of anything more. When the action eased I felt a bit sore and discovered that a piece of shrapnel had nicked the fleshy area above the knee cap. I was told to go to the Regimental Aid Post to have it dressed. I was lucky, a fragment of metal had removed a small portion of flesh above the knee, missing the bone. A clean dressing, a couple of pills, a mug of tea and the inevitable cigarette and I returned back to our position above the sunken road.*

The men had learned valuable lessons from this first enemy bombardment. CSM Ross:

> *A lot of us dug in trenches actually put a cover over the top, anything we could find, even if it was only bushes or twigs or something, so that this anti-personnel stuff didn't get at you.*

They also dug deeper. Ernie Rooke-Matthews:

> *Our slit trench was usually of sufficient depth to enable one to lie the whole body flat below ground level, but we were able to stand in the trench, using the ground around like a table. We were 'on line' which meant we had cable running back to BHQ with a field telephone on each end. We made a shelf for the handset inside the trench as a safety measure. Our main headache was that every time we had shell or mortar bursts the line would go – broken by shrapnel. One of us would then have to go out tracing the line back to the break to effect a repair. We soon discovered that there was no substance in the old soldier's tale that shells didn't hit the same place twice. Signaller's experience is that all too often when effecting a repair more 'flak' would fall on the same spot.*

*

An hour after the first attack the enemy began to re-appear, this time approaching from the north-east, through the Château wood. They were by now aware of the 'A' Company ditch and had dealt it a heavy bombardment, the first of many, and it gradually acquired the name 'Bomb Alley'.[2] Again, the Germans were allowed to get very close before the Paras finally opened up. Sergeant McGeever supported them, this time standing on the jeep, firing the Vickers gun through the hedges, whilst being driven up and down the road. The Germans were forced to withdraw yet again, leaving further dead behind. A relatively quiet period ensued.

*

At the driveway, duty on the Vickers was rotated amongst those who knew how to use it. Sergeant Daniels was one of them:

> *Colour Sergeant Graham came over to me and said, 'Do you fancy a cup of tea? Archie Barrett's brewing up across the road.' I said, 'Nip over and get me one would you?' He said, 'Fetch it yourself.' Well I can't leave the machine gun, but he said, 'I'll look after that.' 'Well what the bloody hell do you know about machine guns?' He said, 'Well I came from the Middlesex didn't I?' I said, 'Let's see you clear the gun.' He rattled it over no problems. So I came from the machine gun pit, just across the road, and BANG! What the bloody hell was that?*

He looked back.

> *I don't know quite what the grenade was that came over the hedge. But then the next two were these little 'blue top' shrapnel grenades. And then I saw another grenade come over the hedge. Jerry had come up alongside this hedge, thrown the grenades over into the pit. When he threw the grenades he was only a couple of yards away. I'm across the road by then. Laying there was Sergeant Holloway, and he'd been orderly room clerk and Quartermaster Sergeant's clerk, so he was not a fighting soldier, never handled weapons much. He was there with a Bren gun, so I said, 'Stanley!' and I grabbed the Bren and the bloody barrel came off. I put the barrel back on quick, I emptied the magazine through the corner of this hedge. I just blazed across. Colour Sergeant Graham was safe enough because he was low down. After I'd fired that magazine, that was it, nothing. We waited, tense, for what was going to happen. Things went quiet. Eventually I went back across the road, got Colour Sergeant Graham back.*
>
> *And so Colour Sergeant Graham got the shrapnel from three, if not four grenades. Every time a grenade exploded he turned back to that gun. He was knocked about with a lot of shrapnel, but it was all sort of 'cocoa tin' shrapnel, and as luck would have it this stick grenade that came over had got a concussion head on. While of course in an open space the concussion wasn't too bad, but if it had been in a room it would have killed us. So he was lucky and he got away with it.*
>
> *I went and had a look through that hedge and I could see a pair*

Colour Sergeant Len Graham.

Colour Sergeant Archie Barrett.

153

of boots, the soles of them were towards me. I could see that the toes were upwards. If you are hugging the earth when you're frightened your toes are down, so I knew he must be dead, so I crawled up and there was this massive great Jerry laid there. He'd got a bandolier of Verey light cartridges over him, and it sounds silly, but this was the way it was. He'd got a Schmeisser slung across him, and he'd also got a rifle and bayonet in his hand. He had three stick grenades in his belt, the concussion grenades, only they hadn't got the shrapnel heads on them. Everything had been hit by a bullet, somewhere. I'm of the opinion that he was the only one who came up there, a death or glory man come up to knock that machine gun out, especially as I sprayed the Bren about. There would have been more than him killed. I went through his pockets and I took out his forage cap and his paybook. I took them back and gave them to Colour Sergeant Graham. I said, 'Here are some souvenirs of the bloke that wounded you.' Being a time-serving soldier he realized the importance of that gun. If it had got into the hands of Jerry, they would have depleted our force in double-quick time.[3]

*

Shortly after, Major Dyer arrived at the Bois des Monts to see Colonel Otway. Sergeant Daniels:

> *That's when he rounded us up, ten or fifteen, something like that, took some of us down there* [Le Mesnil crossroads] *with him. It was 'You, you, you and you come with me!'*

On arriving at the crossroads, Daniels joined the others on the bank behind the hedge, facing the farm. Just up the road Lieutenant Lepper's men had continued to resist in the isolated house. The thick, high wall around the building had played a vital part in their survival because it only gave the enemy two openings to exploit. These were gates at the front and back. Lieutenant Jock Lepper:

Lieutenant 'Jock' Lepper.

> *We had held the position all night and in the morning I posted our one and only Bren gun about twenty-five yards to our rear in a ditch bordering the road that connected with the remainder of the Company. Private Undrill was manning the gun and a short time after he was in position I noticed that he was lying flat on his face. He appeared to have been shot by one of the snipers who were firing from some trees on our left flank. I ordered Corporal Gower to give me covering fire with his rifle whereupon I jumped into the ditch and crawled to Undrill. He was still conscious and I found a bullet hole in the middle of his back. I cut away his smock, tunic and vest in the region of the hole and uncovered a nasty looking wound between his shoulder blades that indicated the bullet had lodged in his lungs. I applied his shell dressing and then crawled along the rest of the ditch towards the Company lines. I attracted the attention of a sentry and yelled for stretcher-bearers and crawled back to Undrill, who was by then unconscious. I got hold of the Bren and magazines, fired a burst at the trees where the snipers were, then got up and dashed back to the farmhouse. Corporal Gower's covering fire had the effect of upsetting the sniper's aim. I remember feeling thankful that I had a small behind.*

His action re-started the firing:

> *Judging by the increase in the racket, the Germans had brought up more machine guns. Within an hour of my return all firing suddenly ceased. For a moment I wondered if my hearing had packed in completely as a German stick grenade had damaged my eardrums in the night. I then saw a surprising sight. Two German prisoners carrying a stretcher accompanied by a medical officer from Brigade HQ were coming towards us. I got up and pointed to where Undrill was lying and the medical officer quickly acknowledged and signed to me to keep my head down. Undrill was safely evacuated together with one of my walking wounded who joined the party.*[4]

154

Lepper, Gower and Tucker remained in a perilous position.

Sergeant Daniels did not have to wait long for a welcome to the hedge position:

> We were getting mortared by 20mm mortars, along the front of the hedge. Major Dyer said to me, 'Sergeant Daniels, can't you stop that bloody mortaring!' So I thought 'Where the hell is he?' I wasn't going to stick my head where these mortar bombs were dropping, so I came down to this stile and looked across. Out in front of the farm there was a well and as I am looking across there, I saw the plume of a little smoke ring as the mortar fired and I thought 'Where did that come from?' As I am looking through my glasses I saw a Jerry pop up to watch the strike of the mortar bomb. Down he went. He was behind the well. A few seconds later he fired again. Up came his head again and had another look, so I thought there might be something going here. He fired again; one, two, three, four, five, six – up came Jerry. He fired again; one, two, three, four, five, six – up he came. He fired again; one, two, three, four, five, six, I pulled the trigger, and Jerry stepped right up into the bullet. Whether he was on his own firing that mortar I don't know, but that was the last of that mortar.

Sergeant Len Daniels.

*

During the afternoon, sporadic fighting continued as the Germans again infiltrated through the Château wood in an area between the Bois des Monts and Brigade HQ, again threatening the road link. Sergeant Arthur Mobsby of 'A' Company was dug in on the south-western corner of the Le Mesnil crossroads:

> A jeep came to us, Red Cross. A bloke stopped and said, 'I've got myself a good job', and it was Eddie Easlea of 'A' Company. He told us that the Battalion was reforming at the Château St Côme.

Easlea's 'good job' was in fact the hazardous task of driving the wounded from the Bois des Monts to the MDS. Later, he was stopped by some Germans who laid the casualties at the side of the road and took off with him, the jeep and pouches that contained Padre Gwinnett's Communion set.

This infiltration proved a continual problem for the jeeps ferrying casualties.

Enemy presence in this area became even more worrying when the sound of tracks could also be heard and Bomb Alley came in for some 'unwelcome attention'. Major Charlton was ordered to form a patrol. Colonel Otway:

> We knew it was either a tank or a self-propelled gun. Something was making life hell for 'A' Company. So I told him to take a few men to find out if they were light tanks coming up for a counter-attack which I thought most unlikely, so I sent him to find out what was happening.

Charlton ran over to the area east of the bungalow and gathered

Sergeant Eddie Easlea.

155

Lieutenant Parfitt and around ten men, including Sergeants Rose and Lukins and Privates Harold Walker, Courtney and Morris. Sid Capon was also there:

> *Because I knew Major Dyer, Charlton said to me, 'Stay there, Major Dyer's coming in with reinforcements'.*

The patrol moved off. Harold 'Johnnie' Walker:

> *We crossed the road, across an open field and then we went into a bit of a wood. I just followed them about thirty to forty yards behind. We reached a bit of a glade and there was a tree stuck in the middle of it. German machine guns opened up. My Sten gun jammed. I dropped down beside the tree and a Bren gunner was there. He said, 'There's snipers up there.' I said, 'I'll crawl back and get the lads in the ditch to give some covering fire.' So I started crawling and one went close to my backside so I got up and ran. I dived through the hedge and got caught in it, and they had to pull me down. I said, 'Give that Bren gunner covering fire,' and he came dashing out. The first thing he said when he reached us was, 'Give us a fag!'[5]*

Harold 'Johnnie' Walker.

The patrol had been caught in the flank by crossfire from two machine guns, which split the group. Charlton, Parfitt, Rose and Courtney were killed and five others wounded. Parfitt's batman, Private Morris, had managed to retaliate, killing several Germans. Ken Walker:

> *I was probably saved by the toss of a coin. Harry Courtney and I tossed a coin and with me winning, he went on the patrol led by Major Charlton.[6]*

The enemy movement had been stopped, but at a painful price.

*

Later in the afternoon Lieutenant Smythe's twenty 'A' Company men moved up to the Bois des Monts. Reg 'Knocker' Knights:

Frank Carey.

Sergeant Paddy Costello.

On arrival at the Bomb Alley area our Platoon Commander, Hugh Smythe, with eight other men, left us to join up with the main body of 'A' Company.

We now had twelve men: Sergeant Albert Woodcock, Corporals Frank Carey, Len Poulter and Paddy Costello, Bailey, myself and six others. Six of us entered Bomb Alley. The other six men moved across the road and dug slit trenches in the wood. Unlike the situation at the Le Mesnil crossroads, our Sten guns were now exactly suited to our task. The thickness of the trees and underbrush in the wood limited our view to about thirty feet.

*

Having spent the best part of a day lying in the ditch, Doug Tottle, who was still unable to see, heard some troops on the move. He began shouting and they came over. These turned out to be 9th Battalion men and they immediately got a stretcher and carried him to the MDS. Tottle was another loss to the Battalion's medical section. Only four men, Captain Watts, Sergeant Spencer, Tottle and Private Anderson had reached the Bois des Monts. Fortunately, during the previous two days three medical orderlies had been acquired from other units, Liddell and Allen of the 12th Battalion and Blakeley of the 7th. However, due to this shortage, all available MDS members of 3 Section of the Field Ambulance, these being Corporal Cranna, Privates Stothers, Sparrow, Newcomb and Bramwell, were ordered to reinforce the Battalion's medical set-up.

Taking a jeep, they were proceeding along the road to the Bois des Monts with John Gwinnett when they were flagged down at a cottage on the roadside. Inside was a Canadian Major who had been sniped through a window while talking to the woman of the house. It was explained that he could not be brought out of the cottage by the front entrance as it was commanded by the sniper hidden in some trees two or three hundred yards away. There was no entrance or windows at the back, and so, using a large lump of timber lying by the roadside, they battered a hole in the wall, carried him out through it and placed him on the jeep. Leaving the rest of the party in the cover of the cottage, Newcomb set off brandishing a Red Cross flag and promising to be back within a quarter of an hour.

9th Battalion medical section. Front left is Sergeant Spencer; beside him is Harold Watts, then Doug Tottle. Front right is Robert Ferguson

Half an hour later he had not reappeared, so they decided to continue on foot.[7] James Bramwell:

I went up there with the Padre, and we had quite an exciting time getting up [there] because we had to crawl half the way when we were almost there, to avoid a sniper. So we arrived rather sort of flustered! We arrived just as there was a tremendous shoot-out going on, with chattering machine guns and so on.... When we got there we expected to find everybody dead. Not at all. It was just one of those things that happened with machine guns. They suddenly all started chattering, and in fact nobody was hurt at all. And so, we found nobody there except in the Dressing Station which was a tool shed behind the villa. Captain Watts, the Medical Officer of the 9th Battalion and his faithful orderly [Sergeant Spencer], who was always with him, was just brewing up tea. Just at that moment the enemy opened up again with mortar bombs and he told me to dig myself a trench at once. I tried to find a place under a tree, and started digging and flopped into a kind of shell-hole and waited, until a bomb landed almost on top of me, just near enough to stop my ears [working] for a time. So then I got up and went back to the tool shed to get my tea.

What was so interesting was arriving at the back part of this villa and finding all this garden or space under the pine trees all full of trenches. There were people popping up on every side like mushrooms with their steel helmets, and lighting their gas cookers, brewing up.[8]

'Popping Up Like Mushrooms'. One of Albert Richards' paintings of the men in the Bois des Monts.

Ron Tucker.   *Corporal Gus Gower.*

Meanwhile, Lieutenant Lepper, Corporal Gower and Private Tucker were still isolated in the house near the crossroads. Ron Tucker:

> *I thought I'd try and make some tea, so I poured some tea and water in the mess tin, we had these little mess stoves.... I sat with my back to the wall, facing the doorway. A shell came through the room, through the wall, made a lovely clean hole and it sort of sucked me with it through the door and threw me in the yard. It didn't explode. And when I went back there was no sign of my mess tin. I've no idea what happened to it. I lost my enthusiasm for making tea after that!*

Around 5.00pm the firing became more intense:

> *We didn't know what the hell was happening. There was a battle going on outside and it just got louder and louder. We knew that there wasn't many at the crossroads, we just imagined that they'd polished them off, and we were going to be the next.*

They were very short of ammunition and began preparing themselves for a 'last ditch stand'. Tucker and his good friend Gus Gower dug a position facing the closed doors and waited:

> *We both agreed not to become POWs and it was Gus who suggested we keep one '36' grenade should we be overrun at the house.*

Suddenly the doors burst open. They were just about to open fire when Captain Robinson appeared, followed by a few men. Ron Tucker:

> *Robinson put his arms around Jock Lepper; there were tears in his eyes. A counter-attack by a Canadian Company had restored the situation.*

As the Paras left, they passed Canadian and German bodies lying about, some only a few feet short of the doorway. The Canadians took over the house.

*

At around 7.00pm, Major Dyer's group left the hedge position to make its way to the Bois des Monts. John Speechley:

> When we moved off I saw all these lads lying five paces away from each other, all facing one way. As I walked along the bank I stepped over his feet, two paces, stepped over his feet, and I'm counting them; eleven, twelve.... They must have been a mixture of our lads and Canadians. At first I thought they were all on watch while we moved off, so I put my feet on the back of one of them, on the back of his boots, and pushed to see if he'd turn round. And I realized the poor buggers were all dead. I don't know whether a Spandau swept them. That upset me.

Suddenly a Spandau did open up:

> Someone gave me a burst as I dived for a tree. Didn't hit me, he hit the tree and I got splinters in my fingers. I thought 'That's better than bullets!'

After a brief halt at Brigade HQ they then headed along a wooded lane with a section in front as an advanced guard. After a while some shots were aimed at them.

> I think it was a Corporal, he stopped one across the shoulder. We had a look at him and I said, 'You're alright' and he had two nicks, two bullets, and they'd just clipped his left shoulder. That didn't come in from the front, that was from behind. It was our own fire.

Major Dyer:

> There were one or two shots, and we all dived down. We stayed down, my blokes f..... and blinding... . It wasn't until I heard some four-letter words coming from the woods that I knew we were back with our own people.

It was around 9.00pm. Sid Capon was waiting for them:

> It was very eerie to tell the truth... all of a sudden you hear a rustle, and it was him! What a welcome relief to see him with these men.

John Speechley:

> I went down the ditch and the first bloke I saw was Sid Capon, and he looked at me and I'd never seen eyes like it. When blokes have had stick, your eyes are like organ stops! He'd had a fair bit of wear and tear! And alright, fair do's, he's been in a bit of a scrape here and before; [but he said] 'And where the f... have you been?', as if nothing had happened down the road! 'I've had my own little war, what d'ya think!' 'Bleedin' things are rough here!' he said.

Seeing that Capon was still without a helmet, Major Dyer ordered him to get one, so he went and found one in a pile of dead men's helmets which was stashed near the Bois des Monts gate.

Colonel Otway greeted Major Dyer:

> The first thing the Colonel said to me was, 'Would you like some milk laced with brandy?', I think it was. So I said, 'Yes I would, very much!' So I downed that, and he said, 'I want you to go and clear that wood over there'.

The Germans had been mortaring the Bois des Monts from the area of the Château, and the Colonel wanted the patrol to make a reconnaissance of the grounds and if possible to capture the mortar positions. Major Dyer went back to his men:

> These blokes were very tired as you can imagine, and there were lots of trees to lean against. So they did, and went straight to sleep standing up.

At 10.00pm Dyer and approximately twenty men, including Captain Robinson, Lieutenant Lepper, Sergeant Daniels and Ron Tucker were waiting to start when shells began to burst in the wood. Everybody fell flat on the ground and, as the explosions crept nearer, they crawled about trying to find slit trenches, but the last and nearest shell burst forty yards away and the patrol was only delayed for about half an hour. By the time they had crossed the road it was nearly dark and entering the wood made it pitch black, so in order to maintain contact, each man had to hold on to the person in front. Bringing up the rear of the column were four stretcher-bearers, Liddell, Blakeley, Sparrow and Bramwell, who were unable to wear Red Cross armbands for fear of giving away the patrol. About halfway to the Château a repeated shout for help could be heard.[5] John Speechley:

> *We were getting nearer and nearer and Major Dyer was shouting, 'Shut up!'*

They came upon the wounded Para lying in a ditch under a thick hedge. He was a survivor of Major Charlton's patrol. The soldier was asked about his officer. John Speechley:

> *He said, 'I think he's dead sir, I haven't heard of him for about an hour.' We got in this opening, a bit of a glen and they'd walked right into that glen and the Krauts had been either side, opened up on them with Spandaus. They'd made a run for it but there were a few left in the middle.*

They found Charlton's body and those of 'Ginger' Parfitt and Sergeant Rose. A Spandau had cut the top of Rose's head clean off. Bramwell and Sparrow were left to tend the wounded man and carry him back to the Bois des Monts while the other two stretcher-bearers continued with the patrol.

Sergeant James Rose.

After about half an hour of stopping and starting, they could not find their way through the wood and became lost. It was decided to split the group in two, one part led by Major Dyer, the other by Sergeant Daniels. Dyer's group retraced its steps to the road and set out once more by the field along the edge of the wood.

As luck would have it Sergeant Daniels' group came out of the wood near the Château and met Dyer's party. They advanced and lay down in a large circle between two rows of trees in front of the Château. Twenty minutes later the patrol moved on 200 yards. A ten minute German mortar bomb barrage then landed on the exact spot that they had just vacated.

The patrol moved to another position where the front of the stables was visible. Jock Lepper ordered Tucker to fire the Bren at each window and doorway. Straw inside caught fire but no one came out. They carried on to the Château and found it deserted, the Germans having withdrawn, leaving only their dead behind. However, during the return journey

Lieutenant Gordon 'Ginger' Parfitt.

they came under sniper fire. Ron Tucker was ordered to fire a few bursts into the suspect trees across the field.

Approaching the Bois des Monts, they were met by CSM Beckwith. Sergeant Daniels:

> *He'd got a Bren gun with him. He whispered, 'I want you to stay out here tonight, and if Jerry comes up, empty the magazine into them and get back as quick as you can.'*

To counter German probing during the night, defensive posts were being pushed forward, outside the Bois des Monts perimeter, to keep the enemy out of grenade-throwing range.

> *'Well,' I said, 'I can't keep my eyes open.' He said, 'I've thought of that, and I've brought you a couple*

of Benzedrine tablets.' I lay there after taking two Benzedrine tablets, and these Benzedrines keep you awake. Being dog-tired they tend to make you hallucinate. You are kind of half-dozing and you wake up.... I could see bloody bushes moving. I could see Jerries running towards these bloody trees. Got the Bren ready, had another look, there's nothing. Several times I dozed, and after a very, very, long night Wally eventually came down and took me back in again.

It was a similar experience for all those on night sentry duty. Sergeant Woodcraft:

Our eyes burnt and felt full of grit. You would bend the knees, stretch the arms, anything to stay awake, but in spite of this, the head would fall forward and you would almost be asleep on your feet.

Nights were especially testing in Bomb Alley. 'Knocker' Knights:

The occasional mortar attacks, the frequent whispered messages that an attack was expected and the possibility that the enemy was in position a few yards away in the woods made sleep almost impossible until ultimately, exhaustion took charge and drove our minds blank.

*

Captain Gordon-Brown's arrival from the crossroads with his 'A' Company party, plus stragglers who had continued to arrive, raised the number at the Bois des Monts to around 270 men, roughly half normal active strength, the strongest it had yet been in Normandy. Gordon-Brown assumed command of 'A' Company, 'B' Company was under Captain Greenway, Major Dyer commanded 'C' Company, Major Smith was now the Colonel's second in command and Lieutenant Slade continued as Battalion Adjutant.

On the supply side, the Battalion's seaborne party had not yet arrived, but this was hardly surprising, considering the strategic situation. However, the only immediate ammunition shortage was 3-inch mortar bombs. Some compo rations and water had arrived from Brigade HQ but barely enough to keep them going. It was a precarious hand-to-mouth existence that left little in reserve, but tiredness was the big problem and the men were taking every opportunity to doze.

*

Unbeknown to the Battalion, under cover of darkness some Germans had moved through Breville and taken up position in the cover of the orchards south-west of the Bois des Monts. Lieutenant Colonel Luard's 13th Parachute Battalion, holding Ranville and Le Mariquet, spotted movement in that area at 3.00am, but could not be sure who it was. And so, in case of an attack, an artillery FOO had been requested from the 5th Parachute Brigade HQ. It was a portent for the day ahead.[9]

CHAPTER TEN

Onslaught
Saturday 10 June

Just before dawn the men at the Bois des Monts 'Stood To', although by first light everything remained quiet. They stood down and morning ablutions began, but this peaceful period was not to last.

At 5.30am the Commandos were subjected to heavy mortar fire, although they were not attacked.

Half an hour later the FOO requested by the 13th Battalion arrived in Ranville and took up position in the church tower. He was asked to register the openings from the suspect orchards, plus two crossroads on the LZ which were likely forming-up points for any attack, and these were immediately subjected to the fire of one field regiment.

Around 7.00am Stirlings appeared overhead on a supply drop, and anti-aircraft fire emanating from the suspected areas confirmed the enemy's presence. Something was brewing.

Twenty-five minutes later a bombardment of the Ranville crossroads began, initiating the first concerted German effort to exploit the 'Breville gap'. The II/857th Grenadier Regiment had been ordered to capture the LZ while the III/857th passed through and consolidated. This was in coordination with a simultaneous assault on the southern flank of the Airborne perimeter, their ultimate target being the precious bridges.

About fifty Germans emerged from the orchards south-west of the Bois des Monts. In Ranville and Le Mariquet the 13th Battalion watched them coming down the slope in extended order. The FOO called in accurate artillery fire, but it could not stop the first wave reaching the large amount of abandoned gliders. By 7.45am the supporting German companies had also left the orchards and a whole Battalion was spread across the fields over a length and depth of around 800 yards. Advancing through the waist-high crops they gradually began forming up amongst the gliders. The 13th Battalion held its fire.

The enemy then emerged from the gliders, heading in two directions; towards the northern end of Ranville and also the eastern side and some orchards by the crossroads. The northern attack was broken up by artillery fire and the few who did manage to infiltrate were duly dealt with.

The advance on the eastern area was met by defensive mortar fire, but all small arms fire was withheld. By 8.25am the Germans had been allowed to reach a crosstracks within thirty yards of the Paras, at which point the 13th Battalion opened sustained fire with automatic weapons, including six captured German machine guns and a Vickers. It halted the attack, but being pinned down, many of the survivors remained spread among the crops and orchards to the east of the village, and they continued to probe.[1]

In conjunction with this assault, at 8.00am an attack from Breville had gone in against No 6 Commando at Amfreville, along with probing forays on Nos 3 and 4 Commandos to their north, and these were continuing.

*

With all the German activity in Breville and on the LZ, Colonel Otway sent a reconnaissance patrol forward to the Château St Côme. Sergeants Doug Woodcraft and Jimmy 'Cocker' Frith led Lance Corporal Jack Watkins, Jock Pattinson, Ken Walker, a Bren gunner and two other 'A' Company riflemen, plus a signalman from Battalion HQ. Sergeant Woodcraft:

> *Our task was to search it and the stables, stay there and report back by radio every fifteen minutes the*

current position. Jimmy Frith and I tossed up who should search the Château or the stables. I won and chose the Château.

They moved forward in bounds along the drive ditches, but before reaching the building Woodcraft gave Ken Walker a specific task:

I was posted amongst a hedge on the left of the Château and some 100 yards from the building as fixed forward observation patrol. This point was overlooking fields towards Breville and was the most likely line of advance of any enemy patrol or attacking force. My line of vision encompassed a wide area, so as soon as Jerry was coming in I had to shoot off, warn them off and we'd pull out.

The patrol carried on into the Château and searched the ground floor. Doug Woodcraft:

Then we went upstairs. Hugging the wall, I cautiously started up, turned a sharp corner and got the shock of my life, for there confronting me was a scruffy figure clad in a camouflage smock, parachutist's helmet with scrim hanging down over his face and pointing a gun at me. Before I could do anything stupid I realized I was looking at myself in a full-length mirror! I leant against the wall for some moments to let my backside return to normal before going on.

I went into the first room. This happened to be the officers' dormitory. All the beds were still made up and personal effects littered the place, including some rather nice Leica cameras. The next room I have always been intrigued by. I crossed to the window and drew the curtains slightly. There were two beds, both strewn with women's dresses, stockings, underclothing etc. as if someone had been packing in a hurry. Whether they were members of German Women's forces or comforts for the officers I do not know.

Lance Corporal Jack Watkins.   **Sergeant Doug Woodcraft.**

Jock Pattinson also went up the stairs, and the landing mirror caused a similar effect on him! What didn't help was the sight of his sunken eyes caused by the strain and lack of sleep of the previous days.

With the Château again being unoccupied, Woodcraft spoke to Pattinson:

Sergeant Woodcraft ordered Corporal Jack Watkins and myself to go through the outhouses of the Château towards the Germans, to establish whether there were any mobile 88mm guns in the vicinity.

They therefore passed through the stables and continued beyond, along the low wall of a kitchen garden.

Geoff 'Jock' Pattinson.

With Jack leading, he stopped, put out his arm and pressed me against the wall. He said, 'When I start to run, follow me back to the outhouses.'

Lance Corporal Watkins:

A German soldier put his head around the end of the wall about seventy-five yards away. All I saw was his head and the nasty end of an automatic weapon.

Jock Pattinson:

We started to run and all hell broke loose. We got to the opening of the barn which was only wide enough for one person, and we fell in. The German was clever. He was firing into the stable knowing that it was all concrete. The bullets were ricocheting around the place. I felt a pain across the back of both legs as though somebody had laid a red-hot poker on them. I don't know whether it was a bullet or a piece that chipped off the wall.

Being 'rather upset' at this he ran out into the cobbled yard and looked over a large corn bail to see where the firing was coming from, but Corporal Watkins called him back. Pattinson was then shocked to find that his boots were full of blood, so they both decided to 'get out of it' and went back through the stables towards the Château where Sergeant Woodcraft was continuing his search of the upstairs rooms:

The last room evidently housed someone of importance because there were large-scale maps of the area on the walls and a roll-top desk which I tried to open but it was locked. I got hold of a poker, inserted it in the lock and heaved and, as if that were a signal, bursts of automatic fire started up beneath the windows. Dropping everything, we tore down the corridor and stairs just in time to meet Jimmy Frith and Jack Watkins running in through the door. Jack Watkins was shouting, 'Look out, Jerry's out there and they've hit Jock.' At that moment, over Jack Watkin's shoulders, I saw Jock run past and off down the drive.

By now our Bren gunner was in action and Jack Watkins was sent out to stoke up some more fire whilst we got the signaller out. We did this by telling him to go to the far side of the room and to run like hell. By the time he got to the door he was flat out and away he went down the drive; we could see sparks as bullets hit the cobbles just behind him.

We now had to get out, but it was impossible to use the door as the Germans were concentrating their fire on it. The woodwork was rapidly being reduced to splinters and pieces of brickwork were flying about. We shouted to Watkins to get back down the drive and we would go out through the French windows on the other side of the room. When we reached these we found they were locked but by running at them together we went out onto the lawn amongst pieces of window frame and broken glass.

We picked ourselves up and ran for the wood the other side of the lawn and just reached it in time to see a small party of Germans come round the far end of the Château in hot pursuit. Instead of running straight through and into the orchard we turned left and found ourselves in a German transport park consisting of horse-drawn vehicles. We took up a position behind one of these and, as the small party of

Germans passed by some twenty yards in front of us, we both opened up with our Stens and, without waiting to see the result, we turned and galloped down through the wood, yelling 'Olly! Olly!', the rallying call of 'A' Company.

As Doug Woodcraft had seen, Pattinson had run past the Château, but then using the building as cover, continued across the field into Bomb Alley. Sergeant Mobsby:

When Geoff came running down the ditch, the blood was pumping out of his wounds. I stopped him and put my field dressing on it. 'Cocker' was laughing his head off when they came down behind Jock!

'Cocker' Frith's amusement arose from the rather unfortunate position of the wound, but it was one of the worst gashes that Mobsby had ever seen. Pattinson was taken over the road to the RAP.[2] During all of this, everyone had forgotten about Ken Walker:

I did not see them but could hear heavy firing of small arms but I could not see any activity from the Château nor any communication from our troops. Then without orders I thought it was prudent to return to HQ and crossing the tall grass or grain in the field I returned to the Battalion. On nearing the driveway this horrible figure stepped out with a revolver in his hand pointing it directly towards me and a voice shouting the words to the effect, 'It's a wonder I didn't blow your f...... head off!' It was Sergeant McGeever protecting his machine gun. He safely negotiated, I made my safe return to HQ.

*

Joe Hughes.

At 10.00am the Paras in Ranville counter-attacked and cleared many of the Germans lying in front of them on the LZ, taking twenty prisoners. The survivors joined others who had earlier taken cover in the nearby woods at Le Mariquet.[3] This had caused another problem because a gap remained in the Airborne perimeter between the 3rd and 5th Parachute Brigades, and the German occupation of one of these woods severed road contact. Private Joe Hughes of the 3rd Brigade Defence Platoon discovered this a little later. He was the assigned escort for the BRASCO (Brigade RASC Officer), Captain Donald Cooper, and a driver on one of the supply trips to the Divisional dump:

The road was not controlled by us and after a while the lorry stopped and the driver shouted there were Jerries blocking the road. I shouted to get going and we went through them. I opened up with my Sten and definitely got three of them. Just as we went through, one of them must have thrown a grenade and it went off in the road behind us. I sprayed them with my Sten to keep their heads down.

We checked the lorry when we arrived at the Div. Dump and the amount of holes in the lorry! It was a wonder we were not wiped out.

This was a situation that could not be allowed to continue for long.

*

By 10.30am the attack on Nos 3 and 6 Commandos had petered out and the Germans, having suffered heavy losses, had been forced back into Breville, although No 4 Commando was still heavily engaged in the Hauger area.

At 11.00am it was the 9th Battalion's turn to receive some 'attention'. The 'A' Company area was attacked through the Château wood, but it was a weak, unsupported company attack and they were smartly driven off.

The pivotal point in the 'A' Company defensive area was the Vickers machine gun of Corporal McGuinness and Private Fenson. Reg 'Knocker' Knights:

> *McGuinness was dug-in at the end of Bomb Alley. I think they'd dug a trench across the corner, and the earth from it formed a bank. The gun fired down the road towards Le Mesnil.*

During their attacks from the east and north-east the Germans had paid a fearful price in learning about this weapon. The ditches on either side of the road were full of decomposing bodies. John Speechley saw McGuinness in action:

> *He was a bit of a lad, 'Let the bastards come up!' He was a hard nut, good soldier though, an Indian 'wallah'. He'd been to India; full of transfers... . He sat there cross-kneed, a few bags and bits of rubbish 'round. He was enjoying himself. All the lads were feeding him at a distance! He was bollocking them, 'Let's have some bleeding rounds!' You didn't have a German on that road. Without that machine gun, trouble, definitely in trouble.*

Consequently, the enemy made several specific attempts to silence this Vickers. 'Knocker' Knights witnessed one when he was just across the road:

Reg Knights is centre-right, Corporal McGuinness at the back.

> *A German machine gun started firing at us from the wooded area up the road. I dived into the nearest trench, which I hadn't dug, and it was only about a foot deep. I was face up and the Germans were firing tracer which was passing across my face, and I couldn't move! I thought if they attack now I've had it. Anyway, Gordon-Brown came out and said, 'Start firing back', so we did and the machine gun stopped. He then said, 'Advance and flush them out.' So we started to creep through the undergrowth when suddenly to my left, across the road, I spotted a German with a rifle and a camouflage net over his face, I think it was one of ours. So I crept nearer, got ready to fire my Sten and the bloody thing clicked. Jammed! I quickly shook it because the Stens were notorious for cross-feeds, and when I looked up he'd dived into the undergrowth, so I sprayed the area.*

Len Poulter discovered the German's body the next day.

Len Poulter (front) and 'Cocker' Frith.

Sergeant Woodcraft witnessed another attempt:

I was crouched over a spirit stove, brewing up, when something made me look at my mate. Before I could speak he motioned me to silence and pointed just over my head, I looked up to see the bushes part and the head and shoulders of a German soldier come into view. How he failed to see us I will never know but all his attention was on the Vickers position. He raised his arm and in his hand was a stick grenade; before he could throw it my mate shot him. As he fell his helmet came off, striking me on the shoulder. In his wallet were photos of his wife and two small children who, unbeknown to them, had just lost their father.

*

During the morning Colonel Otway had been assessing the events that had unfolded and tried to anticipate what was to follow by putting himself in the position of the German commander. Accordingly, half an hour after the attack through the wood, he sent a platoon from 'A' Company over to the driveway, where they occupied about fifty yards of the ditch on the right-hand side. He also placed two Vickers machine guns in ditches astride the main road pointing towards Breville.

At noon, just as the guns had been sited, fifty German infantrymen filed out of the fields between St Côme and Breville, less than 500 yards away. Fred Milward was in the driveway ditch:

A load of Germans came out the hedge on the road, stacked their rifles and started digging along the side of the road as though they were preparing a firing point for an attack on the DZ, across the fields. We'd been there two or three days, they knew we were there, this is the peculiar part. Yet they came there absolutely out in the open.

Two Brens were immediately rushed up from 'B' Company. Sergeant Daniels:

I don't know who was on the machine-gun pit then, but he let fly up the road, and the next thing was a white flag came out. They were called forward and the Germans came out of the ditch. I saw them walking up the road.

They were taken prisoner and duly forwarded to Brigade HQ.

Fifteen minutes after this incident, 'A' Company's advanced position along the drive spotted a

small German patrol approaching them. Sergeant Mobsby:

They came from the west. They were almost on top of us before we could see them. There must have been ten or twelve of them I think. One of them had a radio on his back. We tossed grenades and I think we killed four or five of them. The others must have got away 'cos we didn't take any prisoners.

Some of the Germans had got so close that they actually fell into the platoon's ditch. The 'A' Company men were pulled back inside the defensive perimeter.

At 12.20pm a company of Germans supported by heavy artillery, mortar fire and three tanks, advanced down the slope from Breville, towards the LZ. The 13th Parachute Battalion again blocked the attack in devastating fashion.

*

Sergeant Arthur Mobsby.

168

By 2.00pm a good many of the enemy had accumulated around the Château St Côme and firing erupted, particularly from the stable area. This continued for about an hour until around a company of infantry started to try and edge along each side of the driveway. Two tanks supported them, firing into 'A' and 'HQ' Company areas. John Speechley:

> *The tanks, MkIVs, 75mm guns, they were right down by the horse stables. They turned their turrets and gave us some stick. What I noticed was they were hitting trees and slicing through the foliage but not blowing up. Another one hit a tree and literally chopped the tree clean. The stump fell down beside the main base and stayed trapped in its own foliage. I thought to myself 'Well that bugger never blew up.' It dawned on me that the tanks were fired up with solid shot for tank warfare.*

The mortar section responded but rapidly began to run out of bombs. Sergeant Knight suggested using the PIATS as mortars by firing them at high trajectory into the enemy infantry. Colonel Otway:

> *I thought it a good idea. It didn't work from the point that it caused a lot of casualties; it was rather like a stun grenade. It was a colossal explosion, a hell of a row.*

After a few minutes some of the PIAT bombs set the stables alight.

One of the armoured vehicles advanced as far as the start of the drive's loop, where it opened fire. Ron Phelps:

> *The German tank I saw came out from the Château, facing us through the gate. I don't know exactly what weapon was used to put it off because it appeared to me as though something caught fire on it. It perhaps had been sprayed with a machine gun and caught fire. It wasn't actually destroyed but it was put off. It went back on its way. It retired ungracefully!*

What he had not seen was Sergeant McGeever burst through the driveway entrance with the jeep-mounted Vickers and engage it, and to everyone's amazement and utter delight it 'blew up'. This signalled the end of another attack, as the German infantry gradually began to withdraw from the maelstrom of explosions, burning buildings and squealing horses.

When it had quietened down, CSM Beckwith and another 'B' Company man worked their way forward to the stables in an effort to free some of the horses, but were unable to do anything and several were burned to death.[4]

By now the fields and ditches around the position were choked with rotting German corpses as there was no opportunity for the Paras to bury them. Consequently, the stench of the area was steadily growing worse. Colonel Otway attempted to gain a truce to remove them:

> *I found in the 'house' once of these hailers, I suppose because he was the Mayor of Breville, and I used that. My German was reasonable enough. All they did was shoot at me.*

Later, Padre Gwinnett got hold of a 'white flag' and also made an attempt. Colonel Otway:

> *He had it on a pole to start with and he took it out in front, out into the battlefield and waved it in front of the Germans. He was very brave. When we were collecting wounded and dead, we collected wounded irrespective of whose side they were on. The Germans did stop shooting except for one fool who fired and that was when John Gwinnett, standing up there, turned around and said in the most un-parson like language, 'You stupid bugger. Can't you see my bloody dog collar!'*

*

Enemy sniping had gradually increased during the three days the Battalion had spent in the wood and one sniper in particular was becoming a problem. Arthur Mobsby was in 'Bomb Alley':

> *It was nearly impossible to cross the road as a sniper was using a tree at the end of the ditch as an aiming mark, and anything or any person who passed it were shot at.*
>
> *It was a very unhealthy place to be on the end of 'Bomb Alley'. He was deadly. You only had to get in the wrong spot and BANG! BANG! Snipers have an aiming point and it was the tree. He must have been able to see them coming in and out this trench 'cos he couldn't see anybody in the ditch up the end, or*

Ron Phelps.

Jim Baty.

in the middle, but always seemed to be on the road where we came in there. How Ron Phelps got away with it I don't know, and Jimmy Baty.

Phelps and Baty were 'A' Company runners and they had been crossing and re-crossing the road to supply ammunition for those in Bomb Alley. Phelps also made even more popular journeys:

I used to run around with a bucket of tea. The rations usually came up to me and I dished them out. Blokes [in Bomb Alley] couldn't make their own in the circumstances, so I made a bit of tea every so often, and maybe something to eat and a couple of fags.

Through all this he was suffering severe headaches:

I didn't realize at the time but I had a bit of a swelling on my head. Somebody assumed it was an explosion or something. I didn't seem to notice it to tell the truth. I didn't have any bullet or shrapnel or anything like that. A 'fatty forehead' and the side of my head. You didn't have time to worry about those things.

The sniping of Bomb Alley continued. Gordon Newton:

There was a bloke called 'Lofty' Wingrove, a huge man, never said much at all. He'd been made a Corporal in the field. Me and Wingrove spent all day there. He'd made his place there, and was watching the back. He was well camouflaged. In the evening we

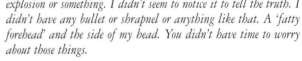

Lance Corporal Fred Wingrove.

170

were ready for an attack... . A sniper was banging away. Wingrove said, 'I'm going to have a crap before it starts.' He took his smock off and his helmet, he had a woolly jumper on, and he went to get over the top of this ditch. The sniper shot him in the head, and he fell back in my arms.

Stretcher-bearers were called and Wingrove was evacuated, grievously wounded but still alive.[5] The culprit continued to use the same tree at the end of Bomb Alley as an aiming point, so the Paras decided to try and do something about it. Sergeant Woodcraft:

> *On this particular occasion he was having a go at the Vickers' position and by the language from that area, the occupants were not amused, so I positioned the Bren gunner and our sniper and ordered them to fire at any likely place. I then tied a mess tin to a stick and waved it backwards and forwards in front of a tree. I was on the point of giving up when 'smack', a bullet hole appeared in the tree trunk just above our heads. Each time he fired I carried out strict butt marking drill; I signalled bulls, inners, magpies and outers, each time marking the strike of the shot by placing the mess tin on the trunk and once, just to stop him getting big-headed, I signalled a miss by waving an aircraft recognition panel.*
>
> *All the time the Bren gunner and sniper were firing into the trees opposite. Whether they got near enough to discourage him or he got tired of it all I don't know but he stopped.*[6]

*

Six hundred yards south-west of the Bois des Monts, the problem of the Germans remaining in the Le Mariquet woods had to be addressed.

At around 3.20pm tanks of 'B' Squadron, 13th/18th Hussars arrived at the western end of the LZ.[7] Lieutenant Colonel Pine-Coffin, CO of the 7th Parachute Battalion, had formulated a plan whereby the tanks, in conjunction with two of his companies, would clear a succession of four woods that the enemy had occupied.[8] The counterattack took the enemy completely by surprise and subsequently three of these were taken, but by the time they were ready to attack the final wood, all six tanks had been knocked out. Fortunately this wood, which was at the road junction below the 3rd Parachute Brigade's HQ, turned out to be unoccupied and the support was not necessary, in fact some Brigade men were waiting at the junction. The two Companies of the 7th remained at the position.

View east across DZ/LZ 'N'. The 13th/18th Hussars attack went straight across the fields in front. (P.R.O. AIR 40/3650)

The Germans suffered around 200 dead and over 150 captured, and the small surviving pockets began making their way back up the slope.

Although the Para losses had been slight, the Hussars had paid a high price, having thirteen killed from the six tanks. Anti-tank guns concealed in the Breville area had knocked them out.[9]

*

For General Gale the attacks on the LZ had made up his mind that Breville had to be captured to close this dangerous gap in the Airborne position. Elements of the 51st Highland Division had moved into the area and were now available to him. The intended use for the Division was to extend the bridgehead southwards, but he decided to divert the 5th Black Watch of 153 Brigade from a proposed attack near Herouvillette, to capture Breville. In the early evening Colonel Otway got his first inkling of what was going to happen:

> I happened to glance down in the fields behind me and saw a group of British soldiers. I looked through my glasses, I saw one of them had red tabs. I thought 'What the hell's going on!' It occurred to me to take an escort because they were wide open and I knew that there were Germans on that road. They were right under fire. I found this Brigadier, this Black Watch Officer, and asked him what was going on. He was very hoity-toity. He said, 'Why?' I said, I was the CO of the 9th. He said he was going to send a Company to attack the Germans on that road and I asked him not to do it. I said that the hedge there was very thick; I didn't know how many Germans there were there but I guess 100 to 150, if not 200.

Otway suggested an alternative start-line and axis to the attack, to the north of the Breville road:

> He haughtily said, 'I know what I'm doing', and I said, 'With the greatest respect sir, I don't think you do.' I then said I would not take any responsibility if you attack across that field.
>
> Got back, rang straight through to James Hill and told him what was happening to try and stop the attack. I had to, to cover myself. Actually, he was very good. He calmed me down and said, 'There's nothing we can do about it'.

The CO of the 5th Black Watch, Lieutenant Colonel Thomson, had been instructed to attack Breville from the western edge of the Bois des Monts. Brigadier Hill:

> I saw the CO [of the Black Watch] and he said, 'The only thing I want is the Château to be in our hands.' I said, 'OK, I'll ensure that the Château is freed. I remember going to Terence Otway and I gave him full marks for this one, and telling him that he had got to take the Château and make certain it was in our hands that evening, when the Black Watch wanted it. And I thought to myself 'Well really, here is a Battalion, absolutely whacked; they've had a hell of a time and now they've got to go and make certain via a strong patrol or company that they get that Château and hand it over to the Black Watch.' And he never belly-ached, he never blanched, he never did anything. He said, 'OK'.

The Château needed to be in safe hands because the Black Watch attack would have been exposed to a counter-attack on its right flank if it were in German possession. Otway also agreed to send a patrol into Breville during the night to try and find out the situation there and arrange for it to report to Colonel Thomson upon returning. This was because by the time the Black Watch reached its RV there would not be enough hours of darkness left to brief and prepare its own patrol.[10]

Thomson therefore decided to make provisional plans for the advance into Breville at first light the next day, but to wait for the patrol's report before finalizing anything.

*

At 7.00pm a mortar barrage began to land on the Bois des Monts and around two companies of Germans followed in its wake, heading towards the 'B' Company area. Bren guns opened up from the bank, and due to the arrival of some bombs from Brigade HQ, were supported by mortar fire. The barrels were worked so hard that they had to be urinated upon to cool them down. Even Colonel Otway took his turn.

The Germans were extremely determined and continued to advance, chanting as they came. The

172

situation was serious. Colonel Otway radioed Brigade HQ for Naval support. The safety limit for this type of shelling was 1000 yards between the target and one's own troops, but the Germans were within 500 yards. Fifteen minutes later the first salvo of shells was on its way.

Five men were waiting in a slit trench near Battalion HQ as part of the 'mobile reserve'. One was the wireless operator, another was Ron Phelps:

The first salvo fell slap bang on top of us. I shall always remember him yelling into the radio to alter the range!

Ernie Rooke-Matthews:

We witnessed the spectacle of one of our officers, Captain the Honourable Paul Greenway, standing on the bank in front, observing the fire and calling out corrections to be passed back via the various links to

the ship, as calm as if he were on a football pitch. Such actions always had a stimulating effect, especially on the ordinary soldiers; they were great morale boosters.

From what Captain Greenway could see, plus information shouted to him by Sergeant Garrett, who was up the tree opposite the driveway gate, the fall of shot was relayed back to Colonel Otway. The Colonel in turn gave the adjustments to the radio operator who passed them on to Brigade. Colonel Otway:

This was deliberate. If our troops were to be hit by shells, only I could take the blame, not Paul or anyone else.

Fred Milward:

Most of their shells fell in front of 'B' Company area. It certainly decimated the Germans, it really did. It was quite heartening really to think they could fire so close and be so accurate. You couldn't mistake them because the bursts were black smoke. Mortars were sort of a dusty colour, but the Arethusa's were big and black. They really did bang 'em in!

Captain Paul Greenway.

Sergeant Daniels:

They sounded like they came over the top of us before they exploded. The air was vibrating! Christ, they did make a commotion, ten times worse than a 'Minnie Werfer'. It put the fear of Christ up me. What the bloody hell is this? I'd got my head down. I managed to get the sole of me boots over me chin-strap! There was a tremendous bloody crash. You heard a couple of cheers go up.

Yet even this did not break the enemy's resolve and some of the leading wave reached the 'B' Company area trenches where hand-to-hand fighting ensued. After several minutes the attackers were finally beaten off, but it was a very close-run thing.

A few prisoners were taken and lined up with their hands above their heads while others were being interrogated and the wounded treated.

The Regimental Aid Post experienced its busiest time to date. During the steady flow of casualties from the mortaring and shelling, the stretcher-bearers had managed to dress, nurse and document the wounded. However, for such a full-scale attack, they had far more to do than they could cope with. All the available rooms in the bungalow, except for one occupied by Colonel Otway, were used as wards for wounded awaiting evacuation. Lightly wounded and those who were beyond aid had to be left on the terrace until space became available. There was no time for anyone to clean up, and it resembled the threshold of a slaughterhouse.

A German, holding his arm, walked unescorted into the tool shed and was met by James Bramwell:

I cut away his smock and the whole arm was hanging there by a ligament, practically severed, hanging

*The tool shed dressing station beside the **Bois des Monts** bungalow.*

by a few shreds of flesh. He pointed below his shoulder to the tourniquet, which he said he had put on himself. When asked if he had had any morphia he said, 'No.' So I just gave him morphia, put him on a stretcher and we carried him into the sort of living room of this villa which was used as a hospital. There he was made as comfortable as possible. Anti-tetanic and anti-gas gangrene sera followed, and he watched the injections calmly. 'Are you going to cut off my arm?' 'Not if I can help it. There is a chance of saving it.' He had seen the arm himself and it was not possible to make the lie much whiter; there was indeed a faint chance if the tourniquet could be removed in time and the severed arteries clipped, of restoring some circulation to the limb. We were using the floor for stretchers and he said his wound didn't hurt. He was quite grey in the face by this time and so I left him to get Captain Watts to come along and have a look. They had already tried to remove the tourniquet and clip the hanging arteries, but there was not sufficient light or space and the attempt failed. Now he was in a bad way. No jeeps had yet managed to get through from the MDS and he was greatly in need of a transfusion. Eventually, he signalled, sent a message to me that he wanted a urine bottle. So I got the flower vase that we were using at the time for that, and put it down. But there seemed no reaction to it, he couldn't make it work at all. He was very ill indeed. I thought it might help to put a hot water bottle on his stomach which seemed to me it might loosen up the situation. I did that and when I tried to put the thing down on his belly he started moving about, tossing, and so that the drip we were giving him was torn out. The dressing was torn off. His arm started pouring blood. I said, 'What the hell's the matter, what's wrong with him?' One of his mates, a wounded German lying beside him said in perfect English, 'He's a victim of our own propaganda. He thinks you're going to castrate him.' No amount of reassurance from the other German was the slightest use. That night, however, the jeeps got through. The patient was evacuated and his arm successfully amputated.

Captain Watts was extremely good with Germans. There was a difficult moment when some stretcher-bearers carried in a German who I think had been hit not very badly, but who was in a state of nervous shock, a very horrible shaking and screaming, like a frightened hare. We tried to see if there was anything wrong with him and we couldn't get near him he was fighting so much. Watts came to try and have a look and sort of put his hand down on his thigh. The man leant forward and bit him. Watts said, 'You bastard,' and smacked him down. Next lull, he came and said, 'You know Bramwell, I shouldn't have said that to that chap. Not really professional you know', which I considered very nice. He was a good doctor.

The MO, Captain Harold Watts.

Among the German wounded was a Colonel, a Deputy Brigade Commander, who had been brought in by four of his own men. He appeared to be covered in wounds, his head swathed in bandages. His uniform, embellished with a high decoration, was soaked in sweat and blood. Field glasses still hung around his neck. While he was being dressed he did not murmur, although the business of slitting his collar and exposing the multiple wounds must have been agony. Captain Johnston had come up from the MDS to help Harold Watts and he injected the German with morphia. To Watts' 'Well done', he growled back in English 'It is nothing.' Colonel Otway arrived to interrogate him, and discovered that he was the acting commander of II/857th Grenadier Regiment. The interrogation began with an exchange of compliments. 'The medical orderlies tell me that you have stood the dressings very bravely.' The German closed his eyes. 'It is nothing to die in battle. I only hope the fight was a fair one.' 'Indeed it was a very fair fight, and you fought bravely. Now tell me, where is your battalion headquarters?' The wounded man opened his eyes, groaned and then wearily closed them again. 'I do not know', he said. Colonel Otway opened a map-case which had been taken from him. A few moments scrutiny and the interrogation was over. 'It was not wise of you to come into battle with marked maps'.[11, 12]

The German stated that his whole battalion had been wiped out in attacks over the last twelve hours and that the rest of his regiment had met a similar fate in their attempts to capture Ranville and Amfreville.

During this interrogation German survivors from the LZ battle began to appear in the fields around the wood. Below the bungalow a four-man standing patrol situated behind the hedge in the south-east corner of the position, saw an organized group of about twenty Germans walking alongside a hedge, straight towards them. The leading man was allowed to get to within ten feet. Jimmy French:

Somebody shot him in the face, poor bastard. Then the others of course opened fire and we opened fire. The first few or so, the ones on the corner, they dropped. The others

Jimmy French.

175

disappeared into the hedge. The eight that were firing, they withdrew and left us in peace for a while. We brought the injured Germans in. Three or four of them were wounded. One of them, I was supporting his arm because his arm had been hit by a bullet. Strangely enough it wasn't bleeding. There was a certain amount of blood there but you'd expect him to be drenched in blood. I left him in the hands of the medics.

Many other Germans were shot or taken prisoner as they tried to get back to Breville or wandered into the Bois des Monts.

*

Apart from the Germans infiltrating the Battalion's radio frequency and trying to trick them into the open, the latter half of the evening was uneventful. Rain began to fall.

The Battalion had either been in action or 'Standing To' most of the day and the men were very tired and hoping for a quiet night. They went through the rituals of cooking, eating, washing, shaving, replenishing ammunition and water, cleaning their weapons and, except the sentries, sleeping. The men on the patrol to the Château prepared themselves.

*

It was dark by the time the Black Watch reached the sunken lane at the Bois des Monts. Mud had made all movement difficult.

When the companies had reported in, Colonel Thomson called an 'O' Group to explain the plan. Unless there was any alteration following the report from the 9th Battalion patrol, the Black Watch would move in the 'advance to contact' formation across the fields and enter Breville from the southeast. 'A' Company was to lead, followed by 'B' and 'C' Companies on the left rear flank. 'D' Company was to relieve the 9th Battalion men around the Château St Côme and occupy it. Shortly after the 'O' Group, an FOO from the 63rd Medium Regiment RA reported for instructions and was asked to bring down fire on the Breville crossroads and village area at first light for about ten minutes prior to the advance. Everyone settled down as best they could to await the dawn.[10]

*

The patrol to the Château comprised of 'C' Company men under Major Dyer, reinforced by four Bren guns. As they were being briefed, Nebelwerfers opened up, and so it was not until just after 11.00pm that they were able to move into Bomb Alley. Having agreed a success signal with those in the ditch, they went forward to clear the wood on the approach to the Château. As they did so, the Bomb Alley men gave them covering fire with Bren and Vickers machine guns.

When they reached their exit point the patrol halted, re-formed and lay down. The Château was clearly visible in the moonlight. They waited while a Battalion mortar barrage was directed against the area immediately in front. When it finished, at Major Dyer's command they all stood up and dashed forward, screaming as they ran. They reached the Château and a grenade was thrown inside. The noise and shouting died down, leaving an eerie silence. The building was deserted. Relieved by this anti-climax, the patrol took up positions of all-round defence. After waiting for an hour and a half the whole patrol moved back into the corner of the wood and took up a new defensive position. They found themselves among dozens of German corpses that had obviously been lying there for a number of days. Sid Capon:

Dead bodies didn't seem to worry us in the short period of time in Normandy, this was an everyday occurrence.

It started to pour with rain again. They were told not to sleep. For the rest of the night the enemy probed towards the Château, and the patrol had a noisy time. However, thanks to the distraction caused, the Bois des Monts was left alone and the remainder of the men had a quiet night.

*

CHAPTER ELEVEN

Tragedy
Sunday 11 June

The patrol to reconnoitre Breville for the Black Watch returned at around 3.00am. Lieutenant Smythe reported to Colonel Thomson that they had encountered some snipers along the road and were fired upon as they neared the crossroads. Walking around a corner, they had nearly bumped straight into some Germans, almost like an act on a stage, and so had not been able to enter Breville but did not think that the village was strongly held. Colonel Thomson therefore confirmed the plan and set the time of the attack for 4.30am.

*

Ron Tucker had been ordered to move his position and was now dug in a few yards below and to the left of the bungalow. Up the slope to his right was a pile of dressings, bandages and boots, but he had not paid it much attention. He awoke to a nasty surprise:

> *The water had run down into my trench, all with blood in it. So I piled some mud around it to take it away and further down* [the slope].

In the mud of the sunken lane, 'A', 'B' and 'C' Companies of the 5th Black Watch prepared for their attack on Breville. Colonel Otway wanted his own troops on the extreme left of the flank and so moved some of the Paras in the 'B' Company area to a position further down the lane.

Near the Château, Major Dyer's patrol was still lying among the German corpses. However, they did not have to wait long for their relief. Sergeant Daniels was in the sunken lane:

> *The Black Watch went through us and the words of this subaltern, two pips, to Wally Beckwith: 'Don't worry about us Sar'nt Major, we can take care of ourselves. The Ladies from Hell are here. You chaps have a rest, you can go home, we won't need you any more.' He came through with this little point patrol. There weren't many of them. I was told to go off with the subaltern down to the Château. And he was just the same with me when I got down to the Château. 'Well Sar'nt, I'll take over here, you can bugger off back.' Of course I had to come back up that ditch and got mortared all the way back.*

Shortly after, 'D' and HQ Companies of the 5th Black Watch crossed to the Château area and began digging in, allowing Dyer's patrol to withdraw to the Bois des Monts. They began crawling along a ditch littered with more dead bodies and a wealth of equipment, when bullets and mortar bombs began to rain down all around them. Due to the ferocity of the fire, progress along the ditch was painfully slow and it took them an hour before finally reaching the Bois des Monts. Fortunately, not a single man was hurt.

Over on the western flank of the position, at exactly 4.30am, 'A' Company, 5th Black Watch emerged from the trees bordering the sunken lane and walked into the field with their rifles at the port. Breville was 750 yards away. Forming up in open order, 7 Platoon on the left, 8 Platoon on the right, Company HQ in the centre and 9 Platoon in the rear, they began to descend a gentle slope. There was little the 9th Battalion could do to assist. Major Dyer:

> *We couldn't use proper fire-power as they were right in front of us. I got as many 2-inch* [mortars] *to fire smoke at extreme range to take them safely forward. But it takes a long time for 2-inch smoke to form a decent cloud, but that was all we could do.*

The supporting artillery opened up as agreed, but the few shells that arrived were not on the required area. There had been no opportunity for the artillery to zero their guns onto the target. After 250 yards the Company arrived at a hedgerow. This gave some cover from which to study the next field. The crossroads and village were beyond the next hedgerow as the field sloped up to their right. There was no sight or sound of the enemy. The Company Commander, Major John McGregor, decided that 7 Platoon should advance on its own, with 8 and 9 Platoons ready to give covering mortar and LMG fire if needed. 7 Platoon passed through two gaps at the lower end of the field and quickly spread out into formation, with two sections in line and one section in the rear. They advanced up the slope with Major McGregor and his runner following a few paces behind the rear section. About forty yards from the next hedge they were hit by intense fire from the front and heavy machine-gun fire from the right. Within seconds the platoon was almost wiped out. The few survivors lying on the ground returned fire, as did the rest of the Company behind the hedge, but then mortars began causing increasing casualties in those platoons. Major McGregor was wounded by two bullets and four pieces of shrapnel. His runner was killed beside him.[1]

The Paras had watched helplessly and in disbelief as the Jocks had walked across. Ron Tucker:

> *They made no attempt to conceal their approach at all. It was broad daylight and they walked uphill towards the Breville road in open order, stretched out across the field. This was where most of them stayed when the enemy opened fire. The rest ran into our lines.*

Sergeant Jenkins:

> *You could hear the machine guns rattling like mad and these lads came running back, screaming. They lost an awful lot of men. That didn't help our morale either. They came back through us, coming back in twos and threes with stretchers. They were milling around and scattered all over. It was terrible.*

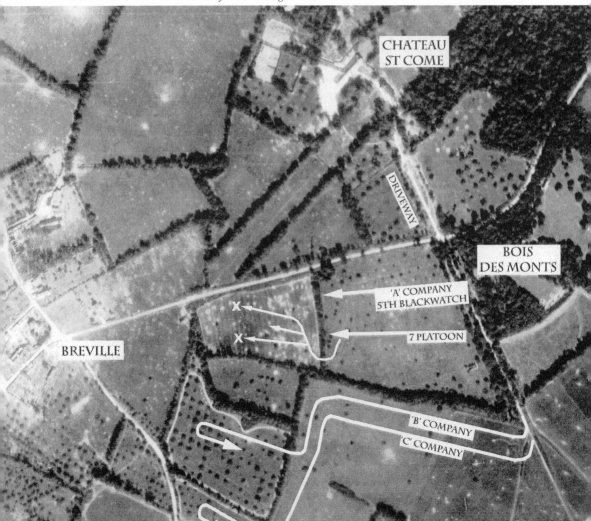

Tanks could be heard moving about in the area of the crossroads. The Black Watch CO, Colonel Thomson, knowing that 'A' Company had been decimated, ordered 'B' Company, under Major Dennis Punton, to work around the left flank to try and approach the crossroads from the south. Using the hedge at the lower end of the field for cover, they passed through the first hedge facing them and entered the next field. Reaching the bottom left-hand corner, they had just moved into the next field, within a hundred yards of the objective, when they encountered withering fire and became pinned down. They were then drawn back along the field, just below the one through which they had advanced, to another hedge. As this occurred, 'C' Company was moving around on their left, attempting a wider left hook to try and come in from the south-west, but this met a similar response. Both companies were forced to fall back.[1] The fields were strewn with bodies and in the sunken lane confusion reigned, with lost, shocked, wounded and dead men everywhere. Stendall Brailsford:

A Bren Gun carrier came up the lane, and laying on some ammunition or whatever it was, was a young fella, face down, with his head to the side. There was a spurt of blood about fifteen inches high coming out where he'd been hit in the brain... . It stopped aside of me, and there was a young officer, and I said, 'What are you going to do about this bloke ? Give me a field dressing, I'll plug it up.' Plugged it up, slung him over my shoulder and carried him into the First Aid post.

Corporal Mick Corboy was dug in below the bungalow, near the lane:

I had the melancholy sight of seeing a succession of jeeps going past delivering bodies to the temporary cemetery at the end of the field.

This cemetery had been established between the bungalow and the tool shed.

The RAP was again overflowing with casualties and some had to be passed straight through to the MDS. The Padres had their hands full, and did what they could in what were shocking circumstances. James Bramwell, 224 Field Ambulance:

Just looking sympathetic and saying a little prayer didn't seem to cut much ice, because my impression was that on the whole, people go down, die slowly, and by that time when they're obviously dying, they're too far gone to care about those kinds of comforts. Unless of course, religion is strong in them. On the whole it must have been a great disappointment for the Padres, hoping that they would have a chance to minister to people.[2]

The full horror of the Black Watch casualties would not be appreciated until a head count was possible, but the danger now was the real possibility of a German counter-attack. With Colonel Otway's help the Black Watch survivors were hastily reorganized in preparation for it.

*

Fortunately, the German counter-attack did not materialize and the remainder of the day was relatively quiet. Such times at the Bois des Monts were few and far between, making the experience almost surreal when they did occur. James Bramwell:

There was an atmosphere, a strangeness of the quiet times when nobody was shouting, when you could hear the cows in the fields down below and the twittering of the birds. You got the feeling of the reflux of nature on the fiendish, of how it would be in a few years time when we'd all gone, when the relatively few scars had been removed. Nobody would ever know.

When it all started again, you knew where you were and that was the end, you'd had your little break. You didn't care about the birds twittering and the cows mooing![2]

Rations for the 9th Battalion were now at a premium. Many were eating the apples from the orchard, but these had an unfortunate side effect – diarrhoea! Ron Tucker:

I was eating the emergency chocolate ration that we had. It was about the size of a sardine tin and about an inch thick, solid dark chocolate, very rich. I was eating into that with some ship's biscuits, y'know, hard tack biscuits. They were supposed to be emergency reserve, well as far as I was concerned, it was an emergency, I was bloomin' hungry!

*

After being informed of the failure of the Black Watch attack, Brigadier Hill decided that the survivors of 'A', 'B' and 'C' Companies of the 5th Black Watch should side-step and join 'D' and HQ Companies around the Château St Côme. Colonel Otway:

> I said to Colonel Thomson, 'I want you to take up position on the far side of the Château to the north and north-east. If any attack came up that way I'll leave it to you'.

At 10.00pm they moved into the Château grounds. 'B' Company and the decimated 'A' Company took up positions on either side of the driveway, 'C' Company went into reserve in the Château wood, and responsibility for Bomb Alley was handed over.[3] 'D' Company remained in and around the Château, and to cover them an anti-tank gun was positioned at the northern end of the Château, just outside what was the kitchen, facing west.

The two commanding officers arranged a link between their battalions halfway down Bomb Alley.

The Black Watch positioned two 6-Pounder anti-tank guns and their crews in the 9th Battalion area, at the north-east corner of their position covering the main road to Breville and the small open space east of the main road and north of the drive.

The late evening passed quietly, with the only incident to affect the Paras being the evacuation of the Intelligence Officer, Lieutenant Worth.

*

At a minute after midnight a 9th Battalion patrol left the Bois des Monts. It was led by Captain Robinson and Sergeant 'Ginger' Woodcock. Accompanying them were some 3rd Parachute Squadron engineers led by Lieutenant Lack. The group of around forty Paras hoped to ambush some vehicles heard moving up earlier in the night. They were also to blow two craters at the junction of a track and the road running north out of Breville, to deny its use to enemy armour.[4] Corporal Corboy:

> I was in the escort patrol under Sergeant Woodcock. There was, as usual, a fair amount of patrolling in the area, and at one point we had to freeze to allow one to pass. Although we were a fighting patrol, our main job was to protect the demolition party.

Jimmy French:

> I was dragged in as a signaller, using a No 18 wireless set which needed two blokes to operate it; one man carrying it on his back while the other walked along behind, working on it. We usually worked in pairs, but on this occasion it wasn't my usual mate.... . Anyhow, I lost the toss and had to carry the bloody thing.
>
> It was a fine night as we left the Bois des Monts, straight up the 'avenue' towards the Château, in single file, my mate and I around the centre of the patrol. When we reached the Château we struck off to the left, through the woods, and then along the hedgerows. A couple of times Jerry sent up flares. Everyone else was on the ground except me with this thundering great R/T set on my back. I had to stand perfectly still in this glaring white light until the flare had burnt itself out. It lasted two or three minutes; it felt like two or three hours.
>
> We had gone three of four hundred yards when a shot, I think it was from a Sten gun, came from three or four places in front of me, and one of the patrol fell wounded in the back. We had no medics or stretcher party with us. Somebody, I don't know who, rendered first aid and supplied a field dressing. We were then ordered to continue on our way back to the Battalion position, leaving the wounded man alone where he fell.

Fred Milward:

> The officer said leave him, which I presume was the right thing to do, because we hadn't done what we'd set out to do. Sergeant Woodcock was incensed. We gave him a shot of morphine and he was left.[5]

They arrived at the road junction.

> We then took up all-round defence while the sappers did their dirty work. We then withdrew a couple of hundred yards, and after a few minutes, a bloody great bang.

The Paras were a little too close to the explosion and were treated to a shower of earth and stones, but no one was injured. Jimmy French:

Jerry, in the vicinity of Breville, does his nut, a lot of noise, small arms fire, flares, and a few moments later a motor vehicle comes belting along the road, no lights, going too fast.

An enemy half-track vehicle raced straight into the first crater. Captain Robinson then ordered the patrol to withdraw to the Battalion position, and for safety, via an alternative route. The patrol arrived back at the Bois des Monts at 3am. Two men, Sergeants Woodcock and Knight, disappeared into the darkness. Shortly after, they came back with the wounded man.

Fred Milward.

*

Whilst the Black Watch were digging-in, a German patrol came into the area making considerable noise, obviously trying to ascertain the location and strength of the defences. The enemy was driven off, but sporadic shelling and mortaring continued.

To reinforce the Black Watch, around twenty men of 10 Platoon, 'C' Company, 1/7th Middlesex Battalion arrived. This was a heavy machine-gun company that supported the battalions of 153 Brigade of the 51st Highland Division, and they were bringing four Vickers machine guns. Twenty-year-old Private Dennis Daly was one of the Carrier drivers:

As we swung into the Château drive we dropped two of the machine guns off and I saw all these dead horses, dead Germans and Paras all over the place. There were fires burning as we went down the drive. All the stables were on fire. The Germans kept firing Verey lights.

Daly drove around the stables into a field where the two remaining guns were sited to the north-west, pointing towards Breville.

*

It had been a tragic day for the 5th Black Watch, a battalion that had done so well in the North African campaign. It's 'A' Company numbered less than platoon strength. Only one officer was left, all the others having been killed or wounded, along with many NCOs. Both 'B' Company, who had lost three Platoon Officers, and 'C' Company with the CO wounded, had also suffered. Overall, the Battalion had lost nineteen officers, eighty-five NCOs and 200 men, and the battle was still yet to be decided.

CHAPTER TWELVE

Day of Decision
Monday 12 June

With the enemy patrols continuing to carry out sporadic attacks on the Black Watch positions, little attention was paid to the 9th Battalion. And so Major Charlton, Lieutenant Parfitt and Sergeant Rose were duly buried in the makeshift cemetery. Ernie Rooke-Matthews:

> *Under the Padre's leadership, comrades who were killed were treated with the utmost respect. In this the medics again played a noble role. The bodies of fallen comrades were removed at the earliest opportunity from the place where they had fallen to a patch at the rear of the bungalow. In the morning, after 'Stand*

The graves beside the Bois des Monts bungalow..

> *To' , our dead comrades would be buried in shallow graves dug in this plot. The Padre gave every man a Christian burial, with some of the man's comrades breaking off from the action to pay homage. These services were family services, not military, very simple, most sincere.*

*

Having landed during the afternoon of D+1, the 9th Battalion seaborne contingent finally managed to reach the Bois des Monts. The party, led by Lieutenant Bill Mills, which included Tommy Tarrant, the REME Armoury sergeant, and Sid Towler, the cook sergeant, brought with them four 3-ton trucks and a water cart.[1] Lieutenant Mills:

> *It was very early in the morning, between 5am and 6am. When we got there they were out of ammunition, out of cigarettes, low on food and they weren't awfully good on water. We had the lot. We emptied every truck, and the trucks were sent straight back to bring up ammunition.*[2]
>
> *All shape of Company formation really had gone. There were chaps all round and they all had to be taken care of. Believe you me, it had got to the stage where you get groups of men to carry out a job, a counter-attack if you like, but whether you could say it was 'A', 'B' or 'C' Company, well... . The spread of men had just been pushed out of all recognition compared with the original idea.*
>
> *I dug a hole just about twenty yards away from the building* [bungalow]. *That was my office. There was a filthy old well there. At the time, all I had to do was to concentrate with my little administrative group, I had a team of four or five chaps, on the job of distributing the food and cigarettes and getting water out. I was very lucky. The LST I came off sent us ashore with enough 'Lucky Strikes' to give every man, I'm only talking about 120 men left at the time, a packet of fags.*

Sergeant Tommy Tarrant.

The day began in earnest at 6.30am when an attack fell upon the Black Watch from the north-east. However, due to the timely arrival of a Royal Artillery Forward Observation Point team on the top floor of the Château, an accurate bombardment was called in to break up the attack.[3,4] A little later, two Middlesex Vickers guns were knocked out and three men killed by a brief mortar bombardment, but for the remainder of the morning a period of calm prevailed.[5]

Sid Towler.

       *

The 'peace' was broken at noon when the whole of the 3rd Parachute Brigade's area began to be bombarded with shell, mortar and Nebelwerfer fire. Fred Milward:

> *The racket when they started shelling and mortaring, it was indescribable. The trees were being blasted over the top of us. The road was littered with branches, absolutely covered, and also inside the Bois des Monts.*

Lieutenant Mills was one of those who had to move around to continue his duties:

> *There was so much shrapnel you just had to ignore it. You could feel it brushing against your face as you were walking around; you could feel the blast against your face.*

The stretcher-bearers of 224 Field Ambulance were also moving around, collecting the wounded. These had to then be carried up the road to meet medical jeeps coming from the MDS, but as they reached a point near the Château wood, mortar bombs began falling within fifty yards. They therefore decided to double with their patients to a point about 400 yards further along the road. Here they were able to pause in comparative safety before continuing to the waiting jeeps.[6]

This bombardment went on unremittingly until 3.00pm, when it became even more intense. It was the heaviest barrage that anyone had experienced. By now the Paras were extremely well dug-in, but the hard, rooted ground had made it extremely difficult for the Black Watch to get down to any

Sergeant Paddy Jenkins.

significant depth and therefore began to sustain casualties from the hail of shrapnel. One of their anti-tank guns was also knocked out.

At the Bois des Monts, amidst the noise, singing could be heard from the area of the sunken lane. Sergeant 'Paddy' Jenkins, an experienced 'Mess Room vocalist', started off the mixture of Paras there in a chorus of:

> *Oh dear what a calamity,*
> *six old maids got stuck in the lavatory,*
> *they were there from Monday to Saturday,*
> *nobody knew they were there.*

The men endured this horrendous barrage for forty-five minutes, and when it finally began to ease, a large number of German infantry, transported in troop carriers, began to approach the Black Watch from across the fields to the north and west. The onslaught fell on 'D' Company and the right-hand platoon of 'B' Company of the Jocks. Their most forward section was immediately overrun and the 'D' Company survivors fell back to the Château area where they formed a defensive line. A few had taken up position in the Château itself, amongst some HQ staff. There

'The Vickers was placed in the landing window (centre). The gaping hole was caused by a 6-inch shell from the *Arethusa*'.

was a pause, a verbal altercation, and then the firing started. Hordes of enemy charged through the copse in front of the Château, attacking in close order without armoured support and suffering heavy casualties, their dead literally piling up as they came on.[7] The Black Watch repelled this initial attack, and in the ensuing lull, a small group of Middlesex led by their Company Officer, Major Pearson went out to check if either of the two Vickers guns knocked out in the early morning, could be salvaged.[8] They returned to the Château with one gun and found it had a hole in the gun casing, and so the water cooling the barrel would leak away. A constant source of water was necessary if it was to be used. The most effective position for the gun was upstairs at the front of the building, and so was placed in a gaping hole that had once been a landing window. Unfortunately, the nearest water supply was in the kitchen and so a human chain was formed to pass the water. Dennis Daly's position in the chain was at the bottom of the stairs. As the Germans attacked again, shouting erupted within the Château, giving him something resembling a running commentary. However, the sound of tracks gradually became more and more apparent above this noise. Dennis Daly, 1/7th Middlesex Battalion:

> I could hear them rattling around. Somebody said they were Shermans. A cheer went up and they're all shouting, 'Shermans!' Then they turned out to be bloody Germans!

The shout had been misheard. Six tanks and assault guns began firing at almost point blank range using solid shot and oil bombs that sent out a flame thirty feet long. A number of enemy troops began to make their way into the stables and a ferocious battle erupted, but the Germans were fought off.[9]

There was only a brief respite before the Germans tried again, this time approaching around the back of the Château and infiltrating through the Château wood. This contained a large amount of Black Watch transport and supplies plus the First Aid Post. Sam Weller, the Black Watch Medical Officer, was wounded and so Tom Nicol, their Padre, was left in charge. Weller was taken to the 9th Battalion RAP where he told Captain Watts that he did not think his Battalion would hold on much longer and asked him to take over the Aid Posts of both battalions.

The Black Watch were slowly but surely being pushed out of the Château wood. Colonel Otway contacted Brigade Headquarters to express his fear that the position might not hold much longer:

> I rang up to report that we were low on ammunition. We were running out of mortar bombs. That was one of the factors, but the most important thing was that if the Black Watch went back through me, what was I going to do?

Brigadier Hill knew that this request for help would not have been made unless it was absolutely necessary, and so went to see the Commanding Officer of the 1st Canadian Parachute Battalion:

> I had no spare bodies so I went to Colonel Bradbrook, whose HQ was 200 yards away at the end of our drive and asked him to help. At that moment German tanks had overrun the road to his right and were shooting up his Company HQ at close range. To his eternal credit he decided that he could deal with this problem and he gave me what he had left of his Reserve Company under Major Hanson, a very hard and excellent commander, together with cooks and any spare men and we set off to the 9th Battalion area.
>
> A young Red Indian aged eighteen, called Private Anderson, informed me that he was going to be my bodyguard.

Hill also gathered some of the 3rd Parachute Squadron engineers.

At 5.00pm the Brigadier set off with pistol in hand, thumbstick in the other, followed by around sixty men.

*

In the Château, every Black Watch and Middlesex man who could carry a rifle had been hurriedly ordered outside to take up a position about fifty yards away in the ditch on the right hand side of the driveway.[10] Dennis Daly:

> They whipped us out to this defensive position. I remember lying prone against some slight rise that you

Lieutenant Hugh Smythe.

could rest your rifle against, and the Germans were coming through what appeared to be Rhododendron bushes of some sort. They weren't all that far away. You didn't need to select a target, it was just a matter of working the bolt and pulling the trigger, and the effect of all those Lee Enfields pouring fire into the bushes was all it needed.

In spite of their losses the enemy just would not give up, causing the situation in the ditch to grow increasingly desperate as the ammunition began to run out. They were on the point of breaking under the German pressure. Lieutenant Hugh Smythe, who was in his slit trench by the main road, saw what was going to happen. He therefore ran up the drive collecting ammunition and jumped down into the ditch, walking the length of the position, reassuring the men and restoring control. This stubborn group continued to hold out in spite of continued point-blank fire from tanks and assault guns.[11]

Elsewhere, some of the Black Watch had started to fall back into the Bois des Monts. Sergeant Mobsby:

> One young lad, I say young lad, I wasn't very old myself, jumped into my trench. He was wearing one of the new steel helmets with this extra bit down the back. 'Have a fag, Sarge,' he said. He was full of remorse, I felt so sorry for him. Having been chased myself.... I had a week in 1940 and know what it's like to be chased. It's much harder being chased than it is chasing.

Lieutenant Mills:

> The Black Watch were coming into our area. I thought to myself, 'Before long we're going to end up hand-to-hand fighting and I'll be lucky if I survive.' I had a bayonet on a Sten. These chaps were coming into the wood. Terence Otway was regrouping them as they came back from the other side of the road. 'Come on occupy this', 'Into there', making them get themselves re-employed immediately. It is the only time in my life when I expected not to live. I was amazed how philosophical about it I was.

Things were becoming so bad that, in order to stop some of the more distressed Black Watch, Otway and another officer were forced to open up in front of their feet with Stens. Every man was needed.

Ernie Rooke-Matthews:

> The German tanks and SP guns were firing right into our positions with shells exploding all over the bungalow area across to the Château. In the road our machine-gun crews, who had been fighting valiantly for some days, were still firing away at the advancing enemy, inflicting heavy casualties. The machine gunners were of course under fire and they suffered losses. Corporal McGuinness and Sergeant McGeever were tireless in their efforts to halt the German attacks. Our mortars also kept up a barrage of fire on the enemy although they themselves were under fire as the German shells and mortars fell deep into the Battalion's positions.

Fortunately, anti-tank shells were again being used instead of high explosive, and so the casualties were nowhere near as bad as they could have been.

Behind the hedge on the road, Lieutenant Slade had found a use for his 'liberated' sword. Lieutenant Mills:

> He kept walking around the positions waving his sword saying, 'Get your heads up, keep your heads up, don't let your heads go down', walking round everywhere amongst all this shrapnel. The idea was, if we took our heads down, the enemy could have rushed in and we wouldn't have had a chance to defend ourselves.

Enemy infantry had penetrated the eastern end of the Château Wood and were fighting their way down the road towards the Bois des Monts. Total confusion reigned as many of the Black Watch who had been forced out of the wood were being rallied into new positions to stop them. Officers were shouting orders, and men, some of them without weapons, were trying to rejoin their disordered formations. Stretcher-bearers were forced to carry the wounded across the fields below the RAP, and onto a lane that led to the road junction below Le Mesnil. A Black Watch stretcher-bearer who had distinguished himself in the 8th Army desert campaigns said that they had not undergone anything like this, even in the worst part of the retreat into Egypt. 'This is hell on earth,' he said.[6]

A few Germans managed to reach the area east of the barn and some hand-to-hand fighting ensued. John Speechley:

> They'd got in that top end, only momentarily. They came across the road, but they didn't realize what they'd walked into and buggered off quick. I believed I'd never make it back. I thought 'We're getting near the end here!'

At this critical moment, to rally morale, the Padre, John Gwinnett, marched through the Bois des Monts gate and over to the right hand corner of the drive, where he proceeded to nail the Battalion's flag to a tree. It was a timely act. Many Paras around the position saw this and word quickly spread. It reinforced their determination. They were not going to move whatever happened.

The tanks and assault guns continued to fire directly into the 'A' and 'B' Company designated areas from close range. The mortar section, still under Sergeant Hennessey and Gus Gower, was reduced to a single serviceable weapon, and this kept up a continuous fire upon the enemy.

Enemy pressure on the pivotal Vickers machine guns at the driveway entrance was intense. Corporal McGuinness:

> My gun was brought up to the crossroads [driveway], Bailey's was in the wood, both facing Breville. Sanderson, a good lad, was right opposite us, his gun facing the Château; he was killed with a mortar bomb, his mates were wounded.

Lieutenant Mills:

> [Lieutenant] 'Corpus' Christie ran into the centre of the wood. 'Anybody here machine gunners?' I said, 'Yes, I am.' He said, 'Come down and get this machine gun into action would you Bill?' They'd got a machine gun very badly sited on the crossroads just by the gate of the Château. So I went down to it and Corporal McGuinness was there. He was not a machine gunner, but he was there at the gun. He was taking cover behind a corpse, one of our blokes laid out in front of him, dead. He said, 'It's bloody murder here y'know Sir!' So I cocked the gun, and down the bottom, as far as I could see down that road, there's a slight dog-leg in it, I could see German infantry crossing the road. So I opened up and got two shots off and she jammed in the number two position which is a very easy position to clear. So I cleared it and I fired again and it did exactly the same. I thought, 'Well, this is crackers.' I took the breech block out and opened the breech to find the

Lieutenant Bill Mills.

187

lands on the machine gun, the tram lines it runs backwards and forwards on, the lands on one side had been hit by shrapnel and dented in. Of course, there was no movement at all, so the machine gun was useless.

I could see what appeared to be a large armoured car along the road, so I thought there's no point in stopping here, so I knew where there was another one in the wood which nobody was operating. I went and got it. If you pick it up by one leg and push it across your shoulders so that the two short legs are down your front, and the one back leg is behind your back, its a very easy load to carry. It's amazing how you can carry the complete gun assembled.

Corporal McGuinness went back to his own gun:

Fenson was hit in the right arm, he just dropped his head. I don't know how I wasn't hit, being Number Two, I was slightly in front of him. I called for the medics but no one came. I told Fenson I was going to see McGeever about moving the gun and bring the medics. I got into the wood and told McGeever the crossroads were a death-trap and I was going to move. I'd no sooner left him, there were bullets flying all over the wood, I dropped into a spare slit trench. Then I heard a tank, I could tell by the sound of the tracks.

Enemy infantry supported by two Mk IV tanks were advancing up the road from Breville. Bill Mills headed for the sunken lane with the Vickers. Near the lane's entrance a Black Watch 6-Pounder anti-tank gun was set in a clump of bushes:

The gun commander, a sergeant, was very badly hurt. That gun never got into action because he and his crew were mauled up so badly. I don't know by what. When I brought the machine gun up, the commander was lying on the ground in absolute agony and our RSM Cunningham was saying, 'Come on get a stretcher-bearer, I want to save a life. For God's sake, I want to save a life.' Other members of the crew were dead.

Mills had to continue down the sunken lane. He found Private Ron Jepp and another machine gunner and set up the Vickers on the slope, not far from the road. Because it had to stand on rough ground they had to hurriedly adjust the back leg.[12]

The leading tank was allowed to close to within forty yards, while the infantry were only twenty yards away. Lieutenant Mills:

We waited until they got very close, it was no good firing at him any earlier. We could see the commander standing thigh-high out of the turret. I was right there with Jepp, I said, 'Right, let him have it', and he took good aim, and missed him unfortunately, but it made him jump down into the tank and drop his lid. It was just one of those things, it didn't kill him, but it stopped him at that point.

Sergeant Knight's PIAT detachment of Privates Paddy MacSorley and Peter Wilson also opened fire from the bank. The leading tank was hit twice on the nose, without any effect. Sergeant Daniels was in his sandbagged position with the MG42s:

I saw this man run out with his three bombs and his PIAT, I guess from the anti-tank platoon... . He hit him in the track with a PIAT 'mortar shell'. We were always told, with a tank get close to it and they couldn't depress their muzzles and do you any harm. Anyway, I saw the smoke from this bomb come up from the track... . Next I saw this 'factory chimney' come round and VRRUMP. My laddo had gone. Just disappeared. There was just a hole with some blackened edges... . But the tank backed up. His track broke but he still kept going, how I don't know.

Stendall Brailsford:

Paddy MacSorley, an ex-India man out of the anti-tank platoon, went down on the left-hand side of the road to Breville in the ditch. I think he got about fifty yards when the tank hit him with a shell. Took him straight out.

I remember saying to somebody, 'Have you got a phosphorous grenade?' He said, 'What do you want it for?' I said, 'I want some smoke down there.' I stepped outside of the gate of the 'cottage', onto the road and threw this phosphorous grenade down towards the tank, which would give me a smoke screen... . The tank backed off! Fired a couple of shells... he did some damage, but he backed off.

You do things in the spur of the moment. I was surprised how you'd do things you'd never dream of doing in other circumstances.

Lieutenant Mills:

He started backing off down the road and as he backed off he was dropping off everything he'd got along the line of that ditch. The shells were arriving, he was firing HE and it was very, very, unpleasant for us. He killed two and wounded about twenty of us. Private Jepp was one of those killed.

Private Wilson was another. One of the shells had blown up close to Sergeant Daniels:

It must have landed just in front of the sandbags. It blew me right back, and Skippels was on the left and Blackwell, I think his name was, the Company Commander's batman, was on the right. Blackwell had his rifle cut clean in half and he didn't get a scratch apart from that. He said, 'Look at this!' He'd just got two bits of the rifle, and the sling held them together. Skippels had the top taken off his shoulder, sliced it off as if it'd been done with a chopper and it was pumping blood. The explosion had knocked me about a bit but I wasn't hurt. It was some time before I realized that through the front of my smock were shrapnel holes.

Corporal McGuinness:

Things went quiet. Fenson had gone, Jepp was dead, he lay just as a No 3 would, about three yards from the gun, which was put out of action beyond repair. It was at this time I saw some of our chaps with toggle ropes, pulling a 6-pounder up a hill. It belonged to the Black Watch, although they had lost some of their crew.... I ran down the hill, put the wheel brakes on, told the driver to reverse. I got the gun hooked up and jumped into the carrier. I told Major Smith I would go with them. We went towards the Château, as near the edge as possible. I was happy, we got the gun ready and loaded and I told the corporal to use his binoculars to see where the shot went. After we estimated the range, the tank was about 600 yards away, but I could see it alright through the telescopic sight. I fired and it was a lucky shot. It stopped, and I put two more shells into it. I was lucky not to have lost my eye. The sight on the left-hand side of the gun nearly caught me. I'd forgot it had a recoil of thirty-two inches. When the gun comes back so does the sight.

With ammunition running low RSM Cunningham and CSM Beckwith saw an undamaged Black Watch carrier that was a hundred yards away beside the Château drive. They sprinted over to it and dived in, but were spotted by another enemy tank coming up the road, and its hull machine-gun opened fire at them. The two Paras started the Carrier and drove it to a 6-pounder anti-tank gun that lay abandoned about

Stendall Brailsford.

Ron Jepp.

189

thirty yards from the entrance. They piled out, loaded and aimed the gun and fired two rounds, missing with both, but the tank had either had enough or run out of ammunition as mercifully it broke off and turned sharply back into the woods.[13]

Inside the Bois des Monts Sergeant Daniels had got Skippels to the RAP:

> There was a little step down from outside onto the quarry floor and it was awash with blood where they'd sat the stretchers down and the blokes were bleeding, and they hadn't had much of a chance to clear up. When I took Skippels in, he was in a bad way and an orderly brought him a mug of tea. Well that mug of tea consisted of that much tea and that much tea leaves. So Skip took a sip and said, 'I don't want it', so I said, 'I'll have it' and got a mouthful of tea leaves. Captain Watts said, 'If you're sick in my waiting room I'll have you shot!', and the place was filthy, you've never seen anything like it! Of course I had no intent of being sick, I just had all these tea leaves in my throat.

Gordon Newton also witnessed the scene at the RAP:

> Private 'Darky' Knight got hit and two of us took him into the villa. The MO said, 'Put him over there,' and gave him a squirt in the arm with a syringe. There were Jocks lying everywhere, badly wounded, dead. Dreadful it was.

With the defensive fire and the withdrawal of their own tanks, the German infantry slowly began to fall back. The enemy armour had destroyed nine Black Watch and Middlesex Carriers, three of them blazing furiously in front of the Château, and the explosions of the ammunition and petrol added to the general confusion.[14]

In this action the last of the 9th Battalion machine-gun platoon had been hit and only one PIAT detachment now survived, but Brigadier Hill's relief force was approaching the area. Bob Sullivan, 3rd Parachute Squadron RE:

> Brigadier Hill and his party of Canadians went ahead and we followed in single file at the rear. We walked along footpaths and hedgerows from 3 Para Brigade HQ, sheltered by trees and the woods, until we came to a track leading into the woods towards the Château St Côme and just beyond the chalet used as an advanced dressing station.

Brigadier Hill encountered the Black Watch:

> I was on the road and they had a very fine Padre [Tom Nicol], a great big fellow, stood about six feet two inches, and he was calming these young chaps of the Black Watch, and of course they were in disarray here.

Bob Sullivan:

> The Canadians and Brigadier Hill dispersed into the woods, and we rested alongside the track awaiting orders. It was utter confusion.

Led by Hill, the Canadians, with bayonets fixed, began to sweep through the Château wood, finding it full of Germans and Black Watch. Jan de Vries, 1st Canadian Parachute Battalion:

> In the run to the Château, as the noise of battle increased and with more shells and bullets flying around, I remember feeling not very heroic. But seeing the Brigadier totally exposed and urging us on gave me a feeling of resolve and let's get this over with.
>
> We passed an open half-circle area where jeeps and Bren carriers were parked close to the trees. They were on our right as we ran past. All the vehicles were on fire and exploding, with dead and wounded lying around, probably hit by mortar

Sapper Bob Sullivan.

or shell fire. When past this area we were at the edge of some trees with thick bush on our right and open areas to our left. While hitting the ground in the trees when a shell burst, I discovered myself crawling through the remains of a Black Watch man and feeling somewhat squeamish. When I noted the Château through the trees we were ordered to dig in and prepare to repulse an attack from our left, which was the direction of Breville.

Brigadier Hill:

We moved up to the far end of the wood near the Château and I remember seeing a German tank cruising up and down at close range but we had no means of dealing with it. At this stage my bodyguard had been shot through the arm but insisted on carrying on. However, by this time, the attack on both the Canadians and the 9th Battalion was petering out.

The Canadians began digging in. Jan de Vries:

The ground under the top ten inches was extremely hard and I never did get more than a foot or so down. There were a number of dead Black Watch men lying around mostly hit by air bursts in the trees that sent shrapnel in all directions, to say nothing of the ear- splitting crack as these air bursts exploded. The section I was in was positioned at the front edge of a small forest or bush with the ground toward Breville rising slightly and then falling away. This tended to limit our field of fire but would also expose the Germans more when they came.

Brigadier Hill went back to the road for further reinforcements. Lance Corporal Alan Graham, 3rd Parachute Squadron RE:

He personally, despite heavy small arms and mortar fire, guided our Troop to its defensive position to the forward area of a wood some fifty to seventy-five yards to the right of the Château. He left us with words of encouragement, and we quickly started digging our 'shell scrapes'. Before we had barely made an impression with our entrenching tools on the thickly rooted forward area of our wooded position, an ominous clanking sound was heard and a German Mk IV tank burst out of a hedge into the open field before us, and started spraying us with small arms fire.

He could see the tank commander standing up in the turret giving commands to his crew:

The tank was barely twenty to thirty yards away with this black-uniformed German calmly talking into his tank microphone. At that moment I am convinced he saw me and actually smiled! The smile soon went as my Troop opened up with rifle, Bren gun and PIAT shots. I personally fired three aimed shots at the tank commander before he ducked back down from the Troop broadside. All my shots must have missed, as the tank started slowly advancing, spraying our area with machine-gun fire.

Lance Sergeant Bill Irving immediately brought his PIAT into action:

I was so concerned with getting the range right that I didn't notice a concrete fence post about ten feet in front of us, and my first shot hit this post and nearly wiped a few of us out!

Lance Corporal Graham:

Standing up, he advanced and fired two shots with his PIAT and hit the tank with, I believe, his second shot.

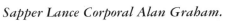

Sapper Lance Corporal Alan Graham.

191

Although not disabled, the tank took off backwards quite quickly and disappeared through the hedge to the right of the Château.[15]

The Germans began to regroup for yet another attack. At the direction of the Brigadier, Sergeant Willard Minard and an artillery officer called through the co-ordinates for heavy fire support from two Allied ships in the Channel, and brought down a barrage equivalent to six regiments of artillery to within a hundred yards of their defensive positions. This heavy shelling halted the enemy advance, but the situation remained serious and so the Brigadier sent some of the Canadians up towards the Château to make sure that the position there was firmly held. The building was re-occupied by a mixture of Canadians, Black Watch and Middlesex.

At 7.30pm further 3rd Parachute Squadron engineers, along with three troops of Sherman tanks of 'B' Squadron, 13th/18th Hussars, left Brigade HQ and took a route below the Bois des Monts and up the sunken lane. Fred Milward:

It was a beautiful feeling after us not seeing any armour up there. We thought 'We're all right now', especially after the battering we'd had.

2 Troop, 13th/18th Hussars was leading. Colonel Otway spoke to the commander of the tanks:

When he arrived he didn't really know what he was supposed to do. So he then said he thought he ought to take them forward and put them out as armoured OPs, hull down... . That seemed a good idea. But I said, 'Do not go up that drive because the Germans are up there to the north-west.' He went up there.

Sergeant Kennedy of the Black Watch was a hundred yards up the driveway in the left-hand ditch:

By now things had quietened down. What firing there was, was getting further away. It was at this point that three Shermans arrived and turned into the avenue. The first one stopped above my position and, without showing himself at the hatch, asked where the Germans were. Before I could answer him, his tank was hit. The two following tanks swung off to the left and into the field to meet the same fate.

Lieutenant Mills:

It was just like a giant blacksmith hitting a giant anvil, three bangs, metal on metal. All three went up in flames.

Derek Vincent

Miraculously, all of the crews managed to escape the burning tanks.[16] Fred Milward:

One of the crew jumped into my trench. He was unable to hear a word I said, deafened by the shell hitting the tank.

Jimmy French:

Suddenly a man jumped into my trench, virtually on top of me. He looked pretty distressed. I said, 'It's alright mate we've got some Shermans coming up.' He said, 'I'm the bloody driver of one of them. It's burning over there!'

A few men stumbled towards Bob Sullivan's trench:

All were blackened by smoke etc, and most were in a state of shock, and mostly incoherent.

Derek Vincent was dug in directly behind the Bois des Monts gate:

During a lull in the shelling I decided it was safe enough to go to the loo. On putting my hand on the side of the trench to lever myself out, I put my hand on the face of a comrade who had had his face blown away. This seemed to unnerve me, particularly as soon afterwards a squadron from the tanks who had brewed up, one of the tank crew came tearing up, through the gate, straight into my trench. He was a bit shaken up naturally, he'd just been brewed up and they were still sending over shell after shell after shell. He said, 'Christ, I'm not stopping here,' and he buggered off. But it unnerved me. The last thing I can remember is shouting, 'No bloody German's coming through the gate unless it's a dead German!' I don't know what happened after that, but I woke up in the building to my rear [the bungalow] *feeling very refreshed after a sleep (I don't know how long for) and not remembering how I got there.*

Lieutenant Douglas Martin.

The tanks of the two remaining troops were withdrawn.

With the ammunition level at the Bois des Monts now getting serious, Colonel Otway ordered Lieutenant Martin, his Brigade Liaison Officer, to fetch some from Brigade HQ. Brigadier Hill said that he could take as much as he wanted but that he may have a problem finding a jeep to bring it back. Martin set off on foot with his batman. At Brigade HQ, he did manage to acquire a jeep, much to the disgust of the driver who was reluctant to part with it. The ammunition was loaded, and with the 'owner' sat beside him and his batman in the back, they set off. Dougie Martin was in a hurry:

> *I said, 'I will drive.' It* [the Battalion] *was near enough running out of ammunition. I was belting down* [the road to the Bois des Monts].

Just as they were approaching the Bois des Monts Martin was hit from behind by a sniper's explosive bullet which carved through the left side of his neck and shoulder before blowing his jaws out. The jeep overturned several times and came to rest ten yards from the Bois des Monts gate. Pandemonium ensued. The Paras immediately fired smoke bombs into the air to try and reach the casualties, but

CSM Wally Beckwith.

these hit branches overhead and the phosphorous began falling onto some Black Watch who were in one of the roadside ditches. CSM Beckwith dashed out and got the Lieutenant into cover. Miraculously, still alive, he was taken into the RAP.[17]

Shortly after, at Brigade HQ, Staff Captain Woodgate heard about Dougie Martin's fate:

When I got news of this, I thought I must try and help my old Battalion, and I filled my jeep with food and ammunition and with my batman manning the Bren gun that I had acquired, we set off for the 9th Battalion. It was an extremely hazardous journey along the road to the crossroads and then a turn left along the road to the Bois des Monts. As we turned at Le Mesnil crossroads, a Canadian Company Commander (I think Major Fuller) dashed up to me and said, 'For God's sake don't go up there, the Germans are all over the place.' I thought the only thing to do was to go on, and I put my foot down, my batman opened up with the Bren, and we drove through the Germans who were on both sides of the road, and they seemed to be falling all over the place. Fortunately the Bren did not jam, nor the jeep founder, and neither my batman nor I were hit.

It became apparent to the Black Watch that German tanks were moving into position to prepare for one last attack. By mere chance, a radio link was established with HMS *Arethusa* by their men in the Château. This again proved to be effective in breaking the German build-up.[18]

Lieutenant Mills:

After a while the enemy started firing Verey lights, and one of the officers, Christie, said, 'Look, these Verey lights. We know what that means, that means they're buggered! Absolutely buggered! They're not coming back.'

He was right. By 8.00pm, the crisis had passed and the position was finally becalmed.

*

Just before 9pm Brigadier Hill returned to Brigade HQ. At around the same time Colonel Otway was talking to Captain Greenway in company with Lieutenants Christie and Pond and Sergeant McGeever on the bank of the sunken lane. Ernie Rooke-Matthews was dug in close by:

It was a pleasant sunny evening. We could now relax as there was quite a lull. Taffy [Pritchard] and I were sitting on the edge of our trench.... . The Commanding Officer was doing his rounds of the Battalion's positions accompanied by Lieutenant Christie, who I assumed was duty officer. He came over to our slit trench to check everything was OK. We were standing together chatting and having a smoke. From time to time in recent evenings an isolated aeroplane had come around and dropped the odd bomb, presumably to let us know that they knew we were there. Suddenly we had not only the plane dropping some small bombs but a small shell burst. By now our reactions were sharp, we would hit the ground whenever we heard the sound of activity.

A concentration of heavy shell fire lasted for ten minutes.

There was a terrific blast, then silence. I was temporarily deafened.... . Then I could hear the shouts, 'Medics, medics'. 'Are you OK Rooke?' It was the sergeant. He helped me to light another cigarette. 'Yes, I'm

Cliff Pritchard.

OK,' I said, my hand trembling as I tried to hold my cigarette.
Taffy was OK.

The blast had blown the Colonel across the road. Greenway was up in a tree, literally spreadeagled across a branch, although luckily he had only suffered concussion. McGeever was also wounded.

An attack was anticipated but nothing followed.[19] Stendall Brailsford had been asleep in his trench and awoke to see Lieutenant Christie:

There was a tree about seven or eight yards away and I saw him sitting with his legs sprawled out, with his head down, with his back against the tree and I thought he was asleep. I went out and nudged him and his head fell down, and shrapnel had taken half his face off... . I reported Christie's death. Somebody helped me carry him over to the field where we buried one or two of the lads... . I buried him... . I made a little cross for him.

Lieutenant Murray Christie.

Hugh Pond had heard the shell coming, dived into a ditch and received a mouthful of dirt and dust that caused him to sneeze. He suffered an agonising pain in his right side and went to move but couldn't. Also suffering from concussion, he was taken to the RAP. After examination, the MO told him that there was no blood but that he must have broken some ribs a week ago in the glider and the sneeze may have split them apart. Adrenalin may have been a factor why he had not felt anything before. He was bound up as tightly as possible, placed on an ambulance jeep and evacuated.

*

During the early morning of this momentous day General Gale had decided to mount a surprise attack in another attempt to close the Breville gap. This time it would be from the area of the 1st Special Service Brigade and be carried out by the 12th Parachute Battalion, a company of the 12th Devons, the 22nd Independent Parachute Company and 'A' Squadron of the 13th/18th Hussars. At 9pm the supporting barrage began, but tragically some of it fell short, and the Airborne men suffered heavy casualties.[20] Yet at 10pm the attack still went in and the 9th Battalion listened to it. Sergeant Knight:

They attacked from Amfreville and you could look down on them and actually see the battle taking place with our boys attacking. They relieved us tremendously by doing that and then they took Breville. Marvellous job. I don't think we'd be here today if they hadn't done that. They lost an awful lot of men though, some killed by our own gunfire.[21]

*

At the Bois des Monts RAP it was 10.30pm before the last batch of wounded men was carried down to the waiting jeeps. Some of the Black Watch bearers were staggering with exhaustion. Every able-bodied man who was not 'Standing To' had helped to carry stretchers. During the worst period of the rush the terrace outside the villa had again been lined with stretcher cases for whom there was no room in the house, and those that were obviously dying lay unattended along the grass verge. Blood-soaked dressings and piles of discarded equipment littered the steps leading to the front door.

Captain Watts had worked continuously during the five days of battle around St Côme and on this day had at one time, 180 wounded in the Aid Post. He had evacuated 183 patients and treated a procession of others while the battle had gone on around him.[22] Padres Gwinnett and Nicol, and the artist, Albert Richards, had worked hard alongside the medics, collecting wounded and also the bodies of the dead. These were laid in the back garden of the bungalow, and were so close together that they were almost piled up.[6]

The Black Watch casualties had again been heavy. The 9th Battalion was also severely depleted. Lieutenant Mills:

> *It was fairly peaceful during the night and this lull came in useful because we hadn't got any water. I'd distributed all the water and I took water out of the well. I filtered that stuff. I used chlorine tablets and the taste removers and managed to make tea for the Battalion to warm everybody up.*
>
> *I took a parade state on the evening of the 12th June and counted only 126 men.*

In effect, the Battalion had suffered nearly 150 casualties since the morning of 10 June. However, the sacrifice of all the formations involved in defending the ridge and capturing Breville had not been in vain. Brigadier Hill:

> *The German losses in both men and material were great and it would be said that we had won a great defensive victory.*

CHAPTER THIRTEEN

Relief

Tuesday 13 June

At around 7.00am, the 2nd Oxfordshire and Buckinghamshire Light Infantry arrived to relieve the 9th Battalion and the 5th Black Watch. They met a scene of utter desolation. Private Dennis Edwards, 'D' Company:

> *All around was evidence of brutal warfare such as I had never seen before. God, I was horrified. I witnessed shell-shock on a massive scale when we came into contact with the Highland Division lads. The poor devils stood around in groups as if in a mass daze, staring at us through vacant and bewildered eyes.*
>
> *I had never seen the result of warfare so grimly portrayed, with every ditch, gully, hedgerow, track and roadway strewn with dead and shattered bodies of British and German alike.*
>
> *Every square foot of ground seemed to be strewn with parts of human bodies, discarded, burnt (and still burning or smouldering) equipment, weapons, clothing ammunition, grenades, guns, vehicles and tanks. Strips of machine gun bullet belts beside twisted and broken weapons. Tins of food, mess tins, packets of biscuits and just about everything else that British and German troops might carry, was scattered everywhere.*
>
> *We moved up the drive that led to the Château St Côme, stepping round what, the day before, had been Sherman tanks and armoured troop carriers. Now they were simply twisted, smouldering and burnt-out wrecks. Beneath one tank was the shrivelled remains of two burnt bodies.*

They moved forward into the Château grounds to seek out any enemy who may still be about, and look for suitable positions in which to dig trenches in anticipation of a counter-attack.

When the Ox and Bucks had settled in, the remnants of the 9th Battalion and 5th Black Watch moved off.[1] The group of Middlesex left the scene with their only surviving Carrier limping noisily along with a broken bogie wheel.

There was no immediate relief for the Paras or the Jocks as they were sent down to the area of the brickworks, opposite Brigade HQ.

The driveway, post-battle.

A carrier knocked out in the area.

The Ox and Bucks could not quite believe the scene of the area they had inherited. Dennis Edwards:

> *They must have been thankful to get away from the place, it must have been sheer hell. Before they left they told us that the whole area had been the scene of vicious hand-to-hand fighting, attack followed by counter-attack and, whilst the battle had been raging, they had been bombarded by the big guns from both sides (including our big Naval guns). When the Scots and Paras had looked like gaining control, the Germans had called for their artillery to blast the area, and when the Germans counter-attacked and drove our lads back, our big guns had blasted the area.*
>
> *Indeed, at one time, all of the big guns from both sides had pounded the area simultaneously whilst hand-to-hand combat had been in progress so that everyone had been caught in the open.*
>
> *From the Scots we learnt about the line of wrecked vehicles along the Château driveway. During the attack the tanks and troop carriers were proceeding slowly along the driveway towards the Château when one of the deadly German 88 SP's came along a parallel hedgerow, poked its long gun through the hedge and, at almost point-blank range, swiftly fired a quick succession of shells that scored direct hits into the sides of every vehicle before anyone had had time to swivel their own guns round and fire back. These 88's were so fast, and so bloody accurate. Before anyone could do anything about them they had gone.*
>
> *The area was crawling with enemy snipers. In the open parkland we presented easy targets as we dug our holes.*
>
> *Opposite our new positions, and just across the driveway, stood what remained of a small coppice which I judged to be about fifty yards by thirty yards. The trees had been torn to shreds. Whole branches ripped off and lying on the ground. Some of the taller ones had had their tops blasted away and the high stumps of the trunks had been set alight and were still smouldering. Within this small area I reckoned that there were at least twenty bodies, British and German. It was difficult to be exact as few were whole and there were many detached arms, legs and heads. British lay across Germans and Germans on top of British.*

There were, however, several dead who had presumably been killed by shell blast and were virtually unmarked. Amidst this dreadful carnage I saw some quite amazing sights. In a hastily dug shallow shell scrape was a Scot laying on his back and in his hand he was holding a set of fanned out playing cards, yet he was completely on his own (At what stage of such a battle a man could have found the time to play a hand of cards I simply could not imagine!) Nearby lay a comrade, a Corporal with an African Star amongst his medal ribbons, he was at the foot of a tree stump, flat upon his stomach and with a Thompson sub-machine gun pulled tightly against his shoulder. His finger was still curled round the trigger and whilst his left eye was tightly closed, his right was wide open and peering intently along the sights of his weapon, obviously taking aim and ready to fire.

Within a few yards, and directly opposite, at the base of another tree-stump, lay a German in an almost identical position, holding a dagger in his still clenched fist. One knee was drawn up beneath his prone body and the other straight out behind him. His arms were in corresponding positions and it appeared as if he was about to crawl forward to attack the Scot. The two appeared to have been killed at the same instant.

A few yards away a German was in the process of opening a box of ammunition and still had a hand on top of the box. Beside him lay his mate behind an empty machine gun. He was looking over his shoulder towards his companion and it was easy to imagine him saying, 'Hurry up, the machine gun is empty', at the moment that death struck them.

There were other unmarked British and Germans in a variety of positions. A German lying flat upon the ground and still clutching a long-handled stick grenade, another with a water bottle pressed to his lips, yet another placing a bandage on the arm of his wounded comrade.

Some were sitting up. Others lying down. Some on their backs with their hands in the air as if to ward off danger, others on their stomachs with faces pressed into the ground, or still clutching a helmet to their heads as if for added protection. The scene was like some grotesque set-piece in a waxworks museum, except

A burnt out barn and derelict carrier.

The rear of the Chateau.

Shermans of the 13th/18th Hussars knocked out in the area.

that these were real people, all killed by the blast of massive shells which left many of them completely unmarked, like a frozen frame from a strip of a movie film. Amidst the bodies was torn and discarded equipment, a German mortar, rolls of blankets, a German Army hand-cart, a wide variety of weapons, some whole and still in good working order, others little more than twisted lumps of wood and metal. Much of this shattered and broken humanity and accessories was covered by large branches from trees, twigs, fresh leaves, strands of barbed wire, lumps and clods of grass and earth and, all around, were deep holes where the big shells had exploded.

The scene was horrifying but the smell was even worse. The air was heavy and sickly with the smell of burnt (and some still burning) flesh, clothing, wood, leaves, grass, petrol, oil and gunpowder. The night-time rain had stopped soon after dawn and been replaced by warm sunshine which was already having its effect upon human flesh.

This was in one small segment of the battlefield. It was repeated all around the grounds of the Château St Côme and along the hilltop to the nearby shattered village of Breville where, amongst other horrific sights, was a weird tableau in which one of the Canadian Paras had been run through the middle of his body by a German rifle and bayonet which had pinned him to a tree. At the same time he had reached over the bent German and plunged his dagger into the middle of his opponent's back. The two had died at some time during the night but in daylight could be seen propping each other up.

The smell of the still burning stables and horses added to the overall and unforgettable putrid stench.[2]

*

The area continued to be shelled and sniped, but Breville remained in Airborne hands and although the men did not realize it at the time, the Germans had been so badly mauled that they would not be able to mount another major assault upon the ridge.

Aftermath

Only a week had passed since the inexperienced 9th Battalion had left Broadwell. Many now lay buried beneath the Normandy soil, others had disappeared without trace, some were terribly wounded. Those left behind were irreparably changed. Veterans. On June 17 they were finally pulled out of the line, retiring to a quarry below Amfreville. Colonel Otway went to see Colonel Pine-Coffin. As he was entering a building, he turned around to see his men stretched out on the grass beside the road, sound asleep. They had fallen where they stood.

*

Today

The Battalion fought many more battles and incurred further losses before the end of the war, but amongst all of this tragedy, a bond between them was cemented.

In 1962 a 9th Parachute Battalion Reunion Club was formed and annual dinners followed which grew in popularity as word of its existence spread.

In 1969 on the 25th Anniversary of D-Day, the first organised coach trip visited the scene of their actions.

Today, although sadly their number has inevitably dwindled, the 9th's Reunion Club is as strong as ever. Sons and grandsons are allowed to become members and those not related, but with an interest in the Battalion, honorary members. Thus the memory of the men and the achievements of the Battalion will be perpetuated.

Annually, 6th Airborne Division veterans travel to Normandy for the D-Day commemorations. The Reunion Club coach forms part of this and is always fully booked. Fred Milward is one of the many regulars:

> Never let it be said we were not scared. I was, and like many more of us, when we carried our boys down to bury them near the Bois des Monts, I wondered where my grave would be. But I was spared, and now every year, with others who made it, I go back to Normandy and honour our dead.

*

The Paras of the 9th Battalion have been 'at odds' with the Commonwealth War Graves Commission concerning losses. The Battalion believes that over 190 men are unaccounted for, presumably lost in the flooded area of Normandy. Certainly, when the known figures are collated, there does appear to be this huge discrepancy. Colonel Otway:

> My own comment is that we were there and know the numbers, which the Civil Servants do not. And we have been in touch with the families of the missing men. When I came out of hospital I travelled all over the place visiting families.

Unfortunately the Battalion's pre D-Day roll call is lost or has not yet come to light, and nearly all of the stick lists that were completed for each plane are also missing. Maybe something will surface in the years ahead.

Whatever the truth, several things ensure that the exploits of the whole Battalion during the first week in Normandy are permanently remembered; a memorial now stands on Walbury Hill near Inkpen, overlooking the site of the Battery mock-up, the Merville Battery still exists and is now a growing tourist attraction, No 1 casemate having been turned into a museum that holds many interesting photos, documents and artefacts and in June 1986, after much work by Frank Delsignore, Sid Capon and the committee, a memorial to the St Côme battle was finally placed at the entrance to the Château driveway.

*

If there is anyone who is able and would like to expand on any of the content within this book, or detail incidents that have not been mentioned, in fact anything to do with the 9th Parachute Battalion, please contact the author via the publisher or by e-mail to neil@mervillebattery.co.uk. Also visit the website at www.mervillebattery.co.uk.

Any information will also be forwarded to the relevant archive.

*

Fates of those men mentioned in the text

The men of the Airborne Division, Commandos and 51st Highland Division remained in the area until their part in the breakout from Normandy in August.

In early September the 6th Airborne Division returned to England. During the three months in action, it had suffered 4,457 casualties; 821 killed, 2709 wounded and 927 missing.

The following is a list of the fates of those men mentioned in the text.

9th Parachute Battalion

Due to the wounds suffered on 12 June, Terence Otway suffered headaches and pains on the left side of his head and neck for weeks after, and on one occasion actually lost his sight for three hours. Finally, on 19 July, he had to be evacuated and was diagnosed as being badly concussed and eventually (after the war), as suffering from nerve damage and a damaged back. Major Napier Crookenden of the 6th Airlanding Brigade assumed command of the Battalion.

Major Edward Charlton, aged 31, is buried in Ranville Cemetery, Grave IA.B.19.

Lt Douglas Catlin, killed in the friendly bombing incident, is buried in Ranville Cemetery, Grave IV.A.F6. Aged 28.

Lt Murray Christie, killed by the explosion in the sunken lane on the 12 June, was 24. He is buried in Ranville Cemetery, Grave IA.J.15.

Lt Mike Dowling, killed in the Merville Battery, has no known grave. He is commemorated on the Bayeux Memorial, Panel 18, Column 1. Aged 34.

Lt Tom Halliburton, aged 24, died on the 7 June from the wounds suffered during the attack on the strong house in Le Plein. He is buried in the Ranville Churchyard, Grave 6.

Lt Alfred Hughes, who must have been dropped very wide was almost certainly killed in a subsequent battle with the enemy. He is buried in Grave 7, St Vaast-en-Auge Churchyard, 29km north-east of Caen. He was 28 years old. (see also Major Alec Pope below)

Lt Gordon Parfitt is buried in Ranville Cemetery, Grave IA.J.19. He was 23 years old.

Lt George Peters, 23 years old, who was killed in the friendly bombing incident, lying beneath Brigadier Hill, is buried in Ranville Cemetery, Grave IV.A.06.

RSM Bill Cunningham, 32-years old, was killed by a shell whilst at the brickworks on 17 June 1944. Ranville Cemetery, Grave IIA.B.12.

CSM Wally Beckwith was killed by a sniper on the 17 August 1944. He was 28 years old. Typically, he was attempting to retrieve a man lying in the open who had been wounded by the sniper. Ranville Cemetery, Grave V.A.C1.

Colour Sgt Albert Davies, who came down into the sea in one of the transport gliders on D-Day is buried in Ranville cemetery, Grave VA.K.2.

Sgt Jimmy Frith, aged 25, was killed on the 19 August 1944. He is buried in Ranville Cemetery, Grave IIA.B.10.

Sgt James Rose, aged 21, who was killed in the Château wood alongside Major Charlton and Lt Parfitt, is buried in Ranville Cemetery, Grave IA.H.20.

Sgt James Young, a member of Brigadier Hill's D-Day morning group, is buried in Ranville Cemetery, Grave IVA.N.6. He was aged 28.

Cpl Fred Wingrove, aged 32, died of his wounds on the 15 June 1944. He is buried in Beaconsfield Cemetery, Bucks., Grave 1531.

L/Cpl Stan Eckert who died on D-Day aged 19, is buried, in Ranville Cemetery, a few yards away from his older brother, Cpl Cyril Eckert of the 7th Battalion, who was killed on the 23 August. Their graves are VI.A.B23 and VI.A.B13 respectively.

L/Cpl Edward Hull, 25 years old, who was killed in the accident before D-Day is buried in Oxford (Botley) Cemetery, Oxfordshire. Plot I/1 Grave 167.

L/Cpl Stanley Plested was killed in the friendly bombing incident and is buried in Ranville Cemetery, Grave VA.F.8. He was aged 24.

L/Cpl Peter Robinson, also killed in the friendly bombing incident, is buried in Ranville Cemetery, Grave IA.B.17. He was aged 24.

Pte George Adsett, Major Parry's batman, killed in the Merville Battery, has no known grave and is commemorated on the Bayeux Memorial, Panel 18, Column 1. He was 21.

Pte Alroy John Armstrong was killed in the friendly bombing incident, and is buried in Ranville Cemetery, Grave IA.E.13. Aged 22.

Emile Corteil and Glenn the Para dog are buried together in Ranville Cemetery, Grave IA.G.13.

Pte Harry Dunk, aged 20, killed on the 7 June at the Le Mesnil crossroads, lies in Ranville Cemetery, Grave IA.H.3.

Pte Thomas 'Jock' Hannen, was killed on D-Day, possibly in the Merville Battery. He has no known grave and is commemorated on the Bayeux Memorial, Panel 18, Column 1. Aged 20.

20 year-old Pte Ron Jepp, the machine-gunner killed on the 12 June by the withdrawing German tank, lies in Ranville Cemetery, Grave IA.G.15.

Pte John 'Paddy' MacSorley, who died on the 12 June while attacking the tanks with a PIAT, is buried in Ranville Cemetery, Grave IA.F.20. He was aged 27.

Pte James Mander, another member of Brigadier Hill's group that was killed in the friendly bombing incident, is buried in Ranville Cemetery, Grave IA.D.13. Aged 19.

Likewise, in the same group, 19 year old Pte Alfred Nicholls is buried in Ranville Cemetery, Grave VA.H.5-8.

Pte Maurice Parris, 18 years old. His body was never found. He is commemorated on the Bayeux Memorial to the missing, Panel 18, Column 1.

Pte Norman Peck, aged 19, was yet another victim of the friendly bombing incident. Buried in Ranville Cemetery, Grave IA.C.13.

Pte Doug Penstone, killed while trying to reach the Airborne perimeter with Terry Jepp (see Appendix 3) is buried in Tilly-sur-Seulles War Cemetery, Grave III.A.6. He was aged 20.

Pte 'Paddy' Roche, aged 20, who suffered a shrapnel wound in the back, was evacuated to the M.D.S., where he was operated on, but died of shock at around 6.00pm on 10 June. He is buried in Ranville Cemetery, Grave IA.E.3.

Pte Peter Sanderson, killed by a mortar bomb at the Chateau driveway on the 12 June, is buried in Ranville Cemetery, Grave IA.J.20.

Pte Patrick Sharples, aged 23, killed in the friendly bombing incident, is buried in Ranville Cemetery, Grave IA.B.17. He was aged 23.

Pte Leonard Tudge, who was wounded and carried to safety by Jack Humfrey at the Le Mesnil Crossroads, returned to the Battalion but was sadly killed on 24 March 1945, aged 20. He is buried in the Reichswald Forrest War Cemetery, Grave 37.B.2.

Pte Percy Walter, 19 years old, another of Brigadier Hill's D-Day morning group, is buried in Ranville Cemetery, Grave IVA.K.6.

Pte Peter Wilson, aged 22, who also died in the action with the tanks, is buried in Ranville Cemetery, Grave IA.E.20.

Bob Abel was wounded in the leg at the Château St Côme and was evacuated to England. Survived.

Sid Capon was badly wounded in the chest and buttock by shrapnel on 24 July 1944. (The same shell killed L/Sgt Reg Fowler). After eight weeks, he returned to the battalion to take part in the Ardennes action.

Frank Delsignore and Fred Garrett were both badly wounded at the Bois des Monts by shrapnel. Both survived.

After being wounded in the throat on D-Day, Roy Wright went into action again and took part in the Rhine Crossing operation. Wounded again but survived the war.

Ernie Rooke-Matthews was wounded later in the campaign. Survived.

Miraculously, although grievously wounded, 'Hal' Hudson, Dougie Martin and Doug Tottle all survived. However, they spent many years recuperating in hospital.

3rd Parachute Brigade

The Brigade-Major, Bill Collingwood, who dislocated his leg while being dragged along outside his Dakota on D-Day, suffered severe injuries to his leg, which never fully recovered. Survived.

Major Alec Pope, who was dropped miles off course, was killed in a subsequent battle with the enemy. He is buried in Grave 1, St Vaast-en-Auge Churchyard, 29km north-east of Caen. He was 25 years old.

Captain Tony Wilkinson, killed on 8 June, is buried in Ranville Cemetery, grave IA.C.20. He was 24 years old.

Signalman S J 'Harry' Courtney, aged 23 of 3rd Parachute Brigade signals, killed while attached to the 9th Battalion, is buried in Ranville Cemetery, Grave IA.H.15. His headstone states that he was killed on 13 June. This is an error. It was 9 June.

3rd Parachute Squadron Royal Engineers

All those mentioned survived the war.

Glider Pilot Regiment

Of the glider pilots, S/Sgt Arnold Baldwin and Sgt Joe Michie survived the war.

S/Sgt Dickie Kerr was killed during the Arnhem operation. He has no known grave and is commemorated on Panel 8 of the Groesbeek Memorial, Holland.

Sgt Harry Walker, aged 29, died on 29 September 1944, during the Arnhem operation. He is buried in the Oosterbeek Cemetery, Grave 24.B.15.

1/7th Middlesex Battalion

The three Middlesex men killed by the brief mortar bombardment in the early morning were Albert Brown, Ben Lyus, Harry Tomlinson. They are all buried in Ranville Cemetery, graves IV.D.5, IV.D.1 and IV.D.23 respectively. Harry Biddell was killed in the Château during the afternoon by a mortar fragment. He lies in Grave IV.D.8.

Lofty Pearson and Dennis Daly survived the war.

5th Black Watch

John McGregor survived the War.

RASC

Driver Raymond Garrett, aged 20, who was driving the medical jeep when it ran over the minefield, died of his wounds on 14 June. He is buried in Hermanville War Cemetery, Grave 1.Q.16.

Appendix 1

The Continuation of Private Fred Glover's Story
following his capture on 6 June, near the Merville Battery

As I was stretchered from the ambulance a glance took in what was obviously a Field Hospital. There was just one large Chateau-like building, the patients being housed in long huts similar to a Nissen. Surgery was carried out in the building and I was taken there. First there was an anaesthetic which consisted of a gauze placed over the mouth and nose with some chloroform then applied.

I recovered to find myself lying on a bed in one of the huts. Looking around it seemed that there were men from many units but none that I could recognise. There is only one incident that comes to mind and that was being approached by a rather sad looking German orderly who asked me, and I quote, 'When are your buddies coming for you?' It transpired that he had been a waiter in New York just prior to the war.

The location of the hospital was in the area of Pont l'Eveque. As far as I am able to recall, my stay was for three days and the procedure of being loaded into an ambulance was repeated and off I go again.

The next location turned out to be a hospital building which I was informed had at one time been known as the American Hospital, for what reason I have no idea. There were, as I remember, three floors and we were housed at the top, there being small wards leading off from a long corridor. One incident I recall was of a soldier from the 15th Scottish Division on his own in a room, empty except for a straw palliase, on which the man lay naked. An orderly explained that he had received a wound to one side of his head and he could not control his bodily functions and he had to be left in this situation but was being treated. I saw this soldier some weeks later and his condition had improved considerably. Anyone reading this, and who was present will I am sure recall the rather ancient German orderly who distributed melted cheese on bread from a basket over his arm and could never understand why he was always short. He never realised that we were using various means of distracting him from his task while others helped themselves to his wares. Surprisingly, there was never a query from the kitchen. It was not all good humour however; there was one particularly unpleasant individual in the person of a middle-aged nursing sister. She delighted in making treatment as painful as possible, sometimes distressing other nurses who were present.

During this period I contracted a mild form of tonsillitis and was conducted to an annex where a doctor gave me a prescription which eased the discomfort. It was then that I learned that we were in or near the town of Evreux.

There were many Hitler Youth working in the building and this was the only experience I witnessed of people actually raising their arm and saying, 'Heil Hitler;' it was an extraordinary sight.

From time to time, groups of us were transported away and it was some time before we discovered that the destination was Paris. At first this was disbelieved but was eventually confirmed. It seemed to me that if there was any chance of avoiding finishing up in a P.O.W. camp somewhere in Germany, perhaps in Paris with the help of the resistance this might just be possible.

It is time for me, together with a number of others to leave. We are put aboard a rather ancient coach with the entry for passengers at the rear. The fairly large windows afforded us quite a good view and this was to prove advantageous as will be seen from what was to follow. We drove slowly through the town and passed a group of what was obviously some unfortunate foreign workers who began to wave, call out and raise their arms in a clenched fist salute. At this, the only guard, seated at the back by the door, leaped out and went berserk, drew a pistol and rushed at the workers shouting and waving the gun in the air. Meanwhile the driver, totally unaware of what had occurred and seeing he had a clear run, put his foot down and started to make off up the road. The guard, suddenly aware of the situation, did a quick about-turn and still waving his gun and shouting, began chasing the coach down the road. Only a few seconds elapsed before his comrade realised what was happening and stopped. The guard arrived sweating profusely and looking very sheepish. All in all it was quite an event, worthy of inclusion in an episode of 'Allo, Allo'! I have often wondered what would have happened had we turned up without him. The eastern front perhaps?

It is true, we are in Paris. There is no mistaking the Eiffel Tower as the coach passes under it on the way to our destination, which turns out to be the Hopital [Ortzlazarette] de la Pitie [on the Boulevard de l'Hopital]. On our arrival, French hospital staff stretcher us inside making various gestures like 'thumbs up' etc; we are among friends. Soon beds are allocated and it is time to take stock. The ward is situated on the top storey and there is just one guard who turns out to be quite a pleasant chap who showed pictures of his family and expressed his fear of being sent to Russia. There is no complaint as regards the treatment received and rations are the same as that provided to the staff.

It is clear that any further movement will be to a camp somewhere in Germany with the fittest being the first to go. In view of this it seems wise to exaggerate one's condition and this some of us did. We had a visit from a propaganda unit. American cigarettes were handed out and photographs taken. As a non-smoker I did not warrant any attention and was not troubled.

One interesting character in the ward was a Naval rating who had landed with the 9th. As a wireless operator his task was to direct gunfire from HMS *Arethusa* on to the Battery should the attack fail. Unfortunately he had trod on a mine and had lost a foot.

Our morale was very high, although tinged with some concern as we had been made aware of the use of the so-called V-weapons. I still wonder how we got away with singing one of the songs from what I think was a Disney cartoon which included some very derogatory remarks about the Fuhrer. I was reminded of this recently by Terry Jepp (now Jefferson), a comrade and friend who I had the good fortune to meet at this time.

Our French friends told us that there had been an evacuation of some of the German personnel and it was feared that there might be plans to move the wounded at short notice. Terry and myself had become acquainted with several young French hospital staff; I will not name them as I believe they are already on record in an item by Terry which can be seen in the [Merville] Battery Museum. Sufficient to say that they were of considerable assistance to us and are always remembered.

It becomes obvious that vigilance is becoming lax and the Germans themselves are aware of increasing activity by the Resistance and it appears that the time is fast approaching when a decision has to be made.

Although feigning difficulty moving very fast, I had made myself available to move between wards helping in any way that I could. This enabled me to get a picture of what was happening. German wounded were being shipped out with some haste and I discovered that some of our own people had also gone, all walking wounded.

It was at this time that I decided to see if our friends could assist as I knew that there was little time left and with the Germans now seemingly more and more concerned with their own predicament, and my movement around the building being taken as read, I reasoned that short of walking through the main gate there should be no difficulty.

This being the case, it was agreed that at nightfall I would get down to the ground floor and, if manageable, would get out of a window in the washroom and if successful, drop down a wall into the grounds of the infirmary next door, and from there be led away by someone who would be waiting.

At the appointed time I did as planned and everything was fine except that the height of the wall had not been determined and as it was dark I had no means of knowing. The fall was a disaster. I reopened my wounds and was in some pain. However, help was at hand and willing hands bore me away. Looking back, I have to say that to class it as an escape might be considered a little over the top. I felt more like a small boy absconding from Boarding School.

Where I was taken is still a mystery to me, sufficient to say that as the night wore on I acquired a taste for Cognac which has never left me.

The following day my helpers brought a doctor to have a look at me. What was revealed next came as a shock. He said that I would need to go back into the hospital as there was an evacuation taking place and the Germans were leaving all Allied wounded behind. At this I felt a little sheepish. It seemed that the efforts of the previous night had been for nothing and I could have stayed put. Probably, to make me feel better, he explained that this situation had only been made known that afternoon and Allied walking wounded had in fact been shipped as late as 11pm that day. Naturally I still like to believe it was worthwhile and have convinced myself that I would have been on that last shipment.

There was some lively discussion and Jean-Luc, who appeared to be in charge of the group and spoke good English, told me that the situation was by no means stable and there were pockets of die-hard Germans and collaborators firing from various vantage points. At this I agreed it would be wiser to wait until the following day.

There were no incidents as I was escorted to the hospital but I was surprised to find that there were still some German staff making frantic efforts to depart. They ignored us. It became apparent that we were no longer under enemy control and during my tour I had the good fortune to meet up with Terry Jepp again. It would appear that he too had evaded the guard and in today's parlance 'had it away on his toes'. The next significant occurrence was my requisitioning of a firearm. I took a walk round the wards to see who remained. On the lower floor there were small annexes where I assume German officers had been housed and I took the opportunity to open the door of just one. There were items of kit stacked ready to move and behind the door a large valise. Without a second's hesitation my hand was in the partially open top and to my astonishment I was holding a holster complete with pistol and spare magazine. What I did next was a reflex action as I stuffed the whole thing inside my shirt and got out of that area as quickly as possible. What the consequences would have been had I been caught one can only guess, but at best I am sure I would have been taken away with the remaining Germans.

Terry and I spent time with the friends we had made and the war had taken a turn for the better. Word began to spread that advance elements of General Leclerc's Free French Division were poised to enter the city and huge crowds began to gather in the boulevards. As the column moved, so it was submerged under a sea of people. The vehicles and tanks could not be seen as the human tide swept over them. These were scenes that defy description and I feel privileged to have witnessed this historic occasion.

It was while we joined in these celebrations that shots were fired from a room on the upper floor of a tall building just behind us. Everyone went to ground and there was a lot of shouting and arm-waving; Terry and I became aware that we had become of interest and realised that it was because I was armed. There seemed to be no alternative but to respond and so I made to move for the entrance to the building with Terry following, 'To keep you company,' as he put it and Arlette Lebrun saying, 'It is necessary to take great care'. We made our way up the stairs with some difficulty, neither of us were too good at moving with any speed, and reached the top storey. At that moment a very elderly lady came towards us shouting and pointing to a room at the end of the corridor. We approached very warily. The door was partially open but there was no sound. On entering in the approved fashion, there was a movement from behind a curtain which was across one corner and I fired two rounds into it. I cannot be certain of whether or not I had hit someone because at that precise moment the room began to disintegrate around us as heavy fire came up from the armoured vehicles down in the road. It was no time to loiter and Terry and I felt we had done enough in the circumstances. We both returned to the hospital and I believe that it was on this night that enemy aircraft dropped a few bombs on the city.

During my wandering, two German orderlies who had apparently decided they wanted out of the war, took me first to a store where the German personnel kit was stored. Here I helped myself to various items of insignia and medals etc. We then moved on to an underground medical facility, operating theatre, X-Ray dept. etc. This building was situated just inside the main gate and had a large swastika in stone over the entrance. I think it was about now that Terry and I lost contact and we went our different ways. For several days I was with Jean-Luc and his group but I was of limited use although I did go with them on a couple of occasions. One of the Free French had given me an American carbine which was useful as there was still sporadic skirmishing taking place. It became increasingly clear that I was in urgent need of medical attention as there was an unpleasant aroma about me and so an American liaison officer was contacted. Arrangements were made for me to be taken to their field hospital and then moved on.

The carbine I passed to the group and then I sought out Marc Vincent, one of the original group who befriended us, and gave him my parachutist's smock. Little enough but I think he was pleased. Gathering my few belongings I board a Jeep and am driven to an American field hospital and receive a warm welcome and treatment. My stay is for a few hours, only then it's on to an airstrip, aboard a C47 and off to England.

Appendix 2
The Commando Liberation of Amfreville/Le Plein

After Captain Westley and Lieutenant Keith Ponsford had been on the recce of the position with Colonel Otway, they returned to the bottom of the hill.

At around 3.30pm, 3 Troop advanced in sections, leapfrogging each other up either side of the road. They neared the top of the hill without incident. In front the road ran between two high walls, with a house on either side. The nearest was the gable end of an outhouse on the left. Trooper 'Ossie' Osbourne was leading with the Bren gun, followed by Troopers 'Dixie' Dean and Jack Barnes. Trooper Stan Scott was behind:

> Top of the house in the apex there was a little window. I don't know why but everybody must have been watching that little window. We spotted the muzzle end of a rifle coming out of it – badly trained infantryman. I don't know how many people fired at it but the window just disappeared with the strikes, and the rifle fell out. We didn't know whether we'd hit the bloke inside or not.

They continued between the walls, reaching a slight bend that opened out into the village. Heavy machine gun fire hit them. A Russian Maxim was firing from in front, and small arms fire was also coming from a nearby building, the village Post Office. Stan Scott:

> That first burst of fire knocked half a dozen of our blokes out. Westley got hit in the wrist and elbow, Paddy Harnett got it through the arse, 'Dixie' Dean got it in the guts, Abbott got his leg cut off... If he'd have waited fifteen seconds he'd have got most of us.

The surviving Commandos immediately returned fire. The only cover was the ground and the contours of the walls. 'Ossie' Osbourne was working the Bren:

> There was a wall on the left with a sort of recessed doorway, a big double one, which 'Tucker' Jennings ran into for cover holding his arse. A bullet shot his water bottle there.

During the ensuing firefight Osbourne saw the enemy machine gunner slump dead. He thought that the skirmish had been won:

> I probably came to a change of mags and realised the firing had ceased. Now I turned round to wave the lads on but they'd withdrawn and I of course followed them back down the hill.

They were all grouped thirty yards back where the wall began on the right-hand side:

I said to Jack Barnes, 'Come on, we'll get Dixie,' he was my No 2. So we went and got Dixie, but he was pretty well gone.

Stan Scott:

He was a big bloke Dixie, he grabbed him by the webbing... It's not all nicey, nicey, like in the pictures. He dragged him back and gave him to me. For some reason or other they'd given me the first-aid kit. I couldn't do anything for Dixie. Within two minutes he was dead. He looked at me and... gone. Then I had Westley. Bandaged up his wrist and elbow and put that in a sling. Paddy Harnett was worried. He's saying to me, 'Have a look at me wedding tackle. Is me wedding tackle alright?'

Much to his relief, it was. Lance-Sergeant Les Hill then said to Osbourne, 'What about Johnny Abbott?' So the two of them went up the hill again. As they bent down to pick him up, the firing re-started and Hill was hit in the head. They had to leave Abbott on the ground. Hill staggered away in a daze, dragging his weapon along the ground behind him. Blood was pouring down his face. As he came back someone said to Stan Scott, 'He's a goner, there's nothing you can do for him.' He just carried straight on down to the bottom of the hill. A 9mm bullet had gone through the front of his helmet, parting his hair and leaving a furrow the size of an index finger across the top of his skull. He was one of the few men wearing a helmet and was only doing so because it had earlier been jangling against his bicycle.

With Captain Westley wounded, Lieutenant Ponsford decided to try again:

After taking command of the Troop I told TSM Coker to reorganise the Troop and cover me and Trooper Osbourne as we went forward to the line of houses... We found a passageway between the houses which gave us a good sight of the village.

They moved along a dirt track. 'Ossie'Osbourne:

As we closed up there, this German sergeant came out of one of the houses, not very aggressively inclined. Somebody gives him a fag. Just after this, Tommy Spencer came up, knocked his f...... fag out, pistol whipped him and queried him. Then I got to the end of that track.

Lieutenant Ponsford:

I then ordered up our 2-inch mortar group and we fired it at any position we thought the enemy may be hiding.

Aiming for the windows, the Post Office was 'plastered' with mortar bombs.

I then called up the Troop and ordered Sergeant Salsbury with his section to clear the row of houses and to leave the men at the upper floor windows ready to give covering fire on the signal.

Lance Sergeant Jimmy Synnott:

My section was to close off the south end of the village but to go no further. We moved off as the attack on the Post Office went in, using the houses on the right side as cover.

Simultaneously another attack went in up the hill road. Lieutenant Ponsford:

We attacked the schoolhouse first, from where the main resistance had been coming from, and lying on the floor we found a paratrooper with one leg blown off. Our medical lads attended to him.

Osbourne was firing at the Post Office windows when suddenly one of the yellow recognition triangles was waved from the back door, and a paratrooper who had been a prisoner came out and vomited.

Lance Sergeant Synnott's section had cleared the other end of the village:

Corporal Ferry and myself searched the houses at the north end, firing and killing two enemy working on a 75mm gun.

They then reached a farm owned by a Monsieur Bernard Saulnier. Jimmy Synnott:

I just asked him, 'Any Bosch?', to which he replied, 'Non.' We patrolled as far as the wall around Amfreville Cemetery. No enemy in sight in Breville but pulled back and dug in at the road junction at Bernard's Farm.

The Troop had swept through the village, killing around eight of the enemy and capturing more than twenty others besides several horse-drawn vehicles. The Germans had made a very hasty exit east, out of the village. 3 Troop did not lose a single man in this second attack. Lieutenant Ponsford:

By this time there was a large welcoming party of French people at the end of the drive leading to the Château Amfreville. As I felt we could expect mortaring from the Germans I asked them in my best schoolboy French to go back to their houses as it was very dangerous where they were. They were soon gone and we took up defensive positions along a hedgerow to the east of the road. Leaving Sergeant Major Coker in charge I went along to arrange our defence of the village with No 6 Commando.

Elements of No 6 Commando had arrived in the southern end of the village around Bernards Farm.

While Lieutenant Ponsford was away, a jeep from the mortar section came up to the No 3 Commando area and turned into the driveway to the Château d'Amfreville. Stan Scott:

Coker went over and was talking to the lads. He picked up a helmet that was in the jeep, put it on top of his head. He had his beret on. He said, 'I'm alright now!' BANG! A shell landed at the entrance to the Château. Billy Moore lost his arm. Coker, just took half his head off. He fell, his brains came out all over his bloody Thompson. A couple of blokes in the jeep were injured. The jeep driver did the right thing, he drove out of it, got away from the area.

This was the TSM that Colonel Otway saw when he drove out of the Château d'Amfreville.

In the following days the 1st Special Service Brigade had to repel heavy enemy attacks, while always carrying out 'aggressive' patrolling. These patrols continued until the whole of the 6th Airborne Division broke out in August.

Appendix 3

Continuation of Private Terry Jepp's experiences after reaching the Vermughens

Whilst the others settled themselves down to sleep, I joined Monique, Yvonne and Adrien in the farmhouse kitchen to try to tell them what the invasion plans were and how we came to be where we were. I did not at that time know that the 9th Battalion had been scattered over an area of thirty square miles, that less than a quarter of them would ever reach the Battery, and that I would never see my twenty-year-old brother Ron, jumping as a member of the machine-gun section, again.

I must at this point explain my constant use of the pronoun 'I'. At twenty-four years of age in 1944, I was an 'old soldier' in the 9th Battalion – old in years when compared with many of my compatriots whose ages were in the early twenties, or really even younger. Also, I was 'old' in experience, having been in the Territorial Army before the war. I had also, uncommonly in my Battalion, had a little experience on active service. And finally, I had previously twice held the rank of full corporal, but having lost it through various foolish misdemeanours. I was still used by my section officer in an 'executive' capacity, although outranked by four corporals and a sergeant. I didn't find it difficult to 'take charge' and others didn't find it difficult to follow me, especially in the circumstances in which we now found ourselves. I was 'known' in the Battalion, largely through my position of medical inspection room corporal, and had the reputation in my own Company of meaning what I said and not tolerating shirkers.

Over the next few days 'La Ferme des Bergheries' became a sort of collecting point for lost paratroopers. They were mainly brought in by civilians from the villages and farms round about; on foot, in farm carts, one even in the box of a tricycle, something like the pre-war 'stop me and buy one' trykes of the Walls' ice cream man. There were also too many people coming in to listen to David's [Duce] radio. Although he was unable to contact any British units, we often picked up their transmissions and were able to listen to the BBC news broadcasts, in English, which we then had to translate for our new friends. Unfortunately, having dumped his spare batteries, David was soon left with a dead radio, so that bit of contact didn't last long.

Some of us began to become concerned about our position. We learned that Cabourg was swarming with Germans, that the coast road was not in British hands, that heavy fighting was taking place from the Bois de Bavent almost to the coast road, and that the British advance had ground to a halt outside Caen. It was time to make a move as it had become obvious that we were not going to be overrun by the British Army for some time to come, and it could only be days before the Germans got wind of our presence. Doug Penstone and I had become quite close friends, decided to make a break for it that night. We spoke to the others, pointing out the danger of remaining, not only to ourselves but more so to the Vermughen family, and out of the twenty-two Paras at that time only seven elected to remain a bit longer. At no time during our stay at the farm did either Adrien or Yvonne indicate by word or deed that we should leave, but more than most I knew that it was becoming increasingly difficult to feed or hide us. Just one small giveaway – by this time the earth closet in the farmyard was full to overflowing, and it was necessary to venture onto the narrow dry strip of land outside the orchard wall to do what had to be done, with the attendant risk of being seen by anyone in Cabourg with field glasses who was scanning the marshes. When I told Yvonne that we were leaving she burst into tears and threw her arms about me. I gathered that she thought that it would be very dangerous and that I should take care.

Whereas 'my' group, consisting of myself and Doug Penstone, 'Mitzi' Green and eight members of various other units, decided to attempt the coast road towards the Orne estuary, another, smaller group opted to try to recross the marshes and head for the Bois de Bavent, which was known to be the D-Day objective of the 8th Battalion. Our signaller, David Duce, along with six others, decided to remain at the farm a day or so longer. It is believed that David was still at the farm when it was surrounded by the Germans, that he became a P.O.W. and eventually remained so until the end of the war in Europe.

We left the farm about 11.00pm and after a couple of minor alarming incidents, we hid up, just before dawn in a small one-up, one-down cottage just west of Le Home, on a small track leading into the dunes. To our horror, as day broke we found that we were very adjacent to a German AA gun site, and from the small window in the gable end of our hideout we could quite clearly see the gun crew moving about. The odd fellow who lived in the house was clearly terrified, but whether he was more frightened of us or the Germans we couldn't tell. All through that day we took it in turns to keep watch on both him and the Jerries, and our hands were never far from our weapons.

Just before dark, when things were quiet, we decided to move out and once more headed west. I believe that it was at this point that some of the group decided to break away and head inland. I think that at this time, besides Mitzi, Doug and myself, there were four or maybe five others and once again we hugged the hedge and ditch on the seaward side of the road. We reasoned that if we came under fire we could always escape into the dunes, with some chance of getting away. And then, just as it was getting really dark, disaster struck! We saw across the road ahead of us a line of 'Teller' mines and knowing that these could be booby-trapped in several different ways, we decided to go round them. Taking the chance on anti-personnel mines in the earth, we pushed through the hedge into the fields. There, just in front of us was a largish pond. Not knowing how deep it might be, and not wanting to get wet feet and legs again, we skirted round it, into the open. Within moments there was a burst of machine-gun fire from the direction of the dunes, and both Doug and I, walking one behind the other, were hit.

It had been agreed before we left the farm that if we ran into trouble and anyone was wounded, their injuries would be treated, their position marked, and they would be left. This was done. I handed over my haversack of dressings to one of the others, and Doug and I were left. There was another burst of MG fire shortly afterwards, but I never heard who was shooting at whom.

Doug Penstone died during the night, of internal haemorrhage, and is buried at Tilly-sur-Seulle, some twenty miles away, the only Para in the cemetery. I can't understand why this is, since Ranville is only about four miles away. Just after dawn the next day I was picked up by a German patrol. One of them was sent back to collect a stretcher, and I was carried back in the direction of Cabourg, then up the long straight road to Descanneville and the Merville Battery, which had been reoccupied by the enemy. As I was borne along this road I passed at least a company of German infantry 'standing to' in the ditch on the right-hand side of the road, their rifles pointing west, in the direction from which I had just been carried. It appears that, unbeknown to either the Germans or ourselves, our 'little band of brothers' had actually passed through the enemy front line in the near dark, and only the fact that we had to break cover had caused us to be spotted.

I received emergency surgery from a partial English-speaking German doctor, one Unterartz Meier, who learned his English from American cowboy novels, and I was moved by stages to Paris via Pont l'Eveque and Evereux. At Ortzlazarette de la Pitie on the Boulevard de la Hopital, I met another 9th Battalion man, one John 'Freddie' Glover, from the G-B Party who were supposed to land by glider in the Battery. Quite independently, but maybe on the same day, we escaped being sent off to Germany and greeted the French 2nd Armoured

Division and the Americans, when they entered Paris. I eventually rejoined the Battalion and served with them until my demobilisation in Palestine in March/April 1946. Mitzi Green also rejoined the 9th and eventually became a sergeant.

On my way home from Palestine, I was given five days compassionate leave to find the grave of my brother Ron, a machine-gunner in the 9th Battalion, who had been killed in action just eight days after his twentieth birthday. I also took the opportunity to find Madame Vermughen and hear the full story of what happened to her and Adrien after we left the farm.

The Germans had attacked the farm and captured the remaining Paras. Adrien Vermughen was tortured and shot in front of his wife. Georges Duval, the farm manager and the farmhand, Jacques Guyovach were also shot. The farm was destroyed. Yvonne Vermughen spent months in prison but was eventually released. Adrien Vermughen was awarded a posthumous Resistance Medal and Yvonne a citation from General Gale.

Appendix 4
Continuation of Lieutenant Douglas Martin's Story
following his serious wounding as recalled by his wife, Eileen

On the day that it happened, she knew that he had been wounded:

I was walking in the office and I had this dreadful pain, and I said to the people in the office, 'Doug's been shot,' and they said, 'Oh stop being fanciful,' you know. It's all in the mind, but it wasn't, it was exactly as I'd imagined it.

He was brought home two days later by sea. He was brought into Basingstoke, Rooksdown Hospital plastic and jaw unit. {The British Hospital}.

The authorities did not ask her to go down on the Wednesday because he was not expected to live.

I had a telegram and I went down in the afternoon of the Thursday {15th}. The only thing recognisable on Dougie was his forehead, that hadn't changed shape, but the rest of his face down to his shoulders... . Where his face had been blown apart, they'd put big stitches just to hold it together. I looked at him and he didn't know me, he just lay in the bed. His eyes were completely dull. And then all of a sudden it was as if someone had turned an electric light on in a room. His eyes suddenly lit up, and she said, 'He remembers you.' I noticed his now paralysed arm and leg. They were enormous, swollen right up and I could see all the injuries up here [around the neck] obviously, and I thought 'Say nothing.' His neck looked just like a shell had carved at it. It carved his neck right out before it blew his jaws out. You could see the nerve endings... . I went down the next day. They'd told me they didn't really think he'd really live. I went up to the nurse who said, 'I'm afraid he's gone.' Of course, I immediately thought he had died, but she meant he was in the ambulance outside! He was being transferred to Hackwood Hospital.

That night my sister came down with me to Hackwood, and he was in the middle of the ward because the surgeon said he'd got to be moved, but they didn't have anywhere else to put him.

They stuck him right in the middle of the ward. He was shaved ready to go down to the theatre, so we couldn't stop that day.

The surgeon who examined him said, 'Get him out of the ward straight away, because he'll kill everyone.' He had gangrenous gas in his neck. That's when they found this huge abscess in his neck. He had a tracheotomy put in. The pus that came out, and the stench... . For about three weeks or more, he had this great wad of cotton wool on his chest. They were changing it every half-hour because it was saturated with pus. He was having penicillin then, an injection every three hours at that time. His behind and everything was like a pepper pot, they couldn't find a place to put it [the needles] in.

Eileen then began a constant bedside vigil. She had been warned that there was an ulcer on his carotid artery and that the wall was very thin. If any blood started to trickle from Dougie's mouth she was to call the Doctor immediately. This meant that his carotid artery had burst and that he only had minutes to live. On 28 June, as she was feeding him, a small trickle of blood began run out of the corner of his mouth.

He was immediately rushed into surgery. If it had happened in the British Hospital... he wouldn't have been saved. Rooksdown House was on two levels, but it was a stone staircase and they could not have got him downstairs to the operating theatre if he'd been there. But Hackwood was a specially built neurological hospital for the Canadian Army and it was all on one level so that they could wheel all the beds and everything without any problems, to the theatre.

They were emptying his lungs because he wasn't allowed to move after the operation for this carotid artery and Hoyle-Campbell {the doctor} saw me afterwards. For five and a half hours he operated on him. He said to me, 'He may wake. If he wakes he may never walk or talk again,' and I went berserk and he caught hold of me and he shook the living daylights out of me. 'I've worked for five and a half hours on this man and now you tell me that.' I said, 'At twenty-two, would you want a lifetime of lying flat on your bed on your back? He wouldn't want that.' He said, 'Well, we'll see if he wakes.' He said, 'He'll wake about eight if he's going to wake'. Well he woke at eight. He 'asked' for a drink.

Well then I had to go and stay with the surgeon and his wife for the two weeks. I used to sit with him every day in the hospital. He was lying in a darkened room with his head down so that the blood could drain away. His carotid artery and all the subsidiary arteries, his jugular vein, were all tied up. The surgeon said to me that your duty is to make sure that he doesn't move a muscle. He used to lie there and hold my hand... and I sat there for what, twelve hours a day. That's when I started to smoke! One day, a few days after this had taken place, I had to go and spend a penny. He was sound asleep I thought. Went up to the toilets which were only a couple of doors away and when I got back , he had forced himself up and I thought 'Oh my God,' because I was afraid that the artery would burst again. So I shouted to Sister Monroe, who was just across the road from where he was in his private room, and she said, 'I told you not to let him move,' and I said 'Well I had to go!' She pushed him down and said, 'Stay there!'

And then they put him into this main ward because he was comatose really, stupefied. She put him right beside her glass [window]. She put the radio on and there was some Canadian jazz music, and it was driving him crazy! I said to Sister Monroe, 'Can he have the music turned off?' and she said, 'No!' 'But he's getting cross.' 'Good', she said, 'The more cross he gets the more stimulating him... When a man who's been very ill is getting better, it is a sign they're improving. The more evil-tempered he becomes, the better pleased we are!'

He was over there six weeks and then he was transferred back to the British Hospital for the rest.

The British Hospital, well, Sir Harold Gillis was marvellous. Over the three-year period he had bone grafts, skin grafts.

The first thing I saw when I went into Rooksdown House for the first time to see him.. I walked through ward 4a which was the other ranks ward which you went through to get to the officers' ward and there was only one bed occupied and there was a chap who we know very well (now) in the corner. He had no face and he had two stumps for arms.... I went into the officers' ward. It was an old mental hospital..., and he was in one of the padded cells.

209

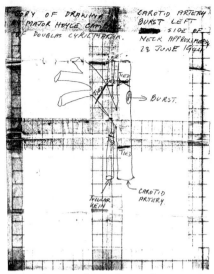

Diagram of Dougie Martin's operation.

He was in hospital from '44 to '47, I think he had about fifteen operations. It was rather wonderful because they used to operate and when they'd recovered sufficiently from the operation, they used to send them home. And he'd have say six weeks at home. He couldn't eat of course, his jaws were all tied up, so I got a feeding cup. I used to do a roast dinner all into this cup and do you know he was the only officer who went back at the end of the six weeks who would be A1 fit for the next operation. It was an experience of a lifetime. Not one that I would advise for everybody to go through! He couldn't walk, he couldn't talk, he had no words.

The boys (in the ward) were wonderful. One day, he'd sang a little tune, God knows what it was, and when I'd gone into the ward that afternoon, they'd sat him up in bed with his officer's jacket on and he had his red beret on his head, and they said, 'Come and listen to Doug, come and listen to Doug!' And of course not a sound came out! They got him walking and they sat me in the lounge and they went and got him. How I sat in that chair I'll never know because his paralysed leg was going this way and he was going that way. But gradually, gradually, he managed to summon his energies and his strength and his concentration, and the only word he had at that time, starting from the Canadian Hospital was, 'Look'. Everything he saw, it was, 'Look, look.' If he wanted something, it was, 'Look, look.' Where that came from I don't know. Now, when he can't think of anything, its 'Can you...' I look because he's usually pointing somewhere!

Now he suffers from Myeloma, [a malignant tumour of the bone marrow] and Dr Barton, his consultant, she feels that his immune system fought so hard against the gangrenous gas at that particular time, that he's been lucky to go as long as he has. He will pick up any infection very easily now. He's been in hospital, he was in there for six weeks a couple of years ago. He was very, very ill. His white cells trigger to the slightest thing now.

Author's note: After fifty-seven years Dougie Martin still has to make regular trips to his consultant. He has learned to walk again, and his speech has improved immeasurably. Dougie and Eileen are truly two remarkable people. In spite of everything they have been through, you could not wish to meet a happier couple. They have one son.

Appendix 5
Controversial Issues Surrounding The Merville Battery

Many controversial issues concerning the Merville Battery have arisen over the years, and by far the most contentious of these have emanated from Lieutenant Alan Jefferson's 1987 book *Assault on the Guns of Merville*. This was the first and only book so far, to interview German members of the Battery, in particular the Commander, Second Lieutenant Raimund Steiner, and his subordinate, Sergeant Major Hans Buskotte. Their testimonies have cast huge doubts over various previously accepted beliefs. Consequently, an undercurrent of doubt and confusion has grown over the assault's necessity, planning, objectives, success, in fact almost everything about it.

Also, in the welter of discussion that has followed, many basic facts also appear to have been overlooked. These matters therefore needed to be re-addressed and a balanced assessment of the facts presented. The following is my attempt.

1. The 'Mystery Glider'
In *Assault on the Guns of Merville* Steiner and Buskotte referred to a 'First Assault' by a glider at around 0026 hours on 6 June. (Note: The Germans were using the same double summer time as the Allies). Vicious fighting ensued, during which all of the assailants were apparently killed. Consequently, the garrison was on full alert for the 9th Battalion's attack. Steiner was actually in an observation post on the beach, west of Merville, and so Buskotte was the senior rank in the Battery during the early hours of D-Day. Up until their statements, no-one had any inkling of this event. It remains cloaked in mystery. However, there are numerous possibilities that could explain the appearance of this glider.

a. One of them is the scenario for the glider to have been part of a Special Forces operation being carried out in the area, but of which as yet nothing is known [Possibly an attack intended for another fortified position nearby, e.g, 'La Redoubte' nearer the coast?].

During my research with the Commandos, by accident this subject arose. In the 1980s a Commando veteran caused uproar when he stated in his local newspaper that he had been part of a Commando force which had attacked the Merville Battery during the early hours of 6 June. The commando later retracted his story, but no explanation of why he claimed this was pursued.

It is almost certain that this was not a deliberate attack on the Merville Battery, especially when we know that 'OBOE', the heavy bombing raid on the Battery [which missed] took place at 0030 hours. If there was some special force attack it would hardly be planned to take place at the exact time as the bombing raid!

Also, I was told that a number of years ago, a Commando had written a book containing details of a secret attack on 'the Battery'. Apparently, the Government at that time [shortly after the war] would not allow him to publish it. The author has since died and the whereabouts of the text, if it still exists, is not known.

b. In the excellent *One Night In June* by Kevin Shannon and Stephen Wright (1994), a transport glider, Chalk No 265, was highlighted as being a possibility for the 'mystery glider'. This apparently contained a jeep, a motorcycle and other kit plus five Canadians. One of the authors was informed by a colleague of the pilots that the glider landing position was ìmined and within a defended area. No other information was available.

Former D-Day glider pilot HN 'Andy' Andrews adds a little to this in his 1997 book, *So, You Want to Fly, Eh?* He recalls talking to the pilots of this glider, Staff Sergeant Lofty Rancom and Sergeant Collard at the first reunion after the war:

Apparently like all of us, Lofty got over the LZ but couldn't see anything. He then was towed up and down the coast about three miles inland looking for the circular wood [a landmark for their LZ]. Eventually in what seemed the closest position, Lofty pulled off, only to land in a minefield and get badly wounded in the arm. He and Collard hid up in a wood hoping their position would be overrun by invading troops.

There is no mention of a battle in this recollection.

Buskotte adds some weight to this possibility as he mentioned that the glider in question contained a jeep, pneumatic drills and flame-throwing equipment. Therefore, maybe not during, but certainly immediately after the 'attack', the Germans must have realised that with so few men involved, it was not a direct attack on the Battery but a glider on another purpose, landing in the wrong place. This was backed-up in a letter to the author, where Herr Steiner states that the aircraft was confirmed as being a transport glider – but an American one. How this was identified as such is not yet known. He also stated that the glider probably had explosives on board as it disappeared without trace after a huge explosion.

A major difference in the letter by Steiner is that he states that all of the Germans who went to deal with the threat were killed, raising the possibility that the occupants of the glider, or some of them, may have escaped.

c. With the notion that the Battery was on full alert, it may be recalled that during his reconnaissance of the Battery, Major Smith decided to cut through the wire to make sure that it was occupied! He stated:

I was a good halfway through the wire when I suddenly heard excited voices half-right about 200 yards away, inside and towards the main entrance of the Battery. A tug aircraft and glider came into view from the right, flying at about 800 feet. This started a frightful hullabaloo in the Battery, which wakened to life as a sleeper with a bucket of cold water thrown over him. There were shouts and cries from everywhere, deep guttural voices booming out orders, these being relayed and acknowledged. I imagined all the available firepower being organised to meet this solitary invader, who was already being chased by a stream of tracer from more distant weapons.

Almost simultaneously four machine guns inside the Battery opened fire with tracer. Neither the glider nor the aircraft faltered, but flew straight on, right over the centre of the Battery. Not more than thirty yards from me a 20mm flak gun opened up.

The aircraft passed and the firing stopped. It must have been hit, but not sufficiently to bring it down, and I saw it disappear, still on the same course, at the same height, and on an even keel.

Major Smith makes no mention of seeing [or smelling] any [smouldering?] remains of a glider or anything else within the Battery.

d. Alan Jefferson, having personally interviewed Sergeant Major Buskotte, casts doubt over the whole event itself in Appendix 3 of his book.

2. The 9th Battalion Attack

a. Number of Machine Guns

The Germans dispute the number of machine guns available to them on the night, stating that only one was in use. However, many different Paras have corroborated the number of machine guns that opened fire [ten)] and all of these men could not have spoken to each other or seen the written accounts that are now available. In para 1c Major Smith mentions the four inside the Battery that are quoted by others later on. Both Sid Knight and Tom Stroud stated categorically that three alone were knocked out on the right hand side of the Battery.

b. The Landing Position of Glider No 27, containing Hugh Pond's Party

I have corresponded quite regularly with Sapper Alex Taylor of 591 Parachute Squadron RE. He was on board this glider and is adamant that it came down to the north of the Battery, in the back garden of the Château de Merville. He has produced a detailed map of the route he believes he took after leaving it. This is at complete odds with the 'official position', which is 500 yards east of the Battery perimeter. Consequently I investigated and found the following.

i. In all of the interviews and correspondence analysed, not one Para on board the glider mentions any such large building in the vicinity. As they were at that spot for about an hour [some books incorrectly state four!] and it was getting light, it is highly unlikely that a château would not be noticed or forgotten by all of those present. Of the many accounts by the assault troops on the ground, all state that it passed over their heads and crashed behind them, and therefore in the 'official position'.

ii. Both Harry Dixon and Fred Glover saw a Pathfinder in a lane after exiting the glider. The Pathfinder navigation devices had been set up to the south-east of the Battery, roughly, the area of the 'official' position.

iii. It may also be remembered that following the assault CSM Dusty Miller was ordered to go and inform the glider party to move to the Calvary. He walked through a minefield that he knew to be a dummy as he had seen two Germans walking through it earlier, when moving along the lane from Gonneville. His ventures during the reconnaissance took him nowhere near the garden of the Château de Merville.

iv. If the glider had come down in the garden of the Château de Merville, both Sid Knight and Tom Stroud, on their diversion mission along the lane that ran along the bottom of the garden, would have witnessed this event first-hand. Neither of their accounts mention any such occurrence. The relevant piece from the pilot, Dickie Kerr's account, is very generalised in its statements and so does not really clarify anything, although he does mention landing 50 yards beyond the perimeter wire.

v. Every aerial photograph taken of the Merville Battery held in the archive at Keele University was checked and no trace of any glider or debris could be found in either position. I also consulted the JARIC at RAF Brampton, which holds other aerial photos. None were held for the relevant time. The absence of any debris may be explained by two of the men. Sergeant 'Dizzy' Brewster, who had to be left behind at the spot, stated that the smouldering wreckage of the glider gradually burned away, leaving little remaining. James Tugwell backed this up.

vi. In June 2000 I met Monsieur Daniel Huet who was living in a house at the bottom of the lane where the 'official' position for the glider landing is situated. He had never been consulted before on the matter. I asked if he knew the position of any glider that landed in the area on D-Day. Without any prompting he stated that one had landed in the early hours of 6 June, then proceeded to take me to the same location as the 'official' position. He then described, in detail, how the remains of the glider were lying and how it had been damaged. All of this tied in with accounts of the Paras in the glider, and in fact the condition that Alex Taylor described.

vii. Later that week in 2000 I took Fred Glover back to the spot. We went through his movements and he is now convinced that the official position is the correct one.

viii. Also in June 2000 I was introduced to Bert Beddowes, a veteran of No 3 Commando who took part in the attack on the Battery on 7 June [see Para 6]. During our walk around the position he described the action and his subsequent capture. By coincidence, he was taken prisoner in what was the back garden of the Château de Merville. Mr Beddowes did not see any remains of a glider there.

ix. Finally, Raimund Steiner informed the author that the glider landed to the east of the Battery, and that it the remnants were later destroyed by artillery fire.

Therefore, all of the evidence leans heavily towards the 'official' position, and so I cannot explain Alex Taylor's opinion, especially as his memory is so good!

c. 2nd Lieutenant Steiner's efforts to reach the Battery from his O.P.
Herr Steiner states that on his attempt to get to the Battery in the early hours of D-Day, fighting was going on around the Franceville crossroads. No British formation was due to be in that area at this stage of the day [unless it was yet another special mission of which we know nothing!] Perhaps it could have been stragglers, but Steiner's description gives the impression of a more sustained battle, something that such groups of Paras were ordered to avoid after landing. Their tasks were the priority. In fact, this incident sounds suspiciously like a battle that took place during the afternoon of 7 June involving 45 RM Commando. They had been ordered to capture Franceville and Merville, but were held up by heavy opposition. The same crossroads became the focal point of some fierce fighting. The attack on the Battery by No 3 Commando was at 2pm on the 7th, and Buskotte was still making the decisions, so Herr Steiner could not have reached the Battery until sometime later in the afternoon or evening.

3. No 1 Casemate – Capture of 9th Battalion Men
Herr Buskotte claimed that around fifteen men of the 9th Battalion made a second attack on No 1 casemate and that three were killed and twelve captured. This seems extremely unlikely, especially when two assault groups had already attacked it anyway. It would have meant a large number of hostile Germans remaining inside the Battery, which was clearly not the case at the immediate end of the fighting. If any such appearance had occurred (ie coming out from underground bunkers) there were plenty of Paras still in the Battery who would have gone to assist. Also, where would the men for yet another attack on No 1 casemate have come from? There were no more available to Colonel Otway after he himself went in. Perhaps this figure comes from the amount of wounded that had either not been found or had to be left behind.

4. Why did HMS *Arethusa* not open fire?
In the absence of a working radio, Navy signallers and mortars, the vital task of informing the *Arethusa* of the Battalion's success could not be done. Although yellow smoke was used, it is highly unlikely that this could have been seen by the *Arethusa* itself and, with difficulty by a spotter plane. Possibly the answer to this question lies in the 1946 book *Operation Neptune* by Commander Kenneth Edwards RN. This states:

> For a considerable time the naval supporting craft could get no reliable information which would enable them to give gunfire support to the airborne troops without risk of firing into our own men.
> The anxiety caused by this shortage of information was most acute with regard to the 'Sallesnelles battery'. This was a battery of 6-inch howitzers east of the River Orne. The plan was for its capture by Airborne troops who were to make crash glider landings in its immediate vicinity. In fact, one glider crash-landed on the battery itself and the battery was duly captured. This, however, was unknown to HMS Arethusa, who was in a position to enfilade the German battery and so facilitate its capture. The trouble was that it was not known whether the battery was in German hands or in the hands of our airborne troops. The fact that the guns of the battery were silent was no criterion, for many of the German batteries had shown inability or disinclination to open fire. The Arethusa was told that she was to open fire at a certain time unless she received orders to the contrary. Then she was told not to open fire until she was certain that the battery was still in German hands. She never was certain and so she did not open fire. It was fortunate, for the battery had been quickly captured by our airborne troops after their crash landings.

And so, although Commander Edwards [or his sources] could not have known of the exact plan of the attack and what happened in detail, he knew the *Arethusa's* task and subsequent dilemma.

The book was written with the help of Admiral Sir Bertram Ramsay, KCB, KBE, MVO, the Allied Naval Commander of the Expeditionary Force, his successor, Sir Harold Burrough and many naval officers who took part in the operation.

5. Did the Merville Guns fire on D-Day?
With regard to the men's reports on putting the guns out of action. Harold Long told me that for the gun that he reached, not having any explosive, they dismantled the breech block and threw the parts in different directions. He stated that this was No 4 casemate, but when discussing this with Barney Ross, who was supposed to go for No 3, there is the possibility that Long could have been No 3. Obviously this gun would not be able to fire again without a new breech block assembly. Johnny Novis stated that he saw an officer dismantling the breech of No 3 gun. A coincidence?

Major Parry oversaw the attempted destruction of No 1 gun. He inspected the gun after the explosion and decided that sufficient damage had been done. Although not an artilleryman, Parry was an experienced officer who had served in France in 1940 and it is hard to believe that he would not have known if the gun could have been able to fire again. Having said that, Gammon bombs would not inflict damage in the hardened steel breech area, and it is not known for certain where the charges were placed.

Various Paras, including Sid Knight, stated that No 2 gun was destroyed by the placement of a shell in the breech and one in the barrel before firing it. Someone would have had to know how to load the gun, there was obviously plenty of propellant around, but this method would certainly have silenced the gun, permanently.

George Hawkins lay wounded in No 4 casemate for nearly four days:

I only ever heard one gun fire. The casement we were in, the gun never fired. And they fired one gun I think. I don't think they fired many, three or four shells, out of that. So the rest of them, didn't use them. The Germans just carried on their normal duties without firing.

There appears to have been, understandably, much confusion in the attempts to damage the guns. This is evident from the various accounts of small parties of men going into casemates when others had already been there and made their attempts, certainly on Nos 2, 3 and 4 casemates.

In 1994 Raimund Steiner met Colonel Otway, Sid Knight and Len Daniels at the Battery for a BBC TV programme. He stated that the guns could not fire because all of the crews had been killed, and that he had only six unwounded men. This is confirmed in a letter to the author. In Alan Jefferson's book, Steiner does not actually state this, but mentions that the guns were undamaged. On the programme, of the guns he continued:

It was not until the afternoon of 6 June that two guns, those in Nos 1 and 2 emplacements, could be 'got going', at the rate of one round every ten minutes.

Yet it may be remembered that Steiner had still not been able to reach the Battery. Therefore, this information can only be that as related to him at the time by Herr Buskotte and/or after Steiner finally arrived himself.

In the invasion plan, if the 9th Battalion was unable to silence the Battery during the morning, 45 Royal Marine Commando had orders to attack it upon arrival during the afternoon. What actually happened was that after crossing the two bridges, the Commando was not informed whether the Battery had been neutralized or not and so just carried on with its orders to head for the Battery and Franceville Plage. A member of the Commando, Derek Cakebread, stated that on approaching Sallenelles, 'C' Troop, which was leading, was fired upon from the north-west. Therefore, the remainder of the Commando took a track heading north-east and decided to dig in about 200 yards to the north-east. Captain John Day of 'B' Troop informed me that the CO, Nicol Gray and Major Jock Rushforth, OC 'C' Troop, made a reconnaissance of the area around the Battery, still uncertain whether the Germans were there or not [Therefore, it was definitely not firing at that stage]. Rushforth informed him later that the situation was clarified when one of the guns in the Battery fired, and the shell seemed to, 'whoosh' right over their heads. However, the rate of fire was very desultory. They began to make plans for an attack when a signal arrived from the 1st Special Service Brigade HQ ordering them not to attack the Battery but to secure Merville village instead. [This obviously ties in to some degree with Steiner's account].

c. As stated by CSM Jack Harries, he went back towards the Battery with a patrol during the afternoon of D-Day and almost certainly 'bumped into' men of 45 RM Commando [probably as they were on the track approaching the Battery]. The Battery was patently not in action at that time.

d. Herr Steiner stated to Alan Jefferson that on D-Day, probably during the afternoon, he ordered Buskotte to open fire and that he gradually carried this out using Nos 1 and 2 guns. The result was an instantaneous backlash of fire from Allied ships and aircraft on the position. As we have seen from previous information, it is highly unlikely that this particular instance was on D-Day and in fact during the first few days, because of the presence of Allied troops in the immediate area.

e. George Hawkins states categorically that the guns did not fire on D-Day, although as previously stated he did hear one gun fire three or four shells during his time there. This was why he could not understand the reason for the Commando attack the following day. If it is surmised that one gun did fire as stated by the Marine Commandos, the rate of fire must have been extremely slow for Hawkins, even though he was badly wounded, not to register the fact. He certainly was very aware of matters during the early evening when the first Germans he had seen during daylight found him!

6. The Commando Attack.

During the morning of 7 June the Commander of the 51st Highland Division made a complaint about the amount of artillery fire Sword beach was being subjected to, ostensibly, he thought, from the Merville Battery. The following action stemmed from there.

Lord Lovat was subsequently ordered by General Gale to attack the Battery. The only available troops at his disposal were Nos 4 and 5 Troops of No 3 Commando. At around 2.00pm, they attacked.

The assault was completed with relative ease, but the Commandos did not have any explosives to deal with the guns either, and as most of the casemate doors were shut,could not get to the guns. Buskotte claims that as the Commandos began to leave the Battery, the defenders wheeled two guns out of the casemates and 'fired at the retreating Commandos'.

I have mentioned this to quite a few Commandos who were on the spot and some of the answers were unprintable! They all vividly recall the problem being two Self-Propelled 88mm guns. Alan Jefferson ties the two together, assuming that the Commandos mistook them for the SPs and the German story also seems to confuse this episode with the Para attack in the early hours of D-Day. A small Commando patrol was actually sent forward to knock the SP88s out, and was not seen again. All were killed or captured.

Finally, it really makes no sense for Buskotte to risk the men and guns in the open when he also says that he had called in an artillery barrage. (In fact shortly after the Commandos began to take up position on the edge of the Battery, a barrage began to fall on them).

7. Conclusions

a. Was the 9th Battalion's attack a success?

Without definite confirmation, the Allied planners had to estimate the calibre of gun being used by the size of the casemates. This meant approximately 155mm, and their calculation was correct. They were not to know that the guns had not yet been fitted. In the absence of any accurate information on this matter, there was no other choice. The calibre meant without question, problems for Sword beach and the shipping etc. In addition, the Battery appears to have been in the charge of very capable, determined and experienced enemy soldiers who would certainly have 'done their worst' if they had been allowed. It had to be dealt with.

b. Was the assault plan too complicated?

I believe that Brigadier Hill answers this fully in his foreword, however, due to the events that followed the drop, this question is now almost irrelevant. Any simple plan would have required a decent amount of men to reach the Battery, not 150 out of 600+ ! No matter what the plan, the drop was the operation that had to be successful.

c. Destruction of the guns

Although the 9th Battalion had the overall task of silencing the Battery, specialist knowledge and explosive were required to destroy the guns themselves. This was the task of the 591 Parachute Squadron Royal Engineers. That they did not reach the Battery was certainly not their fault, but the responsibility for not destroying the guns has perhaps fallen on the 9th due to the lack of people knowing that the engineers were supposed to do it! The Paras subsequent varied, desperate attempts in the darkness to put the guns out of action has possibly contributed to this.

d. Was the 9th Battalion's attack a success?

Another way of addressing this is to ask whether the attack achieved its purpose? In a word, yes. Did the Battery cause Sword beach to be untenable? No. The beach was subjected to a heavy concentration of artillery fire from various other locations, but the landing and reinforcement of the beachhead was not prevented. Although the Battery had not been built to directly bombard the beach, it still had the capability of doing so. The Battery's normal rate of fire would have been six rounds per minute by all four guns, i.e., salvoes of twenty-four rounds per minute. And so important damage was done to the guns/crews to make this fire ineffectual. As mentioned previously, when in later weeks they did fire, the Battery received such a Naval response that it did not induce the urgency to do it too often!

Therefore, for whatever reason, the Battery did not perform to anywhere near its capability. With the failure of the bombing, the only possible reason for this is the consequence of the 9th Battalion attack.

8. Final Word

With all these issues, maybe there is something that has still not been released, or perhaps 'new' accounts will be unearthed at some future date, that may throw light on the subject. Maybe we will just never know for sure.

Sword beach was at worst, not seriously molested by the Merville Battery on D-Day. It did not 'wreak havoc' and prevent the establishment of Sword beachhead. It may also be noted that this would not have been difficult because of the traffic jam that developed during the day. Targets would have been plentiful.

The 9th Parachute Battalion's attack on the Merville Battery saved many lives on Sword beach.

Sources
List of Interviews/Correspondences/Bibliography

9th Parachute Battalion:

Interviews
Lt Col. T Otway
Major I. Dyer (deceased)
Capt. T. Robinson
Lt D. Martin
Lt W. Mills
Stendall Brailsford
John Britton
Mick Corboy
Len Daniels
Robert Ferguson
Jimmy French
Harry Gray
Ron Gregory
George Hawkins
Derek Higgins
Joe Hughes
Jack Humfrey
Paddy Jenkins
Reg Knights
Fred Milward
Arthur Mobsby (deceased)
Alan Mower
Gordon Newton
Johnny Novis
Geoff Pattinson
Ron Phelps
Ernie Rooke-Matthews
Barney Ross
John Speechley

Cyril Thwaites
Ron Tucker
Derek Vincent
Harold 'Johnnie' Walker
Ken Walker
Roy Wright

Correspondences
Jimmy Baty
George Bosher
Alec Durham
Fred Garrett (deceased)
Lt Alan Jefferson
Terry Jepp (now Jefferson)
Walter Johnson
Sid Knight (deceased)
Michael Knight (son)
Don McArthur
Tom Stroud (deceased)
Jack Watkins

Conversations
Peter Bowden
Harry Dixon
Harold Long (deceased)
Doug Smith

Accounts used written by 9th Bn members now deceased:
Major Harold Bestley
Major Allen Parry
Major George Smith
Capt Paul Greenway

Capt 'Hal' Hudson
Lt Jock Lepper
Bob Abel
Arthur Ayre
Frank Delsignore
Fred Dorkins
Jack Harries
Percy Hull
Jim McGuinness
Doug Woodcraft
Capt Ian Johnston, 224 Fd Ambulance

Other Interviews:
Lt Gen. Sir Napier Crookenden
Brig. James Hill
Capt. John Woodgate, 3rd Parachute
    Brigade HQ
Derek Cakebread, 45 RM Commando
Dennis Daly, 1/7th Middlesex
Joe Michie, Glider Pilot Regiment
'Ossie' Osbourne, No 3 Commando
Paul Parris (Brother of Maurice Parris)
Fred Scott, 2nd Ox and Bucks
Stan Scott, No 3 Commando
Eddie Simms, No 6 Commando
Peter Wilson, No 6 Commando

Other Correspondences
Arnold Baldwin, Glider Pilot Regiment
Captain John Day, 45 Royal Marine Commando
Tod' Sweeney, 2nd Ox and Bucks
Dennis Edwards, 2nd Ox and Bucks

Alan Graham, 3rd Parachute Sqdn R.E.
John Shave, 3rd Parachute Sqdn R.E.
Bob Sullivan, 3rd Parachute Sqdn R.E.
George Taylor, 3rd Parachute Sqdn R.E.
P. Kennedy, 5th Black Watch
Major John McGregor, 5th Black Watch
Major Dennis Punton, 5th Black Watch
Rev. Tom Nicol, 5th Black Watch
Cliff Morris, No 6 Commando
Lt Keith Ponsford, No 3 Commando
Jimmy Synnott, No 3 Commando
Alex Taylor, 591 Parachute Sqdn RE
Douglas Coker, 'B' Sqdn, 13th/18th Hussars

George Treloar, 'B' Sqdn, 13th/18th Hussars
Jan de Vries, 1st Canadian Parachute
Battalion

Conversations
Piper Bill Millin, 1st Special Service Brigade
Bill Irving MM, 3rd Parachute Sqdn R.E.
'Nobby' Newell, 45 Royal Marine
Commando
Lt Douglas Smith, 3 Parachute Brigade
HQ, Signals

France:
Monsieur Lechartier, former Mayor of Breville

Mayoress of Gonneville, Mme Anne-Marie
Trevel
Madame Lecomte, wife of local photographer
- Breville
Msr and Mme Courcy (Locals living in the
area), Le Bas de Breville
Monsieur Miguet, owner of the Château St
Côme
Msr and Mme Holtz, owner of the (now)
restaurant where Col. Otway landed.
Louis Adelin, French Historian connected
with 9th Parachute Battalion
Robert Godey

Bibliography
Airborne Forces (The Second World War), Lt. Col T. Otway DSO (HM
Govt.) 1951.
9th Parachute Battalion, The First Six Days, Lt. Gen. Sir Napier
Crookenden KCB, DSO, CBE.
Dropzone Normandy, 1976, Ian Allan Ltd, Lt. Gen. Sir Napier
Crookenden KCB, DSO, CBE.
The Big Drop John Golley, 1982, Jane's.
Brightly Shone the Dawn Johnson & Dunphie, 1980, Frederick
Warne Ltd.
Dawn of D-Day, David Howarth, 1959.
The Longest Day, Cornelius Ryan, 1960, Victor Gollancz Ltd.
Assault on the Guns of Merville, Alan Jefferson, 1987, John Murray
Publishers Ltd.
A Teenager's War, Ron Tucker, 1994, Spellmount.
The Red Devils, The Story of 224 Fd (Para) Ambulance, 1945.
Men of the Red Beret, Max Arthur, 1990, Hutchinson.
Nothing Less Than Victory, Russell Miller, 1993, Michael Joseph.

Visitor's Guide to the Normandy Landing Beaches, Tonie and Valmai
Holt, 1989.
Now It Can Be Told, Gleeson & Waldron, 1952.
True Stories of the Paras, P. Canmer, 1986.
Out of the Clouds, The History of the 1st Canadian Parachute Battalion,
J.A. Wiles, 1981.
Ready For Anything, Julian Thompson, 1989, G Weidenfeld and
Nicolson Ltd.
Go To It! Major John Shave MC, 1948.
The Devils Own Luck, Dennis Edwards, 1999, Pen and Sword
Books Ltd
D-Day, Robert J. Kershaw, 1993, Ian Allan Ltd.
Go To It, Peter Harclerode, 1990, Caxton Editions.
Para! 50 Years of the Parachute Regiment, Peter Harclerode, 1999,
Brockhampton Press.
'D-Day Then and Now', Vol 1, *After The Battle*, 1995.
One Night in June, K. Shannon and S. Wright, 1994, Airlife.
On Wings of Healing, Lt. Col. Howard N. Cole

Official Records

War Diaries, Public Records Office:
9th Parachute Battalion, WO171/1242
5th Black Watch
3rd Parachute Sqdn RE, WO171/1510
3rd Parachute Brigade HQ, WO171/593
6th Airborne Division HQ, WO171/425
13/18th Hussars, WO171/845
No 3 Commando, WO218/65
No 6 Commando, WO218/68
591 Parachute Sqdn RE -
1/7th Middlesex, WO171/
224 Fd (Para) Ambulance, WO222/613
13th Parachute Battalion, WO171/1246
7th Parachute Battalion, WO171/1239
8th Parachute Battalion, WO171/1241
22nd Independent Parachute Company, WO171/1249
4th Airlanding Anti-tank Battery, WO171/960

2nd Ox and Bucks, WO171/1357
Airborne Div. Paras, WO106/4142
Lt J. Loring letter, AIR27/1974
Glider Mission Report, WO171/1283
5th Parachute Brigade HQ, WO171/595
1st Canadian Parachute Battalion, Canadian Military Archive

Taped Interviews, IWM:
James Bramwell, 224 Fd (Para) Ambulance

Medical Records
224 Fd Ambulance Records, Wellcome Centre, Euston

Photos
Airborne Forces Museum
IWM, Film and Photographic Archive
JARIC, RAF Brampton
Keele University
Messieurs Miguet, Lecomte, Courcy,/Madame Trevel
Public Records Office

Notes

Chapter 1
1   RAF Physical Training instructors who were converted to parachuting carried this out.
2   *History of the Essex Regiment.*
3   His 2 I/c, Alastair Pearson, had done such a fine job and been through so much with the 1st Battalion that Flavell could not return
his command. Hill agreed.
4   The War Office thought that he was still in Algiers! When the truth was discovered, three doctors were sent to examine him. He

convinced them of his fitness but consequently they could not allow him any pension for the wounds. This did not bother the Brigadier in the slightest.

5 All information from interviews with Brigadier Hill Nov 2000/Oct 2001.

6 The Divisional number '6' was chosen for security reasons, ie. to keep the Germans guessing about the 'other four Divisions' .

7 *With the 6th Airborne Division in Normandy*, Gen. Richard Gale.

8 In reality, he had been doing both jobs for the preceding couple of months.

9 The figure of 650 comes from a Hal Hudson letter, (the Battalion Adjutant) held in the 9th Bn Archive.

10 Colonel Lindsay was posted to a Scottish Battalion.

11 Contrary to statements written in one or two publications, Colonel Otway stated categorically that this was the first time he had known of the target.
No information had been forthcoming up to that point to indicate a gun battery of any sort.

12 The model had been constructed in accordance with information supplied by aerial photographs and the French Resistance.

13 *The Big Drop*, John Golley. Also confirmed during an interview with Col Otway.

14 The 7th Battalion had moved to the 5th Brigade.

15 Colonel Otway wanted Major Parry, the O.C. 'A' Company, his most experienced officer, beside him during the attack in case anything happened to himself. Parry was deeply disappointed at not being able to lead his Company.

16 *A Teenager's War*, Ron Tucker/Interview Ron Tucker.

17 *Airborne Forces*, Lt Col T. Otway. Also confirmed during interview.

Chapter 2

1 *The 9th Parachute Battalion – The First Six Days.*

2 *Airborne Forces.*

3 The Troubridge Party was named after Admiral Troubridge who performed a reconnaissance before the Battle of Trafalgar.

4 9th Battalion War Diary – May 1944.

5 Map reference 158773.

6 Map reference 150777.

7 This crosstracks was at Map reference 163769.

8 This enemy position was at Map reference 153771.

9 The Firm Base area was between Map references 158773 and 159774.

10 A Bangalore torpedo consisted of a length of light steel tube filled with explosive. Lengths could be connected together as required. The first section had a nose coupling containing a pointed wooden nose block. The torpedo was specifically designed to explode upwards to breach wire obstacles.

11 This information is from the 9th Battalion War Diary. There were also several other plans to cover various contingencies: Should there be no ditch or outer wire (ie, only one belt of wire other than the cattle fence) 'B' Company would lay the torpedoes in the wire. If so, the CO was to order 'REVEILLE' as soon as the gaps were blown and 'C' Company would then assault. If there was no wire or any other obstacle (ie, it has all been removed by OBOE) the following procedure was to be adopted:
> 'B' Company was to remain at the Firm Base.
> 'C' Company was to be led up to the furthest cross tape and lie down.
> The CO was to order 'LIGHTS OUT' as before when the gliders were down.
> Two minutes later, the CO was to order 'REVEILLE' and 'C' Company was to assault.
Should the Battery be 'dead' ie, an assault be unnecessary, when the letter 'M' was flashed from the aircraft, the CO was to order a series of green 2-inch mortar flares. On this signal, the glider pilots were to pick their own LZ and land in the vicinity of the Battery.

12 This Brigade, which comprised of Nos 3, 4 and 6 Commandos and 45 Royal Marine Commando, were to assist the Airborne Division in covering the establishment of the sea-borne British 3rd Division, which was immediately to the west of the Caen Canal. The Commandos were to begin landing by sea on 'SWORD' Beach at around 8.00am, and Nos 3 and 6 Commandos were to head straight for the bridges at Benouville where they were due to arrive in the early afternoon of D-Day. Upon crossing them the Brigade would then come under the overall command of 6th Airborne Division. They were to turn north and take up position along the coast and the northern part of the ridge. No 6 Commando was to head for Breville, while No 3 went to Cabourg. No 4 Commando, which would join the Brigade after capturing Ouistreham, and 45 Commando, would follow later in the afternoon. They were to try and capture the towns of Sallenelles and Franceville-Plage, and clear as much of the enemy as possible from the coastal strip between these places and Cabourg.

13 Initially, it had been planned for the 6th Airlanding Brigade to arrive in the early morning, but in April the Germans had begun erecting anti-glider landing posts in the fields (christened 'Rommels asparagus') and due to this danger, was switched with the 5th Parachute Brigade.

14 Nine of the thirty-two planes were to carry four containers each, and two others, two each.

15 One Sunday afternoon in 1944, Corteil and Private Bolingbroke were caught poaching on Salisbury Plain. Lieutenant Colonel Lindsay handed them a modest punishment. He asked them if they would like to be dog handlers, to which they happily agreed. Bolingbroke's dog was eventually transferred to the 13th Battalion.

16 The Quartermaster was Captain Albert Chilton.

17 He died on 6 June. Everyone was very shocked when they found out a few days later. No one had suspected that the wound was that bad. There is an account in the 'After the Battle' book *D-Day, Then and Now Volume 1* by Father Alberic Stacpoole which raises the possibility that he may have accidentally shot himself. Hopefully, this clarifies the matter.

18 A fourteen-foot arrester parachute was fitted to help slow the glider down just before landing among the Battery casemates. It was deployed by an explosive charge controlled from the cockpit.

19 In some publications it has been stated that the gliders would also slow themselves down by deliberately hitting the casemates with

their wings. Arnold Baldwin and his co-pilot Joe Michie both stated that this was untrue and would not really slow the glider down anyway. Most books state that, 'delivery of these gliders was late, and when, three days before D-Day, six gliders arrived at Brize Norton, three were found to be fitted with the arrester gear and three with the Rebecca sets. A frantic hunt ensued for a further three gliders to modify'.

20 Colonel George Chatterton was the Commanding Officer of the Glider Pilot Regiment.
21 Major Toler was the CO of 'B' Squadron, The Glider Pilot Regiment.
22 Notes on report to Supreme Commander Allied Expeditionary Force (SCAEF), 22 June 1944 – Group Captain Stagg. *D-Day, Then and Now, Volume 1* – After the Battle.

Chapter 3

1 Notes on report to SCAEF, June 22 1944 – Group Captain Stagg – *D-Day, Then and Now – Volume 1* – After the Battle.
2 Major Smith's words.
3 The Paras carrying rifles also used this method. A cord of around twenty feet was attached to the rifle, which was strapped to the leg. A pin was pulled out to release the cord.
4 Each truck was identified by a chalk number to indicate the plane that it would pull up beside.
5 Quote from a *Daily Mail* report.
6 The Colonel believes that he was travelling in the Battalion's third or fourth Dakota.

Chapter 4

1 Due to a heavy drop most of the Eureka beacons were damaged. From subsequent events it is debatable whether this Eureka was actually in working order. Certainly the equipment gliders never found any Eureka working. Andy Andrews, one of these glider pilots, did not see any lights on the DZ. He saw a light 'T' and went for it. This turned out to be close to DZ 'N'.
2 Sid Knight's comments from *Men of the Red Beret*.
3 Notes made by Major Parry in hospital about a week later. Source: General Sir Napier Crookenden.
4 Chalk number 342.
5 Interviews with Colonel Otway, plus *Dawn of D-Day*.
6 John Speechley: *I learned the next day that Dunk had gone through a greenhouse in a garden.*
7 John Speechley: *I think we lost {Harold} 'Ginger' Payne there; he's never been seen* [since].
8 Robert Ferguson joined a group of Paras that remained in the flooded area for two months. By night they carried out nuisance raids on German positions. They were only captured when an American Officer, a downed pilot who had joined them, 'pulled rank' when on a patrol and led them straight into German hands!
9 Reports held in PRO – POW or evading capture reports. Lieutenant Winston and Marine Donald never did reach the Airborne perimeter. By stealth and help from French civilians they headed for Spain. In Bordeaux they were captured by the Gestapo, but, when the Allied breakthrough began they were handed over to the Luftwaffe. Feigning sickness, the Luftwaffe put them in a civilian hospital and departed. The pair arrived back in England in early September.
10 After meeting Lieutenant Browne of the anti-tank platoon and other members of the 9th, they attempted to reach the Airborne perimeter, but were captured after several days on the run.
11 Passwords: 'Punch and Judy' was valid from 0200 on D-1 to 0200 on D-Day. 'V' 'For Victory' was from then until 0200 on D+1. As this was quite soon after the drop, this was possibly a slight error by Hal Hudson.
12 Map reference 168757.
13 Parry Interview – *Brightly Shone The Dawn*.
14 The War Diary of the 22nd Independent Parachute Company states that Private Deakin broke his leg on landing.
15 Wilson has been misquoted in many books as saying it was brandy. The Colonel confirms that it was whisky!
16 Nearly all accounts state that there were no radios either. However, Ernie Rooke-Matthews testimony disproves that. Even so, he still had no-one to talk to! Private Cliff Pritchard had another set – it was unserviceable!
17 9th Battalion Report.

Chapter 5

1 This was almost certainly one of the Divisional gliders due to land on DZ 'N' at 3.20am.
2 Talk by Colonel Otway, Middle Wallop, 1999.
3 Joe Michie and Arnold Baldwin examined the glider later in the morning. Joe Michie: *We saw it in daylight and we were amazed to see that the petohead which was above the cockpit had been broken off and the leading edge of the wings was smashed away where the rope was attached on each side, right back to the main spar and about three or four feet wide. So God knows where we might have been; we might have been above the tug or below the tug. Apparently Dennis Richards said afterwards that it was a 'pretty hairy' experience in the tug.*
4 Report by CO, 'B' Sqdn GPR – 20-6-44 – PRO.
5 As stated in the plan, this crosstracks was about 400 yards east of the Battery at map reference 163769.
6 *Dropzone Normandy.*
7 Allen Parry seemed to forget that he had allocated No 1 casemate to Lieutenant Jefferson. Alan Jefferson stated that this was agreed between them after the war.
8 Account by Leo 'Darky' Duncan.
9 See Appendix 5.
10 One of the Paras near the rear of the glider who was carrying a section of General Wade charge, was hit. He caught fire and it was impossible to do anything for him. This episode was to give Pte James Tugwell nightmares until the day he died.
11 Report by Staff Sergeant Kerr 1944. Courtesy of his son, Neil Kerr.
12 This time was confirmed as correct by Colonel Otway. Also, the gliders were on time.

13 Letters held by General Sir Napier Crookenden and 9th Battalion archive.

14 *Ready for Anything,* (Major Parry's comments).

15 *Men of the Red Beret.*

16 *The Big Drop.*

17 CSM Barney Ross: *Now whether we all got mixed up and he* [Harold Long] *done 3 and I done 4, I don't know. There was no big sign up! I think between us we looked after those two sections.*

18 There is a difference of opinion here. Alan Mower believes that Mike Dowling was not wounded at this point.

19 Len Daniels thought that Hawkins had died. To his amazement he met him on a pilgrimage over thirty years later.

20 Unsigned report by Major Parry in Battalion War Diary dated 27-6-44.

21 *Brightly Shone The Dawn,* states: *Lieutenant Slade then came running bareheaded from the far side of the Battery. He told Major Parry that he himself had checked the other casemates and was satisfied that the guns had been put out of action.*Concerning his wound. In the 1960s, he had to have his leg amputated below the knee due to the injury.

22 The bird got through with its message, 'Hammer', for success, to the correct place.

23 Colonel Otway recalls him saying, *F... your bloody Battery!*

24 Stan Eckert was later found dead by a Royal Marine Commando. A letter was found on the body and was returned to his family:
'Somewhere in France'
Dear Mum,
I am writing this letter at the bottom of a ditch very near the front line and I hope to get it posted pretty soon as my pal and I have a good idea that tomorrow we will be prisoners of war. I am writing this short note here so as if it is ever found by anyone they can forward it for me.
Do you know mum dear, I have never realised how much you meant to me, until now ? If I can get home again, you will see a very different Stan, just wait and see. The same goes for Dad too, and the rest of the Eckerts. There is one thing that worries me, and that is what happened to Cyril. I hope and pray that he is safe and well.
Well mum, just sit and wait for the end of the war when I will be 'home' once again, for good. Don't worry at all will you.
With love to everyone at home, especially you.
*   Your ever loving son.   Stan XXXXX*
Very sadly, his elder brother, Cyril, of the 13th Battalion, was killed on the 23rd August.

25 Later, the German doctor attempted to go back to the Battery for some supplies, but was killed when the Germans opened up with an artillery barrage.

Chapter 6

1 *Red Devils – The Story of 224 Field (Para) Ambulance in Normandy.*

2 Concerning the prisoners, Alan Jefferson stated in his book that the prisoners were put in front as a shield. Colonel Otway stated to the author: *Someone   said that we put the prisoners in front of us. We didn't. I could have been court-martialled for that. The prisoners were behind us all the time.* Sid Capon, Fred Milward and various others back this up. The prisoners were not in front of the column. Perhaps the incident at the Battery where the prisoners were forced to lead through the minefield is the incident that Lieutenant Jefferson recalls.

3 Map reference 165762.

4 The 9th Battalion lost at least 12 men. Those later identified and buried were: Lieutenants Catlin and Peters, Lance Corporal Robinson, Privates Armstrong, Corteil, Mander, Nicholls, Peck, Plested, Sharples,Walter and Young. In 1994, Cyril Thwaites came across a burial list that was made by a man in Gonneville who had buried them. The spelling of Glenn has been taken from the list made by the Frenchman at the time. A 9th Battalion burial party found the bodies later in the year after the breakout from Normandy.

5 Two men, Privates Gent and Skerry took the captured car and reached the remains of the Troarn Bridge.They had to destroy the car and continue on foot. They managed to evade capture until 5 July.

6 On a trip to the Merville Battery in the 1980s, John Speechley met the man who was up the tower – Sergeant   Major Peter Timpf. Timpf was actually the Forward Observation Officer for the Merville Battery. Just as the 9th Battalion's attack had gone in, he had been ordered to take his platoon and clear the area to the south-east behind the guns. This explains how he ended up in Varaville – letter to Alan Jefferson/*Assault on the Guns of Merville.*

7 A château with a very steep roof at map reference 157742.

8 Fred Glover's story continues at Appendix 1.

9 Joe Millward was awarded the MM for this action.

10 *The Big Drop.*

11 *Out of the Clouds - The Story of the 1st Canadian Parachute Battalion.*

12 This was David Haig-Thomas of No 4 Commando. He had jumped with the 3rd Parachute Brigade and was to liaise in the link up between the Commandos and the Brigade.

13 Visibility was no more than a few yards. Possibly the medic saw their silent prostrate bodies, and being under fire, assumed they were dead. Monsieur Godey remained on the ground for quite some time until he was sure it was safe. He then crawled away and returned home. When he got there he told another Frenchman what had happened. Haig-Thomas' body was retrieved and buried in Bavent civilian cemetery, where it remains today. He took a clock and a bone cosh made from a walrus flipper that HT had carried as a lucky talisman. This had been a gift to Haig-Thomas from Baffinland Eskimos during his Cambridge exploration days. It had been splintered with Schmeisser bullets. These were later given to Sam Ryder who passed them to Lord Lovat who duly returned it to his family. *March Past –* Lord Lovat. Johnny Britton believed for fifty years that this boy had been killed and on various trips to Normandy had tried to find out his identity. In 1994, Louis Adelin, a good friend of the 9th Battalion, gave him a shock and introduced him to Robert Godey. He had done a similar thing in 1984 with Lieutenant Smith.

14 These can only have been from the glider which did not reach the River Orne bridge.

15 Divisional HQ had been set up in the Château du Heaume at le Bas de Ranville.

16 In the original plan, Brigadier Hill had earmarked some suitable buildings for an A.D.S. just down the road from Brigade HQ.

17 The Commando liberation of Amfreville/Le Plein is explained at Appendix 2.

18 With the arrival of the Commandos, Lieutenant Pond told Walker and Kerr, the two assault glider pilots, that they were no longer required, but instructed them to take the prisoners with them to Divisional HQ. This they did, reaching Ranville by 6pm and collecting four more prisoners en route, including an officer. Report by C.O. 'B' Sqdn G.P.R. 20-6-44.

19 These were almost certainly members of 45 RM Commando whose job it was to ensure that the Merville Battery was put out of action if the 9th Battalion had failed.

20 Terry Jepp's story, plus that of the Vermughens, continues at Appendix 3.

21 *On Wings of Healing.*

22 Alan Jefferson is adamant that Major Parry went first. However, from Parry's account, plus Hal Hudson's it is apparent that they must have travelled together. Therefore, it is my belief that all three went on the same trip. Walter Johnson also went on one of the two trips.

23 Due to the shortage of aircraft and gliders, only one company of the 12th Devons, the third battalion of the Brigade, was able to be transported. The rest were to follow via the beaches on D+1.

24 When they had landed at RAF Odiham, their pilot, Arnold Baldwin, had reported immediately to Lieutenant Colonel Chatterton, Commander Glider Pilots. A lorry was arranged to take the men back to Brize Norton. Baldwin also reported to his Squadron Commander, Major Toler, asking him to do all in his power to: *Get my Paras to France on the afternoon lift. This he did and Joe* [Michie] *and I waved them off.*

25 Hudson actually thought he was holding Allen Parry's hand.

26 These were 4 and 5 Troops of No 3 Commando.

Chapter 7

1 John Woodgate did not find out until later that Alec Pope, with whom he had swapped planes at such a late hour, had been dropped in the wrong place and killed after a fierce battle near St Vaaste-en-Auge.

2 Telephone discussion with Alan Jefferson. The post-operative report of Captain Gray's surgical team made grisly reading: 'Wounded in the right foot and right buttock (penetrating abdomen). Very shocked, resuscitated with plasma, but did not respond well. At operation, found to have two perforations at the lower end of the ilium, with peritonitis locally. Perforations closed. Buttock wound explored - gas gangrene of gluteuos maximus. Muscle excised in toto. Very weak at end of operation. Plasma given at Post Op'. Source: The 224 Field Ambulance records held in Wellcome Institute Medical Archive

3 Hal Hudson clung desperately to life and on 8 June, although still very weak, was able to be evacuated. The efforts of Gwinnett, Allt and the surgeon had not been in vain.

4 *The Red Devils – The Story of 224 Fd (Para) Ambulance.*

5 The only Colonel there was Peter Young, the revered CO of No 3 Commando. George Hawkins and his two wounded comrades were to remain in No 4 casemate for nearly four days before being evacuated by ambulance. They ended up in Paris at the Ortzlazarette de la Pitie hospital.

6 *'Go To It!',* Lieutenant John Shave.

7 9th Battalion War Diary, PRO

8 *Out of the Clouds – The Story of the 1st Canadian Parachute Battalion.*

9 Commando War Diaries/IWM Film

10 Several accounts state that they became lost. As Colonel Otway has explained in detail, this is incorrect.

11 Later, they listened to news of the invasion on the BBC eight o'clock broadcast.

Chapter 8

1 What they saw was possibly due to an incident which occurred on the evening of D-Day. The following is from *The Red Devils – The Story of 224 Field (Para) Ambulance:*

'During the afternoon RASC Drivers Nicholl and Broad, who were attached to 224 Field Ambulance had used a captured 15-cwt truck to convey casualties from the gun emplacement at 'Gonneville'. [Note: I have not been able to find any further information to corroborate this]. On the way back that evening, the truck was damaged and Corporal Cummings spent several hours repairing it. Sometime after 8pm he had scarcely finished when the call came to go out once more. Guided by one of the captured German medical orderlies, an Unteroffizier Kehlenbach, and scarcely knowing what they were in for, Cummings and Hurry drove along the Breville road and then turned up a long drive where they passed an unattended German machine gun. They had reached a place called the Château St Côme.

At the end of the drive a large house loomed and out tumbled a horde of Germans. Kehlenbach called out something and their first impression was that he had tricked them. But the Germans themselves seemed quite demoralized. Leaving their weapons behind they crowded round the truck, evidently anxious to find out what was happening. Corporal Cummings managed to give the impression that the whole area was swarming with British troops, whereupon a spokesman asked him to accept their surrender. But to return along the road they had come with sixty-three prisoners was an uninviting thought since it was only too plain that at any point they might meet an enemy patrol. While Corporal Cummings was considering this, the Germans were lining up with bundles ready to march off. Two of them were wounded and these were put on the truck and attended to by Jansch who was the only RAMC member of the party. To the disappointment of the would-be prisoners Corporal Cummings would only take the Warrant Officer in charge and drove off saying he would return as soon as possible. Back at Le Mesnil he reported to Lieutenant Philo (RASC) who borrowed two Bren gunners and immediately set off in a jeep with Lance Corporal Young, following Cummings with his German truck. They found the Germans still lined up, impatient to be off, but Lieutenant Philo too, was against marching them back along the road; he needed transport. So he made the Germans get out five trucks of their own. They made a lot of fuss about this, but, amid much shouting and noise they climbed in. At this point someone began to fire red tracer bullets down the drive and Lieutenant Philo decided they must start immediately or never. After what seemed an interminable delay the convoy was assembled and drove off. They reached Brigade HQ safely with all the prisoners and trucks.'

2   This money was handed over to Colonel Otway. However, the Château seemed to be 'awash' with it and some was saved for 'private use' by those who thought it may be legal tender. Those believing otherwise put it to good use as toilet paper. The Courcy family, which lived in le Bas de Breville, also informed the 9th Battalion of (probably) these gliders, meeting Lieutenant Christie on a patrol. The Courcy's had moved home temporarily, to a house on the St Côme estate, north of the Château. When the fighting in the area became heavier, they were forced to leave. They did so during a skirmish between Para and German patrols. The family walked right between the two sides, who withheld their fire until they had passed.

3   The whole property was also known as the Haras de Breville. It had been built around 100 years earlier and purchased by a Monsieur Miguet in 1936. He subsequently moved to Paris and leased the Haras to Lord Derby. Many of Derby's famous racehorses had been bred there and were still in residence.

4   Whoever it was, he survived. Captain Robinson later saw him back at Bulford and he came over and thanked him for saving his life.

5   The Field Ambulance account quotes the occupants as only being four people; Jansch, Thompson (RASC), Garrett plus Tottle. However Doug Tottle's own account states six wounded. There would have been no room for anyone else on the jeep. Garrett must have been the other person because he died of his wounds.

6   IWM Interview with James Bramwell.

7   Although his body was moved to the Divisional Cemetery at Ranville, the stone remains in the Bois des Monts to this day. Most publications state that he was killed on 9 June. However, the Brigade War Diary, plus his own gravestone state 8 June.

8   *The Red Devils – The Story of 224 Field (Para) Ambulance.*

9   Harry Gray remained with the Battalion until the end of the war.

10 Colonel Otway: *I insisted that every person in the Battalion should shave each day. It is amazing how this keeps up morale.*

11 The war reporter, Chester Wilmot, spent this day at the Bois des Monts, during which he made a recording. The BBC now has no knowledge of the whereabouts of this transmission.

Chapter 9

1   Medical archive – Wellcome Institute.

2   The name Bomb Alley also appears to have been given to the whole position by various veterans. However, I have used it purely to describe this ditch.

3   Colour Sergeant Graham was awarded the MM for this action.

4   Private Undrill most probably survived. His name does not appear on the casualty list.

5   Harold Walker: *Years after, I can't remember his name, we had one of the reunion dinners at the White City, and I was sitting there and he comes up and says, 'Give us a fag'.*

6   To find out what had gone wrong, the CO investigated and found that it was probably due to two mistakes. Firstly, the platoon had tried to cross the clearing   in the wood without first ensuring that its flanks were protected by covering fire, and secondly, some of the men rushed a bank behind which they knew there were some enemy, without grenading the far side first. Report on 9th Parachute Battalion – The first six days held in the Battalion War Diary – WO171/1242.

7   *The Red Devils.* While at the MDS Newcomb was ordered to go to Escoville and never returned. He was presumed captured.

8   IWM interview – James Bramwell.

9   War Diary – 13th Parachute Battalion.

Chapter 10

1   War Diary, 13th Parachute Battalion. The crosstracks was at map reference 118734.

2   When Jock Pattinson awoke, the medical orderly who was standing over him said, You're young Pattinson aren't you? Amazingly enough it was George MaCechnie, a friend of Geoff's elder brother from Glasgow. He would later be Best Man at Geoff's wedding. Later, Pattinson was put on a 'stretcher jeep' and driven down to the beachhead. While he was walking down a road towards the beach he saw two Military Policemen ahead. He heard one of them say, 'It's a German, shoot him!' From his ragged appearance, plus the luminous skull and crossbones still visible on his smock, they thought he was one of the enemy. However, Pattinson just managed to identify himself in time!

3   Map reference 125731, 13th Battalion War Diary.

4   Among many good horses to die were Lord Derby's Plassey and Plassey's son Arcot.

5   Fred Wingrove died on 15 June.

6   To this day one can plainly see a group of bullet holes in the trunk of that tree.

7   Map reference 133726.

8   War Diary, 7th Parachute Battalion:
    Tanks would move across the DZ and fire into each wood in turn and would indicate when they had finished firing by means of a smoke shell fired into the wood in question. The infantry would then enter and clear the wood. I ordered a very simple plan which catered for each wood in turn being swept and then mopped up by one company while the other company passed through the first and carried out the same manoeuvre in the next wood. The woods in question were {at map references} 122735 (W), 124733 (X), 124731 (Y) and 133727 (Z). After clearing Z Wood the battalion was to secure road junction 133726 and send out patrols to contact 3 Para Brigade in the area of crossroads 1372. I detailed 'B' Company to clear Woods W, Y and Z and 'A' Company to clear wood X and to secure the road junction at 133726. The infantry start line was the east face of wood 118733 and the time of start was 1600 hours.
    Lieutenant Douglas Coker, 'B' Squadron, 13th/18th Hussars:
    Once over the Orne I swung left with my Troop, then passing through a section of gliders, came down a slope into open fields. My own Troop was leading and my Sherman tank followed about fifty yards behind a Honey (Stuart) manned by the Officer Troop Leader, Lieutenant Trenchant Hardy, of the Recce section.
    Lieutenant Colonel Pine-Coffin:
    The attack started at the appointed hour but difficulty was experienced from the start in co-ordinating with the tanks. These latter came up in pairs and it was hard to know when they were all up as I understood that a squadron was being used, but actually only six tanks appeared at any time. The clearing of W Wood went without a hitch and several Germans were killed and 'A' Company duly passed through and cleared X Wood, where several more Germans

were killed. Two of the tanks were ablaze at this stage.

The Honey had become entangled in parachute cords and ground to a halt. Lieutenant Coker:

It was hit by an anti-tank shot and immediately burst into flames. The turret was like a vast blow torch and needless to say no-one survived. At this stage our advance was halted and in the next moment my own tank was hit and the survivors baled out. My driver, Lance Corporal Miller crawled round to me where I was lying on the ground with wounds in my left leg and right thigh. My driver – we were both unable to walk – was in a poor way and had been quite badly burnt so I got him back by crawling to a Sherman behind us, that of my Troop Sergeant, which was not being fired at.

Lieutenant Colonel Pine-Coffin:

The remaining tanks then fired well into Y Wood, and 'A' Company gave covering fire for 'B' Company's approach to it. When 'B' Company entered the west end of Y Wood a white flag was waved from the north-east corner of it. The wood was thick and it was difficult to sort out the situation as, of course, 'B' Company in the wood were not aware that the Germans were trying to surrender. About forty were taken prisoner here and the sorting out of them delayed 'A' Company.

9   A German officer, interrogated after the war, recalled that these had been knocked out by a roving SP gun situated somewhere between Le Mesnil and Herouvillette. However, both the Hussars survivors and the Paras recall the fire coming from the left – the Breville area.

10 *The Spirit of Angus.*

11 *The Red Devils – The Story of 224 Fd Ambulance.*

12 Colonel Otway: *The maps were important for people 'at the back', not at my level. It showed where the German positions were; way out of our reach.*
6th Airborne Division Diary for 11 June states:

An enemy map, obviously marked in preparation for attack on Ranville on 10th taken from corpse on the DZ after the battle. Four threatening blue arrows converged on the Benouville Bridges, one from Sallenelles two from the Breville area and one from St Honorine. Regimental HQ were marked at map references 166752 and 163731 (857 and 858 Regiments respectively). Ships plastered these areas today.

Chapter 11

1   *The Spirit of Angus.*

2   James Bramwell tape – IWM.

3   Of 'B' Company, 11 Platoon was positioned in the trees and bushes on the left-hand side of the driveway, about fifty yards from the Château. 10 Platoon was placed to their left at approximately the junction between a long avenue of trees and the thick hedge running parallel to the driveway. 12 Platoon was behind them in the same hedge. 'B' Company HQ was in the centre of these positions, in the ditch to the right of the driveway. The remnants of 'A' Company were to the left of the drive, not far from the entrance.

4   Map reference of junction was 136737.

5   Fred Milward believes that the wounded man's name was Tutt. If it was, he survived, as the name Tutt does not appear on the Battalion casualty list.

Chapter 12

1   Bill Mills describes the journey: *We were coming towards the beach to land alongside Ouistreham. Eventually, when we came in, our skipper, an American landing craft, immediately turned right. We dashed up onto the bridge and asked, 'What the hell are you doing?' He said, 'I've got orders from my commander. I'm not to land here until I go further up the coast.' So that cost us hours and hours in time and distance. We thought it was just too hot for him and that was all there was to it. Nothing we could do about it, he was running the ship.*
Instead, they eventually landed along the coast at GOLD Beach, opposite Crepon. This of course entailed a hazardous journey along the coast to reach the 6th Airborne Divisional area.

2   Bill Mills note on water carts: *We got issued with water carts from the First World War. They had shafts for putting between horses. They were very good actually, because their capacity was quite enormous and the great old-fashioned wooden wheels with steel rims round them. We tied them to the backs of jeeps and at least you could take them forward and drop them and then go back for another one, an empty one, and fill it up.*

3   This FOP consisted of three men, Captain D. H. Pullin and gunner signallers Walter Atkinson and Matt Hamilton, all belonging to 'Don' Troop, 304 Battery, 127th Field Regiment. Their battery of 25 Pounders was sited amongst the gliders to the west of the River Orne on DZ 'W'. Arthur Berry Letter/Diary of Captain Pullin.

4   War Diary 127 Field Regt RA, WO171/989.

5   Private Dennis Daly of the 1/7th Middlesex recalls this action:
I'd never been in action before, it was just like being on a manoeuvre in England to me. I thought everybody knows what to do, they've been in the desert, this is what you do! He drove up to the Château to obtain some breakfast:
I drove back to the position, parked the carrier up and it would then be about nine, ten o'clock. I got back into my slit trench to shake the earth off my blankets and straighten myself up and I heard these mortars, just the last few seconds before they arrived, and I dropped in the slit trench, flat down. It seemed a hell of a long time but it must have been thirty seconds or something like that, this salvo of mortars.
And then it all went quiet and I got up and had a look round, and there's Albert Brown, still kneeling down. He'd been brewing up and he hadn't moved and all the back of his head had been caved in... The last thing he'd said to me was, 'D'you know Dennis, I haven't felt scared at all yet.' He didn't even have time to be scared. He was thirty-one and a father figure to us. Ben Lyus was dead, Harry Tomlinson was dead and then all the wounded were shouting for stretcher-bearers. The other gun did not suffer any fatal casualties:
There were three of us out of the gun section that weren't hit. The guns, we thought at the time, were absolutely destroyed so we dropped back from that open field into the stables. They'd been well knocked about, the fires had burnt out but they were in a bit of a rough state.

6   *The Red Devils - The Story of 224 Field Ambulance in Normandy.*

7   Account by Gordon Driscoll, a Black Watch anti-tank gunner positioned beside the Château.

8   Dennis Daly:
As we approached them, my carrier was parked perhaps ten or twelve yards from the guns. These people were on the carrier where I'd left a lot of cigarettes on. So to the three or four of us heading for the guns I said, 'The bloody Paras are nicking my cigarettes.' I never spoke very loudly but we were that close that they heard me, looked up and I realized they were Germans! So they opened up on us. Everyone scattered. Bullets were flying all over the place. We ran like buggery to the gun position, grabbed what we could and I got three boxes of ammo, one under me arm and one in each hand and we hared back.

We managed to get on the other side of a hedge because Lofty {Pearson} was shouting, 'Keep your heads Down,' and he was about six feet two inches, and all he was doing was bending his neck. There was still about four foot of him above this bloody hedge!

We got back to the Château just in time for it to all start again, as though nobody knew what was happening and us going for that gun livened them all up again. It seemed that way.

Major Pearson was later to receive the MC for this action.

9 The following is the Middlesex Diary plus Dennis Daly's account of what happened: Fred Addison, the Middlesex Platoon Sergeant, decided to act. He took a PIAT, went through the kitchen door into the furore outside and fired a bomb clean through the wall of a section of the stable opposite. He reloaded and put another through a door, causing terrific explosions. Dennis Daly:

He didn't even have a steel helmet on. I remember that because a piece of shrapnel took half his cap badge away and that was all he was concerned about. Another group of Germans was spotted trying a stealthy approach behind a cart full of hay. Private Tommy Latham, the Signals carrier driver, pinned it down with the Vickers while Sergeant Addison again ran outside and put a PIAT bomb straight into it, blowing up the cart and the soldiers in one. Latham then inflicted considerable casualties on other retreating enemy. When the Germans tried to re-enter the stable area, Addison acted again. Dennis Daly:

He spotted them forming up in the stables, so he got this PIAT gun and used it as a mortar. I don't know how many rounds he fired but the whole bloody stables went up, Germans and all. Shortly after that it died down a bit.

10 The ammunition for the damaged machine gun had run out, and so the crew of the Middlesex Vickers near the drive entrance was sent up to the Château to bolster its defence. Corporal Harry Biddell, another friend of Daly's came up to the Château. Daly had got hold of a Lee Enfield rifle and taken up position at a ground floor window in one of the back rooms:

Harry Biddell came dancing into the room, he was always acting the goat, laughing and joking. Harry said, 'Sod this for a game of soldiers.' I tried to tell him to slow it down but I was too late. Harry ran up to me at the window. This mortar landed outside the window which was only a low window and he got hit in the stomach. He dropped and I lay down next to him while he died.

11 Here, Daly was knocked out of the battle:

The Germans were taking heavy casualties from the withering fire of our Lee Enfield rifles when I felt an almighty blow on my shoulder, and to my amazement I saw my rifle split in half... It must have been a grenade because they wouldn't have been using mortars on their own people, but they were too close to use anything else. It split the rifle; felt this terrific belt on my shoulder, frightened to look at first, thought I'd lost my bloody arm! Thereafter he could not move it and so went back to the RAP.

12 Bill Mills: *The back leg of the machine gun normally stays firm, as long as you're on flat ground, it's the front legs that you adjusted. The back one is a different clamp altogether, you unwind it a lot. It's a very fine thread.*

13 Colonel Otway recommended Cunningham for the VC and Beckwith the DCM. Neither was awarded. The Colonel was extremely angry about this.

14 Middlesex Diary, Dennis Daly.

15 For this act Bill Irving was awarded the Military Medal.

16 Trooper George Treloare was in one of the tanks, and as he and Troopers Shakeshaft and Rayner got out, the Germans began to machine-gun and mortar the vicinity. George Treloare, 2 Troop, 'B' Squadron, 13th/18th Hussars:

As the mortar bombs began to fall, my best friend, Norman 'Louis' Rayner, dived into a trench and Shakeshaft dived in on top of him. Unfortunately, or fortunately as it turned out, I lay flat on the ground. A mortar bomb hit the edge of the trench. After a time, when it had quietened down a bit, Shakeshaft called out to me and said that Louis had been quiet for some time. We got him out to find a hole in his hat, so we took him to the '6th Airborne Field Dressing Station' {sic} where we found that the piece of shrapnel had gone through Shakeshaft's foot into Louis' head. There Louis died, and Shakeshaft was sent back to Blighty.

17 Dougie Martin's story and a copy of the original diagram made by the surgeon who finally operated on him in England, is at Appendix 4.

18 This incident was extremely fortunate because during the afternoon the *Arethusa* had been hit by a Stuka bomb which damaged her firing table. A signal was sent to the Admiral at 1716 hours requesting permission to weigh anchor and proceed to Portsmouth for repairs. There had been a delay in receiving a reply but in the meantime all FOOs had been advised that she had ceased firing until further notice. Despite her state, the Signals Officer maintained radio contact with the shore and by chance she picked up the Black Watch SOS call for artillery help. The second salvo was equally effective.

19 Ken Walker: *Our Colonel had called some kind of an 'O' Group when according to some reports he and his group were blown up by a bomb dropped from an aircraft. This is not to my recollection, my slit trench was about fifteen yards from Battalion HQ. I heard the loud whistle of a shell which then exploded, I ran to help but was ordered back to my trench although aircraft was in the vicinity I am positive that was not the cause of the killing and wounding of Otway and the others.*

20 Lord Lovat was also badly wounded and had to be evacuated. The CO of the 12th Battalion was killed.

21 *Men of the Red Beret.*

22 Colonel Otway's figure. He actually counted them.

Chapter 13

1 The Ox and Bucks found evidence behind one of the barns of the shooting of Black Watch prisoners. One of them had survived. The Black Watch Padre, the Reverend Nicol remembers:

Joe Wright's D Company was at the Château at one point and must have been over-run, but later retook the position (or some other Company did so) and found a row of bodies lying, obviously shot down in cold blood, but with a gap in the row. It transpired that one soldier had been missed as the Germans ran their machine gun along the line and feigned death, and when the Germans moved on somehow got back to the remnants of the company.

Now this may be quite untrue, but why would it be in my mind: I think that up till that time the soldier concerned had not exactly been a hero, and wasn't believed when he came back with his story of the massacre. But when the bodies of his section were found and the gap in the line he had to be believed. Dennis Daly remembers that the word going around at the time was that his name was Fogarty. He was not believed at first by his friends but months later confirmation of his story was made. They had been lined up in the policies of the Château and shot in the back as they stood.

2 *The Devil's Own Luck.*

Index

(Formations/Personnel/Locations/Various)

Formations:

Supreme Headquarters Allied
  Expeditionary Force (SHAEF) 40, 41
US 82nd Airborne Division, 24
US 101st Airborne Division, 24
British 1st Airborne Division, 15, 16
1st Parachute Battalion, 15
British 6th Airborne Division, 16-17, 29,
  98, 124
22nd Independent Parachute Company, 31,
  44, 147, 195
4th Airlanding anti-tank Battery RA,
  28, 35
3rd Parachute Brigade, 15-17, 20, 23,
  25, 37, 39, 44, 48, 65, 113, 115, 125,
  127, 134, 148, 166, 171, 183, 193
1st Canadian Parachute Battalion, 25,
  31, 37, 39, 48, 54, 94, 98, 99, 106,
  107, 113, 114, 124, 133, 142, 159,
  189, 190, 192, 201
8th Parachute Battalion, 15, 25, 37,
  115,124
3rd Parachute Squadron Royal
  Engineers, 37, 129, 142, 180, 189,
  190, 192,
591 (Antrim) Parachute Squadron
  Royal Engineers, 28, 32, 35
224 Field (Para) Ambulance, 28, 32, 38,
  99, 105, 118, 129, 144, 147, 157, 189
5th Parachute Brigade, 16, 25, 162, 166
7th Parachute Battalion, 15, 124, 171
12th Parachute Battalion, 124, 195
13th Parachute Battalion, 124, 162, 163,
  166, 168
6th Airlanding Brigade, 16, 25, 37, 123
2nd Ox and Bucks Light Infantry, 25,
  124, 197
12th Devons, 124, 195
1st Royal Ulster Rifles, 30, 31, 39, 43, 124

Commando Formations

1st Special Service Brigade, 36, 111,
  115, 119, 124, 133, 146, 163, 195
No 3 Commando, 115, 124, 129, 134,
  163, 166
No 4 Commando, 118, 124, 163, 166, Ap 2
No 6 Commando, 117, 118, 124, 134,
  163, 166, Ap 2
45 RM Commando, 36, 118, Ap 5

Other Formations

51st Highland Division, 172, 181, 197
5th Black Watch, 172, 176-199
Essex Regiment, 10th Holding
  Battalion, 15
Glider Pilot Regiment, 'B' Squadron,
  37, Ap 5
Hussars, 13th/18th, 170-172, 192, 195
Middlesex, 1/7th, 181, 183, 185, 190,
  192, 197
No 8 Field Ambulance, 126
63rd Medium Regiment RA, 176
Royal Air Force
  46 Group, 37
  295 Squadron, 44
  512 Squadron, 37
  570 Squadron, 44

German Formations

857 Grenadier Regiment, 142, 163, 175

Personnel: General

Browning, Major General Frederick, 15,
  16, 23
Eisenhower, General Dwight D, 40
Flavell, Brigadier Edward, 16
Salmon, Major, 16
Stagg, Group Captain J M, 40, 41
Young, Captain Peter, 39, 40

6th Airborne Division

Bray, Lieutenant Colonel Robert, 98

Gale, Major General Richard, 16, 23-25,
  37, 114, 124, 172, 195
MacEwan, Colonel, 114, 115, 118

**22nd Independent Parachute
Company**

De La Tour, Lieutenant Bobby, 42, 72
Wells, Lieutenant Don, 42, 48

3rd Parachute Brigade

Collingwood, Major Bill, 28, 125, 205
Cooper, Captain Donald, 126, 166
Hill, Brigadier James, 15, 16, 20, 25,
  39, 40, 41, 54, 57, 62, 98-101, 113-
  115, 118, 119, 123-125, 127, 137,
  144, 172, 180, 185, 190-192, 194, 196
Hughes, Joe, 166
Jones, Johnnie, 99, 101, 115
Pope, Major Alec, 39, 125, 205
Smith, Lieutenant Douglas, 113, 114
Tilley, Corporal, 146
Wilkinson, Capt Tony, 106, 144-146, 205
Woodgate, Staff Captain John, 39, 65,
  105, 106, 115, 118, 125, 148

1st Canadian Parachute Battalion

Anderson, Pte, 185
Bradbrook, Colonel, 185
De Vries, Jan, 190, 191
Fuller, Major, 194
Griffin, Captain Peter, 106, 114
Hanson, Major, 185
Harvey, Pte, 148
Minard, Sergeant Willard, 192

8th Parachute Battalion

Pearson, Colonel Alastair, 115, 124

3rd Parachute Squadron RE

Docherty, Sergeant, 143
Graham, Lance Corporal Alan, 191
Green, Sapper, 143
Hurst, Lance Corporal, 131, 143
Irving, Lance Sergeant Bill, 191
Lack, Lieutenant, 180
Reynolds, Sapper, 143
Shave, Lieut John, 129-131, 142, 143
Smith, Sapper G, 143
Sullivan, Sapper Bob, 190, 192
Tillbrook, Sapper, 143

591 Parachute Squadron RE

Sanderson, Corporal, 88
Taylor, Sapper Alex, 45, 80, 81, 88, 93, 95

224 Fd (Para) Ambulance

Bramwell, James, 145, 157, 158, 160,
  161, 173-5, 179
Chaundy, Captain, 118
Cracknell, Pte, 99, 100
Cranna, Corporal, 157
Crisp, Staff Sergeant, 99
Garrett, Raymond (RASC), 144, 205
Ginn, Pte, 99
Gray, Captain Tom, 106, 115
Howard, Lance Corporal, 99
Hutton, Pte, 99, 100
Johnston, Captain Ian, 28, 106, 129, 133
Liddell, Pte, 160
Marquis, Captain Bobby, 129
Newcomb, Pte, 157
Park, Driver (RASC), 99
Sargent, Pte, 99, 100
Sparrow, Pte, 157, 160, 161
Stothers, Pte, 157
Thompson, Col, 115
Wright, Pte, 99
Young, Major Alastair, 105, 106, 115, 125

9th Parachute Battalion

Abel, Bob, 77, 109, 110, 205
Adsett, George, 49, 60, 84, 90, 204
Allt, Pte, 122, 123
Anderson, Pte, 157
Armstrong, Alroy, 204

Atkinson, Pte, 62, 63
Backhurst, David, 62, 63, 102, 114
Bailey, Corporal, 157, 187
Barrett, Archie, 153
Baty, Jim, 51, 170
Beckwith, CSM Wally, 134, 136, 137,
  161, 169, 177, 189, 193, 194, 204
Bedford, Sergeant Eric, 78, 85
Berry, Pte, 61, 98
Best, Sergeant Charlie, 150
Bestley, Major Harold, 55, 68, 86, 91,
  92, 97, 122
Blackwell, Pte, 189
Bosher, George, 94, 107
Bowden, Peter, 61
Brailsford, Stendall, 38, 68, 111, 137,
  151, 179, 188, 195
Brewster, Sergeant Stan 'Dizzy', 18, 19, 80
Browne, Lieutenant Brian, 33, 74
Britton, Sergeant John, 56, 57, 113, 114,
  147, 148
Bullock, Sergeant, 103, 104, 122, 129
Capon, Sid, 40, 63, 78, 81, 82, 85, 90,
  91, 92, 141, 156, 160, 176, 204, 205
Carey, Corporal Frank, 157
Cartwright, Les, 50, 78, 93
Catlin, Lieutenant Douglas, 99, 100, 204
Charlton, Major Eddie, 32, 60, 65, 68, 77,
  127, 134, 135, 139, 155, 156, 161,
  182, 204
Christie, Lieutenant Murray, 38, 68, 144,
  187, 194, 195, 204
Colville, 'Darky', 87
Comley, Pte, 97
Courtney, Harry, 156, 205
Corboy, Corporal Mick, 57, 103, 104,
  122, 129, 179, 180
Corteil, Emile, 38, 51, 99, 100, 204
Costello, Corporal Paddy, 157
Cunningham, RSM Bill, 60, 108, 139,
  188, 189, 204
Daniels, Sergeant Len, 30, 54, 68, 78, 81,
  84, 88-91, 94, 97, 108, 135, 139, 146,
  153, 155, 160, 161, 168, 173, 177, 188-190
Davies, Pte, 134
Davies, Colour Sergeant, 67, 204
Delsignore, Frank, 17, 23, 59, 78, 81,
  82, 84, 85, 91, 102, 204, 205
Dixon, Sergeant Harry, 84
Dorkins, Sergeant Fred, 67, 88
Dowling, Lieutenant Mike, 63, 75, 78, 82,
  88, 204
Dowling, Corporal Peter, 55, 56, 68, 104,
  130, 132
Duce, David, 62, 119, Ap 3
Dunk, Harry, 131, 132, 204
Dugan, Pte, 51
Durham, Alex, 132
Durston, Pte, 128
Dyer, Major Ian, 61, 75, 98, 104, 105,
  118, 127, 129, 132, 142, 154, 155,
  160-162, 176, 177
Easlea, Sergeant Eddie, 38, 44, 60, 155
Eckert, Lance Corporal Stan, 93, 204
Fenson, Pte, 76, 109, 134, 166, 188, 189
Fenton, Pte, 142
Ferguson, Corporal Robert, 56
Foster, Pte, 79
French, Jimmy, 54, 105, 118, 175, 176,
  180, 181, 192
Frith, Sergeant Jimmy, 163-167, 204
Garrett, Sergeant Fred, 51-53, 62, 63,
  102, 114, 147, 151, 173, 205
Glenn the Parachute dog, 38, 51, 99,
  100, 204
Glover, Fred, 80, 81, 84, 94, 106, 107, Ap 1,
  Ap 3
Gordon-Brown, Captain Robert, 25, 27,
  66, 79, 80, 106, 122, 132, 149, 162, 167
Gower, Corporal Gus, 61, 98, 142, 154,
  159, 187
Graham, Colour Sergeant Len, 153
Gray, Harry, 147, 148
Green, Lance Corporal 'Mitzi', 62, 119,
  Ap 3

Greenway, Captain the Honourable, Paul,
  74, 77, 114, 115, 162, 173, 194, 195
Gregory, Ron, 39, 41, 45, 78, 135-137, 146
Gwinnett, Padre John, 39-40, 122, 123,
  126, 145, 155, 157, 158, 169, 182,
  187, 195
Halliburton, Lieutenant Tom, 68, 91,
  109, 112, 204
Hannen, Thomas, 89, 205
Harmon, Sid, 59
Harper, Harry, 51, 63
Harper, Sergeant 'Tich', 132
Harries, CSM Jack, 15-16, 18, 20, 35,
  43-44, 45, 50, 64, 67, 68, 72, 75, 84,
  87, 88, 93, 118
Harrold, CSM Bill, 18, 38, 46, 47, 66,
  71, 73, 74, 97, 122
Hart, Pte, 51, 52
Hawkins, George, 88, 89, 92, 123, 129,
  Ap 5
Hearn, Lieutenant Colonel Tom, 15
Hennessey, Sergeant, 148, 187
Higgins, Derek, 33, 61, 151
Holloway, Sergeant 'Stanley', 153
Hudson, Sergeant Havelock, 23, 29, 31,
  38, 53, 58, 60, 64, 65, 68, 75, 86, 89,
  92, 93, 97, 112, 123, 125, 126, 205
Hughes Lieutenant Alfred, 204
Hull, Lance Corporal Edward, 38, 204
Hull, Percy, 102
Humfrey, Jack, 45, 129, 130-132, 143
Hurst, Bill, 105
Hutton, Max, 151
Jefferson, Lieutenant Alan, 68, 75, 78,
  81, 90, 94, 97, 123, 125, Ap 5
Jenkins, Sergeant Bob 'Paddy', 51, 63,
  89, 91, 92, 147, 149, 150, 178, 184
Jepp, Terry, 51, 53, 62, 119, 120, Ap 1, Ap 3
Jepp, Ron, 51, 188, 189, 205
Johnson, Walter, 61, 82, 86, 87, 97, 123
Kightley, Arthur, 61
Knight, 'Darky', 190
Knight, Sergeant Sid, 38, 47, 48, 59, 74,
  76-78, 85, 86, 89, 90, 99, 101, 139,
  169, 181, 188, 195
Knights, Reg 'Knocker', 132, 142, 156,
  162, 166, 167
Lepper, Lieutenant Jock, 61, 98, 142,
  154, 159, 160, 161
Lindsay, Colonel Martin, 17, 23, 29
Long, Colour Sergeant Harold, 60, 68,
  75, 84, 88, 89
Loring, Lieutenant Jimmy, 92
Lukins, Sergeant, 38, 156
MacSorley, 'Paddy', 188, 205
McArthur, Don, 57, 58
McGeever, Sergeant Sammy, 76, 77, 109,
  134, 146-148, 153, 166, 169, 186,
  188, 194, 195
McGuinness, Corporal Jim, 51, 60, 61,
  76, 77, 109, 134, 135, 147, 148, 166,
  167, 186-189
Mander, James, 205
Martin, Lieutenant Douglas, 31, 193,
  194, 205, Ap 4
Mason, Pte, 38
Mead, Tony, 87, 97, 125
Miller, CSMI Dusty, 18, 38, 46, 47, 66,
  69, 71, 73, 74, 95, 99-101, 107-109
Mills, Lieutenant Bill, 182, 183, 186-
  189, 192, 194, 196
Millward, Joe, 109, 110
Milward, Fred, 27, 50, 59, 75, 82, 84,
  85, 91, 107, 108, 146, 148, 173, 180,
  181, 183, 192, 202
Mobsby, Sergeant Arthur, 155, 165, 166,
  168, 169, 186
Morgan, Pte, 78
Morris, Pte, 156
Mower, Alan, 88, 92, 97
Neal, Peter, 39
Newton, Gordon, 39, 40, 66, 73, 79, 80,
  122, 149, 170, 190
Nicholls, Alfred, 205
Novis, Sergeant Johnny, 88, 89, 108

Osborne, Reg, 51, 63, 87, 109
Otway, Lieutenant Colonel Terence, 17, 23, 25, 28-31, 33, 35-36, 44, 53, 64, 65, 68, 72, 74-76, 78, 81, 84-86, 89, 90, 92, 92, 95, 99, 108, 109, 111-113, 115, 116, 127, 134-137, 139, 141, 144, 145, 154, 155, 160, 163, 168, 169, 172-175, 177, 179, 189, 192-195, 202
Page, Pte, 51, 52
Parfitt, Lieutenant Gordon 'Ginger', 68, 141, 156, 161, 182, 204
Parris, Maurice, 38, 99, 205
Parry, Major Allen, 16, 27, 38, 41, 43, 46, 48, 49, 60, 68, 74, 75, 81, 82, 84, 89-91, 94, 95, 97, 123
Pattinson, Geoff, 149, 163-166
Peck, Norman, 204
Penstone, Corporal Doug, 62, 119, 120, 205, Ap 3
Peters, Lieutenant George, 35, 99-101, 204
Phelps, Ron, 45, 139, 169, 170, 173
Picton, Bill, 91
Pinkus, Sergeant, 38
Plested, Lance Corporal Stanley, 204
Pond, Lieutenant Hugh, 28, 66, 80, 84, 95, 99, 134, 194, 195, 204
Poulter, Corporal Len, 157, 167
Pritchard, Cliff 'Taffy', 194
Richards, Captain Albert (War artist, attached), 44, 68, 91, 195
Robinson, Lance Corporal Peter, 204
Robinson, Captain 'Robbie', 61, 62, 100, 101, 113, 119, 124, 127, 143, 159, 160, 180, 181
Roche, Tom 'Paddy', 150, 205
Rooke-Matthews, Ernie, 18, 19, 51, 60, 67, 76, 80, 91, 95, 123, 134, 149, 150, 152, 173, 182, 186, 194, 205
Rose, Sergeant James, 156, 161, 182, 204
Ross, CSM Barney, 35, 58, 72, 75, 84, 86, 87, 151
Russell, Pte, 147
Sanderson, Peter, 187, 205
Salter, Sergeant Hugh, 59
Sharp, Ron, 81
Sharples, Patrick, 205
Sherwood, Reg, 36, 51
Simpson, Vic, 91
Skene, 'Jock', 146
Skippells, Pte, 189, 190
Slade, Lieutenant Dennis, 59, 60, 91, 112, 113, 115, 134, 137, 162, 186
Slater, Dan, 149
Smith, Sergeant Doug, 57, 58
Smith, Major George, 38, 41, 43-49, 54, 65, 69, 71, 73, 74, 77, 81, 94, 99-101, 109-111, 134, 144, 149, 162, 189
Smythe, Lieutenant Hugh, 28, 66, 132, 157, 177, 186
Speechley, John, 50, 55, 104, 142, 160-161, 167, 169, 187
Spencer, Sergeant, 157, 158
Stack, Bill, 17, 36, 51, 56
Stoddart, CSM Frank, 53, 60, 91, 150
Stroud, Tom, 50, 76, 85, 86, 97, 122, 125, 126
Tarrant, Sergeant Tommy, 182
Taylor, Sergeant 'Busty', 94, 118
Tottle, Corporal Doug, 18, 31, 39, 64, 91-94, 144, 157, 205
Towler, Sergeant Sid, 183
Tucker, Ron, 28-29, 61, 98, 104, 129, 142, 156-161, 177, 178, 179
Tudge, Len, 131, 205
Tugwell, James, 219
Thwaites, Cyril, 53, 78, 79, 85, 90
Undrill, Pte, 142, 154
Vallance, Reg, 127, 134
Vincent, Derek, 20, 50, 78, 192
Walker, Harold 'Johnnie', 59, 78, 84, 85, 91, 156
Walker, Sergeant 'John', 76
Walker, Ken, 75, 87, 90, 95, 127, 134,

137, 156, 163, 166
Walter, Percy, 205
Watkins, Corporal Jack, 163-165
Watts, Captain Harold, 59, 64, 68, 77, 91, 97, 113, 139, 157, 158, 174, 175, 185, 190, 195
Wilson, Lance Corporal Joe, 53, 54, 65, 68, 117, 135
Wilson, Peter, 188, 189, 205
Wingrove, Corporal Fred, 170, 176, 204
Woodcock, Sergeant Albert 'Ginger', 18, 19, 149, 157, 180, 181
Woodcraft, Sergeant Doug, 16, 19, 53, 123, 162, 165, 167, 170-71
Worth, Lieutenant Joe, 31, 60, 68, 180
Wright, Roy, 109-112, 118, 205
Young, James - 204

5th Parachute Brigade
7th Parachute Battalion
Blakeley, Pte, 157, 160
Eckert, Corporal Cyril, 204
Pine-Coffin, Lieutenant Colonel Geoffrey, 171, 202

12th Parachute Battalion
Allen, Pte, 157
Liddell, Pte, 157

13th Parachute Battalion
Luard, Lieutenant Colonel Peter, 162

6th Airlanding Brigade
Crookenden, Major Napier, 125, 204

2nd Ox and Bucks
Edwards, Dennis, 197, 198

Glider Pilot Regiment
Baldwin, Staff Sergeant Arnold, 37, 40, 66, 72, 73, 205
Bone, Sergeant, 37, 66, 79, 205
Chatterton, Lieutenant Colonel, 40
Dean, Sergeant, 37, 66, 205
Kerr, Staff Sergeant 'Dickie', 37, 66, 80, 81, 205
Michie, Sergeant Joe, 37, 40, 66, 67, 72, 73, 205
Toler, Major Ian, 40
Walker, Sergeant, 37, 66, 81, 205

1st Special Service Brigade
Abbot, Trooper, Ap 2
Barnes, Trooper Jack, Ap 2
Dean, Trooper 'Dixie', Ap 2
Donald, Marine, 36, 51, 56, 57
Ferry, Corporal, Ap 2
Haig-Thomas, Captain David, 113, 114
Harnett, Trooper, Ap 2
Hill, Lance Sergeant Les, Ap 2
Jennings, Trooper, Ap 2
Lovat, Lord, 115, 117, 118, Ap 2
Osbourne, Trooper 'Ossie', Ap 2
Ponsford, Lieutenant Keith, 116, Ap 2
Ryder, Sam, 113
Scott, Trooper Stan, Ap 2
Synnott, Trooper Jimmy, Ap 2
Westley, Captain Roy, 115, Ap 2
Winston, Lieutenant Peter, 36, 51, 56, 57
Young, Lieutenant Colonel Peter, 129, 134

5th Black Watch
Kennedy, P, 192
Mc Gregor, Major John, 178, 205
Nicol, Reverend Tom, 185, 190, 195
Punton, Major Dennis, 179
Thomson, Lieutenant Colonel, 172, 176, 177, 179
Weller, Doctor Sam, 185

13th/18th Hussars
Coker, Lieutenant Douglas, 221
Treloare, George, 222

1/7th Middlesex Battalion
Biddell, Harry, 205
Brown, Albert, 205
Daly, Dennis, 181, 185, 205
Lyus, Ben, 205
Pearson, Major 'Lofty', 185, 205
Tomlinson, Harry, 205

Royal Air Force
Garnett, Pilot Officer, 79
Mercer, Warrant Officer, 62
Richards, Flight Sergeant Dennis, 66, 67, 72

German Personnel
Buskotte, Sgt Major Hans, Ap 5
Steiner, Lt Raimund, Ap 5

Other
Edward d'Abo, 135
Eileen Martin (nee Hart), 34, Ap 4
French Civilians:
  Barberot Family, 106
  Chadenet, Baronne, 105
  Duval, Georges, 121
  Eve, Monsieur and Madame Arthur, 106
  Godey, Robert, 113, 114
  Magninat, Msr and Mme, 135
  Saulnier, Bernard, Ap 3
  Vermughen Family, 120, 121

Locations:
Amfreville, 109, 117, 124, 127, 133, 134, 146, 175, 199
Bavent, 113, 115, 132, 133
Beja, 16
Benouville, 25, 129
Bois de Bavent, 25, 37, 124
Bois des Monts, 135, 136, 141, 142, 144-148, 148, 149, 154-163, 171-173, 175-177, 179, 182-184, 187, 190, 192-195
Breville, 24, 25, 99, 129, 134-137, 150, 162-164, 168, 172, 175-177, 180, 181, 187, 191, 195, 196, 201
Brigmerston House, 23
Briqueville, 132
Brize Norton, RAF, 37, 40, 66, 125
Broadwell, RAF, 31,38-39, 43, 202
Broadwell Transit Camp, 31, 37, 39, 41, 43, 45
Bulford, 15, 18-20, 23, 29, 143
Bures, 16
Cabourg, 57, 62, 119-122, 129
Caen, 25,
Caen Canal, 24
Caen Canal Bridge, 24-25, 36, 124, 136
Calvary Cross, 32, 36, 94-96, 99
Château d'Amfreville, 110, 115, 117, 118, 134
Château Beneauville-Bavent, 105
Château de Varaville, 99, 113
Château du Mesnil, 106
Château St Côme, 122, 124, 134-141, 146, 155, 160, 161, 163-169, 172, 176, 177, 180, 181, 183-186, 189-192, 195, 197, 198-201, 203, 204
Cirencester, 31
Colombelles, 148
Down Ampney, RAF, 39
Dozule, 103
Ecarde, 115
Escoville, 24
Franceville Plage, 36, 62
Fromagerie du Mesnil, 105, 115, 118
Gonneville, 32, 79, 84, 100, 127
Haras de Retz, 97, 122, 123, 126
Hardwick Hall, 15
Harwell, RAF, 38, 41, 44
Hauger, 25, 107, 111, 146, 166
Herouvillette, 124, 139, 172
Inkpen, 202
Janville, 119

Kiwi Barracks, 15, 18
Le Bas de Ranville, 25, 124
Le Havre, 24, 142
Le Mariquet, 162, 163, 166, 170
Le Mesnil Crossroads, 25, 37, 98, 104, 105, 114, 122-124, 127, 129, 130, 132-136, 139, 142, 144, 149, 154, 155, 157, 187, 194
Le Plein, 25, 36, 99, 102, 107, 109, 111, 113, 115, 117, 124, 127, 148
Longuemare, 107
Longueval, 124
Merville, 25
Merville Battery, 22, 25, 26, 28, 31-32, 35-36, 38, 48, 62, 65, 68-71, 96, 123-124, 127, 129, 146, 202, Ap 5
Merville Battery mock-up, 28
Netheravon, 37
Newbury, 28, 78
North Africa, 15, 101
Odiham, RAF, 73, 125
Petiville, 113
Ranville, 24-25, 98, 105, 114, 118, 124, 134, 139, 148, 162, 163, 166, 175
Rawalpindi, 30
Ringway, 15
River Dives 25, 37, 57, 129
River Divette, 37
River Orne, 24, 25, 57, 124
River Orne Bridge, 24, 25, 36, 136
Robehomme, 37, 106, 114, 129, 132, 133, 147
Salisbury Plain, 55
Sallenelles, 36
Shanghai, 30
Southwick House, 40
St Samson, 37
Tidworth, 16
Troarn, 25, 37, 113, 119, 127, 129
Trouville, 57
Varaville, 24, 37, 47, 57, 62, 98-101, 103, 104, 113, 114, 143
Walbury Hill, 28, 202
Waterloo Station, 19
West Woodhay, 28

Various:
Albemarle, 44, 79
Arethusa, HMS, 36, 91, 99, 124, 174, 194, Ap 5
Bangalore torpedoes, 31, 35, 38, 51, 52, 68, 75, 78
Bellorophon Flag, 39, 187
Benzedrine tablets, 162
Dakota, 38, 44, 49, 51, 61
Diversion Party, 35, 74, 85
Eureka/Rebecca Equipment, 32, 35, 37, 40, 48
Firm Base area, 32, 75
G-B Force, 27, 32, 35, 37, 40, 43, 45, 53, 66, 67, 72, 73, 84
General Wade PHE charge, 32, 35, 66
Gold Beach, 23
Hiwis, 107
Holophane light, 32,
Horsa glider, 27, 37, 79, 81
Juno Beach, 23
NAAFI, 19, 31, 43
Nebelwerfer, 142, 176, 183
OBOE, 32, 48
Omaha Beach, 23
Operation Overlord, 23
RV Party, 32, 38, 41, 43, 45,
Sherman tank, 185, 192
Sword Beach, 23, 36, 124, 129, Ap 5
Taping Party, 38, 74, 77
Troubridge Party, 32, 38, 41, 43, 45, 49, 60, 65, 91
Udine, 106, 132, 133
Utah Beach, 23
War Office, 15, 16
Women's Auxiliary Air Force (WAAF), 29, 43
Women's Voluntary Service (WVS), 40